Analytical Perspectives

BUDGET OF THE U.S. GOVERNMENT

FISCAL YEAR 2022
OFFICE OF MANAGEMENT AND BUDGET

THE BUDGET DOCUMENTS

Budget of the United States Government, Fiscal Year 2022 contains the Budget Message of the President, information on the President's priorities, and summary tables.

Analytical Perspectives, Budget of the United States Government, Fiscal Year 2022 contains analyses that are designed to highlight specified subject areas or provide other significant presentations of budget data that place the budget in perspective. This volume includes economic and accounting analyses, information on Federal receipts and collections, analyses of Federal spending, information on Federal borrowing and debt, baseline or current services estimates, and other technical presentations.

Appendix, Budget of the United States Government, Fiscal Year 2022 contains detailed information on the various appropriations and funds that constitute the budget and is designed primarily for the use of the Appropriations Committees. The Appendix contains more detailed financial information on individual programs and appropriation accounts than any of the other budget documents. It includes for each agency: the proposed text of appropriations language; budget schedules for each account; legislative proposals; narrative explanations of each budget account; and proposed general provisions applicable to the appropriations of entire agencies or group of agencies. Information is also provided on certain activities whose transactions are not part of the budget totals.

GENERAL NOTES

1. All years referenced for budget data are fiscal years unless otherwise noted. All years referenced for economic data are calendar years unless otherwise noted.

2. Detail in this document may not add to the totals due to rounding.

ISBN: 978-1-63671-007-5

TABLE OF CONTENTS

LIST OF CHARTS AND TABLES

LIST OF CHARTS AND TABLES

LIST OF CHARTS

LIST OF TABLES

Tax Expenditures

Special Topics

Aid to State and Local Governments

Information Technology and Cybersecurity Funding

Federal Investment

Research and Development

Credit and Insurance

*Available on the internet at *http://www.whitehouse.gov/omb/analytical-perspectives/*

Federal Drug Control Funding

Technical Budget Analyses

Current Services Estimates

Trust Funds and Federal Funds

Comparison of Actual to Estimated Totals

Detailed Functional Tables

Federal Budget by Agency and Account

*Available on the internet at *http://www.whitehouse.gov/omb/analytical-perspectives/*

INTRODUCTION

1. INTRODUCTION

The *Analytical Perspectives* volume presents analyses that highlight specific subject areas or provide other significant data that place the President's 2022 Budget in context and assist the public, policymakers, the media, and researchers in better understanding the Budget. This volume complements the main *Budget* volume, which presents the President's Budget policies and priorities, and the Budget *Appendix* volume, which provides appropriations language, schedules for budget expenditure accounts, and schedules for selected receipt accounts.

Presidential Budgets have included separate analytical presentations of this kind for many years. The 1947 Budget and subsequent budgets included a separate section entitled *Special Analyses and Tables* that covered four, and later more, topics. For the 1952 Budget, the section was expanded to 10 analyses, including many subjects still covered today, such as receipts, investment, credit programs, and aid to State and local governments. With the 1967 Budget this material became a separate volume entitled *Special Analyses*, and included 13 chapters. The material has remained a separate volume since then, with the exception of the Budgets for 1991–1994, when all of the budget material was included in one volume. Beginning with the 1995 Budget, the volume has been named *Analytical Perspectives*. Since the 2022 Budget is being released following a presidential transition, OMB is publishing an abbreviated *Analytical Perspectives* volume this year. The 2023 Budget will include a more comprehensive *Analytical Perspectives* volume with additional key updates on areas including the Government's mission performance goals and objectives and the President's Management Agenda (PMA), effective utilization of Federal real property, statistics that offer a numerical picture of the United States and an overview of statistical agency budgets and priorities, and the importance of using evidence, evaluation, and data to improve Government effectiveness.

In addition to the information included in this volume, supplemental tables and other materials that are part of the *Analytical Perspectives* volume are available at *http://www.whitehouse.gov/omb/analytical-perspectives*. Tables included at this link are shown in the List of Tables in the front of this volume with an asterisk instead of a page number.

Overview of the Chapters

Economic and Budget Analyses

Economic Assumptions and Overview. This chapter reviews recent economic developments; presents the Administration's assessment of the economic situation and outlook; compares the economic assumptions on which the 2022 Budget is based with the assumptions for last year's Budget and those of other forecasters; provides sensitivity estimates for the effects on the Budget of changes in specified economic assumptions; and reviews past errors in economic projections.

Long-Term Budget Outlook. This chapter assesses the long-term budget outlook under current policies and under the Budget's proposals. It focuses on 25-year projections of Federal deficits and debt to illustrate the long-term impact of the Administration's proposed policies. It also discusses the uncertainties of the long-term budget projections and discusses the actuarial status of the Social Security and Medicare programs.

Federal Borrowing and Debt. This chapter analyzes Federal borrowing and debt and explains the budget estimates. It includes sections on special topics such as trends in debt, debt held by the public net of financial assets and liabilities, investment by Government accounts, and the statutory debt limit.

Management

Strengthening the Federal Workforce. This chapter presents summary data on Federal employment and compensation, and discusses the approach the Administration is taking with Federal human capital management.

Budget Concepts and Budget Process

Budget Concepts. This chapter includes a basic description of the budget process, concepts, laws, and terminology, and includes a glossary of budget terms. It also discusses proposals specific to the 2022 Budget to improve budgeting under certain budget concepts.

Coverage of the Budget. This chapter describes activities that are included in budget receipts and outlays (and are therefore classified as "budgetary") as well as those activities that are not included in the Budget (and are therefore classified as "non-budgetary"). The chapter also defines the terms "on-budget" and "off-budget" and includes illustrative examples.

Federal Receipts

Governmental Receipts. This chapter presents information on estimates of governmental receipts, which consist of taxes and other compulsory collections. It includes descriptions of tax-related legislation enacted in the last year and describes proposals affecting receipts in the 2022 Budget.

Offsetting Collections and Offsetting Receipts. This chapter presents information on collections that offset outlays, including collections from transactions with the public and intragovernmental transactions. In addition, this chapter presents information on "user fees," charges associated with market-oriented activities and regulatory fees. Detailed tables of offsetting receipts and offsetting collections in the Budget are available at the internet address cited above.

Tax Expenditures. This chapter describes and presents estimates of tax expenditures, which are defined as revenue losses from special exemptions, credits, or other preferences in the tax code.

Special Topics

Aid to State and Local Governments. This chapter presents crosscutting information on Federal grants to State and local governments. The chapter also includes a table showing historical grant spending, and a table with budget authority and outlays for grants in the Budget. Tables showing State-by-State spending for major grant programs are available at the internet address cited above.

Information Technology and Cybersecurity. This chapter addresses Federal information technology (IT) and cybersecurity, highlighting initiatives and proposed funding levels to deliver critical citizen services, keep sensitive data and systems secure, and further the vision of modern Government. The Administration will invest in modern, secure technologies and services to drive enhanced efficiency and effectiveness. This will include undertaking complex Government-wide modernization efforts, driving improved delivery of citizen-facing services, and improving the overall management of the Federal IT portfolio. The Administration will also continue its efforts to further build the Federal IT workforce and seek to reduce the Federal Government's cybersecurity risk in order to better serve and protect the American public.

Federal Investment. This chapter discusses federally financed spending that yields long-term benefits. It presents information on annual spending on physical capital, research and development, and education and training.

Research and Development. This chapter presents a crosscutting review of research and development funding in the Budget.

Credit and Insurance. This chapter provides crosscutting analyses of the roles, risks, and performance of Federal credit and insurance programs and Government-sponsored enterprises (GSEs). The chapter covers the major categories of Federal credit (housing, education, small business and farming, energy and infrastructure, and international) and insurance programs (deposit insurance, pension guarantees, disaster insurance, and insurance against terrorism-related risks). Five additional tables address transactions including direct loans, guaranteed loans, and GSEs. These tables are available at the internet address cited above.

Federal Drug Control Funding. This chapter displays enacted and proposed drug control funding for Federal Departments and Agencies.

Technical Budget Analyses

Current Services Estimates. This chapter discusses the conceptual basis of the Budget's current services, or "baseline," estimates, which are generally consistent with the baseline rules in the Balanced Budget and Emergency Deficit Control Act of 1985 (BBEDCA). The chapter presents estimates of receipts, outlays, and the deficit under this baseline. Two detailed tables addressing factors that affect the baseline and providing details of baseline budget authority and outlays are available at the internet address cited above.

Trust Funds and Federal Funds. This chapter provides summary information about the two fund groups in the Budget—Federal funds and trust funds. In addition, for the major trust funds and certain Federal fund programs, the chapter provides detailed information about income, outgo, and balances.

Comparison of Actual to Estimated Totals. This chapter compares the actual receipts, outlays, and deficit for 2020 with the estimates for that year published in the 2020 Budget, published in March 2019.

The following materials are available at the internet address cited above.

Detailed Functional Table

Detailed Functional Table. Table 20–1, "Budget Authority and Outlays by Function, Category, and Program," displays budget authority and outlays for major Federal program categories, organized by budget function (such as healthcare, transportation, or national defense), category, and program.

Federal Budget by Agency and Account

Federal Budget by Agency and Account. Table 21–1, "Federal Budget by Agency and Account," displays budget authority and outlays for each account, organized by agency, bureau, fund type, and account.

Budgets of the Federal Statistical Agencies

Budgets of the Federal Statistical Agencies. Table 22-1, "Budgets of the Federal Statistical Agencies," displays the budgets of the Principle Statistical Agencies recognized by OMB, organized by agency.

Calfed Bay-Delta Program Federal Budget Crosscut

Calfed Bay-Delta Program Crosscut. The Calfed Bay-Delta Program interagency budget crosscut report provides an estimate of Federal funding by each of the participating Federal Agencies with authority and programmatic responsibility for implementing this program, fulfilling the reporting requirements of section 106(c) of Public Law 108–361.

Columbia River Basin Federal Budget Crosscut

Columbia River Basin Federal Budget Crosscut. The Columbia River interagency budget crosscut report includes an estimate of Federal funding by each of the participating Federal agencies to carry out restoration activities within the Columbia River Basin, fulfilling the reporting requirements of section 123 of the Clean Water Act (33 U.S.C. 1275).

ECONOMIC AND BUDGET ANALYSES

2. ECONOMIC ASSUMPTIONS AND OVERVIEW

This chapter presents the economic assumptions that underlie the Administration's 2022 Budget.[1] It provides an overview of the recent performance of the American economy, presents the Administration's projections for key macroeconomic variables, compares them to forecasts prepared by other prominent institutions, and discusses the unavoidable uncertainty inherent in providing long-term forecasts.

This chapter proceeds as follows:

The first section provides an overview of the recent functioning of the U.S. economy, examining the performance of a broad array of key economic indicators.

The second section presents a detailed exposition of the Administration's economic assumptions underlying the 2022 Budget, discussing how key macroeconomic variables are expected to evolve over the years 2021 to 2031.

The third section compares the forecast of the Administration with those of the Congressional Budget Office (CBO), the Federal Open Market Committee of the Federal Reserve, and the Blue Chip panel of private-sector forecasters.

The fourth section discusses the sensitivity of the Administration's projections of Federal receipts and outlays to alternative paths of macroeconomic variables.

The fifth section considers the errors in past Administrations' forecasts, comparing them with the errors in forecasts produced by the CBO and the Blue Chip panel of private professional forecasters.

The sixth section uses information on past accuracy of Administration forecasts to provide understanding and insight into the uncertainty associated with the Administration's current forecast of the budget balance.

Recent Economic Performance[2]

The onset of the COVID-19 pandemic was marked by a sharp recession with steep declines across all prominent U.S. economic indicators. Unlike a typical recession, the effects of the recession were most acutely felt by those in the service and retail sectors, where social distancing behavior limited overall spending and activity. The economy plunged in the second quarter of 2020 and has partially rebounded in the quarters since, yet GDP remains below its pre-pandemic peak. Gains continue to be made in labor force participation while employers have added over 1.5 million jobs since the beginning of 2021.

Looking forward, consumers and businesses alike are showing increasing optimism following the passage of the American Rescue Plan Act of 2021 and significant progress in controlling the pandemic. Both the University of Michigan and Conference Board indicators for consumer sentiment and consumer confidence, respectively, have increased substantially over the past few months. Improvements in consumer sentiment signal increased consumer spending heading into the summer months. Businesses are also exhibiting optimism, as seen in the recent high levels of the ISM Purchasing Managers Index, a survey of business activity at manufacturing companies.

Labor Markets—The headline unemployment rate (U3) spiked to 14.8 percent in April 2020 and has gradually declined to 6.1 percent as of April 2021. While the

---

[1] Economic performance, unless otherwise specified, is discussed in terms of calendar years (January-December). Budget figures are discussed in terms of fiscal years (October-September).

[2] The statistics in this section are based on information available in April 2021.

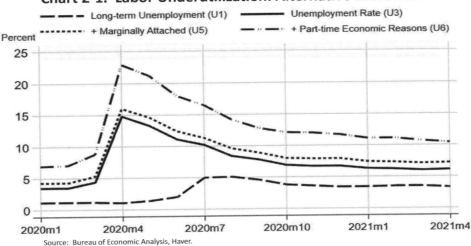

Chart 2-1. Labor Underutilization: Alternative Measures

Source: Bureau of Economic Analysis, Haver.

Chart 2-2. Contributions to Percent Change in 2020 Real GDP

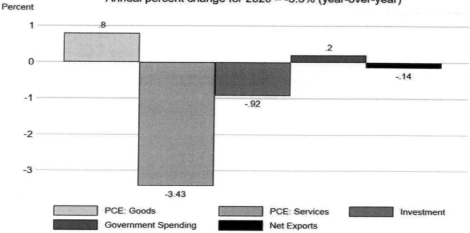

Annual percent change for 2020 = -3.5% (year-over-year)

Source: Bureau of Economic Analysis, Haver, Office of Management and Budget.

decline in the unemployment rate is a positive sign for the economy, and the Blue Chip panel of professional forecasters projects that the unemployment rate will fall to an average of 4.7 percent during 2022, several important labor market indicators still show signs of weakness.

By looking at alternative measures of labor underutilization (Chart 2-1), we can get a clearer picture of the state of employment. The U5 unemployment rate, which includes those workers who identify as marginally attached to the workforce, is 7.2 percent as of April.[3] Including workers who are working part-time for economic reasons (U6), the rate is 10.4 percent. Additionally, not only do millions of Americans remain unemployed—9.8 million as of April, a 72.0 percent increase from February 2020—but the duration of unemployment remains elevat-

ed as well. The long-term unemployment rate (U1), which measures the percent of the labor force unemployed for 15 weeks or longer, is 3.3 percent as of April; this is almost three times as high as the pre-pandemic rate of 1.2 percent from February 2020. Moreover, the median duration of unemployment in April was 19.8 weeks, which is the highest this indicator has been since October 2012.

Consumption—Consumption by private households is the largest component of the country's economy, accounting for over two-thirds of output in 2019. Because of its large share of GDP, consumer spending growth is essential to economic growth in the United States. Real personal consumption expenditures (PCE) declined sharply at the onset of the pandemic (6.9 and 33.2 percent at an annual rate in 2020 Q1 and Q2, respectively), and following a large increase in Q3 (41.0 percent), progress has continued (2.3 percent in Q4 and 10.7 percent in 2021 Q1). As of 2021 Q1, real PCE is only 0.2 percent below where it was at the end of 2019.

---

[3] The BLS defines marginally attached workers as persons who are not in the labor force, want and are available for work, and had looked for a job sometime in the prior 12 months. They are not counted as unemployed because they had not searched for work in the prior 4 weeks.

Chart 2-3. Components of Real Personal Consumption Expenditures

Relative to January 2020

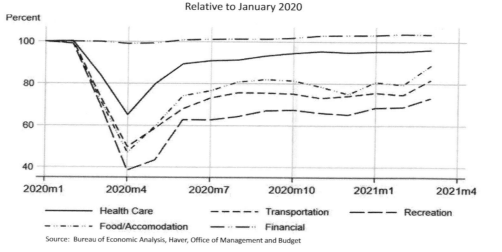

Source: Bureau of Economic Analysis, Haver, Office of Management and Budget

Table 2–1. ECONOMIC ASSUMPTIONS[1]

(Calendar Years, Dollar Amounts In Billions)

	Actual 2019	Projections											
		2020	2021	2022	2023	2024	2025	2026	2027	2028	2029	2030	2031
Gross Domestic Product (GDP)													
Levels, Dollar Amounts in Billions:													
Current Dollars	21,433	20,933	22,411	23,799	24,808	25,778	26,767	27,794	28,860	29,986	31,166	32,414	33,723
Real, Chained (2012) Dollars	19,092	18,423	19,375	20,200	20,652	21,039	21,418	21,803	22,196	22,609	23,039	23,491	23,961
Chained Price Index (2012=100), Annual Average .	112	114	116	118	120	123	125	128	130	133	135	138	141
Percent Change, Fourth Quarter over Fourth Quarter:													
Current Dollars	4.0	-1.2	7.1	5.2	4.0	3.8	3.8	3.8	3.8	3.9	3.9	4.0	4.0
Real, Chained (2012) Dollars	2.3	-2.5	5.2	3.2	2.0	1.8	1.8	1.8	1.8	1.9	1.9	2.0	2.0
Chained Price Index (2012=100)	1.6	1.3	1.8	1.9	2.0	2.0	2.0	2.0	2.0	2.0	2.0	2.0	2.0
Incomes, Billions of Current Dollars													
Domestic Corporate Profits	1,745	1,616	1,529	1,725	1,795	1,861	1,880	1,854	1,828	1,825	1,849	1,900	1,955
Employee Compensation	11,432	11,489	12,247	12,907	13,416	13,909	14,435	15,018	15,642	16,305	17,002	17,730	18,491
Wages and Salaries	9,309	9,369	10,047	10,491	10,918	11,383	11,818	12,296	12,812	13,352	13,930	14,526	15,159
Nonwage Personal Income	5,413	5,409	5,324	5,522	5,806	6,096	6,436	6,747	7,094	7,371	7,650	7,984	8,265
Consumer Price Index (All Urban)[3]:													
Level (1982-1984 = 100), Annual Average	249	252	258	263	269	275	281	287	294	301	307	314	321
Percent Change, Fourth Quarter over Fourth Quarter	1.9	1.3	2.0	2.1	2.2	2.3	2.3	2.3	2.3	2.3	2.3	2.3	2.3
Unemployment Rate, Civilian, Percent													
Annual Average	3.7	8.1	5.5	4.1	3.8	3.8	3.8	3.8	3.8	3.8	3.8	3.8	3.8
Interest Rates, Percent													
91-Day Treasury Bills[2]	2.1	0.4	0.1	0.2	0.4	0.8	1.2	1.5	1.6	1.7	1.8	2.1	2.3
10-Year Treasury Notes	2.1	0.9	1.2	1.4	1.7	2.1	2.4	2.6	2.7	2.8	2.8	2.8	2.8

[1] Based on information available as of mid-February 2021
[2] Average rate, secondary market (bank discount basis)
[3] Seasonally Adjusted

A prominent story of the pandemic has been the extent of the economic damage in specific sectors, particularly services. Chart 2-2 illustrates that a decline in the combined consumption of goods and services accounted for 75 percent of the total decline in real GDP for the year as a whole in 2020. Looking at the composition of services consumption, Chart 2-3 shows that several prominent service sectors are still considerably below pre-pandemic levels.

Nonresidential Fixed Investment—Real nonresidential fixed investment declined at an annual rate of 4.0 percent in 2020 (year-over-year). Equipment and intellectual property investment have recovered strongly in recent quarters, although business structures investment remains slow.

The Government Sector—Topline real government expenditures on consumption and investment increased 1.1 percent in 2020 (year-over-year), which includes a 4.3 percent increase in Federal spending partially offset by a 0.8 percent decline in State and Local spending. Within the Federal spending category, nondefense spending rose 5.6 percent while defense spending increased 3.5 percent.

Federal Reserve Policy—The Federal Reserve's response to the COVID-19 pandemic can be grouped into three main categories: lowering the policy rate, stabilizing financial markets, and supporting the flow of credit in the economy.[4] First, the Fed's monetary policymaking body—the Federal Open Market Committee (FOMC)—quickly lowered the target range for the federal funds rate. The federal funds rate, which serves as the FOMC's policy interest rate, is the rate that banks charge each other for overnight loans. In an effort to forestall negative economic impacts from the pandemic, the FOMC rapidly lowered the federal funds rate from an average of 1.59 in January 2020 to 0.08 by the end of March 2020, and this rate currently sits within the target range of 0 to 0.25 percent as of April 2021. This step helped reduce borrowing costs for households and businesses.

During its March 2021 meeting the FOMC announced it would maintain the target range for the federal funds rate at 0 to 0.25 percent. In its accompanying statement, the Committee repeated that it will not raise the federal funds rate target range "until labor market conditions have reached levels consistent with the Committee's assessments of maximum employment and inflation has risen to 2 percent and is on track to moderately exceed 2 percent for some time."

Second, the Fed took a number of steps to unfreeze key financial markets and to help them run smoothly. In many cases this involved the purchases of securities and assets that were otherwise difficult to sell. These purchases con-

---

[4] See the following Fed blog post for a more detailed description of the Fed's policy response to the pandemic: https://www.stlouisfed.org/open-vault/2020/august/fed-response-covid19-pandemic

veyed to the public that the Fed stands ready to assist important parts of the financial system.

Third, the Fed introduced several temporary lending and funding facilities to support the flow of credit to businesses and households. Overall, the Fed has introduced multiple temporary facilities to support various types of funding and credit markets. Two of the commonly discussed facilities are the Paycheck Protection Program Liquidity Facility, established to help small businesses keep workers on the payroll, and the Main Street Lending Program (a set of five facilities), established to support lending to both small and midsized businesses and non-profit organizations.

Economic Projections

The Administration's forecast was finalized on February 19, with the parameters of that forecast close to the consensus prevailing at that date. The forecast informs the 2022 Budget and assumes implementation of the Administration's policy proposals. Importantly, however, the projections described below were formulated before the details of the American Jobs Plan (AJP) and American Families Plan (AFP) were finalized and therefore do not incorporate the full impact of these policies. The Administration's projections are reported in Table 2-1 and summarized below.

Real GDP—In 2021, as the economy recovers from the COVID-19 pandemic, the Administration forecast assumes a strong recovery in civilian employment, associated with a rebound at a fourth quarter-over-fourth quarter rate of 5.2 percent. As noted below, growth to date in 2021 has been strong, and private forecasters

now project somewhat more rapid 2021 growth than in the Administration forecast. As the economy continues to recover and the employment picture improves, growth is projected to be 3.2 percent in 2022. Real GDP is projected to return to its long-run "potential" level by 2023 and is forecasted to grow at an average of 1.9 percent between 2024 and 2031.

Unemployment—As of December 2020, the unemployment rate stood at 6.7 percent, a substantial recovery from the peak rate of 14.8 percent in April 2020 but still high relative to historical levels. The Administration expects a rapid and strong recovery in unemployment coinciding with progress in controlling the pandemic, with the unemployment rate dropping to 4.7 percent by the end of 2021. The Administration then forecasts unemployment rates will drop to 4.1 percent by 2022 before leveling out at 3.8 percent from 2023-2031.

Interest Rates—Interest rates are expected to rise as the economy recovers from the recession and as inflation rises and then stabilizes around the Federal Reserve target rate of 2 percent. The 91-day Treasury bill rate is expected to steadily rise from an average of 0.1 percent in 2021 to 1.2 percent in 2025, then gradually increase to a terminal rate of 2.3 percent. The 10-year rate follows a similar path as it increases from 1.4 percent in 2021 to 2.4 percent by 2025, reaching 2.8 percent at the end of the budget window, which reflects both the increase in short-term rates and an increase in the term premium for investors committing to holding long-term securities.

General Inflation—The Administration's forecast assumes that inflation will return to a long run trend. Specifically, the Administration's forecast assumes that the Consumer Price Index for all Urban Consumers

Table 2–2.   COMPARISON OF ECONOMIC ASSUMPTIONS IN THE 2021 AND 2022 BUDGETS

	2019	2020	2021	2022	2023	2024	2025	2026	2027	2028	2029	2030
Real GDP (Percent Change)[1]:												
2021 Budget Assumptions	2.5	2.5	3.1	3.0	3.0	3.0	3.0	2.9	2.8	2.8	2.8	2.8
2022 Budget Assumptions	2.3	-2.5	5.2	3.2	2.0	1.8	1.8	1.8	1.8	1.9	1.9	2.0
GDP Price Index (Percent Change)[1]:												
2021 Budget Assumptions	2.3	1.8	2.0	2.0	2.0	2.0	2.0	2.0	2.0	2.0	2.0	2.0
2022 Budget Assumptions	1.6	1.3	1.8	1.9	2.0	2.0	2.0	2.0	2.0	2.0	2.0	2.0
Consumer Price Index (All-Urban; Percent Change)[1]:												
2021 Budget Assumptions	2.2	1.9	2.3	2.3	2.3	2.3	2.3	2.3	2.3	2.3	2.3	2.3
2022 Budget Assumptions	1.9	1.3	2.0	2.1	2.2	2.3	2.3	2.3	2.3	2.3	2.3	2.3
Civilian Unemployment Rate (Percent)[1]:												
2021 Budget Assumptions	3.9	3.7	3.5	3.6	3.8	4.0	4.0	4.0	4.0	4.0	4.0	4.0
2022 Budget Assumptions	3.7	8.1	5.5	4.1	3.8	3.8	3.8	3.8	3.8	3.8	3.8	3.8
91-Day Treasury Bill Rate (Percent)[2]:												
2021 Budget Assumptions	1.9	2.1	1.4	1.5	1.5	1.6	1.7	2.0	2.2	2.4	2.5	2.5
2022 Budget Assumptions	2.1	0.4	0.1	0.2	0.4	0.8	1.2	1.5	1.6	1.7	1.8	2.1
10-Year Treasury Note Rate (Percent)[2]:												
2021 Budget Assumptions	2.9	2.2	2.0	2.2	2.5	2.7	3.0	3.1	3.1	3.1	3.2	3.2
2022 Budget Assumptions	2.1	0.9	1.2	1.4	1.7	2.1	2.4	2.6	2.7	2.8	2.8	2.8

[1] % Change 4Q
[2] Calendar Year Average

Table 2–3.   COMPARISON OF ECONOMIC ASSUMPTIONS [1]

	2020	2021	2022	2023	2024	2025	2026	2027	2028	2029	2030	2031
Real GDP (Year-over-Year):												
2022 Budget	−3.5	5.2	4.3	2.2	1.9	1.8	1.8	1.8	1.9	1.9	2.0	2.0
CBO	−3.4	4.6	2.9	2.2	2.3	2.3	1.9	1.6	1.6	1.6	1.5	1.6
Blue Chip [2]		4.9	3.8	2.3	2.4	2.0	2.0	1.9	1.9	1.9	1.9	1.9
Real GDP (Fourth-Quarter-over-Fourth-Quarter):												
2022 Budget	−2.5	5.2	3.2	2.0	1.8	1.8	1.8	1.8	1.9	1.9	2.0	2.0
Federal Reserve [3]	−2.4	4.2	3.2	2.4	1.8	1.8	1.8	1.8	1.8	1.8	1.8	1.8
Consumer Price Index (CPI-U) (Fourth-Quarter-over-Fourth-Quarter):												
2022 Budget	1.3	2.0	2.1	2.2	2.3	2.3	2.3	2.3	2.3	2.3	2.3	2.3
CBO	1.1	1.9	2.2	2.3	2.3	2.4	2.4	2.5	2.5	2.4	2.4	2.3
Blue Chip [2,4]		2.3	2.1	2.2	2.2	2.2	2.2	2.2	2.2	2.2	2.2	2.2
Federal Reserve, PCE [3,5]	1.2	1.8	1.9	2.0	2.0	2.0	2.0	2.0	2.0	2.0	2.0	2.0
Unemployment Rate: (annual averages)												
2022 Budget	8.1	5.5	4.1	3.8	3.8	3.8	3.8	3.8	3.8	3.8	3.8	3.8
CBO	8.1	5.7	5.0	4.7	4.4	4.1	3.9	3.9	4.0	4.1	4.3	4.3
Blue Chip [2]		5.8	4.7	4.8	4.5	4.3	4.4	4.3	4.3	4.3	4.3	4.3
Federal Reserve [3,6]	6.7	5.0	4.2	3.7	4.1	4.1	4.1	4.1	4.1	4.1	4.1	4.1
Interest Rates:												
91-Day Treasury Bills (discount basis):												
2022 Budget	0.4	0.1	0.2	0.4	0.8	1.2	1.5	1.6	1.7	1.8	2.1	2.3
CBO	0.4	0.1	0.1	0.2	0.3	0.6	1.0	1.4	1.6	1.9	2.2	2.3
Blue Chip [2]		0.1	0.2	0.6	0.9	1.1	1.3	1.7	1.7	1.7	1.7	1.7
10-Year Treasury Notes												
2022 Budget	0.9	1.2	1.4	1.7	2.1	2.4	2.6	2.7	2.8	2.8	2.8	2.8
CBO	0.9	1.1	1.3	1.5	1.8	2.1	2.5	2.7	3.0	3.2	3.3	3.4
Blue Chip [2]		1.2	1.6	1.7	2.0	2.2	2.3	2.5	2.5	2.5	2.5	2.5

Sources: Administration; CBO, The Budget and Economic Outlook: 2021 to 2031, February 2021; October 2020 and February 2021 Blue Chip Economic Indicators, Aspen Publishers, Inc.; Federal Reserve Open Market Committee, December 16, 2020

[1] Calendar Year
[2] 2028-2031 are 5 year averages; 2023-2031 values derived from October 2020 report
[3] Median Projection
[4] Year-over-Year
[5] Personal Consumption Expenditures
[6] Average rate during 4th quarter

(CPI-U) will rise from 1.2 percent in 2020 on a fourth quarter-over-fourth quarter basis to 2.0 percent in 2021 and stabilize at 2.3 percent from 2024 to 2031, a rate consistent with the Federal Open Market Committee's inflation target for a slightly different inflation measure.

Comparison with Other Forecasts

For perspective on the Administration's forecast, this section compares it with forecasts prepared around the same time by the CBO, the Federal Open Market Committee of the Federal Reserve (FOMC), and the Blue Chip panel of private-sector forecasters. There are important differences that should inform such comparisons.

The most important difference between these forecasts is that they make different assumptions about the implementation of the Administration's proposed policies. As already noted, the Administration's forecast assumes impacts of Administration policies, including the American Rescue Plan and components of the American Jobs and American Families Plans. In contrast, the CBO forecast assumes no changes to current law and was formulated prior to passage of the American Rescue Plan. It is not clear to what extent FOMC participants and Blue Chip panelists incorporate policy implementation expectations in their respective outlooks. The Blue Chip panel, in particular, comprises a large number of private-sector forecasters, who have different expectations about the enactment of the Administration's proposed policies and different views about the contribution of those policies to economic growth.

A second difference is that the various forecasts were published on different dates. For example, while the forecast published by the Administration is based on data available in February, the Blue Chip forecasts are drawn from the February survey for 2021 and 2022 values and from the October 2020 survey for the long-term forecast (2023-2031). These were the latest Blue Chip forecasts available at the time the Administration finalized its forecast. In addition, the FOMC projections were released in mid-March, and the CBO forecast was published in early February based on data available in January. During the months that have elapsed since the Administration's forecast was finalized, macroeconomic, policy, and pandemic developments have been mostly positive. Consumer spending has outpaced earlier projections, the Congress has passed the American Rescue Plan, and over one hundred million Americans have been vaccinated. These subsequent developments should be considered when comparing the Administration's forecast with more recent forecasts such as the Blue Chip panel of professional economic forecasters. For example, between February and May of 2021, the Blue Chip panel revised upwards their consensus forecast for 2021 (year-over-year) real GDP growth, from 4.9 percent to 6.6 percent. Likewise, the Blue Chip consensus forecast for the average 2021 unemployment rate was revised downwards from 5.8 to 5.4 percent.

In spite of differences across forecasters, the forecasts are similar in several aspects. All of them project a continued economic recovery and improving labor markets. Interest rates across these various projections are consistent with an environment in which the Federal Reserve holds off on raising its policy rate until late 2022 or early 2023. Rates of inflation are also expected to rise but to remain in line with the Federal Reserve's mandate on low and stable inflation. See Table 2-3 for a comparison.

Real GDP—The Administration forecasts a higher path for real GDP growth than the CBO, a 2.4 percent per year average over the forecast window versus CBO's 2.2 percent average, though consistent with the 2.4 percent average from Blue Chip. The Administration's forecast reflects partial effects of the Administration's proposed policies, while the CBO is required to assume a continuation of current law in its forecast. The Administration's forecast has the same average growth rate over the forecast window as the FOMC although the Fed's forecast assigns more growth in 2021 than the Administration (6.5 percent compared with 5.2 percent) and slightly slower growth over the out-years of the forecast.

Unemployment—On the unemployment rate, the Administration's expectations are largely aligned with those of the other forecasters. In particular, all forecasters expect unemployment to decrease over the forecast window. One minor difference is that the Administration's forecast for unemployment plateaus at 3.8 percent as compared with 4.0 and 4.1 percent for the other projections. Although slightly lower for 2021 through 2023 than the CBO and Blue Chip, the Administration's forecast is slightly higher than the Federal Reserve's forecast during this window.

Interest Rates—The Administration's 91-day interest rate forecast is broadly consistent with the Blue Chip forecast for 2022-2025 and is slightly higher than the CBO's forecast. The Administration expects short-term rates to pick up slowly in 2022 and 2023 and rise from 1.2 to 1.6 percent between 2025-2027. The Blue Chip expects a rise from 1.1 to 1.7 percent, and the CBO expects a rise from 0.4 to 1.7 percent over this period. For both short- and long-term rates, all forecasters agree that they will tend to rise modestly over the coming few years.

General Inflation—Assumptions for CPI-U inflation are similar across the Administration, the CBO, and the Blue Chip. The CBO assumes a CPI-U inflation rate of 2.4 percent in the long run, while the Administration and the Blue Chip are not significantly different at 2.3 and 2.2 percent long-run rates. The Federal Reserve does not predict CPI-U but rather PCE inflation. The Federal Reserve expects PCE inflation to reach the Fed's target of 2.0 percent by 2023 and remain stable thereafter. PCE inflation tends to be lower than CPI-U inflation.

Sensitivity of the Budget to Economic Assumptions

Federal spending and tax collections are heavily influenced by developments in the economy. Income tax receipts are a function of growth in incomes for households and firms. Spending on social assistance programs may rise when the economy enters a downturn, while increases in nominal spending on Social Security and other programs are dependent on consumer price inflation. A robust set of projections for macroeconomic variables assists in budget planning, but unexpected developments in the economy have ripple effects for Federal spending and receipts. This section seeks to provide an understanding of the magnitude of the effects that unforeseen changes in the economy can have on the budget.

To make these assessments, the Administration relies on a set of heuristics that can predict how certain spending and receipt categories will react to a change in a given subset of macroeconomic variables, holding almost everything else constant. These sensitivity analyses provide a sense of the broad changes one would expect after a given development, but they cannot anticipate how policy makers would react and potentially change course in such an event. For example, if the economy were to suffer an unexpected recession, tax receipts would decline and spending on programs such as unemployment insurance would rise. In such a situation, however, policy makers might enact policies that stimulate the economy, leading to secondary and tertiary changes that are difficult to predict. Another caveat is that it is often unrealistic to suppose that one macroeconomic variable might change while others would remain constant. Most macroeconomic variables interact with each other in complex and subtle ways. These are important considerations to bear in mind when examining Table 2-4.

For real GDP growth and employment:

1. The first panel in the table illustrates the effect on the deficit resulting from a one percentage point reduction in real GDP growth, relative to the Administration's forecast, in 2021 that is followed by a subsequent recovery in 2022 and 2023. The unemployment rate is assumed to be half a percentage

Table 2–4. SENSITIVITY OF THE BUDGET TO ECONOMIC ASSUMPTIONS

(Fiscal Years; In Billions of Dollars)

Budget Effect	2021	2022	2023	2024	2025	2026	2027	2028	2029	2030	2031	Total of Budget Effects: 2021-2031
Real Growth and Employment:												
Budgetary effects of 1 percentage point lower real GDP growth:												
(1) For calendar year 2021 only, with real GDP recovery in 2022–2031:[1]												
Receipts	−15.4	−24.4	−12.3	−1.9	0.2	0.2	0.2	0.2	0.2	0.2	0.2	−52.4
Outlays	18.2	25.4	9.7	0.7	1.1	1.3	1.5	1.5	1.6	1.9	2.1	64.9
Increase in deficit (+)	33.6	49.8	22.0	2.6	0.8	1.1	1.2	1.3	1.4	1.7	1.9	117.3
(2) For calendar year 2021 only, with no subsequent recovery:[1]												
Receipts	−15.4	−32.3	−37.5	−39.2	−40.7	−42.5	−44.3	−45.9	−47.6	−49.4	−51.2	−446.0
Outlays	18.2	31.0	29.1	31.6	34.5	37.6	40.3	44.0	47.2	51.8	56.6	421.9
Increase in deficit (+)	33.6	63.3	66.7	70.8	75.2	80.1	84.6	89.8	94.8	101.2	107.9	867.9
(3) Sustained during 2021–2031, with no change in unemployment:												
Receipts	−15.4	−48.5	−88.7	−132.5	−178.7	−229.6	−283.5	−339.3	−398.9	−462.4	−529.9	−2,707.5
Outlays	−1.9	−0.6	−0.3	0.2	1.8	3.7	6.0	7.6	10.6	17.7	26.0	70.7
Increase in deficit (+)	13.5	47.9	88.5	132.7	180.5	233.3	289.5	346.9	409.5	480.1	555.9	2,778.2
Inflation and Interest Rates:												
Budgetary effects of 1 percentage point higher rate of:												
(4) Inflation and interest rates during calendar year 2021 only:												
Receipts	16.9	33.1	34.9	35.0	36.3	37.9	39.4	40.8	42.3	43.8	45.5	405.9
Outlays	44.5	78.8	55.4	55.7	55.8	57.1	55.9	58.6	55.6	59.4	61.8	638.6
Increase in deficit (+)	27.6	45.7	20.6	20.7	19.5	19.2	16.5	17.8	13.3	15.6	16.3	232.7
(5) Inflation and interest rates, sustained during 2021–2031:												
Receipts	16.9	50.8	88.4	128.2	170.9	218.6	269.8	323.4	381.4	444.1	511.7	2,604.2
Outlays	43.3	148.9	227.8	301.8	379.9	461.3	543.3	639.7	717.4	826.3	937.9	5,227.6
Increase in deficit (+)	26.4	98.1	139.4	173.6	209.0	242.8	273.6	316.3	336.0	382.2	426.2	2,623.4
(6) Interest rates only, sustained during 2021–2031:												
Receipts	1.2	2.5	2.9	3.1	3.3	3.6	4.0	4.3	4.5	4.8	5.0	39.2
Outlays	26.3	106.2	154.4	194.0	230.2	267.4	299.7	332.9	363.7	398.3	435.8	2,808.8
Increase in deficit (+)	25.1	103.7	151.5	190.9	226.9	263.8	295.7	328.7	359.2	393.5	430.8	2,769.6
(7) Inflation only, sustained during 2021–2031:												
Receipts	15.7	48.3	85.4	125.1	167.5	214.8	265.5	318.8	376.5	438.8	506.1	2,562.5
Outlays	17.0	42.7	73.5	108.0	149.8	194.1	244.0	307.5	354.8	429.3	503.6	2,424.3
Decrease in deficit (−)	1.3	−5.5	−11.9	−17.1	−17.7	−20.6	−21.5	−11.3	−21.8	−9.6	−2.5	−138.2
Interest Cost of Higher Federal Borrowing:												
(8) Outlay effect of 100 billion increase in borrowing in 2021	0.1	0.1	0.3	0.6	1.2	1.5	1.7	1.9	2.0	2.3	2.5	14.1

[1] The unemployment rate is assumed to be 0.5 percentage point higher per 1 percent shortfall in the level of real GDP.

point higher in 2021 before returning to the baseline level in 2022 and 2023.

2. The next panel in the table reports the effect of a reduction of one percentage point in real GDP growth in 2021 that is not subsequently made up by faster growth in 2022 and 2023. Consistent with this output path, the rate of unemployment is assumed to rise by half a percentage point relative to that assumed in the Administration's forecasts.

3. The third panel in the table shows the impact of a GDP growth rate that is permanently reduced by one percentage point, while the unemployment rate is not affected. This is the sort of situation that would arise if, for example, the economy were to experience a permanent decline in productivity growth.

For inflation and interest rates:

4. The fourth panel in Table 2-4 shows the effect on the budget in the case of a one percentage point higher rate of inflation and a one percentage point higher nominal interest rate in 2021. Both inflation and interest rates return to their assumed levels in 2022. This would result in a permanently higher price

Table 2–5. FORECAST ERRORS, 2002-PRESENT

REAL GDP ERRORS

2-Year Average Annual Real GDP Growth	Administration	CBO	Blue Chip
Mean Error	1.0	0.5	0.7
Mean Absolute Error	1.1	0.7	0.8
Root Mean Square Error	1.5	1.2	1.2
6-Year Average Annual Real GDP Growth			
Mean Error	1.6	1.4	1.2
Mean Absolute Error	1.6	1.4	1.2
Root Mean Square Error	1.7	1.5	1.4

INFLATION ERRORS

2-Year Average Annual Change in the Consumer Price Index	Administration	CBO	Blue Chip
Mean Error	-0.2	-0.2	-0.0
Mean Absolute Error	0.7	0.6	0.6
Root Mean Square Error	0.8	0.8	0.7
6-Year Average Annual Change in the Consumer Price Index			
Mean Error	0.1	0.0	0.3
Mean Absolute Error	0.4	0.3	0.4
Root Mean Square Error	0.5	0.4	0.5

INTEREST RATE ERRORS

2-Year Average 91-Day Treasury Bill Rate	Administration	CBO	Blue Chip
Mean Error	0.5	0.5	0.7
Mean Absolute Error	0.8	0.6	0.8
Root Mean Square Error	1.1	1.0	1.2
6-Year Average 91-Day Treasury Bill Rate			
Mean Error	2.1	2.2	2.3
Mean Absolute Error	2.1	2.2	2.3
Root Mean Square Error	2.3	2.4	2.6

level and nominal GDP level over the course of the forecast horizon.

5. The fifth panel in the table illustrates the effects on the budget deficit of a one percentage point higher inflation rate and interest rate than projected in every year of the forecast.

6. The sixth panel reports the effect on the deficit resulting from an increase in interest rates in every year of the forecast, with no accompanying increase in inflation.

7. The seventh panel in the table reports the effect on the budget deficit of a one percentage point higher inflation rate than projected in every year of the forecast window, while the interest rate remains as forecast.

8. Finally, the table shows the effect on the budget deficit if the Federal Government were to borrow an additional $100 billion in 2021, while all of the other projections remain constant.

9. These simple approximations that inform the sensitivity analysis are symmetric. This means that the effect of, for example, a one percentage point higher rate of growth over the forecast horizon would be of the same magnitude as a one percentage point reduction in growth, though with the opposite sign.

Forecast Errors for Growth, Inflation, and Interest Rates

As with any forecast, the Administration's projections are projections and are subject to error because they are based on a set of assumptions about the underlying milieu comprising social, political, and global conditions. It

Table 2–6.   **DIFFERENCES BETWEEN ESTIMATED AND ACTUAL SURPLUSES OR DEFICITS FOR FIVE-YEAR BUDGET ESTIMATES SINCE 1985**

(As a Percent of GDP)

	Current Year Estimate	Budget Year Estimate	Estimate for Budget Year Plus:			
			One Year (BY + 1)	Two Years (BY + 2)	Three Years (BY + 3)	Four Years (BY + 4)
Mean Error	−0.8	0.2	1.1	1.7	2.4	2.7
Mean Absolute Error	1.2	1.5	2.2	2.7	3.5	3.7
Root Mean Squared Error	1.4	2.1	3.0	3.5	4.5	4.6

is impossible to foresee every eventuality over a one-year horizon, much less over ten or more years. This section evaluates the historical accuracy of past Administrations' forecasts for real GDP growth, inflation, and short-term interest rates from 2002 to the present day, especially relative to the accuracy of forecasts produced by the CBO and Blue Chip panel. For this exercise, forecasts produced by all three entities are compared with realized values of these variables.

The results of this exercise are reported in Table 2-5 and contain three different measures of accuracy. The first is the average forecast error. When a forecaster has an average forecast error of zero, it may be said that the forecast has historically been unbiased, in the sense that realized values of the variables have not been systematically above or below the forecasted value. The second is the average absolute value of the forecast error, which offers a sense of the magnitude of errors. Even if the past forecast errors average to zero, the errors may have been of a very large magnitude, with both positive and negative values. Finally, the table reports the square root of the mean of squared forecast error (RMSE). This metric applies a harsher penalty to forecasts exhibiting large errors. The table reports these measures of accuracy at both the 2-year and the 6-year horizons, thus evaluating the

relative success of different forecasts in the short run and in the medium run.

Past Administrations have forecast 2-year real GDP growth and interest rates that were higher than actually realized, on average, by 1.0 percentage points and 0.5 percentage points, respectively. This is partly due to the assumption that Administration policy proposals contained in the Budget will be enacted, which has not always come to pass. The 2-year average forecast error for inflation is smaller, -0.2 percentage points, and similar to other forecasts.

Uncertainty and the Deficit Projections

This section assesses the accuracy of past budget forecasts for the deficit or surplus, measured at different time horizons. The results of this exercise are reported in Table 2-6, where the average error, the average absolute error, and the RMSE are reported.

In Table 2-6, a negative number means that the Federal Government ran a larger surplus or a smaller deficit than was expected, while a positive number in the table indicates a smaller surplus or a larger deficit. In the current year in which the budget is published, the Administration has tended to understate the surplus (or, equivalently,

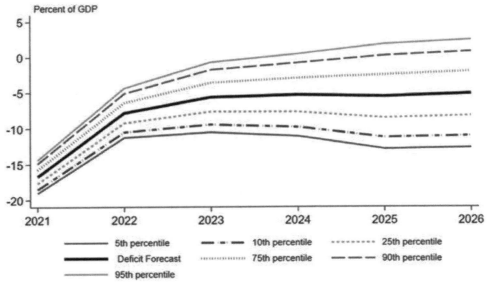

Chart 2-4. **Range of Uncertainty for the Budget Deficit**

overstate the deficit) by an average of 0.8 percent of GDP. For the budget year, however, the historical pattern has been for the budget to understate the deficit by an average of 0.2 percent of GDP.[5] One possible reason for this is that past Administrations' policy proposals have not all been implemented. The forecast errors tend to grow with the time horizon, which is not surprising given that there is much greater uncertainty in the medium run about both the macroeconomic situation and the specific details of policy enactments.

A probabilistic range of outcomes for the deficit over the budget window can be calculated by building off of the historical forecast errors summarized in Table 2-6. This is accomplished by taking the RMSE of previous forecast errors and assuming that these errors are drawn from a normal distribution. This exercise is undertaken at every forecast horizon from the current year through four years after the budget year. Chart 2-4 displays the projected range of possible deficits. In the chart, the middle line represents the Administration's expected fiscal balance and represents the 50th percentile outcome. The rest of the lines in the chart may be read in the following fashion. The top line reports the 95th percentile of the distribution of outcomes over 2021 to 2026, meaning that there is a 95 percent probability that the actual balance in those years will be more negative than expressed by the line. Similarly, there is a 95 percent probability that the balance will be more positive than suggested by the bottom line in the chart.

---

[5] Additionally, the CBO has historically forecasted smaller deficits, on average, than actually materialized.

3. LONG-TERM BUDGET OUTLOOK

The horizon for most numbers in this Budget is 10 years. This 10-year horizon reflects a balance between the importance of considering both the current and future implications of budget decisions made today, and a practical limit on the construction of detailed budget projections for years in the future.

Nonetheless, it can be informative to look further into the future, despite the uncertainty surrounding the assumptions needed for such estimates. This chapter begins by discussing the fiscal outlook under current law over the next 25 years. The second section discusses the fiscal impact of the Administration's policies, finding they will cut deficits and debt over the long run, compared to the baseline. The third section discusses the actuarial projections for Social Security and Medicare. The appendix to this chapter provides further detail on data sources, assumptions, and other methods for estimation.

Long-Run Projections under Continuation of Current Policies

The baseline long-term projections assume that current policy continues for Social Security, Medicare, Medicaid, other mandatory programs, and revenues.[1] Projections for all mandatory programs and revenues maintain consistency with other Federal agency projections. From 2032-2046, total mandatory spending grows by 4.2 percentage points as a share of GDP (Gross Domestic Product), while revenues increase by 3.8 percent. For discretionary spending, it is less clear how to project a continuation of current policy. After the expiration of the statutory caps in 2021, the Administration's 10-year baseline assumes that discretionary funding levels generally grow slightly below the rate of CPI (Consumer Price Index) inflation (about 2.2 percent per year). Thereafter, the baseline long-run projections assume that real per-person discretionary funding remains constant, implying an average growth rate of 2.8 percent per year. The appendix provides additional detail on the methodology behind these projections.

The COVID-19 public health and economic crisis and measures taken to address them significantly increased deficits and debt for 2020 and 2021. In the baseline projections (not including proposed policy), the deficit is 14.9 percent of GDP in 2020 and 16.7 percent of GDP in 2021. The deficit is then projected to fall sharply in 2022 and 2023 and then gradually fall to 4.0 percent of GDP in 2027, though it is projected to rise through the end of the

10-year window and reach 5.0 percent of GDP in 2031. Debt rose to 100.1 percent of GDP in 2020 and is projected to rise to 109.7 percent of GDP in 2022 and 111.2 percent of GDP in 2023 before leveling off to a more gradual ascent, rising to 112.9 percent of GDP in 2031.

Over the past several decades, interest rates have fallen even as debt has risen. This has been a widespread, persistent, and global phenomenon, and it has meant that the burden associated with debt has gone down. Under the baseline projections, real net interest payments will remain at or below 0.5 percent of GDP over the 10-year window, below the approximately one percent average over the last four decades and well below the roughly two percent average level in the 1990s.

Beyond the 10-year horizon, deficits continue to rise under the baseline projections, reaching 5.8 percent of GDP in 2041 before falling back to 5.7 percent of GDP by the end of the 25-year window. Debt is projected to increase gradually from 112.9 percent of GDP in 2031 to 130.8 percent of GDP by 2046, an increase of about 1.2 percentage points per year. Real net interest steadily rises after the 10-year window, but never exceeds 0.7 percent of GDP.

Future budget outcomes depend on a host of unknowns: changing economic conditions, unforeseen international developments, unexpected demographic shifts, and unpredictable technological advances. The longer budget projections are extended, the more the uncertainties increase. These uncertainties make even accurate short-run budget forecasting quite difficult. For example, the Budget's projection of the deficit in five years is 5.1 percent of GDP, but a distribution of probable outcomes ranges from a deficit of 11.0 percent of GDP to a surplus of 0.8 percent of GDP, at the 10th and 90th percentiles, respectively.[2]

Among the risks, the rate of future productivity growth is both highly uncertain and a major driver of the long-term budget outlook. Lower productivity growth would directly reduce the growth of major tax bases while higher productivity growth would have the opposite effect. If productivity were to grow 0.25 percentage points slower per year, we would expect the annual deficits to deteriorate significantly from baseline projections. The same would be true if excess cost growth for healthcare was higher than expected or if interest rates grew faster than expected. These risks are roughly symmetric, so faster productivity growth, less healthcare excess cost growth and lower interest rates would significantly improve the fiscal outlook.

Another primary risk not addressed in the long-run economic assumptions or baseline budget projections is the impact of climate change. Climate change will likely

---

[1]   The long-run baseline projections are consistent with the Budget's baseline concept, which is explained in more detail in Chapter 17, "Current Services Estimates," in this volume. The projections assume full payment of scheduled Social Security and Medicare benefits without regard to the projected depletion of the trust funds for these programs. Additional baseline assumptions beyond the 10-year window are detailed in the appendix to this chapter.

[2] These estimates are derived in Chart 2-4 of Chapter 2, "Economic Assumptions and Overview," in this volume.

Chart 3-1. Comparison of Annual Surplus/Deficit

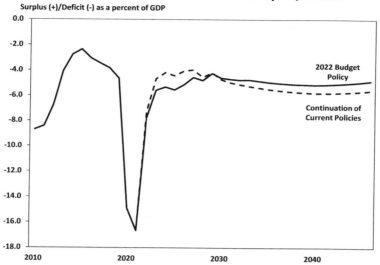

have significant effects on the long-run fiscal outlook. The Administration is undertaking additional analysis to assess these long-run impacts. The Budget's climate policies serve to mitigate long-run impacts of climate change.[3]

Impact of 2022 Budget Policies on the Long-Term Fiscal Outlook

The Budget proposes major investments in infrastructure, education and training, manufacturing, the care economy, and improving economic security, coupled with major reforms to both corporate and individual taxation. Because many of the investments are front-loaded, while the reforms are permanent, the Budget improves the long-term fiscal outlook.

By 2030, the Budget's policies lower annual deficits compared to the baseline projections. To assess long-run impact, this chapter develops more detailed 25-year projections for the impact of the Administration's policies on the budget. As described in the appendix, the projections attempt to make reasonable extensions of policy impact by making assumptions about the growth rates for individual policy proposals beyond the 10-year window. The resulting projections show that the revenue and spending increases in the American Jobs Plan (AJP) and the American Families Plan (AFP) are projected to offset in 15 years, while generating additional savings over the long run. In total, all Budget proposals are offset within two decades and are projected to reduce deficits by more than $2 trillion in the second decade. Table S-2—Effect of Budget Proposals on Projected Deficits, in the main *Budget* volume—shows the deficit impact of the Administration's proposals over the second decade, using the assumptions described here. In the long run, this set of investments and tax reforms will improve the fiscal outlook.

Charts 3-1 and 3-2 illustrate the improvement in deficits and debt. The initial investments in the Administration's

AJP and AFP contribute to a larger deficit in the near term, but that trend reverses, and the plans improve the fiscal outlook over the long term. Beginning in 2030, the AJP and AFP result in a lower deficit through the end of the 25-year window. Similarly, the Budget's policies significantly flatten the projected debt increase compared to the baseline, with debt as a percent of GDP rising by less than 0.6 percentage points per year between 2031 and 2046. Budget proposals would result in further improvement in the fiscal outlook after 25 years.

Notably, these projections may understate the impact that the Budget's policies will have on improving the fiscal outlook because the underlying economic assumptions understate the impact that the Budget's policies will have on economic growth. As noted in the Economic Assumptions chapter, the Administration's economic assumptions incorporate the impact of Administration policies, but were formulated before the details of the AJP and AFP were finalized. Moreover, the Budget makes historic investments in children that will raise their productivity in adulthood, spurring faster economic growth in the long term.

Actuarial Projections for Social Security and Medicare

While the Administration's long-run projections focus on the unified budget outlook, Social Security and Medicare Hospital Insurance (HI) benefits are paid out of trust funds financed by dedicated payroll tax revenues. Projected trust fund revenues fall short of the levels necessary to finance projected benefits over the next 75 years.

The Social Security and Medicare Trustees' reports feature the actuarial balance of the trust funds as a summary measure of their financial status. For each trust fund, the actuarial balance is calculated as the magnitude of change in receipts or program benefits (expressed as a percentage of taxable payroll) that would be needed to preserve a small positive balance in the trust fund at the

---

[3] This additional analysis is part of the broader Administration effort to address climate-related risks, as outlined in Executive Order 13707.

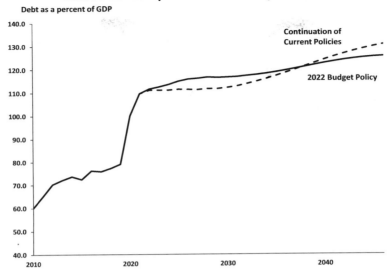

Chart 3-2. Comparison of Publicly Held Debt

end of a specified time period. The estimates cover periods ranging in length from 25 to 75 years.

Table 3-1 shows the projected income rate, cost rate, and annual balance for the Medicare HI and combined OASDI trust funds at selected dates under the Trustees' intermediate assumptions in the 2020 reports. There is a continued imbalance in the long-run projections of the HI program due to revenues that do not match costs over time. According to the 2020 Trustees' report, the HI trust fund reserves are projected to become depleted in 2026, at which point dedicated revenues would be expected to be able to cover 90 percent of scheduled payments.

The 2020 Social Security Trustees' report projects that under current law, there is a long-term mismatch between program revenue and costs. Social Security is currently drawing on its trust fund balances to cover current expenditures. Over time, as the ratio of workers to retirees falls, costs are projected to rise further while revenues excluding interest are projected to rise less rapidly. In the process, the Social Security trust fund reserves, which were built up since 1983, would be drawn down and eventually become depleted in 2035, based on the projections in the 2020 report. At that point, the dedicated revenues could pay for 79 percent of program expenditures in the rest of 2035, declining to 73 percent in 2094. Note that the projections in the 2020 Trustees' report do not reflect the effects of the COVID-19 pandemic on the Social Security program, which may advance reserve depletion to 2034.

The long-term budget projections in this chapter assume that benefits would continue to be paid in full despite the projected depletion of the trust fund reserves to show the long-run cost of maintaining current benefit formulas.

Table 3–1.   INTERMEDIATE ACTUARIAL PROJECTIONS FOR OASDI AND HI, 2020 TRUSTEES' REPORTS

	2019	2020	2030	2040	2090
			Percent of Payroll		
Medicare Hospital Insurance (HI):					
Income Rate	3.3	3.4	3.7	3.8	4.4
Cost Rate	3.4	3.5	4.3	4.8	5.0
Annual Balance	−0.1	−0.2	−0.6	−1.0	−0.6
Projection Interval:			25 years	50 years	75 years
Actuarial Balance			−0.8	−0.8	−0.8
			Percent of Payroll		
Old Age Survivors and Disability Insurance (OASDI):					
Income Rate	12.8	13.0	13.2	13.3	13.4
Cost Rate	13.9	13.9	16.0	16.8	17.9
Annual Balance	−1.0	−0.9	−2.8	−3.5	−4.4
Projection Interval:			25 years	50 years	75 years
Actuarial Balance			−2.0	−2.8	−3.2

TECHNICAL NOTE: SOURCES OF DATA AND METHODS OF ESTIMATING

The long-run budget projections are based on actuarial projections for Social Security and Medicare as well as demographic and economic assumptions. A simplified model of the Federal budget, developed at OMB, is used to compute the budgetary implications of these assumptions after the 10-year budget window.

Demographic and Economic Assumptions.—For the years 2021-2031, the assumptions are drawn from the Administration's economic projections used for the 2022 Budget. The economic assumptions are extended beyond this interval by holding the inflation rate, interest rates, and the unemployment rate constant at the levels assumed in the final year (2031) of the budget forecast. Population growth and labor force growth are extended using the intermediate assumptions from the 2020 Social Security Trustees' report. The projected rate of growth for real GDP is built up from the labor force assumptions and an assumed rate of productivity growth. Productivity growth, measured as real GDP per hour, is assumed to equal its average annual rate of growth in the Budget's economic assumptions: 1.4 percent per year.

Under the Budget's policies, the CPI inflation rate is held constant at 2.3 percent per year, the unemployment rate is held constant at 3.8 percent, the yield to maturity on 10-year Treasury notes is kept at 2.8 percent, and the 91-day Treasury bill rate is kept at 2.2 percent. Consistent with the demographic assumptions in the Trustees' reports, U.S. population growth slows from an average of just over 0.5 percent per year during the budget window to about three-quarters of that rate by the end of the 25-year projection period. Real GDP growth is projected to be less than its historical average of around 2.5 percent per year because the slowdown in population growth and the increase in the share of the population over age 65 reduce labor supply growth. In these projections, real GDP growth averages between 1.7 percent and 1.8 percent per year for the period following the end of the 10-year budget window. The economic and demographic projections described above are set exogenously and do not change in response to changes in the budget outlook.

Baseline Budget Projections.—For the period through 2031, receipts and outlays in the baseline and policy projections follow the 2022 Budget's baseline and policy estimates, respectively. Outside the budget window, discretionary spending grows at the rate of growth in inflation and population. Long-run Social Security spending is projected by the Social Security actuaries using this chapter's long-run economic and demographic assumptions. Medicare benefits are projected based on a projection of beneficiary growth and excess healthcare cost growth from the 2020 Medicare Trustees' report current law baseline. Excess cost growth for private health insurance is assumed to grow at a rate that averages the excess cost growth assumed in the Medicare actuarial assumptions and provided in their Illustrative Alternative. In these projections, private health insurance excess cost growth averages 1.3 percent after 2031. Medicaid outlays are based on the economic and demographic projections in the model, which assume average excess cost growth of approximately 0.9 percentage points above growth in GDP per capita after 2031. Other entitlement programs are projected based on rules of thumb linking program spending to elements of the economic and demographic projections such as the poverty rate. Individual income tax revenues are projected using a microsimulation model that incorporates real bracket creep. Corporate tax and other receipts are projected to grow with GDP.

Policy Budget Projections.—The long-run impact of the President's policy proposals is based on the same set of economic and demographic assumptions, but make the following assumptions for the growth of costs and savings from specific policy proposals.

Discretionary Spending.—Discretionary spending is assumed to grow at the rate of growth in inflation and population outside the budget window, as in the baseline model.

American Jobs Plan Investments.—In general, the proposed outlays for the AJP investments do not continue beyond the budget window. The projections take into account that a small amount of budget authority provided in the first decade is spent outside the budget window.

Made in America Tax Plan.—Other than tax credit expansions, tax provisions in the AJP are assumed to grow at the rate of growth in GDP. Four energy credit expansions (the Energy Investment Credit, the Renewable Production Tax Credit, the Carbon Oxide Sequestration Tax Credit, and the new tax credits for qualified advanced energy manufacturing) can be claimed outside the budget window. The outlays for these credits beyond the budget window are projected separately for each proposal and assume different paths for spend-out, based on guidance from the Department of the Treasury's Office of Tax Analysis (OTA). The remaining energy credits with 2031 outlays will likely have smaller carry-overs; the Budget assumes that their 2032 outlays are half of their 2031 outlays and that their 2033-2046 outlays are zero. For the Low-Income Housing Tax Credit and Neighborhood Homes Investment Tax Credit, the Budget assumes that initial allocations not resulting in credits claimed in the first decade will lead to a declining pattern of credits claimed during 2032-36 before remaining at zero in 2037 and beyond.

American Families Plan.—As a general rule, investments that are expected to be largely paying for wages or providing goods or services that increase in quality are assumed to grow with GDP. Investments that provide constant-quality goods or services are assumed to grow with inflation and population.

Paid Leave and Child Care Initiatives: The 10-year Budget projections assume that providing universal paid family and medical leave, universal preschool, creating a new child care entitlement, and providing pay parity for Head Start teachers and ensuring all early childhood program staff make a $15 minimum wage are fully phased in (with take-up reaching steady state levels) by the tenth year. After that, the budget authority for these provisions is projected based on the GDP growth rate, and the outlay rates for these programs from the budget window are carried through beyond the budget window.

Education Initiatives: Policies to fund free community college and advance affordability for students at Historically Black Colleges and Universities, Tribal Colleges and Universities, and Minority Serving Institutions have their budget authority grow with relevant populations and tuition inflation, as specified in the proposals, with respective outlays growing according to the applicable outlay rate. Increasing the Pell Grant and making recipients of DACA (Deferred Action for Childhood Arrivals) eligible for Pell Grants have their budget authority grow with inflation and population because eligibility is likely to grow with population and the value of the grants is proposed to grow with inflation, and the policies follow the same outlay rate beyond the budget window as during the budget window. Education proposals with flat funding for the first 10 years are assumed to have budget authority grow with inflation and population so that they do not decrease in value in subsequent years. Investments in teacher credentials are funded only in the first five years of the budget window and not beyond.

Nutrition Initiatives: Proposals related to nutrition, including expanding the Summer Electronic Benefit Transfer to all eligible children nationwide, facilitating re-entry for formerly incarcerated individuals through eligibility for the Supplemental Nutrition Assistance Program, and expanding school meal programs, each grow at the rate of inflation and population because the cost of these proposals is affected by food prices, which grow with inflation, while participation will generally grow with population.

Family Coordinators at Veterans Affairs Medical Centers: This proposal grows with GDP because costs would increase with wages.

Investments in Maternal Health: This funding expires before 2031, so funding beyond the budget window is zero.

Tax Investments: These proposals, which include making permanent the American Rescue Plan (ARP) expansion to the Earned Income Tax Credit for workers without children, making permanent ARP changes to the Child and Dependent Care Tax Credit (CDCTC), extending ARP changes to the Child Tax Credit, and making permanent full refundability, were estimated directly by OTA through 2041; the provisions grow in 2042-2046 according to their 2032-2041 growth patterns. The Budget accounts for the CDCTC interaction with the proposed child care entitlement, and the interaction grows at the same rate as the permanent CDCTC. Making permanent the ARP expansion of premium tax credits is projected assuming average excess cost growth of approximately 1.3 percentage points above growth in GDP after 2031.

Offsets: Most tax provisions in the American Families Plan are projected to grow with GDP, based on guidance from OTA. Receipts from Internal Revenue Service (IRS) tax compliance reforms, net of IRS discretionary and mandatory outlay reforms, are assumed to grow with GDP. Capital income proposals were estimated directly by OTA through 2041 and grow at a faster rate than GDP growth based on modeled deferral behavior; the provision grows in 2042-2046 according to its growth pattern in 2032-2041.

4. FEDERAL BORROWING AND DEBT

Debt is the largest legally and contractually binding obligation of the Federal Government. At the end of 2020, the Government owed $21,017 billion of principal to the individuals and institutions who had loaned it the money to fund past deficits. During that year, the Government paid the public approximately $387 billion of interest on this debt.[1] At the same time, the Government also held financial assets, net of financial liabilities other than debt, of $2,993 billion. Therefore, debt held by the public net of financial assets was $18,024 billion.

The $21,017 billion debt held by the public at the end of 2020 represents an increase of $4,216 billion over the level at the end of 2019. This increase is the result of the $3,129 billion deficit in 2020 and other financing transactions that increased the need to borrow by $1,087 billion. Debt held by the public grew from 79.2 percent of Gross Domestic Product (GDP) at the end of 2019 to 100.1 percent of GDP at the end of 2020. The deficit is estimated to increase to $3,669 billion in 2021, and then to fall to $1,837 billion in 2022. The deficit is projected to fall again in 2023, and then to remain relatively stable as a percent of GDP throughout the remainder of the Budget window. Debt held by the public is projected to grow to $24,167 billion (109.7 percent of GDP) at the end of 2021 and $26,265 billion (111.8 percent of GDP) at the end of 2022. After 2022, debt held by the public as a percent of GDP is projected to increase more slowly, reaching 117.0 percent in 2031. Debt held by the public net of financial assets is expected to similarly grow to 98.4 percent of GDP at the end of 2021, 100.1 percent at the end of 2022, and 108.5 percent at the end of 2031.

Trends in Debt Since World War II

Table 4–1 depicts trends in Federal debt held by the public from World War II to the present and estimates from the present through 2031. (It is supplemented for earlier years by Tables 7.1–7.3 in the Budget's *Historical Tables*, available as supplemental budget material.[2]) Federal debt peaked at 106.1 percent of GDP in 1946, just after the end of the war. From that point until the 1970s, Federal debt as a percentage of GDP decreased almost every year because of relatively small deficits, an expanding economy, and unanticipated inflation. With households borrowing large amounts to buy homes and consumer durables, and with businesses borrowing large amounts to buy plant and equipment, Federal debt also decreased almost every year as a percentage of total credit market debt outstanding. The cumulative effect was impressive. From 1950 to 1975, debt held by the public declined from

78.6 percent of GDP to 24.6 percent, and from 53.3 percent of credit market debt to 17.9 percent. Despite rising interest rates during this period, interest outlays became a smaller share of the budget and were roughly stable as a percentage of GDP.

Federal debt relative to GDP is a function of the Nation's fiscal policy as well as overall economic conditions. During the 1970s, large budget deficits emerged as spending grew faster than receipts and as the economy was disrupted by oil shocks and rising inflation. Federal debt relative to GDP and credit market debt stopped declining for several years in the middle of the decade. Federal debt started growing again at the beginning of the 1980s, and increased to almost 48 percent of GDP by 1993. The ratio of Federal debt to credit market debt also rose during this period, though to a lesser extent. Interest outlays on debt held by the public, calculated as a percentage of either total Federal outlays or GDP, increased as well.

The growth of Federal debt held by the public was slowing by the mid-1990s. In addition to a growing economy, two major budget agreements were enacted in the 1990s, implementing spending cuts and revenue increases and significantly reducing deficits. The debt declined markedly relative to both GDP and total credit market debt, with the decline accelerating as budget surpluses emerged from 1998 to 2001. Debt fell from 47.9 percent of GDP in 1993 to 31.5 percent of GDP in 2001. Over that same period, debt fell from 26.2 percent of total credit market debt to 17.4 percent. Interest as a share of outlays peaked at 16.5 percent in 1989 and then fell to 8.9 percent by 2002; interest as a percentage of GDP fell by a similar proportion.

The progress in reducing the debt burden stopped and then reversed course beginning in 2002. The attacks of September 11, 2001, a recession, two major wars, and tax cuts all contributed to increasing deficits, causing debt to rise, both in nominal terms and as a percentage of GDP. Following the recession that began in December 2007, the deficit began increasing rapidly in 2008 and 2009, as the Government intervened in the potential collapse of several major corporations and financial institutions as well as enacting a major stimulus bill. Debt as a percent of GDP continued to grow, increasing from 35.2 percent at the end of 2007 to 79.2 percent in 2019.

As a result of the COVID-19 pandemic and the Government's actions to address the pandemic and support the economy, debt held by the public increased sharply in 2020, growing from 79.2 percent of GDP at the end of 2019 to 100.1 percent at the end of 2020.

In 2021, due largely to continued Government action, such as the American Rescue Plan, to end the pandemic and provide economic stimulus, the deficit is projected to

---

[1] This is 2020 nominal interest on debt held by the public. For a discussion of real net interest, see Chapter 3, "Long-Term Budget Outlook."

[2] The *Historical Tables* are available at *https://www.whitehouse.gov/omb/historical-tables/*.

Table 4–1.   TRENDS IN FEDERAL DEBT HELD BY THE PUBLIC AND INTEREST ON THE DEBT HELD BY THE PUBLIC

(Dollar amounts in billions)

Fiscal Year	Debt held by the public		Debt held by the public as a percent of		Interest on the debt held by the public [3]		Interest on the debt held by the public as a percent of [3]	
	Current dollars	FY 2020 dollars [1]	GDP	Credit market debt [2]	Current dollars	FY 2020 dollars [1]	Total outlays	GDP
1946	241.9	2,635.0	106.1	N/A	4.2	45.5	7.6	1.8
1950	219.0	1,927.7	78.6	53.3	4.8	42.6	11.4	1.7
1955	226.6	1,753.1	55.8	42.1	5.2	40.1	7.6	1.3
1960	236.8	1,623.7	44.3	33.1	7.8	53.6	8.5	1.5
1965	260.8	1,675.6	36.8	26.4	9.6	61.5	8.1	1.4
1970	283.2	1,516.4	27.1	20.3	15.4	82.3	7.9	1.5
1975	394.7	1,556.8	24.6	17.9	25.0	98.6	7.5	1.6
1980	711.9	1,952.4	25.5	18.4	62.8	172.1	10.6	2.2
1985	1,507.3	3,150.5	35.3	22.2	152.9	319.6	16.2	3.6
1990	2,411.6	4,330.7	40.9	22.5	202.4	363.4	16.2	3.4
1995	3,604.4	5,709.1	47.7	26.3	239.2	378.9	15.8	3.2
2000	3,409.8	4,976.9	33.7	18.8	232.8	339.8	13.0	2.3
2005	4,592.2	5,998.4	35.8	17.1	191.4	250.0	7.7	1.5
2010	9,018.9	10,671.0	60.8	25.0	228.2	270.0	6.6	1.5
2015	13,116.7	14,227.3	72.5	30.4	260.6	282.7	7.1	1.4
2016	14,167.6	15,233.3	76.4	31.4	283.8	305.2	7.4	1.5
2017	14,665.4	15,492.8	76.0	31.3	309.9	327.3	7.8	1.6
2018	15,749.6	16,262.9	77.4	31.8	371.4	383.5	9.0	1.8
2019	16,800.7	17,012.0	79.2	32.4	423.3	428.6	9.5	2.0
2020	21,016.7	21,016.7	100.1	36.2	387.4	387.4	5.9	1.8
2021 estimate	24,166.7	23,764.3	109.7	N/A	360.5	354.5	5.0	1.6
2022 estimate	26,264.8	25,361.0	111.8	N/A	355.8	343.6	5.9	1.5
2023 estimate	27,683.1	26,222.3	112.7	N/A	374.9	355.1	6.2	1.5
2024 estimate	29,062.2	26,988.7	113.8	N/A	423.6	393.4	6.8	1.7
2025 estimate	30,538.7	27,803.7	115.2	N/A	500.6	455.8	7.7	1.9
2026 estimate	31,957.9	28,525.3	116.1	N/A	576.9	515.0	8.6	2.1
2027 estimate	33,266.1	29,110.7	116.4	N/A	657.7	575.5	9.5	2.3
2028 estimate	34,690.9	29,762.2	116.8	N/A	729.8	626.1	10.0	2.5
2029 estimate	35,996.2	30,276.4	116.6	N/A	799.3	672.3	10.8	2.6
2030 estimate	37,480.8	30,906.9	116.8	N/A	883.7	728.7	11.3	2.8
2031 estimate	39,059.3	31,576.9	117.0	N/A	970.7	784.8	11.8	2.9

N/A = Not available.

[1] Amounts in current dollars deflated by the GDP chain-type price index with fiscal year 2020 equal to 100.

[2] Total credit market debt owed by domestic nonfinancial sectors. Financial sectors are omitted to avoid double counting, since financial intermediaries borrow in the credit market primarily in order to finance lending in the credit market. Source: Federal Reserve Board flow of funds accounts. Projections are not available.

[3] Interest on debt held by the public is estimated as the interest on Treasury debt securities less the "interest received by trust funds" (subfunction 901 less subfunctions 902 and 903). The estimate of interest on debt held by the public does not include the comparatively small amount of interest paid on agency debt or the offsets for interest on Treasury debt received by other Government accounts (revolving funds and special funds).

increase to $3,669 billion[3] and debt held by the public is projected to grow to 109.7 percent of GDP. The deficit is projected to fall to $1,837 billion in 2022, and debt held by the public is projected to grow more slowly, to 111.8 percent of GDP. After 2022, the deficit is projected to roughly stabilize at around 5 percent as a percent of GDP. As a result, debt held by the public will increase more gradually, reaching 117.0 percent of GDP by 2031. Debt held by the public net of financial assets as a percent of GDP is estimated to grow to 98.4 percent of GDP at the end of 2021, 100.1 percent at the end of 2022, and 108.5 percent by the end of 2031.

Debt Held by the Public and Gross Federal Debt

The Federal Government issues debt securities for two main purposes. First, it borrows from the public to provide for the Federal Government's financing needs, including both the deficit and the other transactions requiring financing, most notably disbursements for direct student loans and other Federal credit programs.[4] Second, it issues debt to Federal Government accounts, primarily trust funds, that accumulate surpluses. By law, trust fund surpluses must generally be invested in Federal securities. The gross Federal debt is defined to consist of both the debt held by the public and the debt held by Government accounts. Nearly all the Federal debt has been issued by the Treasury and is sometimes called "public debt," but a small portion has been issued by other Government agencies and is called "agency debt."[5]

Borrowing from the public, whether by the Treasury or by some other Federal agency, is important because it represents the Federal demand on credit markets. Regardless of whether the proceeds are used for tangible or intangible investments or to finance current consumption, the Federal demand on credit markets has to be financed out of the saving of households and businesses, the State and local sector, or the rest of the world. Borrowing from the public can thus affect the size and composition of assets held by the private sector and the amount of saving imported from abroad and increase the amount of future resources required to pay interest to the public on Federal debt. Borrowing from the public is therefore an important consideration in Federal fiscal policy. Borrowing from the public, however, is an incomplete measure of the Federal impact on credit markets. Different types of Federal activities can affect the credit markets in different ways. For example, under its direct loan programs, the Government uses borrowed funds to acquire financial assets that might otherwise require financing in the cred-

it markets directly. (For more information on other ways in which Federal activities impact the credit market, see the discussion at the end of this chapter.) By incorporating the change in direct loan and other financial assets, debt held by the public net of financial assets adds useful insight into the Government's financial condition.

Issuing debt securities to Government accounts performs an essential function in accounting for the operation of these funds. The balances of debt represent the cumulative surpluses of these funds due to the excess of their tax receipts, interest receipts, and other collections over their spending. The interest on the debt that is credited to these funds accounts for the fact that some earmarked taxes and user fees will be spent at a later time than when the funds receive the monies. The debt securities are assets of those funds but are a liability of the general fund to the funds that hold the securities, and are a mechanism for crediting interest to those funds on their recorded balances. These balances generally provide the fund with authority to draw upon the U.S. Treasury in later years to make future payments on its behalf to the public. Public policy may result in the Government's running surpluses and accumulating debt in trust funds and other Government accounts in anticipation of future spending.

However, issuing debt to Government accounts does not have any of the current credit market effects of borrowing from the public. It is an internal transaction of the Government, made between two accounts that are both within the Government itself. Issuing debt to a Government account is not a current transaction of the Government with the public; it is not financed by private savings and does not compete with the private sector for available funds in the credit market. While such issuance provides the account with assets—a binding claim against the Treasury— those assets are fully offset by the increased liability of the Treasury to pay the claims, which will ultimately be covered by the collection of revenues or by borrowing. Similarly, the current interest earned by the Government account on its Treasury securities does not need to be financed by other resources.

The debt held by Government accounts may differ from the estimated amount of the account's obligations or responsibilities to make future payments to the public. For example, if the account records the transactions of a social insurance program, the debt that it holds does not necessarily represent the actuarial present value of estimated future benefits (or future benefits less taxes) for the current participants in the program; nor does it necessarily represent the actuarial present value of estimated future benefits (or future benefits less taxes) for the current participants plus the estimated future participants over some stated time period. The future transactions of Federal social insurance and employee retirement programs, which own 90 percent of the debt held by Government accounts, are important in their own right and need to be analyzed separately. This can be done through information published in the actuarial and financial reports for these programs.[6]

---

[3] The estimated deficit for 2021 is based on partial year actual data and generally incorporates actuals through March.

[4] For the purposes of the Budget, "debt held by the public" is defined as debt held by investors outside of the Federal Government, both domestic and foreign, including U.S. State and local governments and foreign governments. It also includes debt held by the Federal Reserve.

[5] The term "agency debt" is defined more narrowly in the budget than customarily in the securities market, where it includes not only the debt of the Federal agencies listed in Table 4–4, but also certain Government-guaranteed securities and the debt of the Government-sponsored enterprises listed in Table 15–7 in the supplemental materials to the "Credit and Insurance" chapter. (Table 15–7 is available on the internet at: *https://www.whitehouse.gov/omb/analytical-perspectives/*.)

[6] Extensive actuarial analyses of the Social Security and Medicare programs are published in the annual reports of the boards of trustees

Table 4–2. FEDERAL GOVERNMENT FINANCING AND DEBT

(In billions of dollars)

	Actual 2020	Estimate										
		2021	2022	2023	2024	2025	2026	2027	2028	2029	2030	2031
Financing:												
Unified budget deficit	3,129.2	3,668.7	1,837.0	1,371.9	1,359.0	1,469.8	1,414.2	1,303.5	1,423.7	1,306.8	1,477.2	1,567.9
Other transactions affecting borrowing from the public:												
Changes in financial assets and liabilities: [1]												
Change in Treasury operating cash balance	1,399.2	−1,031.7	....	....	....	....	....	....	....	....	....	....
Net disbursements of credit financing accounts:												
Direct loan and Troubled Asset Relief Program (TARP) equity purchase accounts	198.3	159.3	110.0	43.7	16.8	3.5	2.5	1.4	−1.5	−3.9	4.6	7.6
Guaranteed loan accounts	−499.2	354.3	153.6	4.9	5.7	5.5	4.9	5.5	4.7	4.6	4.5	4.5
Subtotal, net disbursements	−300.9	513.7	263.7	48.6	22.5	9.0	7.4	6.9	3.2	0.7	9.1	12.1
Net purchases of non-Federal securities by the National Railroad Retirement Investment Trust	−0.5	*	−2.1	−1.8	−1.8	−1.8	−1.8	−1.7	−1.6	−1.5	−1.2	−1.0
Net change in other financial assets and liabilities [2]	−11.1	....	....	....	....	....	....	....	....	....	....	....
Subtotal, changes in financial assets and liabilities ...	1,086.8	−518.0	261.6	46.9	20.6	7.2	5.6	5.3	1.6	−0.9	8.0	11.1
Seigniorage on coins	−*	−0.6	−0.5	−0.5	−0.5	−0.5	−0.5	−0.5	−0.6	−0.6	−0.6	−0.6
Total, other transactions affecting borrowing from the public	1,086.7	−518.6	261.1	46.4	20.1	6.6	5.1	4.7	1.0	−1.4	7.4	10.5
Total, requirement to borrow from the public (equals change in debt held by the public)	4,216.0	3,150.1	2,098.1	1,418.3	1,379.1	1,476.5	1,419.3	1,308.2	1,424.7	1,305.4	1,484.6	1,578.5
Changes in Debt Subject to Statutory Limitation:												
Change in debt held by the public	4,216.0	3,150.1	2,098.1	1,418.3	1,379.1	1,476.5	1,419.3	1,308.2	1,424.7	1,305.4	1,484.6	1,578.5
Change in debt held by Government accounts	17.0	173.0	121.5	163.0	201.8	105.6	64.9	−93.1	−208.7	−120.2	−233.7	−273.4
Less: change in debt not subject to limit and other adjustments	0.8	1.4	0.9	1.1	1.1	−0.3	0.5	1.0	0.3	*	−1.1	−1.0
Total, change in debt subject to statutory limitation	4,233.8	3,324.5	2,220.4	1,582.4	1,582.0	1,581.8	1,484.7	1,216.1	1,216.3	1,185.2	1,249.8	1,304.0
Debt Subject to Statutory Limitation, End of Year:												
Debt issued by Treasury	26,881.0	30,204.3	32,423.5	34,004.6	35,585.7	37,167.4	38,651.7	39,867.0	41,082.5	42,267.0	43,516.9	44,820.9
Less: Treasury debt not subject to limitation (−) [3]	−7.7	−6.5	−5.3	−4.1	−3.2	−3.2	−2.8	−2.0	−1.1	−0.5	−0.5	−0.5
Agency debt subject to limitation	*	*	*	*	*	*	*	*	*	*	*	*
Adjustment for discount and premium [4]	47.2	47.2	47.2	47.2	47.2	47.2	47.2	47.2	47.2	47.2	47.2	47.2
Total, debt subject to statutory limitation [5]	26,920.4	30,244.9	32,465.3	34,047.7	35,629.7	37,211.4	38,696.1	39,912.2	41,128.6	42,313.7	43,563.6	44,867.6
Debt Outstanding, End of Year:												
Gross Federal debt: [6]												
Debt issued by Treasury	26,881.0	30,204.3	32,423.5	34,004.6	35,585.7	37,167.4	38,651.7	39,867.0	41,082.5	42,267.0	43,516.9	44,820.9
Debt issued by other agencies	21.5	21.3	21.6	21.7	21.6	21.8	21.7	21.5	22.1	22.7	23.8	24.8
Total, gross Federal debt	26,902.5	30,225.6	32,445.1	34,026.3	35,607.2	37,189.3	38,673.5	39,888.6	41,104.6	42,289.8	43,540.6	44,845.7
As a percent of GDP	128.1%	137.2%	138.1%	138.5%	139.4%	140.3%	140.5%	139.5%	138.4%	137.0%	135.7%	134.3%
Held by:												
Debt held by Government accounts	5,885.8	6,058.8	6,180.3	6,343.2	6,545.0	6,650.6	6,715.5	6,622.4	6,413.7	6,293.5	6,059.8	5,786.4
Debt held by the public [7]	21,016.7	24,166.7	26,264.8	27,683.1	29,062.2	30,538.7	31,957.9	33,266.1	34,690.9	35,996.2	37,480.8	39,059.3
As a percent of GDP	100.1%	109.7%	111.8%	112.7%	113.8%	115.2%	116.1%	116.4%	116.8%	116.6%	116.8%	117.0%

*$50 million or less.

[1] A decrease in the Treasury operating cash balance (which is an asset) is a means of financing a deficit and therefore has a negative sign. An increase in checks outstanding (which is a liability) is also a means of financing a deficit and therefore also has a negative sign.

[2] Includes checks outstanding, accrued interest payable on Treasury debt, uninvested deposit fund balances, allocations of special drawing rights, and other liability accounts; and, as an offset, cash and monetary assets (other than the Treasury operating cash balance), other asset accounts, and profit on sale of gold.

[3] Consists primarily of debt issued by the Federal Financing Bank.

[4] Consists mainly of unamortized discount (less premium) on public issues of Treasury notes and bonds (other than zero-coupon bonds) and unrealized discount on Government account series securities.

[5] Legislation enacted August 2, 2019 (P.L. 116-37), temporarily suspends the debt limit through July 31, 2021.

[6] Treasury securities held by the public and zero-coupon bonds held by Government accounts are almost all measured at sales price plus amortized discount or less amortized premium. Agency debt securities are almost all measured at face value. Treasury securities in the Government account series are otherwise measured at face value less unrealized discount (if any).

[7] At the end of 2020, the Federal Reserve Banks held $4,445.5 billion of Federal securities and the rest of the public held $16,571.2 billion. Debt held by the Federal Reserve Banks is not estimated for future years.

This Budget uses a variety of information sources to analyze the condition of Social Security and Medicare, the Government's two largest social insurance programs. The excess of future Social Security and Medicare benefits relative to their dedicated income is very different in concept and much larger in size than the amount of Treasury securities that these programs hold.

For all these reasons, debt held by the public and debt held by the public net of financial assets are both better gauges of the effect of the budget on the credit markets than gross Federal debt.

Government Deficits or Surpluses and the Change in Debt

Table 4–2 summarizes Federal borrowing and debt from 2020 through 2031.[7] In 2020, the Government borrowed $4,216 billion, increasing the debt held by the public from $16,801 billion at the end of 2019 to $21,017 billion at the end of 2020. The debt held by Government accounts grew by $17 billion, and gross Federal debt increased by $4,233 billion to $26,902 billion.

Debt held by the public.—The Federal Government primarily finances deficits by borrowing from the public, and it primarily uses surpluses to repay debt held by the public.[8] Table 4–2 shows the relationship between the Federal deficit or surplus and the change in debt held by the public. The borrowing or debt repayment depends on the Government's expenditure programs and tax laws, on the economic conditions that influence tax receipts and outlays, and on debt management policy. The sensitivity of the budget to economic conditions is analyzed in Chapter 2, "Economic Assumptions and Overview," in this volume.

The total or unified budget consists of two parts: the on-budget portion; and the off-budget Federal entities, which have been excluded from the budget by law. Under present law, the off-budget Federal entities are the two Social Security trust funds (Old-Age and Survivors Insurance and Disability Insurance) and the Postal Service Fund.[9] The on-budget and off-budget surpluses or deficits are added together to determine the Government's financing needs.

---

of these funds. The actuarial estimates for Social Security, Medicare, and the major Federal employee retirement programs are summarized in the *Financial Report of the United States Government*, prepared annually by the Department of the Treasury in coordination with the Office of Management and Budget, and presented in more detail in the financial statements of the agencies administering those programs.

[7] For projections of the debt beyond 2031, see Chapter 3, "Long-Term Budget Outlook."

[8] Treasury debt held by the public is measured as the sales price plus the amortized discount (or less the amortized premium). At the time of sale, the book value equals the sales price. Subsequently, it equals the sales price plus the amount of the discount that has been amortized up to that time. In equivalent terms, the book value of the debt equals the principal amount due at maturity (par or face value) less the unamortized discount. (For a security sold at a premium, the definition is symmetrical.) For inflation-protected notes and bonds, the book value includes a periodic adjustment for inflation. Agency debt is generally recorded at par.

[9] For further explanation of the off-budget Federal entities, see Chapter 7, "Coverage of the Budget."

Over the long run, it is a good approximation to say that "the deficit is financed by borrowing from the public" or "the surplus is used to repay debt held by the public." However, the Government's need to borrow in any given year has always depended on several other factors besides the unified budget surplus or deficit, such as the change in the Treasury operating cash balance. These other factors—"other transactions affecting borrowing from the public"—can either increase or decrease the Government's need to borrow and can vary considerably in size from year to year. The other transactions affecting borrowing from the public are presented in Table 4–2 (where an increase in the need to borrow is represented by a positive sign, like the deficit).

In 2020 the deficit was $3,129 billion while these other factors increased the need to borrow by $1,087 billion, or 26 percent of total borrowing from the public. As a result, the Government borrowed $4,216 billion from the public. The other factors are estimated to reduce borrowing by $519 billion (16 percent of total borrowing from the public) in 2021, and increase borrowing by $261 billion (12 percent) in 2022. In 2023–2031, these other factors are expected to impact borrowing by annual amounts ranging from a $1 billion decrease to a $46 billion increase.

Three specific factors presented in Table 4–2, and discussed below, have historically been especially important.

Change in Treasury operating cash balance.—The cash balance increased by $1,399 billion in 2020, to $1,782 billion. This was a significantly larger change than in previous years; over the prior 10 years, annual increases and decreases in the cash balance ranged from $2 billion to $252 billion. The higher 2020 cash balance was needed to manage the changes to outlays and receipts associated with the COVID-19 impacts and the Federal response. For risk management purposes, Treasury seeks to maintain a cash balance roughly equal to one week of Government outflows, with a minimum balance of about $150 billion. The operating cash balance is projected to decrease by $1,032 billion, to $750 billion, at the end of 2021. Changes in the operating cash balance, while occasionally large, are inherently limited over time. Decreases in cash—a means of financing the Government—are limited by the amount of past accumulations, which themselves required financing when they were built up. Increases are limited because it is generally more efficient to repay debt.

Net financing disbursements of the direct loan and guaranteed loan financing accounts.—Under the Federal Credit Reform Act of 1990 (FCRA), the budgetary program account for each credit program records the estimated subsidy costs—the present value of estimated net losses—at the time when the direct or guaranteed loans are disbursed. The individual cash flows to and from the public associated with the loans or guarantees, such as the disbursement and repayment of loans, the default payments on loan guarantees, the collection of interest and fees, and so forth, are recorded in the credit program's non-budgetary financing account. Although the non-budgetary financing account's cash flows to and from the public are not included in the deficit (except for their impact on subsidy costs), they affect Treasury's net borrowing requirements.[10]

In addition to the transactions with the public, the financing accounts include several types of intragovernmental transactions. They receive payment from the credit program accounts for the subsidy costs of new direct loans and loan guarantees and for any upward reestimate of the costs of outstanding direct and guaranteed loans. They also receive interest from Treasury on balances of uninvested funds. The financing accounts pay any negative subsidy collections or downward reestimate of costs to budgetary receipt accounts and pay interest on borrowings from Treasury. The total net collections and gross disbursements of the financing accounts, consisting of transactions with both the public and the budgetary accounts, are called "net financing disbursements." They occur in the same way as the "outlays" of a budgetary account, even though they do not represent budgetary costs, and therefore affect the requirement for borrowing from the public in the same way as the deficit.

The intragovernmental transactions of the credit program, financing, and downward reestimate receipt accounts do not affect Federal borrowing from the public. Although the deficit changes because of the budgetary account's outlay to, or receipt from, a financing account, the net financing disbursement changes in an equal amount with the opposite sign, so the effects are cancelled out. On the other hand, financing account disbursements to the public increase the requirement for borrowing from the public in the same way as an increase in budget outlays that are disbursed to the public in cash. Likewise, receipts from the public collected by the financing account can be used to finance the payment of the Government's obligations, and therefore they reduce the requirement for Federal borrowing from the public in the same way as an increase in budgetary receipts.

Credit net financing disbursements reduced borrowing by $301 billion in 2020. Credit financing accounts are projected to increase borrowing by $514 billion in 2021 and by $264 billion in 2022. From 2023 to 2031, the credit financing accounts are expected to increase borrowing by amounts ranging from $1 billion to $49 billion.

In some years, large net upward or downward reestimates in the cost of outstanding direct and guaranteed loans may cause large swings in the net financing disbursements. In 2021, upward reestimates for student loans are partly offset by downward reestimates for Small Business Administration Disaster Assistance loans and Federal Housing Administration (FHA) guarantees, resulting in a net upward reestimate of $3.8 billion. In 2020, there was a net upward reestimate of $51.1 billion.

Net purchases of non-Federal securities by the National Railroad Retirement Investment Trust (NRRIT).— This trust fund, which was established by the Railroad Retirement and Survivors' Improvement Act of 2001, invests its assets primarily in private stocks and bonds. The Act required special treatment of the purchase or sale

of non-Federal assets by the NRRIT trust fund, treating such purchases as a means of financing rather than as outlays. Therefore, the increased need to borrow from the public to finance NRRIT's purchases of non-Federal assets is part of the "other transactions affecting borrowing from the public" rather than included as an increase in the deficit. While net purchases and redemptions affect borrowing from the public, unrealized gains and losses on NRRIT's portfolio are included in both the "other transactions" and, with the opposite sign, in NRRIT's net outlays in the deficit, for no net impact on borrowing from the public. In 2020, net decreases, including redemptions and losses, were $0.5 billion. A $21 million net increase is projected for 2021 and net annual decreases ranging from $1.0 billion to $2.1 billion are projected for 2022 and subsequent years.[11]

Debt held by Government accounts.—The amount of Federal debt issued to Government accounts depends largely on the surpluses of the trust funds, both on-budget and off-budget, which owned 89 percent of the total Federal debt held by Government accounts at the end of 2020. Net investment may differ from the surplus due to changes in the amount of cash assets not currently invested. In 2020, there was a total trust fund deficit of $53 billion,[12] while trust fund investment in Federal securities fell by $29 billion. The remainder of debt issued to Government accounts is owned by a number of special funds and revolving funds. The debt held in major accounts and the annual investments are shown in Table 4–5.

Debt Held by the Public Net of Financial Assets and Liabilities

While debt held by the public is a key measure for examining the role and impact of the Federal Government in the U.S. and international credit markets and for other purposes, it provides incomplete information on the Government's financial condition. The U.S. Government holds significant financial assets, which can be offset against debt held by the public and other financial liabilities to achieve a more complete understanding of the Government's financial condition. The acquisition of those financial assets represents a transaction with the credit markets, broadening those markets in a way that is analogous to the demand on credit markets that borrowing entails. For this reason, debt held by the public is also an incomplete measure of the impact of the Federal Government in the United States and international credit markets.

One transaction that can increase both borrowing and assets is an increase to the Treasury operating cash balance. When the Government borrows to increase the Treasury operating cash balance, that cash balance also represents an asset that is available to the Federal Government. Looking at both sides of this transaction—

---

[10] The FCRA (sec. 505(b)) requires that the financing accounts be non-budgetary. They are non-budgetary in concept because they do not measure cost. For additional discussion of credit programs, see Chapter 15, "Credit and Insurance," and Chapter 6, "Budget Concepts."

[11] The budget treatment of this fund is further discussed in Chapter 6, "Budget Concepts."

[12] 2020 was the first time in several decades that the trust funds group ran a deficit rather than a surplus, due to the impacts of the COVID-19 pandemic and the Federal response. For further discussion of trust funds, see Chapter 18, "Trust Funds and Federal Funds."

the borrowing to obtain the cash and the asset of the cash holdings—provides much more complete information about the Government's financial condition than looking at only the borrowing from the public. Another example of a transaction that simultaneously increases borrowing from the public and Federal assets is Government borrowing to issue direct loans to the public. When the direct loan is made, the Government is also acquiring an asset in the form of future payments of principal and interest, net of the Government's expected losses on the loan. Similarly, when NRRIT increases its holdings of non-Federal securities, the borrowing to purchase those securities is offset by the value of the asset holdings.

The acquisition or disposition of Federal financial assets very largely explains the difference between the deficit for a particular year and that year's increase in debt held by the public. Debt held by the public net of financial assets is a measure that is conceptually closer to the measurement of Federal deficits or surpluses; cumulative deficits and surpluses over time more closely equal the debt held by the public net of financial assets than they do the debt held by the public.

Table 4–3 presents debt held by the public net of the Government's financial assets and liabilities. Treasury debt is presented in the Budget at book value, with no adjustments for the change in economic value that results from fluctuations in interest rates. The balances of credit financing accounts are based on projections of future cash flows. For direct loan financing accounts, the balance generally represents the net present value of anticipated future inflows such as principal and interest payments from borrowers. For guaranteed loan financing accounts,

the balance generally represents the net present value of anticipated future outflows, such as default claim payments net of recoveries, and other collections, such as program fees. NRRIT's holdings of non-Federal securities are marked to market on a monthly basis. Government-sponsored enterprise stock and Air carrier worker support warrants and notes are measured at market value.

Due largely to the $1,399 billion increase in the Treasury operating cash balance, partly offset by other transactions, net financial assets grew by $1,087 billion, to $2,993 billion, in 2020. This $2,993 billion in net financial assets included a cash balance of $1,782 billion, net credit financing account balances of $1,147 billion, and other assets and liabilities that aggregated to a net asset of $65 billion. At the end of 2020, debt held by the public was $21,017 billion, or 100.1 percent of GDP. Therefore, debt held by the public net of financial assets was $18,024 billion, or 85.8 percent of GDP. As shown in Table 4–3, the value of the Government's net financial assets is projected to fall, to $2,483 billion in 2021. The projected 2021 decrease is principally due to the anticipated decrease in the Treasury operating cash balance, partly offset by the expected increase in the value of the credit financing accounts. While debt held by the public is expected to increase from 100.1 percent to 109.7 percent of GDP during 2021, debt held by the public net of financial assets is expected to increase from 85.8 percent to 98.4 percent of GDP.

Debt securities and other financial assets and liabilities do not encompass all the assets and liabilities of the Federal Government. For example, accounts payable occur in the normal course of buying goods and services;

Table 4–3. DEBT HELD BY THE PUBLIC NET OF FINANCIAL ASSETS AND LIABILITIES

(Dollar amounts in billions)

	Actual 2020	Estimate										
		2021	2022	2023	2024	2025	2026	2027	2028	2029	2030	2031
Debt Held by the Public:												
Debt held by the public	21,016.7	24,166.7	26,264.8	27,683.1	29,062.2	30,538.7	31,957.9	33,266.1	34,690.9	35,996.2	37,480.8	39,059.3
As a percent of GDP	100.1%	109.7%	111.8%	112.7%	113.8%	115.2%	116.1%	116.4%	116.8%	116.6%	116.8%	117.0%
Financial Assets Net of Liabilities:												
Treasury operating cash balance	1,781.7	750.0	750.0	750.0	750.0	750.0	750.0	750.0	750.0	750.0	750.0	750.0
Credit financing account balances:												
Direct loan and TARP equity purchase accounts	1,613.3	1,772.6	1,882.6	1,926.3	1,943.1	1,946.6	1,949.1	1,950.6	1,949.0	1,945.1	1,949.7	1,957.3
Guaranteed loan accounts	−466.7	−112.4	41.3	46.2	51.9	57.3	62.2	67.7	72.4	77.0	81.6	86.1
Subtotal, credit financing account balances	1,146.5	1,660.2	1,923.9	1,972.5	1,995.0	2,004.0	2,011.4	2,018.3	2,021.5	2,022.2	2,031.3	2,043.4
Government-sponsored enterprise stock [1]	108.9	108.9	108.9	108.9	108.9	108.9	108.9	108.9	108.9	108.9	108.9	108.9
Air carrier worker support warrants and notes [2]	5.3	13.0	13.0	13.0	13.0	13.0	12.5	11.9	11.9	11.9	11.9	6.6
Non-Federal securities held by NRRIT	24.0	24.0	21.9	20.1	18.3	16.5	14.7	13.1	11.4	9.9	8.7	7.7
Other assets net of liabilities	−73.4	−73.4	−73.4	−73.4	−73.4	−73.4	−73.4	−73.4	−73.4	−73.4	−73.4	−73.4
Total, financial assets net of liabilities	2,993.0	2,482.7	2,744.4	2,791.2	2,811.9	2,819.0	2,824.2	2,828.8	2,830.4	2,829.5	2,837.5	2,843.3
Debt Held by the Public Net of Financial Assets and Liabilities:												
Debt held by the public net of financial assets	18,023.6	21,684.0	23,520.5	24,891.9	26,250.4	27,719.6	29,133.8	30,437.3	31,860.5	33,166.7	34,643.3	36,216.0
As a percent of GDP	85.8%	98.4%	100.1%	101.3%	102.8%	104.5%	105.8%	106.5%	107.3%	107.5%	107.9%	108.5%

*$50 million or less.

[1] Treasury's warrants to purchase 79.9 percent of the common stock of the enterprises expire after September 7, 2028. The warrants were valued at $13 billion at the end of 2020.

[2] Of the notes and warrants issued under Air carrier worker support (Payroll support program), $0.5 billion are scheduled to expire by the end of 2026, $0.6 billion are scheduled to expire by the end of 2027, and $5.3 billion are scheduled to expire by the end of 2031.

Social Security benefits are due and payable as of the end of the month but, according to statute, are paid during the next month; and Federal employee salaries are paid after they have been earned. Like debt securities sold in the credit market, these liabilities have their own distinctive effects on the economy. The Federal Government also has significant holdings of non-financial assets, such as land, mineral deposits, buildings, and equipment. The different types of assets and liabilities are reported annually in the financial statements of Federal agencies and in the *Financial Report of the United States Government*, prepared by the Treasury in coordination with OMB.

Treasury Debt

Nearly all Federal debt is issued by the Department of the Treasury. Treasury meets most of the Federal Government's financing needs by issuing marketable securities to the public. These financing needs include both the change in debt held by the public and the refinancing—or rollover—of any outstanding debt that matures during the year. Treasury marketable debt is sold at public auctions on a regular schedule and, because it is very liquid, can be bought and sold on the secondary market at narrow bid-offer spreads. Treasury also sells to the public a relatively small amount of nonmarketable securities, such as savings bonds and State and Local Government Series securities (SLGS).[13] Treasury nonmarketable debt cannot be bought or sold on the secondary market.

Treasury issues marketable securities in a wide range of maturities, and issues both nominal (non-inflation-protected) and inflation-protected securities. Treasury's marketable securities include:

Treasury Bills—Treasury bills have maturities of one year or less from their issue date. In addition to the regular auction calendar of bill issuance, Treasury issues cash management bills on an as-needed basis for various reasons such as to offset the seasonal patterns of the Government's receipts and outlays. In 2020, Treasury began issuing cash management bills on a weekly basis in relation to the financing needed due to the impacts of the COVID-19 pandemic and the Government's response.

Treasury Notes—Treasury notes have maturities of more than one year and up to 10 years.

Treasury Bonds—Treasury bonds have maturities of more than 10 years. The longest-maturity securities issued by Treasury are 30-year bonds. In 2020, Treasury began issuing a monthly 20-year bond.

Treasury Inflation-Protected Securities (TIPS)—Treasury inflation-protected—or inflation-indexed—securities are coupon issues for which the par value of the security rises with inflation. The principal value is adjusted daily to reflect inflation as measured by changes in the Consumer Price Index (CPI-U-NSA, with a two-month lag). Although the principal value may be adjusted downward if inflation is negative, at maturity, the securities will be redeemed at the greater of their inflation-adjusted principal or par amount at original issue.

Floating Rate Securities—Floating rate securities have a fixed par value but bear interest rates that fluctuate based on movements in a specified benchmark market interest rate. Treasury's floating rate notes are benchmarked to the Treasury 13-week bill. Currently, Treasury is issuing floating rate securities with a maturity of two years.

Historically, the average maturity of outstanding debt issued by Treasury has been about five years. The average maturity of outstanding debt was 63 months at the end of 2020.

In addition to quarterly announcements about the overall auction calendar, Treasury publicly announces in advance the auction of each security. Individuals can participate directly in Treasury auctions or can purchase securities through brokers, dealers, and other financial institutions. Treasury accepts two types of auction bids: competitive and noncompetitive. In a competitive bid, the bidder specifies the yield. A significant portion of competitive bids are submitted by primary dealers, which are banks and securities brokerages that have been designated to trade in Treasury securities with the Federal Reserve System. In a noncompetitive bid, the bidder agrees to accept the yield determined by the auction.[14] At the close of the auction, Treasury accepts all eligible noncompetitive bids and then accepts competitive bids in ascending order beginning with the lowest yield bid until the offering amount is reached. All winning bidders receive the highest accepted yield bid.

Treasury marketable securities are highly liquid and actively traded on the secondary market, which enhances the demand for Treasuries at initial auction. The demand for Treasury securities is reflected in the ratio of bids received to bids accepted in Treasury auctions; the demand for the securities is substantially greater than the level of issuance. Because they are backed by the full faith and credit of the United States Government, Treasury marketable securities are considered to be credit "risk-free." Therefore, the Treasury yield curve is commonly used as a benchmark for a wide variety of purposes in the financial markets.

Whereas Treasury issuance of marketable debt is based on the Government's financing needs, Treasury's issuance of nonmarketable debt is based on the public's demand for the specific types of investments. Increases in outstanding balances of nonmarketable debt, such as occurred in 2020, reduce the need for marketable borrowing.[15]

Agency Debt

A few Federal agencies other than Treasury, shown in Table 4–4, sell or have sold debt securities to the public and, at times, to other Government accounts. Currently, new debt is issued only by the Tennessee Valley Authority (TVA) and the Federal Housing Administration; the remaining agencies are repaying past borrowing. Agency debt was $21.5 billion at the end of 2020. Agency debt is

---

[13] Under the SLGS program, the Treasury offers special low-yield securities to State and local governments and other entities for temporary investment of proceeds of tax-exempt bonds.

[14] Noncompetitive bids cannot exceed $5 million per bidder.

[15] Detail on the marketable and nonmarketable securities issued by Treasury is found in the *Monthly Statement of the Public Debt*, published on a monthly basis by the Department of the Treasury.

around one-tenth of one percent of Federal debt held by the public. Primarily as a result of TVA activity, agency debt is estimated to fall to $21.3 billion at the end of 2021 and then increase to $21.6 billion at the end of 2022.

The predominant agency borrower is TVA, which had borrowings of $21.4 billion from the public as of the end of 2020, or over 99 percent of the total debt of all agencies other than Treasury. TVA issues debt primarily to finance capital projects.

TVA has traditionally financed its capital construction by selling bonds and notes to the public. Since 2000, it has also employed two types of alternative financing methods, lease financing obligations and prepayment obligations. Under the lease financing obligations method, TVA signs long-term contracts to lease some facilities and equipment. The lease payments under these contracts ultimately secure the repayment of third-party capital used to finance construction of the facility. TVA retains substantially all of the economic benefits and risks related to ownership of the assets.[16] Under the prepayment obligations method, TVA's power distributors may prepay a portion of the price of the power they plan to purchase in the future. In return, they obtain a discount on a specific quantity of the future power they buy from TVA. The quantity varies, depending on TVA's estimated cost of borrowing.

OMB determined that each of these alternative financing methods is a means of financing the acquisition of assets owned and used by the Government, or of refinancing debt previously incurred to finance such assets. They are equivalent in concept to other forms of borrowing from the public, although under different terms and conditions. The budget therefore records the upfront cash

proceeds from these methods as borrowing from the public, not offsetting collections.[17] The budget presentation is consistent with the reporting of these obligations as liabilities on TVA's balance sheet under generally accepted accounting principles. At the end of 2020, lease financing obligations were $1.3 billion and there were no outstanding obligations for prepayments. Table 4–4 presents lease financing obligations separately from TVA bonds and notes to distinguish between the types of borrowing.

Although the FHA generally makes direct disbursements to the public for default claims on FHA-insured mortgages, it may also pay claims by issuing debentures. Issuing debentures to pay the Government's bills is equivalent to selling securities to the public and then paying the bills by disbursing the cash borrowed, so the transaction is recorded as being simultaneously an outlay and borrowing. The debentures are therefore classified as agency debt.

A number of years ago, the Federal Government guaranteed the debt used to finance the construction of a building for the Architect of the Capitol, and subsequently exercised full control over the design, construction, and operation of the building. This arrangement is equivalent to direct Federal construction financed by Federal borrowing. The construction expenditures and interest were

---

[16] This arrangement is at least as governmental as a "lease-purchase without substantial private risk." For further detail on the current budgetary treatment of lease-purchase without substantial private risk, see OMB Circular No. A–11, Appendix B.

[17] This budgetary treatment differs from the treatment in the *Monthly Treasury Statement of Receipts and Outlays of the United States Government* (Monthly Treasury Statement) Table 6 Schedule C, and the *Combined Statement of Receipts, Outlays, and Balances of the United States Government* Schedule 3, both published by the Treasury. These two schedules, which present debt issued by agencies other than Treasury, exclude the TVA alternative financing arrangements. This difference in treatment is one factor causing minor differences between debt figures reported in the Budget and debt figures reported by Treasury. The other factors are adjustments for the timing of the reporting of Federal debt held by NRRIT and treatment of the Federal debt held by the Securities Investor Protection Corporation and the Public Company Accounting Oversight Board.

Table 4–4.   AGENCY DEBT

(In millions of dollars)

	2020 Actual		2021 Estimate		2022 Estimate	
	Borrowing/ Repayment(–)	Debt, End-of-Year	Borrowing/ Repayment(–)	Debt, End-of-Year	Borrowing/ Repayment(–)	Debt, End-of-Year
Borrowing from the public:						
Housing and Urban Development:						
Federal Housing Administration	....	19	....	19	....	19
Architect of the Capitol	–12	58	–13	45	–14	31
Tennessee Valley Authority:						
Bonds and notes..	–1,293	20,074	16	20,090	422	20,512
Lease financing obligations	–105	1,346	–242	1,104	–71	1,033
Total, borrowing from the public	–1,409	21,496	–239	21,258	337	21,595
Borrowing from other funds:						
Tennessee Valley Authority [1]	1	1	....	1	....	1
Total, borrowing from other funds	1	1	....	1	....	1
Total, agency borrowing	–1,408	21,497	–239	21,259	337	21,596
Memorandum:						
Tennessee Valley Authority bonds and notes, total	–1,292	20,075	16	20,091	422	20,513

[1] Represents open market purchases by the National Railroad Retirement Investment Trust.

therefore classified as Federal outlays, and the borrowing was classified as Federal agency borrowing from the public.

Several Federal agencies borrow from the Bureau of the Fiscal Service (Fiscal Service) or the Federal Financing Bank (FFB), both within the Department of the Treasury. Agency borrowing from the FFB or the Fiscal Service is not included in gross Federal debt. It would be double counting to add together (a) the agency borrowing from the Fiscal Service or FFB and (b) the Treasury borrowing from the public that is needed to provide the Fiscal Service or FFB with the funds to lend to the agencies.

Debt Held by Government Accounts

Trust funds, and some special funds and public enterprise revolving funds, accumulate cash in excess of current needs in order to meet future obligations. These cash surpluses are generally invested in Treasury securities.

The total investment holdings of trust funds and other Government accounts increased by $17 billion in 2020. Net investment by Government accounts is estimated to be $173 billion in 2021 and $121 billion in 2022, as shown in Table 4–5. The holdings of Federal securities by Government accounts are estimated to grow to $6,180 billion by the end of 2022, or 19 percent of the gross Federal debt. The percentage is estimated to decrease gradually over the next 10 years.

The Government account holdings of Federal securities are concentrated among a few funds: the Social Security Old-Age and Survivors Insurance and Disability Insurance trust funds; the Medicare Hospital Insurance and Supplementary Medical Insurance trust funds; and four Federal employee retirement funds. These Federal employee retirement funds include two trust funds, the Military Retirement Fund and the Civil Service Retirement and Disability Fund (CSRDF), and two special funds, the uniformed services Medicare-Eligible Retiree Health Care Fund (MERHCF) and the Postal Service Retiree Health Benefits Fund (PSRHBF). At the end of 2022, these Social Security, Medicare, and Federal employee retirement funds are estimated to own 79 percent of the total debt held by Government accounts. During 2020–2022, the Military Retirement Fund has a large surplus and is estimated to invest a total of $253 billion, 81 percent of total net investment by Government accounts. Some Government accounts are projected to have net disinvestment in Federal securities during 2020–2022.

Technical note on measurement.—The Treasury securities held by Government accounts consist almost entirely of the Government account series. Most were issued at par value (face value), and the securities issued at a discount or premium are traditionally recorded at par in the OMB and Treasury reports on Federal debt. However, there are two kinds of exceptions.

First, Treasury issues zero-coupon bonds to a very few Government accounts. Because the purchase price is a small fraction of par value and the amounts are large, the holdings are recorded in Table 4–5 at par value less unamortized discount. The only Government accounts that held zero-coupon bonds during 2020 are the Nuclear

Waste Disposal Fund in the Department of Energy, the Military Retirement Fund, and MERHCF. The unamortized discount on zero-coupon bonds held by these three funds was $24.3 billion at the end of 2020.

Second, Treasury subtracts the unrealized discount on other Government account series securities in calculating "net Federal securities held as investments of Government accounts." Unlike the discount recorded for zero-coupon bonds and debt held by the public, the unrealized discount is the discount at the time of issue and is not amortized over the term of the security. In Table 4–5 it is shown as a separate item at the end of the table and not distributed by account. The amount was $1.4 billion at the end of 2020.

Debt Held by the Federal Reserve

The Federal Reserve acquires marketable Treasury securities as part of its exercise of monetary policy. For purposes of the Budget and reporting by the Department of the Treasury, the transactions of the Federal Reserve are considered to be non-budgetary, and accordingly the Federal Reserve's holdings of Treasury securities are included as part of debt held by the public.[18] Federal Reserve holdings were $4,445 billion (21 percent of debt held by the public) at the end of 2020. Over the last 10 years, the Federal Reserve holdings have averaged 17 percent of debt held by the public. The historical holdings of the Federal Reserve are presented in Table 7.1 in the Budget's *Historical Tables*. The Budget does not project Federal Reserve holdings for future years.

Limitations on Federal Debt

Definition of debt subject to limit.—Statutory limitations have usually been placed on Federal debt. Until World War I, the Congress ordinarily authorized a specific amount of debt for each separate issue. Beginning with the Second Liberty Bond Act of 1917, however, the nature of the limitation was modified in several steps until it developed into a ceiling on the total amount of most Federal debt outstanding. This last type of limitation has been in effect since 1941. The limit currently applies to most debt issued by the Treasury since September 1917, whether held by the public or by Government accounts; and other debt issued by Federal agencies that, according to explicit statute, is guaranteed as to principal and interest by the U.S. Government.

The third part of Table 4–2 compares total Treasury debt with the amount of Federal debt that is subject to the limit. Nearly all Treasury debt is subject to the debt limit.

A large portion of the Treasury debt not subject to the general statutory limit was issued by the Federal Financing Bank. The FFB is authorized to have outstanding up to $15 billion of publicly issued debt. The FFB has on occasion issued this debt to CSRDF in exchange for equal amounts of regular Treasury securities. The FFB securities have the same interest rates and maturities as the Treasury securities for which they were exchanged.

---

[18] For further detail on the monetary policy activities of the Federal Reserve and the treatment of the Federal Reserve in the Budget, see Chapter 7, "Coverage of the Budget."

Table 4–5.   DEBT HELD BY GOVERNMENT ACCOUNTS[1]

(In millions of dollars)

Description	Investment or Disinvestment (–)			Holdings, End of 2022 Estimate
	2020 Actual	2021 Estimate	2022 Estimate	
Investment in Treasury debt:				
Judicial Branch:				
Judicial Officers' Retirement Fund	111	127	123	1,104
Commerce:				
Public Safety Trust Fund	105	4,519	100	12,285
Defense--Military:				
Host Nation Support Fund for Relocation	61	–422	–199	1,167
Energy:				
Nuclear Waste Disposal Fund [1]	1,740	508	514	43,361
Uranium Enrichment Decontamination Fund	–837	–836	6	21
Health and Human Services:				
Federal Hospital Insurance Trust Fund	–64,890	–13,736	1,289	121,288
Federal Supplementary Medical Insurance Trust Fund	–17,239	99,528	5,042	192,047
Vaccine Injury Compensation Fund	118	75	84	4,126
Child Enrollment Contingency Fund	....	15,979	6	15,985
Homeland Security:				
Aquatic Resources Trust Fund	86	67	54	2,204
Oil Spill Liability Trust Fund	460	724	725	8,764
National Flood Insurance Reserve Fund	120	860	600	3,105
Housing and Urban Development:				
Federal Housing Administration Mutual Mortgage Insurance Capital Reserve	17,336	12,891	9,681	90,509
Guarantees of Mortgage-Backed Securities Capital Reserve	–7,258	3,859	2,790	15,049
Interior:				
Bureau of Land Management Permanent Operating Funds	82	82	82	1,207
Abandoned Mine Reclamation Fund	–46	–41	–27	2,565
Federal Aid in Wildlife Restoration Fund	40	80	62	2,202
Environmental Improvement and Restoration Fund	24	15	14	1,571
Natural Resource Damage Assessment Fund	132	104	100	2,100
National Parks and Public Land Legacy Restoration Fund	....	1,615	938	2,553
Justice:				
Assets Forfeiture Fund	1,118	1	–36	3,189
U.S. Victims of State Sponsored Terrorism Fund	–872	*	....	168
Labor:				
Unemployment Trust Fund	–33,847	–7,089	9,157	52,583
Pension Benefit Guaranty Corporation	8,840	3,474	4,265	53,292
State:				
Foreign Service Retirement and Disability Trust Fund	663	599	370	20,950
Transportation:				
Airport and Airway Trust Fund	–7,118	5,735	–652	12,983
Highway Trust Fund	–16,112	–1,113	–10,968	....
Aviation Insurance Revolving Fund	10	35	11	2,348
Treasury:				
Exchange Stabilization Fund	–11,453	12,256	367	23,793
Treasury Forfeiture Fund	74	79	84	1,381
Gulf Coast Restoration Trust Fund	136	101	113	1,895
Comptroller of the Currency Assessment Fund	13	5	5	1,993
Veterans Affairs:				
Servicemembers' Group Life Insurance Fund	961	1,262	630	3,154
National Service Life Insurance Trust Fund	–510	–498	–405	1,043
Veterans Special Life Insurance Fund	–135	–156	–146	920
Corps of Engineers:				
Harbor Maintenance Trust Fund	–222	780	–928	8,912

Table 4–5. DEBT HELD BY GOVERNMENT ACCOUNTS [1]—Continued
(In millions of dollars)

Description	Investment or Disinvestment (–)			Holdings, End of 2022 Estimate
	2020 Actual	2021 Estimate	2022 Estimate	
Other Defense-Civil:				
Military Retirement Fund [1]	79,613	72,628	100,630	1,080,285
Medicare-Eligible Retiree Health Care Fund [1]	11,947	5,268	15,825	287,217
Education Benefits Fund	–29	–24	–23	1,003
Environmental Protection Agency:				
Hazardous Substance Superfund	–318	70	70	5,073
Leaking Underground Storage Tank Trust Fund	122	200	40	1,135
International Assistance Programs:				
Overseas Private Investment Corporation	–5,864	....	....	....
Development Finance Corporation Corporate Capital Account	6,165	94	–450	5,809
Office of Personnel Management:				
Civil Service Retirement and Disability Trust Fund	22,381	20,369	19,202	1,001,654
Postal Service Retiree Health Benefits Fund	–2,743	–2,808	–3,308	35,752
Employees Life Insurance Fund	930	623	624	50,376
Employees and Retired Employees Health Benefits Fund	529	3,634	1,527	33,492
Social Security Administration:				
Federal Old-Age and Survivors Insurance Trust Fund [2]	6,817	–64,800	–42,313	2,704,100
Federal Disability Insurance Trust Fund [2]	690	–7,412	2,741	92,538
District of Columbia:				
Federal Pension Fund	18	71	23	3,909
Farm Credit System Insurance Corporation:				
Farm Credit System Insurance Fund	221	307	504	5,964
Federal Deposit Insurance Corporation:				
Deposit Insurance Fund	4,934	5,269	6,883	121,101
National Credit Union Administration:				
Share Insurance Fund	1,334	1,463	2,395	20,468
Central Liquidity Facility	702	30	32	1,095
Postal Service:				
Postal Service Fund [2]	5,650	–4,154	–7,129	3,708
Railroad Retirement Board:				
Railroad Retirement Board trust funds	–917	599	234	2,536
Securities Investor Protection Corporation [3]	289	279	265	4,224
United States Enrichment Corporation Fund	14	–248	–496	973
Other Federal funds	–70	46	295	5,214
Other trust funds	–345	172	154	3,322
Unrealized discount [1]	13,386	....	....	–1,392
Total, investment in Treasury debt [1]	**17,032**	**173,017**	**121,454**	**6,180,270**
Investment in agency debt:				
Railroad Retirement Board:				
National Railroad Retirement Investment Trust	1	....	....	1
Total, investment in agency debt [1]	**1**	....	....	**1**
Total, investment in Federal debt [1]	**17,033**	**173,017**	**121,454**	**6,180,271**
Memorandum:				
Investment by Federal funds (on-budget)	26,957	61,993	42,056	759,279
Investment by Federal funds (off-budget)	5,650	–4,154	–7,129	3,708
Investment by trust funds (on-budget)	–36,467	187,391	126,099	2,622,036
Investment by trust funds (off-budget)	7,507	–72,213	–39,572	2,796,638
Unrealized discount [1]	13,386	....	....	–1,392

* $500 thousand or less.

[1] Debt held by Government accounts is measured at face value except for Treasury zero-coupon bonds, which are recorded at market or redemption price; and the unrealized discount on Government account series, which is not distributed by account. If recorded at face value, at the end of 2020 the debt figure would be $12.3 billion higher for the Nuclear Waste Disposal Fund, $9.2 billion higher for the Military Retirement Fund, and $2.8 billion higher for the Medicare-Eligible Retiree Health Care Fund than recorded in this table. Changes are not estimated in the unrealized discount.

[2] Off-budget Federal entity.

[3] Amounts on calendar-year basis.

Most recently, the FFB issued: $9 billion to the CSRDF on October 1, 2013, with maturity dates from June 30, 2015, through June 30, 2024; and $3 billion of securities to the CSRDF on October 15, 2015, with maturity dates from June 30, 2026, through June 30, 2029. The outstanding balance of FFB debt held by CSRDF was $7 billion at the end of 2020 and is projected to be $6 billion at the end of 2021.

The other Treasury debt not subject to the general limit consists almost entirely of silver certificates and other currencies no longer being issued. It was $478 million at the end of 2020 and is projected to gradually decline over time.

The sole agency debt currently subject to the general limit, $209 thousand at the end of 2020, is certain debentures issued by the Federal Housing Administration.[19]

Some of the other agency debt, however, is subject to its own statutory limit. For example, the Tennessee Valley Authority is limited to $30 billion of bonds and notes outstanding.

The comparison between Treasury debt and debt subject to limit also includes an adjustment for measurement differences in the treatment of discounts and premiums. As explained earlier in this chapter, debt securities may be sold at a discount or premium, and the measurement of debt may take this into account rather than recording the face value of the securities. However, the measurement differs between gross Federal debt (and its components) and the statutory definition of debt subject to limit. An adjustment is needed to derive debt subject to limit (as defined by law) from Treasury debt. The amount of the adjustment was $47 billion at the end of 2020 compared with the total unamortized discount (less premium) of $64 billion on all Treasury securities.

Changes in the debt limit.—The statutory debt limit has been changed many times. Since 1960, the Congress has passed 85 separate acts to raise the limit, revise the definition, extend the duration of a temporary increase, or temporarily suspend the limit.[20]

The seven most recent laws addressing the debt limit have each provided for a temporary suspension followed by an increase in an amount equivalent to the debt that was issued during that suspension period in order to fund commitments requiring payment through the specified end date. The Bipartisan Budget Act of 2018 suspended the $20,456 billion debt ceiling from February 9, 2018, through March 1, 2019, and then raised the debt limit on March 2, 2019, by $1,532 billion to $21,988 billion. The Bipartisan Budget Act of 2019 suspended the $21,988 billion debt ceiling from August 2, 2019, through July 31, 2021.

At many times in the past several decades, including 2018 and 2019, the Government has reached the statutory debt limit before an increase has been enacted. When this has occurred, it has been necessary for the Treasury to take "extraordinary measures" to meet the Government's obligation to pay its bills and invest its trust funds while remaining below the statutory limit.

One such extraordinary measure is the partial or full suspension of the daily reinvestment of the Thrift Savings Plan (TSP) Government Securities Investment Fund (G-Fund).[21] The Treasury Secretary has statutory authority to suspend investment of the G-Fund in Treasury securities as needed to prevent the debt from exceeding the debt limit. Treasury determines each day the amount of investments that would allow the fund to be invested as fully as possible without exceeding the debt limit. The TSP G-Fund had an outstanding balance of $292 billion at the end of April 2021. The Treasury Secretary is also authorized to suspend investments in the CSRDF and to declare a debt issuance suspension period, which allows him or her to redeem a limited amount of securities held by the CSRDF. The Postal Accountability and Enhancement Act of 2006 provides that investments in the Postal Service Retiree Health Benefits Fund shall be made in the same manner as investments in the CSRDF.[22] Therefore, Treasury is able to take similar administrative actions with the PSRHBF. The law requires that when any such actions are taken with the G-Fund, the CSRDF, or the PSRHBF, the Treasury Secretary is required to make the fund whole after the debt limit has been raised by restoring the forgone interest and investing the fund fully. Another measure for staying below the debt limit is disinvestment of the Exchange Stabilization Fund. The outstanding balance in the Exchange Stabilization Fund was $13 billion at the end of April.

As the debt has neared the limit, including in 2019, Treasury has also suspended the issuance of SLGS to reduce unanticipated fluctuations in the level of the debt. At times, Treasury has also adjusted the schedule for auctions of marketable securities.

In addition to these steps, Treasury has previously exchanged Treasury securities held by the CSRDF with borrowing by the FFB, which, as explained above, is not subject to the debt limit. This measure was most recently taken in October 2015.

The debt limit has always been increased prior to the exhaustion of Treasury's limited available administrative actions to continue to finance Government operations when the statutory ceiling has been reached. Failure to enact a debt limit increase before these actions were exhausted would have significant and long-term negative consequences. The Federal Government would be forced to delay or discontinue payments on its broad range of obligations, including Social Security and other payments to individuals, Medicaid and other grant payments to States, individual and corporate tax refunds, Federal employee salaries, payments to vendors and contractors, principal and interest payments on Treasury securities, and other obligations. If Treasury were unable to make timely interest payments or redeem securities, investors would

---

[19] At the end of 2020, there were also $18 million of FHA debentures not subject to limit.

[20] The Acts and the statutory limits since 1940 are listed in Table 7.3 of the Budget's *Historical Tables*, available at *https://www.whitehouse.gov/omb/historical-tables/*.

[21] The TSP is a defined contribution pension plan for Federal employees. The G-Fund is one of several components of the TSP.

[22] Both the CSRDF and the PSRHBF are administered by the Office of Personnel Management.

cease to view U.S. Treasury securities as free of credit risk and Treasury's interest costs would increase. Because interest rates throughout the economy are benchmarked to the Treasury rates, interest rates for State and local governments, businesses, and individuals would also rise. Foreign investors would likely shift out of dollar-denominated assets, driving down the value of the dollar and further increasing interest rates on non-Federal, as well as Treasury, debt.

The debt subject to limit is estimated to increase to $30,245 billion by the end of 2021 and to $32,465 billion by the end of 2022. The Budget anticipates timely congressional action to address the statutory limit as necessary before exhaustion of Treasury's extraordinary measures.

Federal funds financing and the change in debt subject to limit.—The change in debt held by the public, as shown in Table 4–2, and the change in debt held by the public net of financial assets are determined primarily by the total Government deficit or surplus. The debt subject to limit, however, includes not only debt held by the public but also debt held by Government accounts. The change in debt subject to limit is therefore determined both by the factors that determine the total Government deficit or surplus and by the factors that determine the change in debt held by Government accounts. The effect of debt held by Government accounts on the total debt subject to limit can be seen in the second part of Table 4–2. The change in debt held by Government accounts is equal to 5 percent of the estimated total 2021 increase in debt subject to limit.

The Budget is composed of two groups of funds, Federal funds and trust funds. The Federal funds, in the main, are derived from tax receipts and borrowing and are used for the general purposes of the Government. The trust funds, on the other hand, are financed by taxes or other receipts dedicated by law for specified purposes, such as for paying Social Security benefits or making grants to State governments for highway construction.[23]

A Federal funds deficit must generally be financed by borrowing, which can be done either by selling securities to the public or by issuing securities to Government accounts that are not within the Federal funds group. Federal funds borrowing consists almost entirely of Treasury securities that are subject to the statutory debt limit. Very little debt subject to statutory limit has been issued for reasons except to finance the Federal funds deficit. The change in debt subject to limit is therefore determined primarily by the Federal funds deficit, which is equal to the difference between the total Government deficit or surplus and the trust fund surplus. Trust fund surpluses are almost entirely invested in securities subject to the debt limit, and trust funds hold most of the debt held by Government accounts. The trust fund surplus reduces the total budget deficit or increases the total budget surplus, decreasing the need to borrow from the public or increasing the ability to repay borrowing from the public. When the trust fund surplus is invested in Federal securities, the debt held by Government accounts increases, offsetting the decrease in debt held by the public by an equal amount. Thus, there is no net effect on gross Federal debt.

Table 4–6 derives the change in debt subject to limit. In 2020 the Federal funds deficit was $3,076 billion, and other factors increased financing requirements by $1,087 billion. The change in the Treasury operating cash balance increased financing requirements by $1,399 billion, partly offset by the net financing disbursements of credit financing accounts and other Federal fund factors, which together reduced financing requirements by $312 billion. In addition, special funds and revolving funds, which are part of the Federal funds group, invested a net of $33 billion in Treasury securities. Adjustments are also made for the difference between the trust fund surplus or deficit and the trust funds' investment or disinvestment in Federal securities (including the changes in NRRIT's investments in non-Federal securities) and for the change in unrealized discount on Federal debt held by Government accounts. As a net result of all these factors, $4,233 billion in financing was required, increasing gross Federal debt by that amount. Since Federal debt not subject to limit fell by $3 billion and the adjustment for discount and premium changed by $2 billion, the debt subject to limit increased by $4,234 billion, while debt held by the public increased by $4,216 billion.

Debt subject to limit is estimated to increase by $3,325 billion in 2021 and by $2,220 billion in 2022. The projected increases in the debt subject to limit are caused by the continued Federal funds deficit, supplemented by the other factors shown in Table 4–6. While debt held by the public increases by $18,043 billion from the end of 2020 through 2031, debt subject to limit increases by $17,947 billion, due to projected outyear net disinvestment by Government accounts.

Foreign Holdings of Federal Debt

Foreign holdings of Federal debt are presented in Table 4–7. During most of American history, the Federal debt was held almost entirely by individuals and institutions within the United States. In the late 1960s, foreign holdings were just over $10 billion, less than 5 percent of the total Federal debt held by the public. Foreign holdings began to grow significantly in the early 1970s, and then remained about 15–20 percent of total Federal debt until the mid-1990s. During 1995–97, growth in foreign holdings accelerated, reaching 33 percent by the end of 1997. Since 2004, foreign holdings of Federal debt have generally represented around 40 percent or more of outstanding debt. Foreign holdings increased to 48 percent by the end of 2008 and then remained relatively stable through 2015. After 2015, foreign holdings began to decline as a percent of total Federal debt held by the public, falling from 47 percent at the end of 2015 to 40 percent at the end of 2018. In 2019, foreign holdings increased slightly, to 41 percent.

By the end of 2020, foreign holdings of Treasury debt had grown to $7,069 billion, but fell to 34 percent of the total debt held by the public.[24] The dollar increase in foreign holdings was about 3 percent of total Federal bor-

---

[23] For further discussion of the trust funds and Federal funds groups, see Chapter 18, "Trust Funds and Federal Funds."

[24] The debt calculated by the Bureau of Economic Analysis is different, though similar in size, because of a different method of valuing securities.

Table 4–6. FEDERAL FUNDS FINANCING AND CHANGE IN DEBT SUBJECT TO STATUTORY LIMIT

(In billions of dollars)

Description	Actual 2020	Estimate										
		2021	2022	2023	2024	2025	2026	2027	2028	2029	2030	2031
Change in Gross Federal Debt:												
Federal funds deficit	3,076.4	3,783.4	1,983.2	1,504.2	1,527.9	1,541.4	1,445.8	1,173.8	1,176.8	1,146.1	1,199.2	1,245.7
Other transactions affecting borrowing from the public—Federal funds [1]	1,087.2	–518.6	263.2	48.1	21.9	8.4	6.9	6.4	2.6	0.1	8.5	11.5
Increase (+) or decrease (–) in Federal debt held by Federal funds	32.6	57.8	34.9	31.8	34.1	35.2	34.4	36.7	38.3	40.6	44.4	48.8
Adjustments for trust fund surplus/deficit not invested/disinvested in Federal securities [2]	23.4	0.5	–61.8	–2.9	–3.0	–3.0	–3.0	–1.8	–1.7	–1.7	–1.2	–1.1
Change in unrealized discount on Federal debt held by Government accounts	13.4	....	....	....	....	....	....	....	....	....	....	....
Total financing requirements	4,233.0	3,323.1	2,219.5	1,581.3	1,580.9	1,582.1	1,484.2	1,215.1	1,216.1	1,185.1	1,250.9	1,305.0
Change in Debt Subject to Limit:												
Change in gross Federal debt	4,233.0	3,323.1	2,219.5	1,581.3	1,580.9	1,582.1	1,484.2	1,215.1	1,216.1	1,185.1	1,250.9	1,305.0
Less: increase (+) or decrease (–) in Federal debt not subject to limit	–3.0	–1.4	–0.9	–1.1	–1.1	0.3	–0.5	–1.0	–0.3	–*	1.1	1.0
Less: change in adjustment for discount and premium [3]	2.2	....	....	....	....	....	....	....	....	....	....	....
Total, change in debt subject to limit	4,233.8	3,324.5	2,220.4	1,582.4	1,582.0	1,581.8	1,484.7	1,216.1	1,216.3	1,185.2	1,249.8	1,304.0
Memorandum:												
Debt subject to statutory limit [4]	26,920.4	30,244.9	32,465.3	34,047.7	35,629.7	37,211.4	38,696.1	39,912.2	41,128.6	42,313.7	43,563.6	44,867.6

* $50 million or less.

[1] Includes Federal fund transactions that correspond to those presented in Table 4–2, but that are for Federal funds alone with respect to the public and trust funds.

[2] Includes trust fund holdings in other cash assets and changes in the investments of the National Railroad Retirement Investment Trust in non-Federal securities.

[3] Consists of unamortized discount (less premium) on public issues of Treasury notes and bonds (other than zero-coupon bonds).

[4] Legislation enacted August 2, 2019 (P.L. 116–37), temporarily suspends the debt limit through July 31, 2021.

rowing from the public in 2020 and 12 percent over the last five years. Increases in foreign holdings have been almost entirely due to decisions by foreign central banks, corporations, and individuals, rather than the direct marketing of these securities to foreign investors. All of the foreign holdings of Federal debt are denominated in dollars.

In 2020, foreign central banks and other foreign official institutions owned 59 percent of the foreign holdings of Federal debt; private investors owned the rest. At the end of 2020, the nations holding the largest shares of U.S. Federal debt were Japan, which held 18 percent of all foreign holdings, and China, which held 15 percent.

Foreign holdings of Federal debt are around 20-25 percent of the foreign-owned assets in the United States, depending on the method of measuring total assets. The foreign purchases of Federal debt securities do not measure the full impact of the capital inflow from abroad on the market for Federal debt securities. The capital inflow supplies additional funds to the credit market generally, and thus affects the market for Federal debt. For example, the capital inflow includes deposits in U.S. financial intermediaries that themselves buy Federal debt.

Federal, Federally Guaranteed, and Other Federally Assisted Borrowing

The Government's effects on the credit markets arise not only from its own borrowing but also from the direct loans that it makes to the public and the provision of assistance to certain borrowing by the public. The Government guarantees various types of borrowing by individuals, businesses, and other non-Federal entities, thereby providing assistance to private credit markets. The Government is also assisting borrowing by States through the Build America Bonds program, which subsidizes the interest that States pay on such borrowing. In addition, the Government has established private corporations—Government-sponsored enterprises—to provide financial intermediation for specified public purposes; it exempts the interest on most State and local government debt from income tax; it permits mortgage interest to be deducted in calculating taxable income; and it insures the deposits of banks and thrift institutions, which themselves make loans.

Federal credit programs and other forms of assistance are discussed in Chapter 15, "Credit and Insurance," in this volume. Detailed data are presented in tables accompanying that chapter.

Table 4–7. FOREIGN HOLDINGS OF FEDERAL DEBT
(Dollar amounts in billions)

Fiscal Year	Debt held by the public			Change in debt held by the public [2]	
	Total	Foreign [1]	Percentage foreign	Total	Foreign
1965	260.8	12.2	4.7	3.9	0.3
1970	283.2	14.0	4.9	5.1	3.7
1975	394.7	66.0	16.7	51.0	9.1
1980	711.9	126.4	17.8	71.6	1.3
1985	1,507.3	222.9	14.8	200.3	47.3
1990	2,411.6	463.8	19.2	220.8	72.0
1995	3,604.4	820.4	22.8	171.3	138.4
2000	3,409.8	1,038.8	30.5	−222.6	−242.6
2005	4,592.2	1,929.6	42.0	296.7	135.1
2010	9,018.9	4,324.2	47.9	1,474.2	753.6
2011	10,128.2	4,912.1	48.5	1,109.3	587.9
2012	11,281.1	5,476.1	48.5	1,152.9	564.0
2013	11,982.7	5,652.8	47.2	701.6	176.7
2014	12,779.9	6,069.2	47.5	797.2	416.4
2015	13,116.7	6,105.9	46.6	336.8	36.7
2016	14,167.6	6,155.9	43.5	1,050.9	50.0
2017	14,665.4	6,301.9	43.0	497.8	146.0
2018	15,749.6	6,225.9	39.5	1,084.1	−76.0
2019	16,800.7	6,923.5	41.2	1,051.1	697.6
2020	21,016.7	7,069.2	33.6	4,216.0	145.7

[1] Estimated by Treasury Department. These estimates exclude agency debt, the holdings of which are believed to be small. The data on foreign holdings are recorded by methods that are not fully comparable with the data on debt held by the public. Projections of foreign holdings are not available.

[2] Change in debt held by the public is defined as equal to the change in debt held by the public from the beginning of the year to the end of the year.

MANAGEMENT

5. STRENGTHENING THE FEDERAL WORKFORCE

"Our Constitution opens with the words, 'We the People.' It's time we remembered that We the People are the government. You and I. Not some force in a distant capital. Not some powerful force we have no control over. It's us. It's 'We the people.'" – President Biden

Even before the inauguration, President-elect Biden recorded a message to the Federal career workforce to establish how he would manage the civil service: "I'm thinking of you and I have the utmost trust in your capabilities. I'll be President for all Americans, just as you are civil servants for all Americans. And together, together, we'll lead with core values that have guided me throughout my career in public service, as I imagine they have guided you in your careers."

After decades of under-investment in a modern-day workforce, a failure to partner with labor unions, and ongoing, unwarranted attacks on its independence, the civil service is in need of repair and rebuilding and the Administration has already taken swift action to deliver on that goal. The reason for doing so is critical. As President Biden stated in his April 28, 2021, address to Congress: "We have to prove that democracy still works. That our government still works – and can deliver for the people."

This chapter provides an overview of actions the Administration has already taken and how the Budget will support additional efforts to strengthen, empower, and reenergize the Federal workforce. As in previous years, this chapter provides an annual update on the status of the U.S. civil service, including tables and charts that describe its size, location, demographics, costs, and projections. The chapter also reviews the actions that the Administration has taken during the first 100 days and its plans to help ensure the Federal workforce can meet the opportunities and challenges before us – both now and in the future.

First Actions

The Administration is committed to empowering, rebuilding, and protecting the Federal workforce, which is why the Budget provides for a 2.7 percent pay increase for the Federal civilian workforce. Proposed funding also will help executive departments and agencies (Agencies) implement the policy established in Executive Order (E.O.) 14003, issued on January 22, 2021, aimed at protecting the Federal workforce. As the Order stated, "career civil servants are the backbone of the Federal workforce, providing the expertise and experience necessary for the critical functioning of the Federal Government. It is the policy of the United States to protect, empower, and rebuild the career Federal workforce." Furthermore, the Administration is taking initial steps to revitalize the

national security workforce—whose expertise and work keep this country safe.

Before the hard work could begin on new efforts, the President immediately halted the previous administration's actions aimed at politicizing the civil service, destroying Federal employee unions, and decreasing diversity. In E.O. 14003, the Biden-Harris Administration eliminated Schedule F, which threatened the foundations of the civil service; restored and expanded collective bargaining power and worker protections for Federal workers; and directed the Office of Personnel Management (OPM) to make recommendations to the President to promote a $15 per hour minimum wage for Federal employees. E.O. 14025, "Worker Organizing and Empowerment," (April 26, 2021) tasked the Vice-President and Agency leadership with proposing ways to facilitate union organizing and worker power in the public and private sectors. Signed on April 27, 2021, E.O. 14026 requires contractors to pay a $15 minimum wage for any employees on Federal contracts, an increase from the current $10.95 per hour. This E.O. also ends the practice that allowed certain government contractors to pay a subminimum wage to people with disabilities under certain circumstances. The E.O. will put in motion actions to end that practice so that persons with disabilities start receiving at least the new $15 per hour minimum wage.

The Budget supports the steps that the President took on his first day in office to protect the health and safety of Federal employees and contractors from COVID-19 by directing Agencies to finalize and implement workplace health and safety plans aligned with the Centers for Disease Control and Prevention's (CDC's) science-based guidelines. Too many federal workers – like many other critical workers across the country – fell ill and died after contracting COVID-19 providing critical services for their fellow Americans, like ensuring our food is safe, caring for our veterans, responding to natural disasters, and keeping Government operations and services open with minimal disruption.

Federal Workforce Trends and Updates

The Federal workforce's current staff level is 2.2 million (See Tables 5-1 and 5-2). Using data from the Bureau of Labor Statistics on full-time, full-year workers, Table 5-3 breaks out all Federal and private sector jobs into 22 occupational groups to demonstrate the differences in composition between the Federal and private workforces. Table 5-4 summarizes total pay and benefit costs. Charts 5-1 and 5-2 present trends in educational levels for the Federal and private sector workforces over the past two decades. Chart 5-3 shows the trends in average age in both the Federal and private sectors. Chart 5-4 and

Chart 5-5 show the location of Federal employees in 1978 and again in 2021. Chart 5-6 reflects the changing nature of work, comparing the number of employees in each General Schedule grade in 1950 versus 2021, showing an almost complete shift from lower-grade to higher-grade types of work.

Civil Service Diversity, Equity, Inclusion, and Accessibility

Since the modern merit-based civil service started in 1883, the make-up of the Federal workforce has continued to evolve. The Federal workforce often has taken the lead in expanding job opportunities for highly qualified Americans who were denied positions elsewhere because of their race, gender, disability, sexual orientation, or other characteristics. This Administration seeks to permanently end the lingering biases against all such groups while simultaneously bringing in their untapped abilities to help agencies meet their missions. The Federal Government is the Nation's largest employer, including both the civilian and uniformed services. It also funds millions of positions through contracts, grants, and research awards. How the Federal Government manages its workforce often amplifies similar changes in State, local, and private sector personnel management. In addition to the equal opportunity laws that all employers must follow, the U.S. Government generally maintains a higher standard than the private sector by adhering to the Federal Merit System Principles in Government employment. Unfortunately, our civil service hiring processes have not maximally supported these ideals, and the current makeup of the Federal workforce does not reflect the overall civilian population in many career fields and management ranks.

During the first 100 days of the new Administration, the President issued an initial series of executive actions to direct agencies to make quick progress to ensure that the Federal workforce represents the full talent of the Nation. E.O. 13985, "Advancing Racial Equity and Support for Underserved Communities Through the Federal Government," (January 20, 2021) established that affirmatively advancing equity, civil rights, racial justice, and equal opportunity is the responsibility of the entire Government. Additionally, the President's National Security Memorandum on "Revitalizing America's Foreign Policy and National Security Workforce, Institutions, and Partnerships" (February 4, 2021) ordered a series of actions by agencies to seek to ensure that our national security workforce reflects and draws on the richness and diversity of the country it represents. Management research continually demonstrates that diverse, equitable, inclusive, and accessible workplaces yield higher performing organizations. This Budget invests in Federal employees and the opportunity to "build back better."

The Federal Government made progress increasing representation of underrepresented groups from December 2019 to December 2020. According to data from OPM in December 2020, the Federal civilian workforce self-identified as 61.5 percent White; 18.4 percent Black, which is an increase from 18.2 percent the previous year; 9.4 percent Hispanic of all races, which is an increase from 9.2 percent; 6.9 percent Asian/Pacific Islander, which is an increase from 6.6 percent; 1.6 percent Native American/ Alaskan Native, which remained the same; and 1.9 percent more than one race. Men make up 55.7 percent of all permanent Federal employees and women represent 44.3 percent, which is up from 43.9 percent. Veterans make up 30.7 percent of the Federal workforce. By comparison, veterans represent about 6 percent of the private sector non-agricultural workforce. In addition, 18.3 percent of all Federal employees self-identify as having a disability, which includes the approximately 2.6 percent who have a "targeted disability," such as blindness. Table 5-5 shows the staffing trends since 2016.

The Federal workforce continues to become older on average. Almost 30 percent (635,397) of employees are older than 55, while 8.1 percent (176,805) of employees are younger than 30. By comparison, in the private sector, 23 percent of the workforce is younger than 30. Every single agency has fewer employees younger than 30 today than they had in 2010. The number of paid internships dropped from more than 60,000 in 2010 to about 4,000 in 2020, reducing the opportunity for many to serve. Chart 5-7 shows the widening age gap at the 24 large and mid-sized agencies since 2007. This gap carries into each career field. As an example, Chart 5-8 demonstrates the growing age disparity in the information technology sector that in particular shows the drop since 2010, when Federal internships and hiring programs for recent graduates became subject to new restrictions. The Budget recommends that agencies identify barriers and challenges to hiring interns, ensure internships are included in workforce planning, and directs them to identify options to increase internship opportunities.

Human Capital Management Operations and Modernization

In calendar year 2020, USAJOBS.gov hosted over 330,000 job announcements, facilitated 1.25 billion job searches, and enabled individuals to begin more than 18 million applications for Federal jobs. More than 5,000 job announcements related to the Government's COVID-19 response led individuals to begin nearly a million applications. And OPM's Retirement Services processed almost 100,000 new retirement cases and about 30,000 survivor claims. The Federal Employees Health Benefits Program added six new health plan options and had an average premium increase of 3.6 percent for the 2021 benefit year. Additionally, the various responsible agencies completed about 2.5 million background investigations.

As the President's Management Agenda takes shape, OPM, OMB, and the Chief Human Capital Officers (CHCO) Council continue to collaborate on major workforce reforms. For example, OPM is compiling and developing comprehensive guidance for agencies on hiring flexibilities and competitive hiring best practices to facilitate a talent surge into Government. This work includes developing regulations to make it easier to bring back former employees by allowing agencies to rehire at a grade commensurate with the experience achieved while working outside of Government, rather

Table 5–1. FEDERAL CIVILIAN EMPLOYMENT IN THE EXECUTIVE BRANCH

(Civilian employment as measured by full-time equivalents (FTE) in thousands, excluding the Postal Service)

Agency	Actual		Estimate		Change: 2021 to 2022	
	2019	2020	2021	2022	FTE	Percent
Cabinet agencies						
Agriculture	81.4	79.3	88.2	91.5	3.2	3.7%
Commerce	45.0	83.2	46.4	43.0	−3.4	−7.4%
Defense--Military Programs	741.5	776.8	777.4	786.0	8.5	1.1%
Education	3.6	3.7	4.0	4.2	0.1	3.4%
Energy	14.0	14.1	15.0	16.0	0.9	6.2%
Health and Human Services	73.0	75.1	79.7	82.9	3.1	3.9%
Homeland Security	192.4	197.5	198.8	198.4	−0.4	−0.2%
Housing and Urban Development	7.4	7.6	8.0	8.8	0.8	9.6%
Interior	61.6	60.6	63.4	67.0	3.7	5.8%
Justice	111.9	114.2	116.5	117.9	1.4	1.2%
Labor	14.8	14.5	15.3	17.3	2.1	13.5%
State	25.3	24.9	25.0	25.4	0.3	1.3%
Transportation	53.1	53.5	54.3	54.7	0.4	0.7%
Treasury	88.0	90.7	97.5	103.5	6.0	6.1%
Veterans Affairs	375.8	389.4	406.3	425.5	19.1	4.7%
Other agencies—excluding Postal Service						
Consumer Financial Protection Bureau	1.5	1.4	1.5	1.6	*	3.2%
Corps of Engineers--Civil Works	23.2	24.0	24.2	24.2	....	....
Environmental Protection Agency	13.6	13.9	14.4	15.4	1.1	7.4%
Equal Employment Opportunity Commission	2.1	1.9	2.0	2.3	0.3	15.0%
Federal Communications Commission	1.4	1.4	1.5	1.6	0.1	5.3%
Federal Deposit Insurance Corporation	5.9	5.8	5.9	5.9	*	0.2%
Federal Trade Commission	1.1	1.1	1.1	1.3	0.1	9.6%
General Services Administration	11.0	11.4	12.1	12.3	0.3	2.2%
International Assistance Programs	5.3	5.7	5.7	6.0	0.3	4.6%
National Aeronautics and Space Administration	17.2	17.2	17.8	17.9	0.1	0.3%
National Archives and Records Administration	2.6	2.8	2.8	3.0	0.1	5.2%
National Credit Union Administration	1.1	1.1	1.2	1.2	....	....
National Labor Relations Board	1.3	1.2	1.2	1.4	0.2	13.2%
National Science Foundation	1.4	1.4	1.5	1.6	0.1	7.4%
Nuclear Regulatory Commission	2.9	2.8	2.9	2.9	*	0.4%
Office of Personnel Management	5.5	2.5	2.2	2.2	*	0.7%
Other Defense Civil Programs	1.0	1.0	1.1	1.1	*	2.3%
Securities and Exchange Commission	4.4	4.4	4.5	4.7	0.2	3.7%
Small Business Administration	4.2	4.8	10.0	10.0	*	0.2%
Smithsonian Institution	5.1	4.9	5.3	5.3	0.1	1.3%
Social Security Administration	61.2	60.3	60.2	61.5	1.3	2.1%
Tennessee Valley Authority	10.0	10.0	10.0	10.0	....	....
U.S. Agency for Global Media	1.6	1.7	1.5	1.5	....	....
All other small agencies	11.9	11.9	12.9	13.5	0.6	4.5%
Total, Executive Branch civilian employment	2,085.5	2,179.9	2,199.4	2,250.0	50.6	2.3%

* 50 or less.

than limiting such employees to the grade level where they were when they left. OPM intends to reinvigorate the existing Pathways Programs for student trainees and recent graduates by issuing regulations for post-secondary and recent graduate hiring authorities in section 1108 of the National Defense Authorization Act for Fiscal Year 2019 (Public Law 115-232; 5 U.S.C. 3115-16). OPM also will examine and update the existing Pathways Program regulations accordingly.

The Administration is leading efforts to reform how the Executive Branch conducts background checks for its workforce through the Security Clearance, Suitability, and Credentialing Performance Accountability Council (PAC) established by E.O. 13467 (2008) and chaired by OMB's Deputy Director for Management. The PAC is spearheading several transformative reforms through the Trusted Workforce 2.0 initiative that will introduce continuous vetting, reduce the amount of time needed to

Table 5–2. TOTAL FEDERAL EMPLOYMENT
(As measured by Full-Time Equivalents)

Description	2020 Actual	2021 Estimate	2022 Estimate	Change: 2021 to 2022 FTE	Change: 2021 to 2022 Percent
Executive Branch Civilian:					
All Agencies, Except Postal Service	2,179,917	2,199,387	2,249,971	50,584	2.2%
Postal Service [1]	569,288	579,741	563,690	−16,051	−2.8%
Subtotal, Executive Branch Civilian	2,749,205	2,779,128	2,813,661	34,533	1.2%
Executive Branch Uniformed Military:					
Department of Defense [2]	1,389,398	1,399,318	1,381,998	−17,320	−1.3%
Department of Homeland Security (USCG)	41,244	42,252	42,703	451	1.1%
Commissioned Corps (DOC, EPA, HHS)	6,371	6,366	6,679	313	4.7%
Subtotal, Uniformed Military	1,437,013	1,447,936	1,431,380	−16,556	−1.2%
Subtotal, Executive Branch	4,186,218	4,227,064	4,245,041	17,977	0.4%
Legislative Branch [3]	33,673	34,495	34,914	419	1.2%
Judicial Branch	33,242	33,665	34,198	533	1.6%
Grand Total	4,253,133	4,295,224	4,314,153	18,929	0.4%

[1] Includes Postal Rate Commission.

[2] Includes activated Guard and Reserve members on active duty. Does not include Full-Time Support (Active Guard & Reserve (AGRSs)) paid from Reserve Component appropriations.

[3] FTE data not available for the Senate (positions filled were used for actual year and extended at same level).

conduct background checks for new hires, and improve the mobility of the workforce, all without sacrificing the Nation's security.

The resiliency of the Federal workforce has been on full display during the COVID-19 pandemic, as civil servants have continued to deliver on their Agencies' missions despite unprecedented challenges. Agencies have established COVID-19 Agency safety teams and safety plans to help ensure the protection of their workforces. The CHCO community has collaborated to determine how to move formerly in-person work to the virtual environment. An overwhelming majority of respondents to the 2020 Federal Employee Viewpoint Survey reported a high level of ability to meet customers' needs, as well as agencies' sustained performance and quality of work. OPM, GSA, and OMB will capture best practices, convene diverse stakeholder groups inside and outside of Government, evaluate options, and develop guidance to assist agencies to adapt as the country continues to emerge from the COVID-19 pandemic.

As the Administration and the country move forward, it is imperative that the Federal Government have the tools and human resources personnel to evolve and compete with the overall labor market. The Budget supports building additional capacity and capability for agencies to strengthen the workforce, recruit and hire talent, and ensure agencies can recruit specific technical talent where there are longstanding gaps. It requires CHCO Act Agencies to create and fund talent teams at the component level and to participate in or contribute to, as allowable, a centralized, Government-wide hiring assessment support team to improve hiring outcomes for critical positions, including more technical or hard-to-fill positions, in particular.

The Budget acknowledges the complex and longstanding challenges facing the Federal Government while reflecting a commitment to innovation, improvement, and performance. The Federal workforce is composed of dedicated public servants who work to improve the lives of the American people. The Budget demonstrates the Administration's commitment to them.

Table 5–3. OCCUPATIONS OF FEDERAL AND PRIVATE SECTOR WORKFORCES

(Grouped by Average Private Sector Salary)

Occupational Groups	Percent	
	Federal Workers	Private Sector Workers
Highest Paid Occupations Ranked by Private Sector Salary		
Lawyers and judges	3%	1%
Engineers	4%	2%
Scientists and social scientists	5%	1%
Managers	13%	14%
Pilots, conductors, and related mechanics	3%	0%
Doctors, nurses, psychologists, etc.	8%	7%
Miscellaneous professionals	17%	10%
Administrators, accountants, HR personnel	6%	2%
Inspectors	1%	0%
Total Percentage	**60%**	**38%**
Medium Paid Occupations Ranked by Private Sector Salary		
Sales including real estate, insurance agents	1%	6%
Other miscellaneous occupations	3%	5%
Automobile and other mechanics	2%	3%
Law enforcement and related occupations	8%	1%
Office workers	2%	5%
Social workers	2%	1%
Drivers of trucks and taxis	1%	3%
Laborers and construction workers	3%	10%
Clerks and administrative assistants	12%	10%
Manufacturing	2%	7%
Total Percentage	**36%**	**50%**
Lowest Paid Occupations Ranked by Private Sector Salary		
Other miscellaneous service workers	2%	6%
Janitors and housekeepers	1%	2%
Cooks, bartenders, bakers, and wait staff	1%	4%
Total Percentage	**4.0%**	**11.7%**

Source: 2015-2020 Current Population Survey, IPUMS-CPS, University of Minnesota, www.ipums.org.
Notes: Federal workers exclude the military and Postal Service, but include all other Federal workers in the Executive, Legislative, and Judicial Branches. However, the vast majority of these employees are civil servants in the Executive Branch. Private sector workers exclude the self-employed. Neither category includes state and local government workers. This analysis is limited to full-time, full-year workers, i.e. those with at least 1,500 annual hours of work.

Table 5–4.   PERSONNEL PAY AND BENEFITS
(In millions of dollars)

Description	2020 Actual	2021 Estimate	2022 Estimate	Change: 2021 to 2022	
				Dollars	Percent
Civilian Personnel Costs:					
Executive Branch (excluding Postal Service):					
Pay	214,206	218,826	230,009	11,183	5.1%
Benefits	97,482	100,424	104,689	4,265	4.2%
Subtotal	311,688	319,250	334,698	15,448	4.8%
Postal Service:					
Pay	39,829	39,748	39,770	22	0.1%
Benefits	14,377	12,376	13,072	696	5.6%
Subtotal	54,206	52,124	52,842	718	1.4%
Legislative Branch:					
Pay	2,403	2,531	2,669	138	5.5%
Benefits	876	953	1,043	90	9.4%
Subtotal	3,279	3,484	3,712	228	6.5%
Judicial Branch:					
Pay	3,526	3,819	4,088	269	7.0%
Benefits	1,202	1,224	1,249	25	2.0%
Subtotal	4,728	5,043	5,337	294	5.8%
Total, Civilian Personnel Costs	373,901	379,901	396,589	16,688	4.4%
Military Personnel Costs					
Department of Defense--Military Programs:					
Pay	107,927	110,932	113,728	2,796	2.5%
Benefits	51,700	57,030	60,479	3,449	6.0%
Subtotal	159,627	167,962	174,207	6,245	3.7%
All other Executive Branch uniform personnel:					
Pay	3,895	4,020	4,143	123	3.1%
Benefits	701	728	785	57	7.8%
Subtotal	4,596	4,748	4,928	180	3.8%
Total, Military Personnel Costs	164,223	172,710	179,135	6,425	3.7%
Grand total, personnel costs	**538,124**	**552,611**	**575,724**	**23,113**	**4.2%**
ADDENDUM					
Former Civilian Personnel:					
Pensions	92,663	95,153	98,498	3,345	3.5%
Health benefits	13,186	13,312	13,969	657	4.9%
Life insurance	42	42	43	1	2.4%
Subtotal	105,891	108,507	112,510	4,003	3.7%
Former Military Personnel:					
Pensions	64,482	65,988	67,720	1,732	2.6%
Health benefits	10,905	11,811	12,297	486	4.1%
Subtotal	75,387	77,799	80,017	2,218	2.9%
Total, Former Personnel	181,278	186,306	192,527	6,221	3.3%

Table 5–5. HIRING TRENDS SINCE 2016

Federal Civilian Workforce	SEP 2016	SEP 2017	SEP 2018	SEP 2019	SEP 2020	JAN 2021
Total Federal Workforce Count [1]	2,097,038	2,087,747	2,100,802	2,132,812	2,181,106	2,167,192
Average Age	47.1	47.2	47.1	47.1	47.0	47.0
Total Under 30	7.88%	7.55%	7.76%	8.07%	8.39%	8.06%
Total 55 and over	28.16%	28.79%	28.99%	29.17%	29.11%	29.04%
Male	56.70%	56.60%	56.44%	56.27%	55.90%	55.64%
Female	43.29%	43.38%	43.52%	43.72%	44.10%	44.36%
All Disabilities	9.46%	10.49%	12.38%	13.89%	15.33%	18.15%
Targeted Disabilities (These totals are included in the total disability #'s above)	1.10%	2.69%	2.66%	2.61%	2.56%	2.55%
Veteran	29.33%	29.43%	29.34%	29.15%	28.78%	28.82%
American Indian or Alaskan Native	1.71%	1.69%	1.66%	1.63%	1.62%	1.59%
Asian	5.86%	5.99%	6.10%	6.01%	6.17%	6.43%
Black/African American	17.91%	18.15%	18.21%	18.02%	18.06%	18.35%
Native Hawaiian or Pacific Islander	0.49%	0.51%	0.52%	0.52%	0.54%	0.56%
More Than One Race	1.47%	1.60%	1.73%	1.82%	1.91%	1.93%
Hispanic/Latino (H/L)	8.46%	8.75%	9.08%	9.14%	9.33%	9.41%
White	64.04%	63.26%	62.63%	61.22%	60.86%	61.45%

Source: U.S. Office of Personnel Management

[1] Total count varies slightly from other sources because of date and data collection method

Chart 5-1. Masters Degree or Above By Year for Federal and Private Sectors

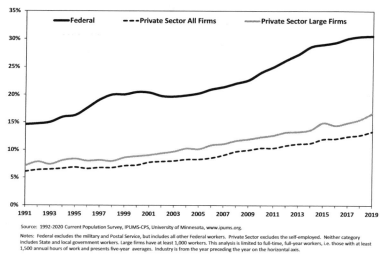

Source: 1992-2020 Current Population Survey, IPUMS-CPS, University of Minnesota, www.ipums.org.

Notes: Federal excludes the military and Postal Service, but includes all other Federal workers. Private Sector excludes the self-employed. Neither category includes State and local government workers. Large firms have at least 1,000 workers. This analysis is limited to full-time, full-year workers, i.e. those with at least 1,500 annual hours of work and presents five-year averages. Industry is from the year preceding the year on the horizontal axis.

Chart 5-2. High School Graduate or Less By Year for Federal and Private Sectors

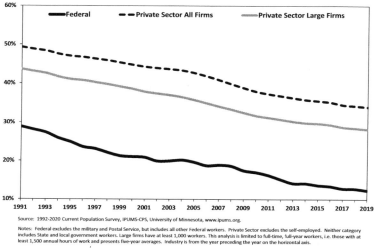

Source: 1992-2020 Current Population Survey, IPUMS-CPS, University of Minnesota, www.ipums.org.

Notes: Federal excludes the military and Postal Service, but includes all other Federal workers. Private Sector excludes the self-employed. Neither category includes State and local government workers. Large firms have at least 1,000 workers. This analysis is limited to full-time, full-year workers, i.e. those with at least 1,500 annual hours of work and presents five-year averages. Industry is from the year preceding the year on the horizontal axis.

Chart 5-3. Average Age by Year for Federal and Private Sectors

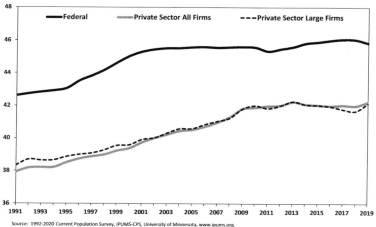

Source: 1992-2020 Current Population Survey, IPUMS-CPS, University of Minnesota, www.ipums.org.

Notes: Federal excludes the military and Postal Service, but includes all other Federal workers. Private Sector excludes the self-employed. Neither category includes State and local government workers. Large firms have at least 1,000 workers. This analysis is limited to full-time, full-year workers, i.e. those with at least 1,500 annual hours of work and presents five-year averages. Industry is from the year preceding the year on the horizontal axis.

Chart 5-4. GOVERNMENT-WIDE ON-BOARD U.S. DISTRIBUTION 10–1–1978

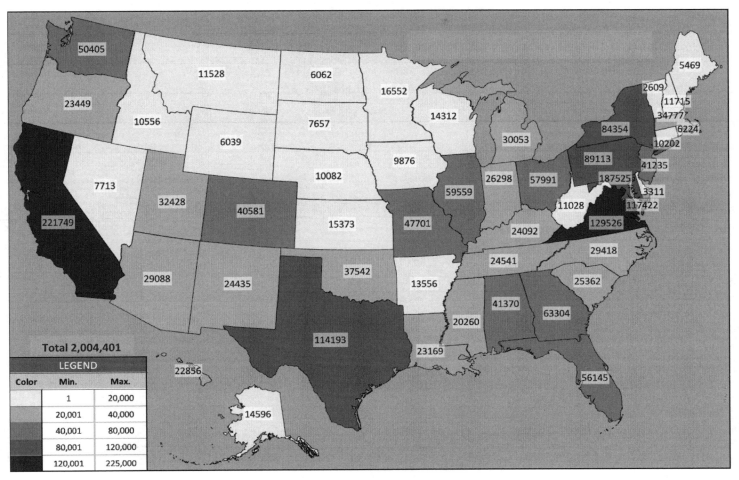

Total 2,004,401

Color	Min.	Max.
	1	20,000
	20,001	40,000
	40,001	80,000
	80,001	120,000
	120,001	225,000

LEGEND

Source: Office of Personnel Management.

Chart 5-5. GOVERNMENT-WIDE ON-BOARD U.S. DISTRIBUTION 1–1–2021

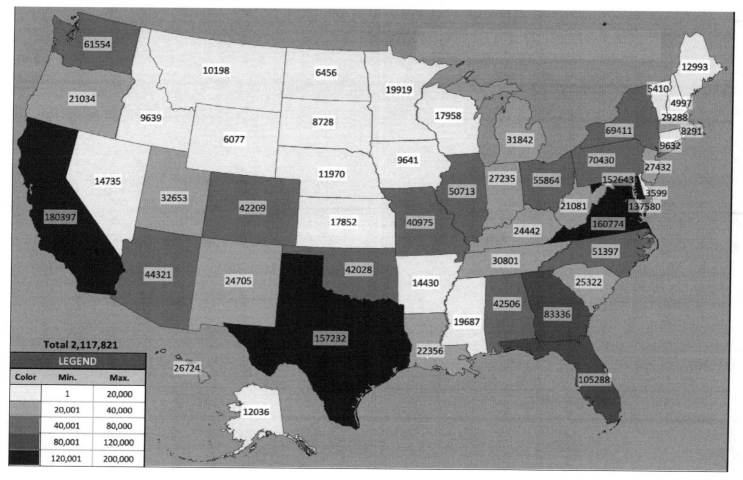

Total 2,117,821

LEGEND		
Color	Min.	Max.
	1	20,000
	20,001	40,000
	40,001	80,000
	80,001	120,000
	120,001	200,000

Source: Office of Personnel Management.

5-6. The Changing General Schedule Workforce

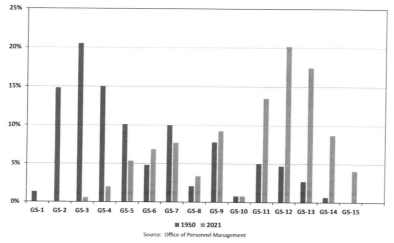

■ 1950 ■ 2021

Source: Office of Personnel Management

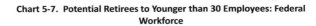

Chart 5-7. Potential Retirees to Younger than 30 Employees: Federal Workforce

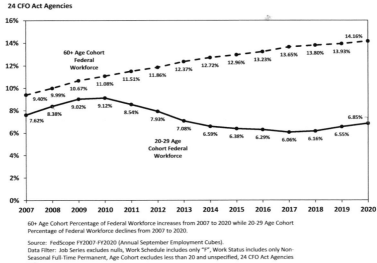

60+ Age Cohort Percentage of Federal Workforce increases from 2007 to 2020 while 20-29 Age Cohort Percentage of Federal Workforce declines from 2007 to 2020.

Source: FedScope FY2007-FY2020 (Annual September Employment Cubes).
Data Filter: Job Series excludes nulls, Work Schedule includes only "F", Work Status includes only Non-Seasonal Full-Time Permanent, Age Cohort excludes less than 20 and unspecified, 24 CFO Act Agencies only.
Data Range: FY2007-FY2020, Age Cohorts 20-29, 30-39, 40,49, 50-59, and 60+.

Chart 5-8. Potential Retires to Younger than 30 Employees: Federal IT Workforce Vs. Federal Workforce

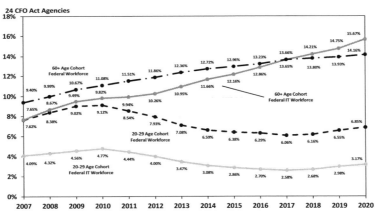

60+ Age Cohort Federal IT Workforce increases from 2007 to 2020 while 20-29 Age Cohort Federal IT Workforce declines slightly.

Source: FedScope FY2007-FY2020 (Annual September Employment Cubes).
Data Filter: Job Series excludes nulls, Work Schedule includes only "F", Work Status includes only Non-Seasonal Full-Time Permanent, Age Cohort excludes less than 20 and unspecified, 24 CFO Act Agencies only.
Data Range: FY2007-FY2020, Age Cohorts 20-29, 30-39, 40,49, 50-59, and 60+).

BUDGET CONCEPTS AND BUDGET PROCESS

6. BUDGET CONCEPTS

The budget system of the United States Government provides the means for the President and the Congress to decide how much money to spend, what to spend it on, and how to raise the money they have decided to spend. Through the budget system, they determine the allocation of resources among the agencies of the Federal Government and between the Federal Government and the private sector. The budget system focuses primarily on dollars, but it also allocates other resources, such as Federal employment. The decisions made in the budget process affect the Nation as a whole, State and local governments, and individual Americans. Many budget decisions have worldwide significance. The Congress and the President enact budget decisions into law. The budget system ensures that these laws are carried out.

This chapter provides an overview of the budget system and explains some of the more important budget concepts. It includes summary dollar amounts to illustrate major concepts, and enumerates specific policies or presentation choices in the 2022 Budget associated with some of these concepts. Other chapters of the budget documents dis-

cuss these concepts and more detailed amounts in greater depth.

The following section discusses the budget process, covering formulation of the President's Budget, action by the Congress, budget enforcement, and execution of enacted budget laws. The next section provides information on budget coverage, including a discussion of on-budget and off-budget amounts, functional classification, presentation of budget data, types of funds, and full-cost budgeting. Subsequent sections discuss the concepts of receipts and collections, budget authority, and outlays. These sections are followed by discussions of Federal credit; surpluses, deficits, and means of financing; Federal employment; and the basis for the budget figures. A glossary of budget terms appears at the end of the chapter.

Various laws, enacted to carry out requirements of the Constitution, govern the budget system. The chapter refers to the principal ones by title throughout the text and gives complete citations in the section just preceding the glossary.

THE BUDGET PROCESS

The budget process has three main phases, each of which is related to the others:

1. Formulation of the President's Budget;

2. Action by the Congress; and

3. Execution of enacted budget laws.

Formulation of the President's Budget

The Budget of the United States Government consists of several volumes that set forth the President's fiscal policy goals and priorities for the allocation of resources by the Government. The primary focus of the Budget is on the budget year—the next fiscal year for which the Congress needs to make appropriations, in this case 2022. (Fiscal year 2022 will begin on October 1, 2021, and end on September 30, 2022.) The Budget also covers the nine years following the budget year in order to reflect the effect of budget decisions over the longer term. It includes the funding levels provided for the current year, in this case 2021, which allows the reader to compare the President's Budget proposals with the most recently enacted levels. The Budget also includes data on the most recently completed fiscal year, in this case 2020, so that the reader can compare budget estimates to actual accounting data.

In a normal year (excluding transitions between Administrations), the President begins the process of formulating the budget by establishing general budget and fiscal policy guidelines, usually by late spring of each year. Based on these guidelines, the Office of Management and Budget (OMB) works with the Federal agencies to establish specific policy directions and planning levels to guide the preparation of their budget requests.

During the formulation of the budget, the President, the Director of OMB, and other officials in the Executive Office of the President continually exchange information, proposals, and evaluations bearing on policy decisions with the Secretaries of the Departments and the heads of the other Government agencies. Decisions reflected in previously enacted budgets, including the one for the fiscal year in progress, reactions to the last proposed budget (which the Congress is considering at the same time the process of preparing the forthcoming budget begins), and evaluations of program performance all influence decisions concerning the forthcoming budget, as do projections of the economic outlook, prepared jointly by the Council of Economic Advisers, OMB, and the Department of the Treasury.

Agencies normally submit their budget requests to OMB, where analysts review them and identify issues that OMB officials need to discuss with the agencies. OMB and the agencies resolve many issues themselves. Others require the involvement of White House policy officials and the President. This decision-making process is usually completed by late December. At that time, the final stage of developing detailed budget data and the preparation of the budget documents begins.

The decision-makers must consider the effects of economic and technical assumptions on the budget estimates. Interest rates, economic growth, the rate of inflation, the unemployment rate, and the number of people eligible for various benefit programs, among other factors, affect Government spending and receipts. Small changes in these assumptions can alter budget estimates by many billions of dollars. (Chapter 2, "Economic Assumptions and Overview," provides more information on this subject.)

Thus, the budget formulation process involves the simultaneous consideration of the resource needs of individual programs, the allocation of resources among the agencies and functions of the Federal Government, and the total outlays and receipts that are appropriate in light of current and prospective economic conditions.

The law governing the President's Budget requires the transmittal of the following fiscal year's Budget to the Congress on or after the first Monday in January but not later than the first Monday in February of each year. The budget is usually scheduled for transmission to the Congress on the first Monday in February, giving the Congress eight months to act on the budget before the fiscal year begins. In years when a Presidential transition has taken place, this timeline for budget release is commonly extended to allow the new administration sufficient time to take office and formulate its budget policy. While there is no specific timeline set for this circumstance, the detailed budget is usually completed and released in April or May. However, in order to aid the congressional budget process (discussed below), new administrations often release a budget blueprint that contains broad spending outlines and descriptions of major policies and priorities earlier in the year.

Congressional Action[1]

The Congress considers the President's Budget proposals and approves, modifies, or disapproves them. It can change funding levels, eliminate programs, or add programs not requested by the President. It can add or eliminate taxes and other sources of receipts or make other changes that affect the amount of receipts collected.

The Congress does not enact a budget as such. Through the process of adopting a planning document called a budget resolution, the Congress agrees on targets for total spending and receipts, the size of the deficit or surplus, and the debt limit. The budget resolution provides the framework within which individual congressional committees prepare appropriations bills and other spending and receipts legislation. The Congress provides funding for specified purposes in appropriations acts each year. It

also enacts changes each year in other laws that affect spending and receipts.

In making appropriations, the Congress does not vote on the level of outlays (spending) directly, but rather on budget authority, which is the authority provided by law to incur financial obligations that will result in outlays. In a separate process, prior to making appropriations, the Congress usually enacts legislation that authorizes an agency to carry out particular programs, authorizes the appropriation of funds to carry out those programs, and, in some cases, limits the amount that can be appropriated for the programs. Some authorizing legislation expires after one year, some expires after a specified number of years, and some is permanent. The Congress may enact appropriations for a program even though there is no specific authorization for it or its authorization has expired.

The Congress begins its work on its budget resolution shortly after it receives the President's Budget. Under the procedures established by the Congressional Budget Act of 1974 (Congressional Budget Act), the Congress decides on budget targets before commencing action on individual appropriations. The Act requires each standing committee of the House and Senate to recommend budget levels and report legislative plans concerning matters within the committee's jurisdiction to the Budget Committee in each body. The House and Senate Budget Committees then each design and report, and each body then considers, a concurrent resolution on the budget. The congressional timetable calls for the House and Senate to resolve differences between their respective versions of the congressional budget resolution and adopt a single budget resolution by April 15 of each year.

In the report on the budget resolution, the Budget Committees allocate the total on-budget budget authority and outlays set forth in the resolution to the Appropriations Committees and the other committees that have jurisdiction over spending. These committee allocations are commonly known as "302(a)" allocations, in reference to the section of the Congressional Budget Act that provides for them. The Appropriations Committees are then required to divide their 302(a) allocations of budget authority and outlays among their subcommittees. These subcommittee allocations are known as "302(b)" allocations. There are procedural hurdles associated with considering appropriations bills that would breach an Appropriations subcommittee's 302(b) allocation. Similar procedural hurdles exist for considering legislation that would cause the 302(a) allocation for any committee to be breached. The Budget Committees' reports may discuss assumptions about the level of funding for major programs. While these assumptions do not bind the other committees and subcommittees, they may influence their decisions.

Budget resolutions may include "reserve funds," which permit adjustment of the resolution allocations as necessary to accommodate legislation addressing specific matters, such as healthcare or tax reform. Reserve funds are most often limited to legislation that is deficit neutral, including increases in some areas offset by decreases in

---

[1] For a fuller discussion of the congressional budget process, see Bill Heniff Jr., *Introduction to the Federal Budget Process* (Congressional Research Service Report 98–721), and Robert Keith and Allen Schick, *Manual on the Federal Budget Process* (Congressional Research Service Report 98–720, archived).

others. The budget resolution may also contain "reconciliation directives" (discussed further below).

Since the concurrent resolution on the budget is not a law, it does not require the President's approval. However, the Congress considers the President's views in preparing budget resolutions, because legislation developed to meet congressional budget allocations does require the President's approval. In some years, the President and the joint leadership of Congress have formally agreed on plans to reduce the deficit or balance the budget. These agreements were then reflected in the budget resolution and legislation passed for those years.

If the Congress does not pass a budget resolution, the House and Senate typically adopt one or more "deeming resolutions" in the form of a simple resolution or as a provision of a larger bill. A deeming resolution may serve nearly all functions of a budget resolution, except it may not trigger reconciliation procedures in the Senate.

Once the Congress approves the budget resolution, it turns its attention to enacting appropriations bills and authorizing legislation. The Appropriations Committee in each body has jurisdiction over annual appropriations. These committees are divided into subcommittees that hold hearings and review detailed budget justification materials prepared by the Executive Branch agencies within the subcommittee's jurisdiction. After a bill has been drafted by a subcommittee, the full committee and the whole House, in turn, must approve the bill, sometimes with amendments to the original version. The House then forwards the bill to the Senate, where a similar review follows. If the Senate disagrees with the House on particular matters in the bill, which is often the case, the two bodies form a conference committee (consisting of some Members of each body) to resolve the differences. The conference committee revises the bill and returns it to both bodies for approval. When the revised bill is agreed to, first in the House and then in the Senate, the Congress sends it to the President for approval or veto.

Since 1977, when the start of the fiscal year was established as October 1, there have been only three fiscal years (1989, 1995, and 1997) for which the Congress agreed to and enacted every regular appropriations bill by that date. When one or more appropriations bills are not enacted by this date, the Congress usually enacts a joint resolution called a "continuing resolution" (CR), which is an interim or stop-gap appropriations bill that provides authority for the affected agencies to continue operations at some specified level until a specific date or until the regular appropriations are enacted. Occasionally, a CR has funded a portion or all of the Government for the entire year.

The Congress must present these CRs to the President for approval or veto. In some cases, Congresses have failed to pass a CR or Presidents have rejected CRs because they contained unacceptable provisions. Left without funds, Government agencies were required by law to shut down operations—with exceptions for some limited activities—until the Congress passed a CR the President would approve. Shutdowns have lasted for periods of a day to several weeks.

The Congress also provides budget authority in laws other than appropriations acts. In fact, while annual appropriations acts fund the majority of Federal programs, they account for only about a third of the total spending in a typical year. Authorizing legislation controls the rest of the spending, which is commonly called "mandatory spending." A distinctive feature of these authorizing laws is that they provide agencies with the authority or requirement to spend money without first requiring the Appropriations Committees to enact funding. This category of spending includes interest the Government pays on the public debt and the spending of several major programs, such as Social Security, Medicare, Medicaid, unemployment insurance, and Federal employee retirement. Almost all taxes and most other receipts also result from authorizing laws. Article I, Section 7 of the Constitution provides that all bills for raising revenue shall originate in the House of Representatives. In the House, the Ways and Means Committee initiates tax bills; in the Senate, the Finance Committee has jurisdiction over tax laws.

BUDGET CALENDAR

The following timetable highlights the scheduled dates for significant budget events during a normal budget year:

Between the 1st Monday in January and the 1st Monday in February	President transmits the budget
Six weeks later	Congressional committees report budget estimates to Budget Committees
April 15	Action to be completed on congressional budget resolution
May 15	House consideration of annual appropriations bills may begin even if the budget resolution has not been agreed to.
June 10	House Appropriations Committee to report the last of its annual appropriations bills.
June 15	Action to be completed on "reconciliation bill" by the Congress.
June 30	Action on appropriations to be completed by House
July 15	President transmits Mid-Session Review of the Budget
October 1	Fiscal year begins

The budget resolution often includes reconciliation directives, which require authorizing committees to recommend changes in laws that affect receipts or mandatory spending. They direct each designated committee to report amendments to the laws under the committee's jurisdiction that would achieve changes in the levels of receipts or mandatory spending controlled by those laws. These directives specify the dollar amount of changes that each designated committee is expected to achieve, but do not specify which laws are to be changed or the changes to be made. However, the Budget Committees' reports on the budget resolution frequently discuss assumptions about how the laws would be changed. Like other assumptions in the report, they do not bind the committees of jurisdiction but may influence their decisions. A reconciliation instruction may also specify the total amount by which the statutory limit on the public debt is to be changed.

The committees subject to reconciliation directives draft the implementing legislation. Such legislation may, for example, change the tax code, revise benefit formulas or eligibility requirements for benefit programs, or authorize Government agencies to charge fees to cover some of their costs. Reconciliation bills are typically omnibus legislation, combining the legislation submitted by each reconciled committee in a single act.

The Senate considers such omnibus reconciliation acts under expedited procedures that limit total debate on the bill. To offset the procedural advantage gained by expedited procedures, the Senate places significant restrictions on the substantive content of the reconciliation measure itself, as well as on amendments to the measure. Any material in the bill that is extraneous or that contains changes to the Federal Old-Age and Survivors Insurance and the Federal Disability Insurance programs is not in order under the Senate's expedited reconciliation procedures. Non-germane amendments are also prohibited. Reconciliation acts, together with appropriations acts for the year, are usually used to implement broad agreements between the President and the Congress on those occasions where the two branches have negotiated a comprehensive budget plan. Reconciliation acts have sometimes included other matters, such as laws providing the means for enforcing these agreements.

Budget Enforcement

The Federal Government uses budget enforcement mechanisms to control revenues, spending, and deficits. The Statutory Pay-As-You-Go Act of 2010, enacted on February 12, 2010, reestablished a statutory procedure to enforce a rule of deficit neutrality on new revenue and mandatory spending legislation. The Budget Control Act of 2011 (BCA), enacted on August 2, 2011, amended the Balanced Budget and Emergency Deficit Control Act of 1985 (BBEDCA) by reinstating limits ("caps") on the amount of discretionary budget authority that can be provided through the annual appropriations process. The BCA also created a Joint Select Committee on Deficit Reduction that was instructed to develop a bill to reduce the Federal deficit by at least $1.5 trillion over a 10-year

period, and imposed automatic spending cuts to achieve $1.2 trillion of deficit reduction over nine years after the Joint Committee process failed to achieve its deficit reduction goal. The original enforcement mechanisms established by the BCA—the caps on spending in annual appropriations and instructions to calculate reductions to achieve the $1.2 trillion deficit reduction goal—expire at the end of fiscal year 2021, although the sequestration of mandatory spending has been extended through 2030.

BBEDCA divides spending into two types—discretionary spending and direct (or mandatory) spending. Discretionary spending is controlled through annual appropriations acts. Funding for salaries and other operating expenses of Government agencies, for example, is generally discretionary. Direct spending (also referred to as mandatory spending) is controlled by permanent laws. Medicare and Medicaid payments, unemployment insurance benefits, and farm price supports are examples of mandatory spending. Receipts are included under the same statutory enforcement rules that apply to mandatory spending because permanent laws generally control receipts.

Direct spending enforcement. The Statutory Pay-As-You-Go Act of 2010 requires that new legislation changing mandatory spending or revenue must be enacted on a "pay-as-you-go" (PAYGO) basis; that is, that the cumulative effects of such legislation must not increase projected on-budget deficits. PAYGO is a permanent requirement, and it does not impose a cap on spending or a floor on revenues. Instead, PAYGO requires that legislation reducing revenues must be fully offset by cuts in mandatory programs or by revenue increases, and that any bills increasing mandatory spending must be fully offset by revenue increases or cuts in mandatory spending.

This requirement of deficit neutrality is not enforced on a bill-by-bill basis, but is based on two scorecards that tally the cumulative budgetary effects of PAYGO legislation as averaged over rolling 5- and 10-year periods, starting with the budget year. Any impacts of PAYGO legislation on the current year deficit are counted as budget year impacts when placed on the scorecard. PAYGO is enforced by sequestration. Within 14 business days after a congressional session ends, OMB issues an annual PAYGO report. If either the 5- or 10-year scorecard shows net costs in the budget year column, the President is required to issue a sequestration order implementing across-the-board cuts to nonexempt mandatory programs by an amount sufficient to offset those net costs. The PAYGO effects of legislation may be directed in legislation by reference to statements inserted into the *Congressional Record* by the chairmen of the House and Senate Budget Committees. Any such estimates are determined by the Budget Committees and are informed by, but not required to match, the cost estimates prepared by the Congressional Budget Office (CBO). If this procedure is not followed, then the PAYGO effects of the legislation are determined by OMB. Provisions of mandatory spending or receipts legislation that are designated in that legislation as an emergency requirement are not scored as PAYGO budgetary effects.

The PAYGO rules apply to the outlays resulting from outyear changes in mandatory programs made in appropriations acts and to all revenue changes made in appropriations acts. However, outyear changes to mandatory programs as part of provisions that have zero net outlay effects over the sum of the current year and the next five fiscal years are not considered under the PAYGO rules.

The PAYGO rules do not apply to increases in mandatory spending or decreases in receipts that result automatically under existing law. For example, mandatory spending for benefit programs, such as unemployment insurance, rises when the number of beneficiaries rises, and many benefit payments are automatically increased for inflation under existing laws.

The House and Senate impose points of order against consideration of tax or mandatory spending legislation that would violate the PAYGO principle, although the time periods covered by these rules and the treatment of previously enacted costs or savings may differ in some respects from the requirements of the Statutory Pay-As-You-Go Act of 2010.

BBEDCA Section 251A reductions. The failure of the Joint Select Committee on Deficit Reduction to propose, and the Congress to enact, legislation to reduce the deficit by at least $1.5 trillion triggered automatic reductions to discretionary and mandatory spending in fiscal years 2013 through 2021. The reductions were implemented through a combination of sequestration of mandatory spending and reductions in the discretionary caps, with some modifications as provided for in the American Taxpayer Relief Act of 2012, and the Bipartisan Budget Acts (BBAs) of 2013, 2015, 2018, and 2019.

By amending section 251A of BBEDCA, the mandatory sequestration provisions were extended beyond 2021 by the BBA of 2013, which extended sequestration through 2023; Public Law 113-82, commonly referred to as the Military Retired Pay Restoration Act, which extended sequestration through 2024; the BBA of 2015, which extended sequestration through 2025; the BBA of 2018, which extended sequestration through 2027; the BBA of 2019, which extended sequestration through 2029; and Public Law 116-136, commonly referred to as the CARES Act, which extended sequestration through 2030.

Starting in 2022, section 251A of BBEDCA requires that the same percentage reductions for non-exempt mandatory defense and non-defense spending will be applied each year at the rate established in 2021. Those reductions are 5.7 percent for non-defense accounts, 8.3 percent for defense accounts, and 2 percent for Medicare and community and migrant health centers. [2] Since the percentage reduction is known in advance, the 2022 Budget will present these reductions at the account level.

Previously, the Budget reflected the reductions starting in the budget year in a central allowance account.

Discretionary cap enforcement. BBEDCA specified spending limits ("caps") on discretionary budget authority for 2012 through 2021. Similar enforcement mechanisms were established by the Budget Enforcement Act of 1990 and were extended in 1993 and 1997, but expired at the end of 2002. The threat of sequestration if the caps were breached proved sufficient to ensure compliance with the discretionary spending limits.

When caps were in place, BBEDCA required OMB to adjust the caps each year for: changes in concepts and definitions; appropriations designated by the Congress and the President as emergency requirements; and appropriations designated by the Congress and the President for Overseas Contingency Operations/Global War on Terrorism (OCO/GWOT). BBEDCA also specified cap adjustments (which are limited to fixed amounts) for: appropriations for continuing disability reviews and redeterminations by the Social Security Administration; the healthcare fraud and abuse control program at the Department of Health and Human Services; appropriations designated by the Congress as being for disaster relief; appropriations for reemployment services and eligibility assessments; appropriations for wildfire suppression at the Department of Agriculture and the Department of the Interior; and, for 2020 only, appropriations provided for the 2020 Census at the Department of Commerce.

The 2022 Budget does not propose new caps on discretionary funding. The caps in place from 2012 through 2021, especially after Joint Committee enforcement was triggered, led to a serious erosion in discretionary resources, particularly for non-defense funding, and contributed to a decade of under-investments in core public services and programs.

However, the 2022 Budget does support retaining several of the aforementioned cap adjustments as "allocation adjustments" to be used pursuant to the Congressional Budget Act in the Congressional Budget Resolution. The Budget does not retain all the BBEDCA adjustments (specifically, the Administration shifts funds that had been designated as OCO to the base) but it still provides funds for anomalous or above-base activities such as program integrity, disaster relief, and wildfire suppression that continue to be presented outside of the base allocation for certain accounts. In anticipation of most of these useful mechanisms being retained as part of the annual budget and appropriations process, the Budget includes the following adjustments above the base level of discretionary funding:

- **Program Integrity.** This allocation adjustment continues to recognize that certain discretionary activities focused on program integrity in the largest benefit programs (Social Security, Medicare, Medicaid, and Unemployment Insurance) have a return on investment (ROI) in the form of savings for these programs. The allocation adjustment, shown in the 2022 Budget as an additional amount for program integrity activities in the specific benefit program's discretionary request, encourages the Congress to

---

[2] The CARES Act, as amended by Public Law 117-7, suspended the Medicare sequestration from May 1, 2020 to December 31, 2021 and specified that, notwithstanding the 2 percent limit on Medicare sequestration in the BCA, the reduction in the Medicare program should be 2 percent in the first 5.5 months of 2030, a 4 percent reduction in the second 6 months of 2030, and a 0 percent reduction in the remaining half month of 2030.

continue proposing those adjustments and reaping the savings associated with this activity. The Administration also supports additional program integrity funding through an allocation adjustment to support ongoing enforcement of tax payments by the Internal Revenue Service. Savings derived from the program integrity allocation adjustments on the discretionary side are assumed to continue into the outyears. Because the savings are only generated if the funding is provided in annual discretionary appropriations, savings in the mandatory benefit programs are shown as a legislative proposal not subject to Pay-As-You-Go procedures. This allows the scorekeeping community to recognize the benefits of this spending within established scorekeeping guidelines. Details for each program are below:

- Internal Revenue Service (IRS): The Budget proposes to establish and fund a new IRS program integrity allocation adjustment for program integrity activities starting in 2022. The IRS base appropriation funds current tax administration activities, including all tax enforcement and compliance program activities, in the Enforcement and Operations Support accounts. The additional $417 million adjustment in 2022 funds new and continuing investments in expanding and improving the effectiveness and efficiency of the IRS's tax enforcement program. The activities are estimated to generate and protect $50 billion in revenue over 10 years and cost approximately $7 billion, resulting in an estimated net savings of $43 billion. (Separately, the Budget also proposes new mandatory funding for IRS enforcement activities.)

- Social Security: The Social Security Administration (SSA) takes seriously its responsibilities to ensure eligible individuals receive the benefits to which they are entitled, and to safeguard the integrity of benefit programs to better serve recipients. The proposed $1.7 billion in discretionary funding, including a $1.4 billion allocation adjustment, allows SSA to conduct continuing disability reviews (CDRs) and Supplemental Security Income (SSI) redeterminations to confirm that participants remain eligible to receive benefits, and it supports anti-fraud cooperative disability investigation units and special attorneys for fraud prosecutions. Access to approximately $20 billion in discretionary funding over 10 years, including approximately $17 billion in allocation adjustments, would produce $73 billion in gross Federal savings ($54 billion from allocation adjustments), with net deficit savings of approximately $37 billion in the 10-year window and additional savings in the outyears (the Budget excludes funding for the now withdrawn proposed rule regarding increasing the number and frequency of CDRs).

- Health Care Fraud and Abuse Control (HCFAC): The 2022 Budget requests $873 million in discretionary HCFAC funding. Of this, $556 million is additional new budget authority for the allocation adjustment. Over 10 years, the Budget invests $6.3 billion in additional new budget authority, yielding $13.1 billion in mandatory savings to Medicare and Medicaid. The 2022 allocation adjustment includes funding to invest in Medicare medical review, address new program integrity work stemming from the COVID-19 public health emergency, and handle work associated with Medicaid expansion and the federally facilitated exchanges.

- Unemployment Insurance (UI): The 2022 Budget proposes $250 million in discretionary funding, of which $133 million is an allocation adjustment, for Reemployment Services and Eligibility Assessments (RESEA), which addresses individual reemployment needs of UI claimants and prevents and detects improper benefit payments. This level is consistent with the enacted level in the Congressional Budget Act, which allows for the adjustment for congressional budget procedures through 2027, and the budgetary treatment is the same as the other adjustments. Program integrity funding in 2028 through 2031 continues at a level that results from applying the rate of inflation in the current services baseline to the 2027 amount. The mandatory savings over ten years are $6.1 billion, which includes an estimated $1.8 billion reduction in State unemployment taxes. When netted against the discretionary costs for the cap adjustment funding, the 10-year net savings for the program is $913 million.

- **Disaster Relief.** The 2022 Budget maintains the same methodology for determining the funding ceiling for disaster relief used in previous budgets. At the time the 2022 Budget was prepared, OMB estimated the total adjustment available for disaster funding for 2022 at $18.9 billion after accounting for 2021 enacted appropriations. This ceiling estimate is based on three components: a 10-year average of disaster relief funding provided in prior years that excludes the highest and lowest years ($10.1 billion); 5 percent of Robert T. Stafford Disaster Relief and Emergency Assistance Act emergencies since 2012 ($8.7 billion); and carryover from the previous year ($0.1 billion). For 2022, the Administration is requesting $18.8 billion in funding for the Federal Emergency Management Agency's (FEMA) Disaster Relief Program and more than $0.1 billion for the Small Business Administration's Disaster Loans Program. These amounts cover the costs of Presidentially-declared major disasters, including identified costs for previously declared catastrophic events and the estimated annual cost of non-catastrophic events expected to obligate in 2022. The Administration's request also addresses the significant and unprecedented recovery needs from COVID-19 pandemic. Consistent with past practice, the 2022 request level does not seek to pre-fund anticipated needs in other programs arising out of disasters that have yet to occur. After 2022, the Administration does not have adequate information about known or future requirements necessary to estimate the total amount that will be requested in future years. Accordingly, the Budget does not explicitly request any disaster relief funding in any year after the budget year and includes a placeholder in each of the outyears that is equal to the 10-year average ($10.1 billion) of disaster relief currently estimated under the formula for the 2022 ceiling. This funding level does not reflect a specific request but a placeholder amount that, along with other outyear appropriations levels, will be decided on an annual basis as part of the normal budget development process.

- **Wildfire Suppression.** The 2022 Budget requests funding as an allocation adjustment for wildfire suppression operations at the level authorized in the Stephen Sepp Wildfire Suppression Funding and Forest Management Activities Act. The Budget funds a base level that is equal to the average costs over ten years for wildfire suppression operations that were requested in the President's 2015 Budget for the Department of Agriculture's Forest Service and the Department of the Interior (DOI), and seeks the full $2.5 billion adjustment authorized, with $2.1 billion for Forest Service and $0.3 billion included for DOI. Providing the full level authorized in 2022 will ensure that adequate resources are available to fight wildland fires, protect communities, and safeguard human life during the most severe wildland fire season. After 2022, the Budget includes a placeholder for wildfire suppression that is equal to the 2022 request level. Those amounts will be refined in subsequent Budgets, as data on costs for wildfire suppression operations are updated annually.

Budget Execution

Government agencies may not spend or obligate more than the Congress has appropriated, and they may use funds only for purposes specified in law. The Antideficiency Act prohibits them from spending or obligating funds in advance or in excess of an appropriation, unless specific authority to do so has been provided in law. Additionally, the Antideficiency Act requires the President to apportion the budgetary resources available for most executive branch agencies. The President has delegated this authority to OMB. Some apportionments are by time periods (usually by quarter of the fiscal year), some are by projects or activities, and others are by a combination of both. Agencies may request OMB to reapportion funds during the year to accommodate changing circumstances. This system helps to ensure that funds do not run out before the end of the fiscal year.

During the budget execution phase, the Government sometimes finds that it needs more funding than the Congress has appropriated for the fiscal year because of unanticipated circumstances. For example, more might be needed to respond to a severe natural disaster. Under such circumstances, the Congress may enact a supplemental appropriation.

On the other hand, the President may propose to reduce a previously enacted appropriation, through a "rescission" or "cancellation" of those funds. How the President proposes this reduction determines whether it is considered a rescission or a cancellation. A rescission is a reduction in previously enacted appropriations proposed pursuant to the Impoundment Control Act (ICA). The ICA allows the President, using the specific authorities in that Act, to transmit a "special message" to the Congress to inform them of these proposed rescissions, at which time the funding can be withheld from obligation for up to 45 days on the OMB-approved apportionment. Agencies are instructed not to withhold funds without the prior approval of OMB. If the Congress does not act to rescind these funds within the 45-day period, the funds are made available for obligation.

The President can also propose reductions to previously enacted appropriations outside of the ICA; in these cases, these reductions are referred to as cancellations. Cancellation proposals are not subject to the requirements and procedures of the ICA and amounts cannot be withheld from obligation. The 2022 President's Budget includes $4.3 billion in proposed cancellations.

COVERAGE OF THE BUDGET

Federal Government and Budget Totals

The budget documents provide information on all Federal agencies and programs. However, because the laws governing Social Security (the Federal Old-Age and Survivors Insurance and the Federal Disability Insurance trust funds) and the Postal Service Fund require that the receipts and outlays for those activities be excluded from the budget totals and from the calculation of the deficit or surplus, the budget presents on-budget and off-budget totals. The off-budget totals include the Federal transactions excluded by law from the budget totals. The on-budget and off-budget amounts are added together to derive the totals for the Federal Government. These are sometimes referred to as the unified or consolidated budget totals.

It is not always obvious whether a transaction or activity should be included in the budget. Where there is a question, OMB normally follows the recommendation of the 1967 President's Commission on Budget Concepts to be comprehensive of the full range of Federal agencies, programs, and activities. In recent years, for example, the budget has included the transactions of the Affordable Housing Program funds, the Universal Service Fund, the Public Company Accounting Oversight Board, the Securities Investor Protection Corporation, Guaranty Agencies Reserves, the National Railroad Retirement Investment Trust, the United Mine Workers Combined

Benefits Fund, the Federal Financial Institutions Examination Council, Electric Reliability Organizations (EROs) established pursuant to the Energy Policy Act of 2005, the Corporation for Travel Promotion, and the National Association of Registered Agents and Brokers.

In contrast, the budget excludes tribal trust funds that are owned by Indian Tribes and held and managed by the Government in a fiduciary capacity on the Tribes' behalf. These funds are not owned by the Government, the Government is not the source of their capital, and the Government's control is limited to the exercise of fiduciary duties. Similarly, the transactions of Government-sponsored enterprises, such as the Federal Home Loan Banks, are not included in the on-budget or off-budget totals. Federal laws established these enterprises for public policy purposes, but they are privately owned and operated corporations. Nevertheless, because of their public charters, the budget discusses them and reports summary financial data in the Budget *Appendix* and in some detailed tables.

The budget also excludes the revenues from copyright royalties and spending for subsequent payments to copyright holders where (1) the law allows copyright owners and users to voluntarily set the rate paid for the use of protected material, and (2) the amount paid by users of copyrighted material to copyright owners is related to the frequency or quantity of the material used. The budget excludes license royalties collected and paid out by the Copyright Office for the retransmission of network broadcasts via cable collected under 17 U.S.C. 111 because these revenues meet both of these conditions. The budget includes the royalties collected and paid out for license fees for digital audio recording technology under 17 U.S.C. 1004, since the amount of license fees paid is unrelated to usage of the material.

The *Appendix* includes a presentation for the Board of Governors of the Federal Reserve System for information only. The amounts are not included in either the on-budget or off-budget totals because of the independent status of the System within the Government. However, the Federal Reserve System transfers its net earnings to the Treasury, and the budget records them as receipts.

Chapter 7 of this volume, "Coverage of the Budget," provides more information on this subject.

Functional Classification

The functional classification is used to organize budget authority, outlays, and other budget data according to the major purpose served—such as agriculture, transportation, income security, and national defense. There are 20 major functions, 17 of which are concerned with broad areas of national need and are further divided into subfunctions. For example, the Agriculture function comprises the subfunctions Farm Income Stabilization and Agricultural Research and Services. The functional classification meets the Congressional Budget Act requirement for a presentation in the budget by national needs and agency missions and programs. The remaining three functions—Net Interest, Undistributed Offsetting

Table 6–1. TOTALS FOR THE BUDGET AND THE FEDERAL GOVERNMENT

(In billions of dollars)

	2020 Actual	Estimate	
		2021	2022
Budget authority:			
Unified	7,735	7,090	6,212
On-budget	6,774	6,063	5,134
Off-budget	962	1,027	1,078
Receipts:			
Unified	3,421	3,581	4,174
On-budget	2,456	2,637	3,142
Off-budget	965	944	1,033
Outlays:			
Unified	6,550	7,249	6,011
On-budget	5,598	6,232	4,931
Off-budget	952	1,018	1,081
Deficit (–) / Surplus (+):			
Unified	–3,129	–3,669	–1,837
On-budget	–3,142	–3,595	–1,789
Off-budget	13	–73	–48

Receipts, and Allowances—enable the functional classification system to cover the entire Federal budget.

The following criteria are used in establishing functional categories and assigning activities to them:

- A function encompasses activities with similar purposes, emphasizing what the Federal Government seeks to accomplish rather than the means of accomplishment, the objects purchased, the clientele or geographic area served (except in the cases of functions 450 for Community and Regional Development, 570 for Medicare, 650 for Social Security, and 700 for Veterans Benefits and Services), or the Federal agency conducting the activity (except in the case of subfunction 051 in the National Defense function, which is used only for defense activities under the Department of Defense—Military).

- A function must be of continuing national importance, and the amounts attributable to it must be significant.

- Each basic unit being classified (generally the appropriation or fund account) usually is classified according to its primary purpose and assigned to only one subfunction. However, some large accounts that serve more than one major purpose are subdivided into two or more functions or subfunctions.

In consultation with the Congress, the functional classification is adjusted from time to time as warranted. Detailed functional tables, which provide information on Government activities by function and subfunction, are available online at *https://www.whitehouse.gov/omb/analytical-perspectives/* and on *OMB's website*.

Agencies, Accounts, Programs, Projects, and Activities

Various summary tables in the *Analytical Perspectives* volume of the Budget provide information on budget authority, outlays, and offsetting collections and receipts arrayed by Federal agency. A table that lists budget authority and outlays by budget account within each agency and the totals for each agency of budget authority, outlays, and receipts that offset the agency spending totals is available online at: *https://www.whitehouse.gov/ omb/analytical-perspectives/* and on *OMB's website*. The *Appendix* provides budgetary, financial, and descriptive information about programs, projects, and activities by account within each agency.

Types of Funds

Agency activities are financed through Federal funds and trust funds.

Federal funds comprise several types of funds. Receipt accounts of the *general fund*, which is the greater part of the budget, record receipts not earmarked by law for a specific purpose, such as income tax receipts. The general fund also includes the proceeds of general borrowing. General fund appropriations accounts record general fund expenditures. General fund appropriations draw from general fund receipts and borrowing collectively and, therefore, are not specifically linked to receipt accounts.

Special funds consist of receipt accounts for Federal fund receipts that laws have designated for specific purposes and the associated appropriation accounts for the expenditure of those receipts.

Public enterprise funds are revolving funds used for programs authorized by law to conduct a cycle of business-type operations, primarily with the public, in which outlays generate collections.

Intragovernmental funds are revolving funds that conduct business-type operations primarily within and between Government agencies. The collections and the outlays of revolving funds are recorded in the same budget account.

Trust funds account for the receipt and expenditure of monies by the Government for carrying out specific purposes and programs in accordance with the terms of a statute that designates the fund as a trust fund (such as the Highway Trust Fund) or for carrying out the stipulations of a trust where the Government itself is the beneficiary (such as any of several trust funds for gifts and donations for specific purposes). *Trust revolving funds* are trust funds credited with collections earmarked by law to carry out a cycle of business-type operations.

The Federal budget meaning of the term "trust," as applied to trust fund accounts, differs significantly from its private-sector usage. In the private sector, the beneficiary of a trust usually owns the trust's assets, which are managed by a trustee who must follow the stipulations of the trust. In contrast, the Federal Government owns the assets of most Federal trust funds, and it can raise or lower future trust fund collections and payments, or change the purposes for which the collections are used, by changing existing laws. There is no substantive difference between a trust fund and a special fund or between a trust revolving fund and a public enterprise revolving fund.

However, in some instances, the Government does act as a true trustee of assets that are owned or held for the benefit of others. For example, it maintains accounts on behalf of individual Federal employees in the Thrift Savings Fund, investing them as directed by the individual employee. The Government accounts for such funds in *deposit funds*, which are not included in the budget. (Chapter 18 of this volume, "Trust Funds and Federal Funds," provides more information on this subject.)

Budgeting for Full Costs

A budget is a financial plan for allocating resources—deciding how much the Federal Government should spend in total, program by program, and for the parts of each program and deciding how to finance the spending. The budgetary system provides a process for proposing policies, making decisions, implementing them, and reporting the results. The budget needs to measure costs accurately so that decision makers can compare the cost of a program with its benefits, the cost of one program with another, and the cost of one method of reaching a specified goal with another. These costs need to be fully included in the budget up front, when the spending decision is made, so that executive and congressional decision makers have the information and the incentive to take the total costs into account when setting priorities.

The budget includes all types of spending, including both current operating expenditures and capital investment, and to the extent possible, both are measured on the basis of full cost. Questions are often raised about the measure of capital investment. The present budget provides policymakers the necessary information regarding investment spending. It records investment on a cash basis, and it requires the Congress to provide budget authority before an agency can obligate the Government to make a cash outlay. However, the budget measures only costs, and the benefits with which these costs are compared, based on policy makers' judgment, must be presented in supplementary materials. By these means, the budget allows the total cost of capital investment to be compared up front in a rough way with the total expected future net benefits. Such a comparison of total costs with benefits is consistent with the formal method of cost-benefit analysis of capital projects in government, in which the full cost of a capital asset as the cash is paid out is compared with the full stream of future benefits (all in terms of present values). (Chapter 13 of this volume, "Federal Investment," provides more information on capital investment.)

RECEIPTS, OFFSETTING COLLECTIONS, AND OFFSETTING RECEIPTS

In General

The budget records amounts collected by Government agencies two different ways. Depending on the nature of the activity generating the collection and the law that established the collection, they are recorded as either:

Governmental receipts, which are compared in total to outlays (net of offsetting collections and offsetting receipts) in calculating the surplus or deficit; or

Offsetting collections or *offsetting receipts*, which are deducted from gross outlays to calculate net outlay figures.

Governmental Receipts

Governmental receipts are collections that result from the Government's exercise of its sovereign power to tax or otherwise compel payment. Sometimes they are called receipts, budget receipts, Federal receipts, or Federal revenues. They consist mostly of individual and corporation income taxes and social insurance taxes, but also include excise taxes, compulsory user charges, regulatory fees, customs duties, court fines, certain license fees, and deposits of earnings by the Federal Reserve System. Total receipts for the Federal Government include both on-budget and off-budget receipts (see Table 6–1, "Totals for the Budget and the Federal Government," which appears earlier in this chapter.) Chapter 8 of this volume, "Governmental Receipts," provides more information on governmental receipts.

Offsetting Collections and Offsetting Receipts

Offsetting collections and offsetting receipts are recorded as offsets to (deductions from) spending, not as additions on the receipt side of the budget. These amounts are recorded as offsets to outlays so that the budget totals represent governmental rather than market activity and reflect the Government's net transactions with the public. They are recorded in one of two ways, based on interpretation of laws and longstanding budget concepts and practice. They are offsetting collections when the collections are authorized by law to be credited to expenditure accounts and are generally available for expenditure without further legislation. Otherwise, they are deposited in receipt accounts and called offsetting receipts; many of these receipts are available for expenditure without further legislation as well.

Offsetting collections and offsetting receipts result from any of the following types of transactions:

- *Business-like transactions or market-oriented activities with the public*—these include voluntary collections from the public in exchange for goods or services, such as the proceeds from the sale of postage stamps, the fees charged for admittance to recreation areas, and the proceeds from the sale of Government-owned land; and reimbursements for damages. The budget records these amounts as *offsetting collections from non-Federal sources* (for offsetting collections) or as *proprietary receipts* (for offsetting receipts).

- *Intragovernmental transactions*—collections from other Federal Government accounts. The budget records collections by one Government account from another as *offsetting collections from Federal sources* (for offsetting collections) or as *intragovernmental receipts* (for offsetting receipts). For example, the General Services Administration rents office space to other Government agencies and records their rental payments as offsetting collections from Federal sources in the Federal Buildings Fund. These transactions are exactly offsetting and do not affect the surplus or deficit. However, they are an important accounting mechanism for allocating costs to the programs and activities that cause the Government to incur the costs.

- *Voluntary gifts and donations*—gifts and donations of money to the Government, which are treated as offsets to budget authority and outlays.

- *Offsetting governmental transactions*—collections from the public that are governmental in nature and should conceptually be treated like Federal revenues and compared in total to outlays (e.g., tax receipts, regulatory fees, compulsory user charges, custom duties, license fees) but required by law or longstanding practice to be misclassified as offsetting. The budget records amounts from non-Federal sources that are governmental in nature as *offsetting governmental collections* (for offsetting collections) or as *offsetting governmental receipts* (for offsetting receipts).

Offsetting Collections

Some laws authorize agencies to credit collections directly to the account from which they will be spent and, usually, to spend the collections for the purpose of the account without further action by the Congress. Most revolving funds operate with such authority. For example, a permanent law authorizes the Postal Service to use collections from the sale of stamps to finance its operations without a requirement for annual appropriations. The budget records these collections in the Postal Service Fund (a revolving fund) and records budget authority in an amount equal to the collections. In addition to revolving funds, some agencies are authorized to charge fees to defray a portion of costs for a program that are otherwise financed by appropriations from the general fund and usually to spend the collections without further action by the Congress. In such cases, the budget records the offsetting collections and resulting budget authority in the program's general fund expenditure account. Similarly, intragovernmental collections authorized by some laws may be recorded as offsetting collections and budget authority in revolving funds or in general fund expenditure accounts.

Sometimes appropriations acts or provisions in other laws limit the obligations that can be financed by offsetting collections. In those cases, the budget records budget authority in the amount available to incur obligations, not in the amount of the collections.

Offsetting collections credited to expenditure accounts automatically offset the outlays at the expenditure account level. Where accounts have offsetting collections, the budget shows the budget authority and outlays of the account both gross (before deducting offsetting collections) and net (after deducting offsetting collections). Totals for the agency, subfunction, and overall budget are net of offsetting collections.

Offsetting Receipts

Collections that are offset against gross outlays but are not authorized to be credited to expenditure accounts are credited to receipt accounts and are called offsetting receipts. Offsetting receipts are deducted from budget authority and outlays in arriving at total net budget authority and outlays. However, unlike offsetting collections credited to expenditure accounts, offsetting receipts do not offset budget authority and outlays at the account level. In most cases, they offset budget authority and outlays at the agency and subfunction levels.

Proprietary receipts from a few sources, however, are not offset against any specific agency or function and are classified as undistributed offsetting receipts. They are deducted from the Government-wide totals for net budget authority and outlays. For example, the collections of rents and royalties from outer continental shelf lands are undistributed because the amounts are large and for the most part are not related to the spending of the agency that administers the transactions and the subfunction that records the administrative expenses.

Similarly, two kinds of intragovernmental transactions—agencies' payments as employers into Federal employee retirement trust funds and interest received by trust funds—are classified as undistributed offsetting receipts. They appear instead as special deductions in computing total net budget authority and outlays for the Government rather than as offsets at the agency level. This special treatment is necessary because the amounts are so large they would distort measures of the agency's activities if they were attributed to the agency.

User Charges

User charges are fees assessed on individuals or organizations for the provision of Government services and for the sale or use of Government goods or resources. The payers of the user charge must be limited in the authorizing legislation to those receiving special benefits from, or subject to regulation by, the program or activity beyond the benefits received by the general public or broad segments of the public (such as those who pay income taxes or customs duties). Policy regarding user charges is established in OMB Circular A–25, "User Charges." The term encompasses proceeds from the sale or use of Government goods and services, including the sale of natural resources (such as timber, oil, and minerals) and proceeds from asset sales (such as property, plant, and equipment). User charges are not necessarily dedicated to the activity they finance and may be credited to the general fund of the Treasury.

The term "user charge" does not refer to a separate budget category for collections. User charges are classified in the budget as receipts, offsetting receipts, or offsetting collections according to the principles explained previously.

See Chapter 9, "Offsetting Collections and Offsetting Receipts," for more information on the classification of user charges.

BUDGET AUTHORITY, OBLIGATIONS, AND OUTLAYS

Budget authority, obligations, and outlays are the primary benchmarks and measures of the budget control system. The Congress enacts laws that provide agencies with spending authority in the form of budget authority. Before agencies can use these resources—obligate this budget authority—OMB must approve their spending plans. After the plans are approved, agencies can enter into binding agreements to purchase items or services or to make grants or other payments. These agreements are recorded as obligations of the United States and deducted from the amount of budgetary resources available to the agency. When payments are made, the obligations are liquidated and outlays recorded. These concepts are discussed more fully below.

Budget Authority and Other Budgetary Resources

Budget authority is the authority provided in law to enter into legal obligations that will result in immediate or future outlays of the Government. In other words, it is the amount of money that agencies are allowed to commit to be spent in current or future years. Government officials may obligate the Government to make outlays only to the extent they have been granted budget authority.

In deciding the amount of budget authority to request for a program, project, or activity, agency officials estimate the total amount of obligations they will need to incur to achieve desired goals and subtract the unobligated balances available for these purposes. The amount of budget authority requested is influenced by the nature of the programs, projects, or activities being financed. For current operating expenditures, the amount requested usually covers the needs for the fiscal year. For major procurement programs and construction projects, agencies generally must request sufficient budget authority in the first year to fully fund an economically useful segment of a procurement or project, even though it may be obligated over several years. This full funding policy is intended to ensure that the decision-makers take into account all costs and benefits at the time decisions are made to provide resources. It also avoids sinking money into a procurement or project without being certain if or when future funding will be available to complete the procurement or project, as well as saddling future agency budgets with must-pay bills to complete past projects.

Budget authority takes several forms:

- **Appropriations**, provided in annual appropriations acts or authorizing laws, permit agencies to incur obligations and make payment;

- **Borrowing authority**, usually provided in permanent laws, permits agencies to incur obligations but requires them to borrow funds, usually from the general fund of the Treasury, to make payment;

- **Contract authority**, usually provided in permanent law, permits agencies to incur obligations in advance of a separate appropriation of the cash for payment or in anticipation of the collection of receipts that can be used for payment; and

- **Spending authority from offsetting collections**, usually provided in permanent law, permits agencies to credit offsetting collections to an expenditure account, incur obligations, and make payment using the offsetting collections.

Because offsetting collections and offsetting receipts are deducted from gross budget authority, they are referred to as negative budget authority for some purposes, such as Congressional Budget Act provisions that pertain to budget authority.

Authorizing statutes usually determine the form of budget authority for a program. The authorizing statute may authorize a particular type of budget authority to be provided in annual appropriations acts, or it may provide one of the forms of budget authority directly, without the need for further appropriations.

An appropriation may make funds available from the general fund, special funds, or trust funds, or authorize the spending of offsetting collections credited to expenditure accounts, including revolving funds. Borrowing authority is usually authorized for business-like activities where the activity being financed is expected to produce income over time with which to repay the borrowing with interest. The use of contract authority is traditionally limited to transportation programs.

New budget authority for most Federal programs is normally provided in annual appropriations acts. However, new budget authority is also made available through permanent appropriations under existing laws and does not require current action by the Congress. Much of the permanent budget authority is for trust funds, interest on the public debt, and the authority to spend offsetting collec-

tions credited to appropriation or fund accounts. For most trust funds, the budget authority is appropriated automatically under existing law from the available balance of the fund and equals the estimated annual obligations of the funds. For interest on the public debt, budget authority is provided automatically under a permanent appropriation enacted in 1847 and equals interest outlays.

Annual appropriations acts generally make budget authority available for obligation only during the fiscal year to which the act applies. However, they frequently allow budget authority for a particular purpose to remain available for obligation for a longer period or indefinitely (that is, until expended or until the program objectives have been attained). Typically, budget authority for current operations is made available for only one year, and budget authority for construction and some research projects is available for a specified number of years or indefinitely. Most budget authority provided in authorizing statutes, such as for most trust funds, is available indefinitely. If budget authority is initially provided for a limited period of availability, an extension of availability would require enactment of another law (see "Reappropriation" later in this chapter).

Budget authority that is available for more than one year and not obligated in the year it becomes available is carried forward for obligation in a following year. In some cases, an account may carry forward unobligated budget authority from more than one prior year. The sum of such amounts constitutes the account's **unobligated balance**. Most of these balances had been provided for specific uses such as the multiyear construction of a major project and so are not available for new programs. A small part may never be obligated or spent, primarily amounts provided for contingencies that do not occur or reserves that never have to be used.

Amounts of budget authority that have been obligated but not yet paid constitute the account's **unpaid obligations**. For example, in the case of salaries and wages, one to three weeks elapse between the time of obligation and the time of payment. In the case of major procurement and construction, payments may occur over a period of several years after the obligation is made. Unpaid obligations (which are made up of accounts payable and undelivered orders) net of the accounts receivable and unfilled customers' orders are defined by law as the **obligated balances**. Obligated balances of budget authority at the end of the year are carried forward until the obligations are paid or the balances are cancelled. (A general law provides that the obligated balance of budget authority that was made available for a definite period is automatically cancelled five years after the end of the period.) Due to such flows, a change in the amount of budget authority available in any one year may change the level of obligations and outlays for several years to come. Conversely, a change in the amount of obligations incurred from one year to the next does not necessarily result from an equal change in the amount of budget authority available for that year and will not necessarily result in an equal change in the level of outlays in that year.

The Congress usually makes budget authority available on the first day of the fiscal year for which the appropriations act is passed. Occasionally, the appropriations language specifies a different timing. The language may provide an ***advance appropriation***—budget authority that does not become available until one fiscal year or more beyond the fiscal year for which the appropriations act is passed. ***Forward funding*** is budget authority that is made available for obligation beginning in the last quarter of the fiscal year (beginning on July 1) for the financing of ongoing grant programs during the next fiscal year. This kind of funding is used mostly for education programs, so that obligations for education grants can be made prior to the beginning of the next school year. For certain benefit programs funded by annual appropriations, the appropriation provides for ***advance funding***—budget authority that is to be charged to the appropriation in the succeeding year, but which authorizes obligations to be incurred in the last quarter of the current fiscal year if necessary to meet benefit payments in excess of the specific amount appropriated for the year. When such authority is used, an adjustment is made to increase the budget authority for the fiscal year in which it is used and to reduce the budget authority of the succeeding fiscal year.

The 2022 Budget includes $28,768 million in discretionary advance appropriations for 2023 and freezes them at this level in subsequent years, consistent with limits established in recent congressional budget resolutions. Outside of this limit, the Administration continues advance appropriations for the Department of Veterans Affairs' medical care accounts and proposes new advance appropriations for the Department of Health and Human Services' Indian Health Service accounts. In addition, the Administration proposes new mandatory advance appropriations for the Department of Agriculture's Supplemental Nutrition Assistance Program. For a detailed table of accounts that have received advance appropriations since 2020 or for which the Budget requests advance appropriations for 2023 and beyond, please refer to the Advance Appropriations chapter in the *Appendix*.

Provisions of law that extend into a new fiscal year the availability of unobligated amounts that have expired or would otherwise expire are called ***reappropriations***. Reappropriations of expired balances that are newly available for obligation in the current or budget year count as new budget authority in the fiscal year in which the balances become newly available. For example, if a 2018 appropriations act extends the availability of unobligated budget authority that expired at the end of 2017, new budget authority would be recorded for 2018. This scorekeeping is used because a reappropriation has exactly the same effect as allowing the earlier appropriation to expire at the end of 2017 and enacting a new appropriation for 2018.

For purposes of BBEDCA and the Statutory Pay-As-You-Go Act of 2010 (discussed earlier under "Budget Enforcement"), the budget classifies budget authority as ***discretionary*** or ***mandatory***. This classification indicates whether an appropriations act or authorizing legislation controls the amount of budget authority that is available. Generally, budget authority is discretionary if provided in an annual appropriations act and mandatory if provided in authorizing legislation. However, the budget authority provided in annual appropriations acts for certain specifically identified programs is also classified as mandatory by OMB and the congressional scorekeepers. This is because the authorizing legislation for these programs entitles beneficiaries—persons, households, or other levels of government—to receive payment, or otherwise legally obligates the Government to make payment and thereby effectively determines the amount of budget authority required, even though the payments are funded by a subsequent appropriation.

The 2022 Budget proposes two reclassifications of programs that historically have been funded as discretionary. The first proposal reclassifies the appropriations for the Contract Support Costs (CSCs) and Payments for Tribal Leases accounts in the Department of Health and Human Services' Indian Health Service and the Department of the Interior's Bureau of Indian Affairs. Specifically, the Budget proposes that, beginning in 2023, the CSCs and Payments for Tribal Leases accounts will continue to be funded through the annual appropriations process but will be reclassified as mandatory funding. The second proposal reclassifies Indian water rights settlements funding at the Department of the Interior starting in 2023 by providing full funding for currently enacted settlements in authorizing legislation rather than through the annual appropriations process. The Budget proposes to offset the increase in mandatory funding resulting from both reclassifications by reducing overall discretionary spending by amounts equal to baseline inflation of the programs.

Sometimes, budget authority is characterized as current or permanent. Current authority requires the Congress to act on the request for new budget authority for the year involved. Permanent authority becomes available pursuant to standing provisions of law without appropriations action by the Congress for the year involved. Generally, budget authority is current if an annual appropriations act provides it and permanent if authorizing legislation provides it. By and large, the current/permanent distinction has been replaced by the discretionary/mandatory distinction, which is similar but not identical. Outlays are also classified as discretionary or mandatory according to the classification of the budget authority from which they flow (see "Outlays" later in this chapter).

The amount of budget authority recorded in the budget depends on whether the law provides a specific amount or employs a variable factor that determines the amount. It is considered ***definite*** if the law specifies a dollar amount (which may be stated as an upper limit, for example, "shall not exceed ..."). It is considered ***indefinite*** if, instead of specifying an amount, the law permits the amount to be determined by subsequent circumstances. For example, indefinite budget authority is provided for interest on the public debt, payment of claims and judgments awarded by the courts against the United States, and many entitlement programs. Many of the laws that authorize collections to be credited to revolving, special, and trust funds make all of the collections available for expenditure for the authorized purposes of the fund, and such authority is considered to be indefinite budget authority because the amount of collections is not known in advance of their collection.

Obligations

Following the enactment of budget authority and the completion of required apportionment action, Government agencies incur obligations to make payments (see earlier discussion under "Budget Execution"). Agencies must record obligations when they incur a legal liability that will result in immediate or future outlays. Such obligations include the current liabilities for salaries, wages, and interest; and contracts for the purchase of supplies and equipment, construction, and the acquisition of office space, buildings, and land. For Federal credit programs, obligations are recorded in an amount equal to the estimated subsidy cost of direct loans and loan guarantees (see "Federal Credit" later in this chapter).

Outlays

Outlays are the measure of Government spending. They are payments that liquidate obligations (other than most exchanges of financial instruments, of which the repayment of debt is the prime example). The budget records outlays when obligations are paid, in the amount that is paid.

Agency, function and subfunction, and Government-wide outlay totals are stated net of offsetting collections and offsetting receipts for most budget presentations. (Offsetting receipts from a few sources do not offset any specific function, subfunction, or agency, as explained previously, but only offset Government-wide totals.) Outlay totals for accounts with offsetting collections are stated both gross and net of the offsetting collections credited to the account. However, the outlay totals for special and trust funds with offsetting receipts are not stated net of the offsetting receipts. In most cases, these receipts offset the agency, function, and subfunction totals but do not offset account-level outlays. However, when general fund payments are used to finance trust fund outlays to the public, the associated trust fund receipts are netted against the bureau totals to prevent double-counting budget authority and outlays at the bureau level.

The Government usually makes outlays in the form of cash (currency, checks, or electronic fund transfers). However, in some cases agencies pay obligations without disbursing cash, and the budget nevertheless records outlays for the equivalent method. For example, the budget records outlays for the full amount of Federal employees' salaries, even though the cash disbursed to employees is net of Federal and State income taxes withheld, retirement contributions, life and health insurance premiums, and other deductions. (The budget also records receipts for the amounts withheld from Federal employee paychecks for Federal income taxes and other payments to the Government.) When debt instruments (bonds, deben-

tures, notes, or monetary credits) are used in place of cash to pay obligations, the budget records outlays financed by an increase in agency debt. For example, the budget records the acquisition of physical assets through certain types of lease-purchase arrangements as though a cash disbursement were made for an outright purchase. The transaction creates a Government debt, and the cash lease payments are treated as repayments of principal and interest.

The budget records outlays for the interest on the public issues of Treasury debt securities as the interest accrues, not when the cash is paid. A small portion of Treasury debt consists of inflation-indexed securities, which feature monthly adjustments to principal for inflation and semi-annual payments of interest on the inflation-adjusted principal. As with fixed-rate securities, the budget records interest outlays as the interest accrues. The monthly adjustment to principal is recorded, simultaneously, as an increase in debt outstanding and an outlay of interest.

Most Treasury debt securities held by trust funds and other Government accounts are in the Government account series. The budget normally states the interest on these securities on a cash basis. When a Government account is invested in Federal debt securities, the purchase price is usually close or identical to the par (face) value of the security. The budget generally records the investment at par value and adjusts the interest paid by Treasury and collected by the account by the difference between purchase price and par, if any.

For Federal credit programs, outlays are equal to the subsidy cost of direct loans and loan guarantees and are recorded as the underlying loans are disbursed (see "Federal Credit" later in this chapter).

The budget records refunds of receipts that result from overpayments by the public (such as income taxes withheld in excess of tax liabilities) as reductions of receipts, rather than as outlays. However, the budget records payments to taxpayers for refundable tax credits (such as earned income tax credits) that exceed the taxpayer's tax liability as outlays. Similarly, when the Government makes overpayments that are later returned to the Government, those refunds to the Government are recorded as offsetting collections or offsetting receipts, not as governmental receipts.

Not all of the new budget authority for 2022 will be obligated or spent in 2022. Outlays during a fiscal year may liquidate obligations incurred in the same year or in prior years. Obligations, in turn, may be incurred against budget authority provided in the same year or against unobligated balances of budget authority provided in prior years. Outlays, therefore, flow in part from budget authority provided for the year in which the money is spent and in part from budget authority provided for prior years. The ratio of a given year's outlays resulting from budget authority enacted in that or a prior year to the original amount of that budget authority is referred to as the outlay rate for that year.

As shown in the accompanying chart, $4,474 billion of outlays in 2022 (74 percent of the outlay total) will be made from that year's $6,212 billion total of proposed new

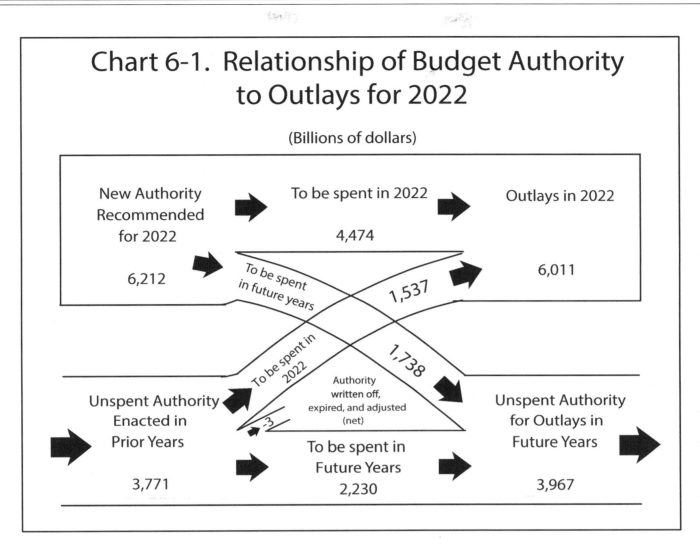

Chart 6-1. Relationship of Budget Authority to Outlays for 2022

(Billions of dollars)

New Authority Recommended for 2022

6,212

To be spent in 2022

4,474

Outlays in 2022

6,011

To be spent in future years

1,537

To be spent in 2022

1,738

Authority written off, expired, and adjusted (net)

-3

Unspent Authority Enacted in Prior Years

3,771

To be spent in Future Years

2,230

Unspent Authority for Outlays in Future Years

3,967

budget authority (a first-year outlay rate of 72 percent). Thus, the remaining $1,537 billion of outlays in 2022 (26 percent of the outlay total) will be made from budget authority enacted in previous years. At the same time, $1,738 billion of the new budget authority proposed for 2022 (28 percent of the total amount proposed) will not lead to outlays until future years.

As described earlier, the budget classifies budget authority and outlays as discretionary or mandatory. This classification of outlays measures the extent to which actual spending is controlled through the annual appropriations process. About 25 percent of total outlays in 2020 ($1,627 billion) were discretionary and the remaining 75 percent ($4,923 billion in 2020) were mandatory spending and net interest. Such a large portion of total spending is mandatory because authorizing rather than appropriations legislation determines net interest ($345 billion in 2020) and the spending for a few programs with large amounts of spending each year, such as Social Security ($1,090 billion in 2020) and Medicare ($769 billion in 2020).

The bulk of mandatory outlays flow from budget authority recorded in the same fiscal year. This is not necessarily the case for discretionary budget authority and outlays. For most major construction and procurement projects and long-term contracts, for example, the budget authority available at the time the projects are initiated covers the entire estimated cost of the project even though the work will take place and outlays will be made over a period extending beyond the year for which the budget authority is enacted. Similarly, discretionary budget authority for most education and job training activities is appropriated for school or program years that begin in the fourth quarter of the fiscal year. Most of these funds result in outlays in the year after the appropriation.

FEDERAL CREDIT

Some Government programs provide assistance through direct loans or loan guarantees. A ***direct loan*** is a disbursement of funds by the Government to a non-Federal borrower under a contract that requires repayment of such funds with or without interest and includes economically equivalent transactions, such as the sale of Federal assets on credit terms. A ***loan guarantee*** is any guarantee, insurance, or other pledge with respect to the payment of all or a part of the principal or interest on any debt obligation of a non-Federal borrower to a non-Federal lender. The Federal Credit Reform Act of 1990, as amended (FCRA), prescribes the budgetary treatment for Federal credit programs. Under this treatment, the budget records obligations and outlays up front, for the net cost to the Government (subsidy cost), rather than recording the cash flows year by year over the term of the loan. FCRA treatment allows the comparison of direct loans and loan guarantees to each other, and to other methods of delivering assistance, such as grants.

The cost of direct loans and loan guarantees, sometimes called the "subsidy cost," is estimated as the present value of expected payments to and from the public over the term of the loan, discounted using appropriate Treasury interest rates.[3] Similar to most other kinds of programs, agencies can make loans or guarantee loans only if the Congress has appropriated funds sufficient to cover the subsidy costs, or provided a limitation in an appropriations act on the amount of direct loans or loan guarantees that can be made.

The budget records the subsidy cost to the Government arising from direct loans and loan guarantees—the budget authority and outlays—in ***credit program accounts***. When a Federal agency disburses a direct loan or when a non-Federal lender disburses a loan guaranteed by a Federal agency, the program account disburses or outlays an amount equal to the estimated present value cost, or subsidy, to a non-budgetary credit ***financing account***. The financing accounts record the actual transactions with the public. For a few programs, the estimated subsidy cost is negative because the present value of expected Government collections exceeds the present value of expected payments to the public over the term of the loan. In such cases, the financing account pays the estimated subsidy cost to the program's negative subsidy receipt account, where it is recorded as an offsetting receipt. In a few cases, the offsetting receipts of credit accounts are dedicated to a special fund established for the program and are available for appropriation for the program.

The agencies responsible for credit programs must reestimate the subsidy cost of the outstanding portfolio of direct loans and loan guarantees each year. If the estimated cost increases, the program account makes an additional payment to the financing account equal to the change in cost. If the estimated cost decreases, the financing account pays the difference to the program's downward reestimate receipt account, where it is recorded as an offsetting receipt. The FCRA provides permanent indefinite appropriations to pay for upward reestimates.

If the Government modifies the terms of an outstanding direct loan or loan guarantee in a way that increases the cost as the result of a law or the exercise of administrative discretion under existing law, the program account records obligations for the increased cost and outlays the amount to the financing account. As with the original subsidy cost, agencies may incur modification costs only if the Congress has appropriated funds to cover them. A modification may also reduce costs, in which case the amounts are generally returned to the general fund, as the financing account makes a payment to the program's negative subsidy receipt account.

Credit financing accounts record all cash flows arising from direct loan obligations and loan guarantee commitments. Such cash flows include all cash flows to and from the public, including direct loan disbursements and repayments, loan guarantee default payments, fees, and recoveries on defaults. Financing accounts also record intragovernmental transactions, such as the receipt of subsidy cost payments from program accounts, borrowing and repayments of Treasury debt to finance program activities, and interest paid to or received from the Treasury. The cash flows of direct loans and of loan guarantees are recorded in separate financing accounts for programs that provide both types of credit. The budget totals exclude the transactions of the financing accounts because they are not a cost to the Government. However, since financing accounts record all credit cash flows to and from the public, they affect the means of financing a budget surplus or deficit (see "Credit Financing Accounts" in the next section). The budget documents display the transactions of the financing accounts, together with the related program accounts, for information and analytical purposes.

The budgetary treatment of direct loan obligations and loan guarantee commitments made prior to 1992 was grandfathered in under FCRA. The budget records these on a cash basis in ***credit liquidating accounts***, the same as they were recorded before FCRA was enacted. However, this exception ceases to apply if the direct loans or loan guarantees are modified as described above. In that case, the budget records the subsidy cost or savings of the modification, as appropriate, and begins to account for the associated transactions under FCRA treatment for direct loan obligations and loan guarantee commitments made in 1992 or later.

Under the authority provided in various acts, certain activities that do not meet the definition in FCRA of a direct loan or loan guarantee are reflected pursuant to FCRA. For example, the Emergency Economic Stabilization Act of 2008 (EESA) created the Troubled Asset Relief Program (TARP) under the Department of the Treasury, and authorized Treasury to purchase or guarantee troubled assets until October 3, 2010. Under the TARP, Treasury purchased equity interests in financial institutions. Section 123 of the EESA provides the Administration the author-

---

[3] Present value is a standard financial concept that considers the time-value of money. That is, it accounts for the fact that a given sum of money is worth more today than the same sum would be worth in the future because interest can be earned.

ity to treat these equity investments on a FCRA basis, recording outlays for the subsidy as is done for direct loans and loan guarantees. The budget reflects the cost to the Government of TARP direct loans, loan guarantees, and equity investments consistent with the FCRA and Section 123 of EESA, which requires an adjustment to the FCRA discount rate for market risks. Similarly, Treasury equity purchases under the Small Business Lending Fund are treated pursuant to the FCRA, as provided by the Small Business Jobs Act of 2010. The Coronavirus Aid, Relief, and Economic Security (CARES) Act authorized certain investments in programs and facilities established by the Federal Reserve. Section 4003 of the CARES Act provided that these amounts be treated in accordance with FCRA.

BUDGET DEFICIT OR SURPLUS AND MEANS OF FINANCING

When outlays exceed receipts, the difference is a deficit, which the Government finances primarily by borrowing. When receipts exceed outlays, the difference is a surplus, and the Government automatically uses the surplus primarily to reduce debt. The Federal debt held by the public is approximately the cumulative amount of borrowing to finance deficits, less repayments from surpluses, over the Nation's history.

Borrowing is not exactly equal to the deficit, and debt repayment is not exactly equal to the surplus, because of the other transactions affecting borrowing from the public, or other means of financing, such as those discussed in this section. The factors included in the other means of financing can either increase or decrease the Government's borrowing needs (or decrease or increase its ability to repay debt). For example, the change in the Treasury operating cash balance is a factor included in other means of financing. Holding receipts and outlays constant, increases in the cash balance increase the Government's need to borrow or reduce the Government's ability to repay debt, and decreases in the cash balance decrease the need to borrow or increase the ability to repay debt. In some years, the net effect of the other means of financing is minor relative to the borrowing or debt repayment; in other years, the net effect may be significant.

Borrowing and Debt Repayment

The budget treats borrowing and debt repayment as a means of financing, not as receipts and outlays. If borrowing were defined as receipts and debt repayment as outlays, the budget would always be virtually balanced by definition. This rule applies both to borrowing in the form of Treasury securities and to specialized borrowing in the form of agency securities. The rule reflects the common-sense understanding that lending or borrowing is just an exchange of financial assets of equal value—cash for Treasury securities—and so is fundamentally different from, say, paying taxes, which involve a net transfer of financial assets from taxpayers to the Government.

In 2020, the Government borrowed $4,216 billion from the public, bringing debt held by the public to $21,017 billion. This borrowing financed the $3,129 billion deficit in that year, as well as the net impacts of the other means of financing, such as changes in cash balances and other accounts discussed below.

In addition to selling debt to the public, the Department of the Treasury issues debt to Government accounts, primarily trust funds that are required by law to invest in Treasury securities. Issuing and redeeming this debt does not affect the means of financing, because these transactions occur between one Government account and another and thus do not raise or use any cash for the Government as a whole.

(See Chapter 4 of this volume, "Federal Borrowing and Debt," for a fuller discussion of this topic.)

Exercise of Monetary Power

Seigniorage is the profit from coining money. It is the difference between the value of coins as money and their cost of production. Seigniorage reduces the Government's need to borrow. Unlike the payment of taxes or other receipts, it does not involve a transfer of financial assets from the public. Instead, it arises from the exercise of the Government's power to create money and the public's desire to hold financial assets in the form of coins. Therefore, the budget excludes seigniorage from receipts and treats it as a means of financing other than borrowing from the public. The budget also treats proceeds from the sale of gold as a means of financing, since the value of gold is determined by its value as a monetary asset rather than as a commodity.

Credit Financing Accounts

The budget records the net cash flows of credit programs in credit financing accounts. These accounts include the transactions for direct loan and loan guarantee programs, as well as the equity purchase programs under TARP that are recorded on a credit basis consistent with Section 123 of EESA. Financing accounts also record equity purchases under the Small Business Lending Fund consistent with the Small Business Jobs Act of 2010, and certain investments in programs and facilities established by the Federal Reserve consistent with Section 4003 of the CARES Act. Credit financing accounts are excluded from the budget because they are not allocations of resources by the Government (see "Federal Credit" earlier in this chapter). However, even though they do not affect the surplus or deficit, they can either increase or decrease the Government's need to borrow. Therefore, they are recorded as a means of financing.

Financing account disbursements to the public increase the requirement for Treasury borrowing in the same way as an increase in budget outlays. Financing account receipts from the public can be used to finance the payment of the Government's obligations and therefore reduce the requirement for Treasury borrowing from the public in the same way as an increase in budget receipts.

Deposit Fund Account Balances

The Treasury uses non-budgetary accounts, called deposit funds, to record cash held temporarily until ownership is determined (for example, earnest money paid by bidders for mineral leases) or cash held by the Government as agent for others (for example, State and local income taxes withheld from Federal employees' salaries and not yet paid to the State or local government or amounts held in the Thrift Savings Fund, a defined contribution pension fund held and managed in a fiduciary capacity by the Government). Deposit fund balances may be held in the form of either invested or uninvested balances. To the extent that they are not invested, changes in the balances are available to finance expenditures without a change in borrowing and are recorded as a means of financing other than borrowing from the public. To the extent that they are invested in Federal debt, changes in the balances are reflected as borrowing from the public (in lieu of borrowing from other parts of the public) and are not reflected as a separate means of financing.

United States Quota Subscriptions to the International Monetary Fund (IMF)

The United States participates in the IMF primarily through a quota subscription. Financial transactions with the IMF are exchanges of monetary assets. When the IMF temporarily draws dollars from the U.S. quota, the United States simultaneously receives an equal, offsetting, inter-est-bearing, Special Drawing Right (SDR)-denominated claim in the form of an increase in the U.S. reserve position in the IMF. The U.S. reserve position in the IMF increases when the United States makes deposits in its account at the IMF when the IMF temporarily uses members' quota resources to make loans and decreases when the IMF returns funds to the United States as borrowing countries repay the IMF (and the cash flows from the reserve position to the Treasury letter of credit).

The U.S. transactions with the IMF under the quota subscriptions do not increase the deficit in any year, and the budget excludes these transfers from budget outlays and receipts, consistent with the budgetary treatment for exchanges of monetary assets recommended by the President's Commission on Budget Concepts in 1967. The only exception is that interest earnings on U.S. deposits in its IMF account are recorded as offsetting receipts. Other exchanges of monetary assets, such as deposits of cash in Treasury accounts at commercial banks, are likewise not included in the Budget. However, the Congress has historically expressed interest in showing some kind of budgetary effect for U.S. transactions with the IMF.[4]

---

[4] For a more detailed discussion of the history of the budgetary treatment of U.S. participation in the quota and New Arrangements to Borrow (NAB), see pages 139-141 in the *Analytical Perspectives* volume of the 2016 Budget. As discussed in that volume, the budgetary treatment of the U.S. participation in the NAB is similar to the quota. See pages 85-86 of the *Analytical Perspectives* volume of the 2018 Budget for a more complete discussion of the changes made to the budgetary presentation of quota increases in Title IX of the Department of State, Foreign Operations, and Related Programs Appropriations Act, 2016.

FEDERAL EMPLOYMENT

The Budget includes information on civilian and military employment. It also includes information on related personnel compensation and benefits and on staffing requirements at overseas missions. Chapter 5 of this volume, "Strengthening the Federal Workforce," provides employment levels measured in full-time equivalents (FTEs). Agency FTEs are the measure of total hours worked by an agency's Federal employees divided by the total number of one person's compensable work hours in a fiscal year.

BASIS FOR BUDGET FIGURES

Data for the Past Year

The past year column (2020) generally presents the actual transactions and balances as recorded in agency accounts and as summarized in the central financial reports prepared by the Department of the Treasury for the most recently completed fiscal year. Occasionally, the Budget reports corrections to data reported erroneously to Treasury but not discovered in time to be reflected in Treasury's published data. In addition, in certain cases the Budget has a broader scope and includes financial transactions that are not reported to Treasury (see Chapter 19 of this volume, "Comparison of Actual to Estimated Totals," for a summary of these differences).

Data for the Current Year

The current year column (2021) includes estimates of transactions and balances based on the amounts of budgetary resources that were available when the Budget was prepared. In cases where the Budget proposes policy changes effective in the current year, the data will also reflect the budgetary effect of those proposed changes.

Data for the Budget Year

The Budget year column (2022) includes estimates of transactions and balances based on the amounts of budgetary resources that are estimated to be available, including new budget authority requested under current authorizing legislation, and amounts estimated to result from changes in authorizing legislation and tax laws.

The Budget *Appendix* generally includes the appropriations language for the amounts proposed to be appropriated under current authorizing legislation. In a few cases, this language is transmitted later because the exact requirements are unknown when the budget is transmitted. The *Appendix* generally does not include appropriations language for the amounts that will be requested under proposed legislation; that language is usually transmitted later, after the legislation is enacted. Some tables in the budget identify the items for later transmittal and the related outlays separately. Estimates of the total requirements for the Budget year include both the amounts requested with the transmittal of the budget and the amounts planned for later transmittal.

Data for the Outyears

The budget presents estimates for each of the nine years beyond the budget year (2023 through 2031) in order to reflect the effect of budget decisions on objectives and plans over a longer period.

Allowances

The budget may include lump-sum allowances to cover certain transactions that are expected to increase or decrease budget authority, outlays, or receipts but are not, for various reasons, reflected in the program details. For example, the budget might include an allowance to show the effect on the budget totals of a proposal that would affect many accounts by relatively small amounts, in order to avoid unnecessary detail in the presentations for the individual accounts.

Baseline

The Budget baseline is an estimate of the receipts, outlays, and deficits or surpluses that would occur if no changes were made to current laws and policies during the period covered by the Budget. The baseline assumes that receipts and mandatory spending, which generally are authorized on a permanent basis, will continue in the future consistent with current law and policy. The baseline assumes that the future funding for most discretionary programs, which generally are funded annually, will equal the most recently enacted appropriation, adjusted for inflation.

Baseline outlays represent the amount of resources that the Government would use over the period covered by the Budget on the basis of laws currently enacted.

The baseline serves several useful purposes:

- It may warn of future problems, either for Government fiscal policy as a whole or for individual tax and spending programs.

- It may provide a starting point for formulating the President's Budget.

- It may provide a benchmark against which the President's Budget and alternative proposals can be compared to assess the magnitude of proposed changes.

The baseline rules in BBEDCA provide that funding for discretionary programs is inflated from the most recent enacted appropriations using specified inflation rates. Occasionally, exceptions are needed to provide more meaningful comparisons for discretionary spending. This year, the baseline removes the extension of certain emergency spending provided to address the public health and economic effects of the COVID-19 public health emergency (funding that was provided and designated as emergency funding for 2021 in Division M of Public Law 116-260). (Chapter 17 of this volume, "Current Services Estimates," provides more information on the baseline.)

PRINCIPAL BUDGET LAWS

The Budget and Accounting Act of 1921 created the core of the current Federal budget process. Before enactment of this law, there was no annual centralized budgeting in the Executive Branch. Federal Government agencies usually sent budget requests independently to congressional committees with no coordination of the various requests in formulating the Federal Government's budget. The Budget and Accounting Act required the President to coordinate the budget requests for all Government agencies and to send a comprehensive budget to the Congress. The Congress has amended the requirements many times and portions of the Act are codified in Title 31, United States Code. The major laws that govern the budget process are as follows:

Article 1, section 8, clause 1 of the Constitution, which empowers the Congress to lay and collect taxes.

Article 1, section 9, clause 7 of the Constitution, which requires appropriations in law before money may be spent from the Treasury and the publication of a regular statement of the receipts and expenditures of all public money.

Antideficiency Act (codified in Chapters 13 and 15 of Title 31, United States Code), which prescribes rules and procedures for budget execution.

Balanced Budget and Emergency Deficit Control Act of 1985, as amended, which establishes limits on discretionary spending and provides mechanisms for enforcing mandatory spending and discretionary spending limits.

Chapter 11 of Title 31, United States Code, which prescribes procedures for submission of the President's budget and information to be contained in it.

Congressional Budget and Impoundment Control Act of 1974 (Public Law 93–344), as amended. This Act comprises the:

- ***Congressional Budget Act of 1974***, as amended, which prescribes the congressional budget process;

- ***Impoundment Control Act of 1974***, *as amended,* which controls certain aspects of budget execution; and

- ***Federal Credit Reform Act of 1990, as amended (2 USC 661–661f),*** which the Budget Enforcement Act of 1990 included as an amendment to the Congressional Budget Act to prescribe the budget treatment for Federal credit programs.

Chapter 31 of Title 31, United States Code, which provides the authority for the Secretary of the Treasury to issue debt to finance the deficit and establishes a statutory limit on the level of the debt.

Chapter 33 of Title 31, United States Code, which establishes the Department of the Treasury as the authority for making disbursements of public funds, with the authority to delegate that authority to executive agencies in the interests of economy and efficiency.

Government Performance and Results Act of 1993 (Public Law 103–62, as amended) which emphasizes managing for results. It requires agencies to prepare strategic plans, annual performance plans, and annual performance reports.

Statutory Pay-As-You-Go Act of 2010, which establishes a budget enforcement mechanism generally requiring that direct spending and revenue legislation enacted into law not increase the deficit.

GLOSSARY OF BUDGET TERMS

Account refers to a separate financial reporting unit used by the Federal Government to record budget authority, outlays and income for budgeting or management information purposes as well as for accounting purposes. All budget (and off-budget) accounts are classified as being either expenditure or receipt accounts and by fund group. Budget (and off-budget) transactions fall within either of two fund groups: (1) Federal funds and (2) trust funds. (Cf. Federal funds group and trust funds group.)

Accrual method of measuring cost means an accounting method that records cost when the liability is incurred. As applied to Federal employee retirement benefits, accrual costs are recorded when the benefits are earned rather than when they are paid at some time in the future. The accrual method is used in part to provide data that assists in agency policymaking, but not used in presenting the overall budget of the United States Government.

Advance appropriation means appropriations of new budget authority that become available one or more fiscal years beyond the fiscal year for which the appropriation act was passed.

Advance funding means appropriations of budget authority provided in an appropriations act to be used, if necessary, to cover obligations incurred late in the fiscal year for benefit payments in excess of the amount specifically appropriated in the act for that year, where the budget authority is charged to the appropriation for the program for the fiscal year following the fiscal year for which the appropriations act is passed.

Agency means a department or other establishment of the Government.

Allowance means a lump-sum included in the budget to represent certain transactions that are expected to increase or decrease budget authority, outlays, or receipts but that are not, for various reasons, reflected in the program details.

Balanced Budget and Emergency Deficit Control Act of 1985 (BBEDCA) refers to legislation that altered the budget process, primarily by replacing the earlier fixed targets for annual deficits with a Pay-As-You-Go requirement for new tax or mandatory spending legislation and with caps on annual discretionary funding. The Statutory Pay-As-You-Go Act of 2010, which is a standalone piece of legislation that did not directly amend the BBEDCA, reinstated a statutory pay-as-you-go rule for revenues and mandatory spending legislation, and the Budget Control Act of 2011, which did amend BBEDCA, reinstated discretionary caps on budget authority.

Balances of budget authority means the amounts of budget authority provided in previous years that have not been outlayed.

Baseline means a projection of the estimated receipts, outlays, and deficit or surplus that would result from continuing current law or current policies through the period covered by the budget.

Budget means the Budget of the United States Government, which sets forth the President's comprehensive financial plan for allocating resources and indicates the President's priorities for the Federal Government.

Budget authority (BA) means the authority provided by law to incur financial obligations that will result in outlays. (For a description of the several forms of budget authority, see "Budget Authority and Other Budgetary Resources" earlier in this chapter.)

Budget Control Act of 2011 refers to legislation that, among other things, amended BBEDCA to reinstate discretionary spending limits on budget authority through 2021 and restored the process for enforcing those spending limits. The legislation also increased the statutory debt ceiling; created a Joint Select Committee on Deficit Reduction that was instructed to develop a bill to reduce the Federal deficit by at least $1.5 trillion over a 10-year period; and provided a process to implement alternative spending reductions in the event that legislation achieving at least $1.2 trillion of deficit reduction was not enacted.

Budget resolution—see concurrent resolution on the budget.

Budget totals mean the totals included in the budget for budget authority, outlays, receipts, and the surplus or deficit. Some presentations in the budget distinguish on-budget totals from off-budget totals. On-budget totals reflect the transactions of all Federal Government entities except those excluded from the budget totals by law. Off-budget totals reflect the transactions of Government entities that are excluded from the on-budget totals by law. Under current law, the off-budget totals include the Social Security trust funds (Federal Old-Age and Survivors Insurance and Federal Disability Insurance Trust Funds) and the Postal Service Fund. The budget combines the on- and off-budget totals to derive unified (i.e. consolidated) totals for Federal activity.

Budget year refers to the fiscal year for which the budget is being considered, that is, with respect to a session of Congress, the fiscal year of the Government that starts on October 1 of the calendar year in which that session of the Congress begins.

Budgetary resources mean amounts available to incur obligations in a given year. The term comprises new budget authority and unobligated balances of budget authority provided in previous years.

Cap means the legal limits for each fiscal year under BBEDCA on the budget authority and outlays (only if applicable) provided by discretionary appropriations.

Cap adjustment means either an increase or a decrease that is permitted to the statutory cap limits for each fiscal year under BBEDCA on the budget authority and outlays (only if applicable) provided by discretionary appropriations only if certain conditions are met. These conditions may include providing for a base level of funding, a designation of the increase or decrease by the Congress, (and in some circumstances, the President) pursuant to a section of the BBEDCA, or a change in concepts and definitions of funding under the cap. Changes in concepts and definitions require consultation with the Congressional Appropriations and Budget Committees. As noted above, while there are no discretionary caps in place for 2022, the 2022 Budget retains several cap adjustments as "allocation adjustments" to be used pursuant to the Congressional Budget Act in the Congressional Budget Resolution.

Cash equivalent transaction means a transaction in which the Government makes outlays or receives collections in a form other than cash or the cash does not accurately measure the cost of the transaction. (For examples, see the section on "Outlays" earlier in this chapter.)

Collections mean money collected by the Government that the budget records as a governmental receipt, an offsetting collection, or an offsetting receipt.

Concurrent resolution on the budget refers to the concurrent resolution adopted by the Congress to set budgetary targets for appropriations, mandatory spending legislation, and tax legislation. These concurrent resolutions are required by the Congressional Budget Act of 1974, and are generally adopted annually.

Continuing resolution means an appropriations act that provides for the ongoing operation of the Government in the absence of enacted appropriations.

Cost refers to legislation or administrative actions that increase outlays or decrease receipts. (Cf. savings.)

Credit program account means a budget account that receives and obligates appropriations to cover the subsidy cost of a direct loan or loan guarantee and disburses the subsidy cost to a financing account.

Current services estimate—see Baseline.

Debt held by the public means the cumulative amount of money the Federal Government has borrowed from the public and not repaid.

Debt held by the public net of financial assets means the cumulative amount of money the Federal Government has borrowed from the public and not repaid, minus the current value of financial assets such as loan assets, bank deposits, or private-sector securities or equities held by the Government and plus the current value of financial liabilities other than debt.

Debt held by Government accounts means the debt the Department of the Treasury owes to accounts within the Federal Government. Most of it results from the surpluses of the Social Security and other trust funds, which are required by law to be invested in Federal securities.

Debt limit means the maximum amount of Federal debt that may legally be outstanding at any time. It includes both the debt held by the public and the debt held by Government accounts, but without accounting for offsetting financial assets. When the debt limit is reached, the Government cannot borrow more money until the Congress has enacted a law to increase the limit.

Deficit means the amount by which outlays exceed receipts in a fiscal year. It may refer to the on-budget, off-budget, or unified budget deficit.

Direct loan means a disbursement of funds by the Government to a non-Federal borrower under a contract that requires the repayment of such funds with or without interest. The term includes the purchase of, or participation in, a loan made by another lender. The term also includes the sale of a Government asset on credit terms of more than 90 days duration as well as financing arrangements for other transactions that defer payment for more than 90 days. It also includes loans financed by the Federal Financing Bank (FFB) pursuant to agency loan guarantee authority. The term does not include the acquisition of a federally guaranteed loan in satisfaction of default or other guarantee claims or the price support "loans" of the Commodity Credit Corporation. (Cf. loan guarantee.)

Direct spending—see mandatory spending.

Disaster funding means a discretionary appropriation that is enacted that the Congress designates as being for disaster relief. Such amounts are a cap adjustment to the limits on discretionary spending under BBEDCA. The total adjustment for this purpose cannot exceed a ceiling for a particular year that is defined as the total of the average funding provided for disaster relief over the previous 10 years (excluding the highest and lowest years) and the unused amount of the prior year's ceiling (excluding the portion of the prior year's ceiling that was itself due to any unused amount from the year before). Disaster relief is defined as activities carried out pursuant to a determination under section 102(2) of the Robert T. Stafford Disaster Relief and Emergency Assistance Act.

Discretionary spending means budgetary resources (except those provided to fund mandatory spending programs) provided in appropriations acts. (Cf. mandatory spending.)

Emergency requirement means an amount that the Congress has designated as an emergency requirement. Such amounts are not included in the estimated budgetary effects of PAYGO legislation under the requirements of the Statutory Pay-As-You-Go Act of 2010, if they are mandatory or receipts. Such a discretionary appropriation that is subsequently designated by the President as an emergency requirement results in a cap adjustment to the limits on discretionary spending under BBEDCA.

Entitlement refers to a program in which the Federal Government is legally obligated to make payments or provide aid to any person who, or State or local government that, meets the legal criteria for eligibility. Examples include Social Security, Medicare, Medicaid, and the Supplemental Nutrition Assistance Program (formerly Food Stamps).

Federal funds group refers to the moneys collected and spent by the Government through accounts other than those designated as trust funds. Federal funds include general, special, public enterprise, and intragovernmental funds. (Cf. trust funds group.)

Financing account means a non-budgetary account (an account whose transactions are excluded from the budget totals) that records all of the cash flows resulting from post-1991 direct loan obligations or loan guarantee commitments. At least one financing account is associated with each credit program account. For programs that make both direct loans and loan guarantees, separate financing accounts are required for direct loan cash flows and for loan guarantee cash flows. (Cf. liquidating account.)

Fiscal year means the Government's accounting period. It begins on October 1 and ends on September 30, and is designated by the calendar year in which it ends.

Forward funding means appropriations of budget authority that are made for obligation starting in the last quarter of the fiscal year for the financing of ongoing grant programs during the next fiscal year.

General fund means the accounts in which are recorded governmental receipts not earmarked by law for a specific purpose, the proceeds of general borrowing, and the expenditure of these moneys.

Government-sponsored enterprises mean private enterprises that were established and chartered by the Federal Government for public policy purposes. They are classified as non-budgetary and not included in the Federal budget because they are private companies, and their securities are not backed by the full faith and credit of the Federal Government. However, the budget presents statements of financial condition for certain Government sponsored enterprises such as the Federal National Mortgage Association. (Cf. off-budget.)

Intragovernmental fund—see Revolving fund.

Liquidating account means a budget account that records all cash flows to and from the Government resulting from pre-1992 direct loan obligations or loan guarantee commitments. (Cf. financing account.)

Loan guarantee means any guarantee, insurance, or other pledge with respect to the payment of all or a part of the principal or interest on any debt obligation of a non-Federal borrower to a non-Federal lender. The term does not include the insurance of deposits, shares, or other withdrawable accounts in financial institutions. (Cf. direct loan.)

Mandatory spending means spending controlled by laws other than appropriations acts (including spending for entitlement programs) and spending for the Supplemental Nutrition Assistance Program, formerly food stamps. Although the Statutory Pay-As-You-Go Act of 2010 uses the term direct spending to mean this, mandatory spending is commonly used instead. (Cf. discretionary spending.)

Means of financing refers to borrowing, the change in cash balances, and certain other transactions involved in financing a deficit. The term is also used to refer to the debt repayment, the change in cash balances, and certain other transactions involved in using a surplus. By definition, the means of financing are not treated as receipts or outlays and so are non-budgetary.

Obligated balance means the cumulative amount of budget authority that has been obligated but not yet outlayed. (Cf. unobligated balance.)

Obligation means a binding agreement that will result in outlays, immediately or in the future. Budgetary resources must be available before obligations can be incurred legally.

Off-budget refers to transactions of the Federal Government that would be treated as budgetary had the Congress not designated them by statute as "off-budget." Currently, transactions of the Social Security trust funds and the Postal Service are the only sets of transactions that are so designated. The term is sometimes used more broadly to refer to the transactions of private enterprises that were established and sponsored by the Government, most especially "Government-sponsored enterprises" such as the Federal Home Loan Banks. (Cf. budget totals.)

Offsetting collections mean collections that, by law, are credited directly to expenditure accounts and deducted from gross budget authority and outlays of the expenditure account, rather than added to receipts. Usually, they are authorized to be spent for the purposes of the account without further action by the Congress. They result from business-like transactions with the public, including payments from the public in exchange for goods and services, reimbursements for damages, and gifts or donations of money to the Government and from intragovernmental transactions with other Government accounts. The authority to spend offsetting collections is a form of budget authority. (Cf. receipts and offsetting receipts.)

Offsetting receipts mean collections that are credited to offsetting receipt accounts and deducted from gross budget authority and outlays, rather than added to receipts. They are not authorized to be credited to expenditure accounts. The legislation that authorizes the offsetting receipts may earmark them for a specific purpose and either appropriate them for expenditure for that purpose or require them to be appropriated in annual appropriation acts before they can be spent. Like offsetting collections, they result from business-like transactions or market-oriented activities with the public, including payments from the public in exchange for goods and services, reimbursements for damages, and gifts or donations of money to the Government and from intragovernmental transactions with other Government accounts. (Cf. receipts, undistributed offsetting receipts, and offsetting collections.)

On-budget refers to all budgetary transactions other than those designated by statute as off-budget. (Cf. budget totals.)

Outlay means a payment to liquidate an obligation (other than the repayment of debt principal or other disbursements that are "means of financing" transactions). Outlays generally are equal to cash disbursements, but also are recorded for cash-equivalent transactions, such as the issuance of debentures to pay insurance claims, and in a few cases are recorded on an accrual basis such as interest on public issues of the public debt. Outlays are the measure of Government spending.

Outyear estimates mean estimates presented in the budget for the years beyond the budget year of budget authority, outlays, receipts, and other items (such as debt).

Overseas Contingency Operations/Global War on Terrorism (OCO/GWOT) means a discretionary appropriation that is enacted that the Congress and, subsequently, the President have so designated on an account by account basis. Such a discretionary appropriation that is designated as OCO/GWOT results in a cap adjustment to the limits on discretionary spending under BBEDCA. Funding for these purposes has most recently been associated with the wars in Iraq and Afghanistan.

Pay-as-you-go (PAYGO) refers to requirements of the Statutory Pay-As-You-Go Act of 2010 that result in a sequestration if the estimated combined result of new legislation affecting direct spending or revenue increases the on-budget deficit relative to the baseline, as of the end of a congressional session.

Public enterprise fund—see Revolving fund.

Reappropriation means a provision of law that extends into a new fiscal year the availability of unobligated amounts that have expired or would otherwise expire.

Receipts mean collections that result from the Government's exercise of its sovereign power to tax or otherwise compel payment. They are compared to outlays in calculating a surplus or deficit. (Cf. offsetting collections and offsetting receipts.)

Revolving fund means a fund that conducts continuing cycles of business-like activity, in which the fund charges for the sale of products or services and uses the proceeds to finance its spending, usually without requirement for annual appropriations. There are two types of revolving funds: Public enterprise funds, which conduct business-like operations mainly with the public, and intragovernmental revolving funds, which conduct business-like operations mainly within and between Government agencies. (Cf. special fund and trust fund.)

Savings refers to legislation or administrative actions that decrease outlays or increase receipts. (Cf. cost.)

Scorekeeping means measuring the budget effects of legislation, generally in terms of budget authority, receipts, and outlays, for purposes of measuring adherence to the Budget or to budget targets established by the Congress, as through agreement to a Budget Resolution.

Sequestration means the cancellation of budgetary resources. The Statutory Pay-As-You-Go Act of 2010 requires such cancellations if revenue or direct spending legislation is enacted that, in total, increases projected deficits or reduces projected surpluses relative to the baseline. The Balanced Budget and Emergency Deficit Control Act of 1985, as amended, requires annual across-the-board cancellations to selected mandatory programs through 2030.

Special fund means a Federal fund account for receipts or offsetting receipts earmarked for specific purposes and the expenditure of these receipts. (Cf. revolving fund and trust fund.)

Statutory Pay-As-You-Go Act of 2010 refers to legislation that reinstated a statutory pay-as-you-go requirement for new tax or mandatory spending legislation. The law is a standalone piece of legislation that cross-references BBEDCA but does not directly amend that legislation. This is a permanent law and does not expire.

Subsidy means the estimated long-term cost to the Government of a direct loan or loan guarantee, calculated on a net present value basis, excluding administrative costs and any incidental effects on governmental receipts or outlays.

Surplus means the amount by which receipts exceed outlays in a fiscal year. It may refer to the on-budget, off-budget, or unified budget surplus.

Supplemental appropriation means an appropriation enacted subsequent to a regular annual appropriations act, when the need for additional funds is too urgent to be postponed until the next regular annual appropriations act.

Trust fund refers to a type of account, designated by law as a trust fund, for receipts or offsetting receipts dedicated to specific purposes and the expenditure of these receipts. Some revolving funds are designated as trust funds, and these are called trust revolving funds. (Cf. special fund and revolving fund.)

Trust funds group refers to the moneys collected and spent by the Government through trust fund accounts. (Cf. Federal funds group.)

Undistributed offsetting receipts mean offsetting receipts that are deducted from the Government-wide totals for budget authority and outlays instead of being offset against a specific agency and function. (Cf. offsetting receipts.)

Unified budget includes receipts from all sources and outlays for all programs of the Federal Government, including both on- and off-budget programs. It is the most comprehensive measure of the Government's annual finances.

Unobligated balance means the cumulative amount of budget authority that remains available for obligation under law in unexpired accounts. The term "expired balances available for adjustment only" refers to unobligated amounts in expired accounts.

User charges are charges assessed for the provision of Government services and for the sale or use of Government goods or resources. The payers of the user charge must be limited in the authorizing legislation to those receiving special benefits from, or subject to regulation by, the program or activity beyond the benefits received by the general public or broad segments of the public (such as those who pay income taxes or custom duties).

7. COVERAGE OF THE BUDGET

The Federal budget is the central instrument of national policy making. It is the Government's financial plan for proposing and deciding the allocation of resources to serve national objectives. The budget provides information on the cost and scope of Federal activities to inform decisions and to serve as a means to control the allocation of resources. When enacted, it establishes the level of public goods and services provided by the Government.

Federal Government activities can be either "budgetary" or "non-budgetary." Those activities that involve direct and measurable allocation of Federal resources are budgetary. The payments to and from the public resulting from budgetary activities are included in the budget's accounting of outlays and receipts. Federal activities that do not involve direct and measurable allocation of Federal resources are non-budgetary and are not included in the budget's accounting of outlays and receipts. More detailed information about outlays and receipts may be found in Chapter 6, "Budget Concepts," of this volume.

The budget documents include information on some non-budgetary activities because they can be important instruments of Federal policy and provide insight into the scope and nature of Federal activities. For example, the budget documents show the transactions of the Thrift Savings Program (TSP), a collection of investment funds managed by the Federal Retirement Thrift Investment Board (FRTIB). Despite the fact that the FRTIB is budgetary and one of the TSP funds is invested entirely in Federal securities, the transactions of these funds are non-budgetary because current and retired Federal employees own the funds. The Government manages these funds only in a fiduciary capacity.

The budget also includes information on cash flows that are a means of financing Federal activity, such as for credit financing accounts. However, to avoid double-counting, means of financing amounts are not included in the estimates of outlays or receipts because the costs of the underlying Federal activities are already reflected in the deficit.[1] This chapter provides details about the budgetary and non-budgetary activities of the Federal Government.

Budgetary Activities

The Federal Government has used the unified budget concept—which consolidates outlays and receipts from Federal funds and trust funds, including the Social Security trust funds—since 1968, starting with the 1969 Budget. The 1967 President's Commission on Budget Concepts (the Commission) recommended the change to include the financial transactions of all of the Federal Government's programs and agencies. Thus, the budget includes information on the financial transactions of all 15 Executive Departments, all independent agencies (from all three branches of Government), and all Government corporations.[2]

The budget shows outlays and receipts for on-budget and off-budget activities separately to reflect the legal distinction between the two. Although there is a legal distinction between on-budget and off-budget activities, conceptually there is no difference between them. Off-budget Federal activities reflect the same kinds of governmental roles as on-budget activities and result in outlays and receipts. Like on-budget activities, the Government funds and controls off-budget activities. The "unified budget" reflects the conceptual similarity between on-budget and off-budget activities by showing combined totals of outlays and receipts for both.

Many Government corporations are entities with business-type operations that charge the public for services at prices intended to allow the entity to be self-sustaining, although some operate at a loss in order to provide subsidies to specific recipients. Often these entities are more independent than other agencies and have limited exemptions from certain Federal personnel requirements to allow for flexibility.

All accounts in Table 21-1, "Federal Budget by Agency and Account," in the supplemental materials to this volume are budgetary.[3] The majority of budgetary accounts are associated with the Departments or other entities that are clearly Federal agencies. Some budgetary accounts reflect Government payments to entities that the Government created or chartered as private or non-Federal entities. Some of these entities receive all or a majority of their funding from the Government. These include the Corporation for Public Broadcasting, Gallaudet University, Howard University, the Legal Services Corporation, the National Railroad Passenger Corporation (Amtrak), the Smithsonian Institution, the State Justice Institute, and the United States Institute of Peace. A related example is the Standard Setting Board, which is not a Federally created entity but since 2003 has received a majority of funding through a federally

---

[1] For more information on means of financing, see the "Budget Deficit or Surplus and Means of Financing" section of Chapter 6, "Budget Concepts," in this volume.

[2] Government corporations are Government entities that are defined as corporations pursuant to the Government Corporation Control Act, as amended (31 U.S.C. 9101), or elsewhere in law. Examples include the Commodity Credit Corporation, the Export-Import Bank of the United States, the Federal Crop Insurance Corporation, the Federal Deposit Insurance Corporation, the Millennium Challenge Corporation, the Overseas Private Investment Corporation (now the U.S. International Development Finance Corporation), the Pension Benefit Guaranty Corporation, the Tennessee Valley Authority, the African Development Foundation (22 U.S.C. 290h-6), the Inter-American Foundation (22 U.S.C. 290f), the Presidio Trust (16 U.S.C. 460bb note), and the Valles Caldera Trust (16 U.S.C. 698v-4).

[3] Table 21-1 can be found at: *https://www.whitehouse.gov/omb/analytical-perspectives*.

Table 7–1. COMPARISON OF TOTAL, ON-BUDGET, AND OFF-BUDGET TRANSACTIONS[1]

(In billions of dollars)

Year	Receipts			Outlays			Surplus or deficit (–)		
	Total	On-budget	Off-budget	Total	On-budget	Off-budget	Total	On-budget	Off-budget
1981	599.3	469.1	130.2	678.2	543.0	135.3	–79.0	–73.9	–5.1
1982	617.8	474.3	143.5	745.7	594.9	150.9	–128.0	–120.6	–7.4
1983	600.6	453.2	147.3	808.4	660.9	147.4	–207.8	–207.7	–.1
1984	666.4	500.4	166.1	851.8	685.6	166.2	–185.4	–185.3	–.1
1985	734.0	547.9	186.2	946.3	769.4	176.9	–212.3	–221.5	9.2
1986	769.2	568.9	200.2	990.4	806.8	183.5	–221.2	–237.9	16.7
1987	854.3	640.9	213.4	1,004.0	809.2	194.8	–149.7	–168.4	18.6
1988	909.2	667.7	241.5	1,064.4	860.0	204.4	–155.2	–192.3	37.1
1989	991.1	727.4	263.7	1,143.7	932.8	210.9	–152.6	–205.4	52.8
1990	1,032.0	750.3	281.7	1,253.0	1,027.9	225.1	–221.0	–277.6	56.6
1991	1,055.0	761.1	293.9	1,324.2	1,082.5	241.7	–269.2	–321.4	52.2
1992	1,091.2	788.8	302.4	1,381.5	1,129.2	252.3	–290.3	–340.4	50.1
1993	1,154.3	842.4	311.9	1,409.4	1,142.8	266.6	–255.1	–300.4	45.3
1994	1,258.6	923.5	335.0	1,461.8	1,182.4	279.4	–203.2	–258.8	55.7
1995	1,351.8	1,000.7	351.1	1,515.7	1,227.1	288.7	–164.0	–226.4	62.4
1996	1,453.1	1,085.6	367.5	1,560.5	1,259.6	300.9	–107.4	–174.0	66.6
1997	1,579.2	1,187.2	392.0	1,601.1	1,290.5	310.6	–21.9	–103.2	81.4
1998	1,721.7	1,305.9	415.8	1,652.5	1,335.9	316.6	69.3	–29.9	99.2
1999	1,827.5	1,383.0	444.5	1,701.8	1,381.1	320.8	125.6	1.9	123.7
2000	2,025.2	1,544.6	480.6	1,789.0	1,458.2	330.8	236.2	86.4	149.8
2001	1,991.1	1,483.6	507.5	1,862.8	1,516.0	346.8	128.2	–32.4	160.7
2002	1,853.1	1,337.8	515.3	2,010.9	1,655.2	355.7	–157.8	–317.4	159.7
2003	1,782.3	1,258.5	523.8	2,159.9	1,796.9	363.0	–377.6	–538.4	160.8
2004	1,880.1	1,345.4	534.7	2,292.8	1,913.3	379.5	–412.7	–568.0	155.2
2005	2,153.6	1,576.1	577.5	2,472.0	2,069.7	402.2	–318.3	–493.6	175.3
2006	2,406.9	1,798.5	608.4	2,655.1	2,233.0	422.1	–248.2	–434.5	186.3
2007	2,568.0	1,932.9	635.1	2,728.7	2,275.0	453.6	–160.7	–342.2	181.5
2008	2,524.0	1,865.9	658.0	2,982.5	2,507.8	474.8	–458.6	–641.8	183.3
2009	2,105.0	1,451.0	654.0	3,517.7	3,000.7	517.0	–1,412.7	–1,549.7	137.0
2010	2,162.7	1,531.0	631.7	3,457.1	2,902.4	554.7	–1,294.4	–1,371.4	77.0
2011	2,303.5	1,737.7	565.8	3,603.1	3,104.5	498.6	–1,299.6	–1,366.8	67.2
2012	2,450.0	1,880.5	569.5	3,526.6	3,019.0	507.6	–1,076.6	–1,138.5	61.9
2013	2,775.1	2,101.8	673.3	3,454.9	2,821.1	633.8	–679.8	–719.2	39.5
2014	3,021.5	2,285.9	735.6	3,506.3	2,800.2	706.1	–484.8	–514.3	29.5
2015	3,249.9	2,479.5	770.4	3,691.9	2,948.8	743.1	–442.0	–469.3	27.3
2016	3,268.0	2,457.8	810.2	3,852.6	3,077.9	774.7	–584.7	–620.2	35.5
2017	3,316.2	2,465.6	850.6	3,981.6	3,180.4	801.2	–665.4	–714.9	49.4
2018	3,329.9	2,475.2	854.7	4,109.0	3,260.5	848.6	–779.1	–785.3	6.2
2019	3,463.4	2,549.1	914.3	4,447.0	3,540.3	906.6	–983.6	–991.3	7.7
2020	3,421.2	2,455.7	965.4	6,550.4	5,598.0	952.4	–3,129.2	–3,142.3	13.1
2021 estimate	3,580.8	2,636.6	944.1	7,249.5	6,231.9	1,017.5	–3,668.7	–3,595.3	–73.4
2022 estimate	4,174.2	3,141.6	1,032.6	6,011.1	4,930.6	1,080.6	–1,837.0	–1,789.0	–48.0
2023 estimate	4,641.0	3,569.4	1,071.6	6,013.0	4,870.5	1,142.4	–1,371.9	–1,301.1	–70.9
2024 estimate	4,827.8	3,710.2	1,117.6	6,186.8	4,974.3	1,212.5	–1,359.0	–1,264.1	–94.9
2025 estimate	5,037.9	3,879.3	1,158.6	6,507.7	5,220.4	1,287.3	–1,469.8	–1,341.1	–128.7
2026 estimate	5,332.1	4,125.3	1,206.8	6,746.3	5,385.7	1,360.6	–1,414.2	–1,260.4	–153.8

[1] Off-budget transactions consist of the Social Security Trust funds and the Postal Service fund.

mandated assessment on public companies under the Sarbanes-Oxley Act. Although the Federal payments to these entities are budgetary, the entities themselves are non-budgetary.

Whether the Government created or chartered an entity does not alone determine its budgetary status. The Commission recommended that the budget be comprehensive but it also recognized that proper budgetary classification required weighing all relevant factors regarding establishment, ownership, and control of an entity while erring on the side of inclusiveness. Generally, entities that are primarily Government owned or controlled are classified as budgetary. OMB determines the budgetary classification of entities in consultation with the Congressional Budget Office (CBO) and the Budget Committees of the Congress.

One recent example of a budgetary classification was for the Puerto Rico Financial Oversight Board, created in June 2016 by the Puerto Rico Oversight, Management, and Economic Stability Act (P. L. 114–187). By statute, this oversight board is not a department, agency, establishment, or instrumentality of the Federal Government, but is an entity within the territorial government financed entirely by the territorial government. Because the flow of funds from the territory to the oversight board is mandated by Federal law, the budget reflects the allocation of resources by the territorial government to the territorial entity as a receipt from the territorial government and an equal outlay to the oversight board, with net zero deficit impact. Because the oversight board itself is not a Federal entity, its operations are not included in the budget.

Another example involved the National Association of Registered Agents and Brokers (NARAB). NARAB allows for the adoption and application of insurance licensing, continuing education, and other nonresident producer qualification requirements on a multi-State basis. In other words, NARAB streamlines the ability of a non-resident insurer to become a licensed agent in another State. In exchange for providing enhanced market access, NARAB collects fees from its members. The Terrorism Risk Insurance Reauthorization Act of 2015 established the association. In addition to being statutorily established—which in itself is an indication that the entity is governmental—NARAB has a board of directors appointed by the President and confirmed by the Senate. It must also submit bylaws and an annual report to the Department of the Treasury and its primary function involves exercising a regulatory function.

Off-budget Federal activities.—Despite the Commission's recommendation that the budget be comprehensive, every year since 1971 at least one Federal program or agency has been presented as off-budget because of a legal requirement.[4] The Government funds such off-budget Federal activities and administers them according to Federal legal requirements. However, their net costs are excluded, by law, from the rest of the budget totals, also known as the "on-budget" totals.

Off-budget Federal activities currently consist of the U.S. Postal Service and the two Social Security trust funds: Old-Age and Survivors Insurance and Disability Insurance. Social Security has been classified as off-budget since 1986 and the Postal Service has been classified as off-budget since 1990.[5] Other activities that had been designated in law as off-budget at various times before 1986 have been classified as on-budget by law since at least 1985 as a result of the Balanced Budget and Emergency Deficit Control Act of 1985 (P. L. 99–177). Activities that were off-budget at one time but that are now on-budget are classified as on-budget for all years in historical budget data.

Social Security is the largest single program in the unified budget and it is classified by law as off-budget; as a result, the off-budget accounts constitute a significant part of total Federal spending and receipts. Table 7–1 divides total Federal Government outlays, receipts, and the surplus or deficit between on-budget and off-budget amounts. Within this table, the Social Security and Postal Service transactions are classified as off-budget for all years to provide a consistent comparison over time.

Non-Budgetary Activities

The Government characterizes some important Government activities as non-budgetary because they do not involve the direct allocation of resources.[6] These activities can affect budget outlays or receipts even though they have non-budgetary components.

Federal credit programs: budgetary and non-budgetary transactions.—Federal credit programs make direct loans or guarantee private loans to non-Federal borrowers. The Federal Credit Reform Act of 1990 (FCRA), as amended by the Balanced Budget Act of 1997, established the current budgetary treatment for credit programs. Under FCRA, the budgetary cost of a credit program, known as the "subsidy cost," is the estimated lifetime cost to the Government of a loan or a loan guarantee on a net present value basis, excluding administrative costs.

Outlays equal to the subsidy cost are recorded in the budget up front, as they are incurred—for example, when a loan is made or guaranteed. Credit program cash flows to and from the public are recorded in non-budgetary

---

[4] While the term "off-budget" is sometimes used colloquially to mean non-budgetary, the term has a meaning distinct from non-budgetary. Off-budget activities would be considered budgetary, absent legal requirement to exclude these activities from the budget totals.

[5] See 42 U.S.C. 911, and 39 U.S.C. 2009a, respectively. The off-budget Postal Service accounts consist of the Postal Service Fund, which is classified as a mandatory account, and the Office of the Inspector General and the Postal Regulatory Commission, both of which are classified as discretionary accounts. The Postal Service Retiree Health Benefits Fund is an on-budget mandatory account with the Office of Personnel Management. The off-budget Social Security accounts consist of the Federal Old-Age and Survivors Insurance trust fund and the Federal Disability Insurance trust fund, both of which have mandatory and discretionary funding.

[6] Tax expenditures, which are discussed in Chapter 10 of this volume, are an example of Government activities that could be characterized as either budgetary or non-budgetary. Tax expenditures refer to the reduction in tax receipts resulting from the special tax treatment accorded certain private activities. Because tax expenditures reduce tax receipts and receipts are budgetary, tax expenditures clearly have budgetary effects. However, the size and composition of tax expenditures are not explicitly recorded in the budget as outlays or as negative receipts and, for this reason, tax expenditures might be considered a special case of non-budgetary transactions.

financing accounts and the information is included in budget documents to provide insight into the program size and costs. For more information about the mechanisms of credit programs, see Chapter 6 of this volume, "Budget Concepts." More detail on credit programs is in Chapter 15 of this volume, "Credit and Insurance."

Deposit funds.—Deposit funds are non-budgetary accounts that record amounts held by the Government temporarily until ownership is determined (such as earnest money paid by bidders for mineral leases) or held by the Government as an agent for others (such as State income taxes withheld from Federal employees' salaries and not yet paid to the States). The largest deposit fund is the Government Securities Investment Fund, also known as the G-Fund, which is part of the TSP, the Government's defined contribution retirement plan. The Federal Retirement Thrift Investment Board manages the fund's investment for Federal employees who participate in the TSP (which is similar to private-sector 401(k) plans). The Department of the Treasury holds the G-Fund assets, which are the property of Federal employees, only in a fiduciary capacity; the transactions of the Fund are not resource allocations by the Government and are therefore non-budgetary.[7] For similar reasons, Native American-owned funds that are held and managed in a fiduciary capacity are also excluded from the budget.

Government-Sponsored Enterprises (GSEs).—GSEs are privately owned and therefore distinct from Government corporations. The Federal Government has chartered GSEs such as the Federal National Mortgage Association (Fannie Mae), the Federal Home Loan Mortgage Corporation (Freddie Mac), the Federal Home Loan Banks, the Farm Credit System, and the Federal Agricultural Mortgage Corporation to provide financial intermediation for specified public purposes. Although Federally chartered to serve public-policy purposes, GSEs are classified as non-budgetary because they are intended to be privately owned and controlled—with any public benefits accruing indirectly from the GSEs' business transactions. Estimates of the GSEs' activities can be found in a separate chapter of the Budget *Appendix*, and their activities are discussed in Chapter 15 of this volume, "Credit and Insurance."

In September 2008, in response to the financial market crisis, the director of the Federal Housing Finance Agency (FHFA)[8] placed Fannie Mae and Freddie Mac into conservatorship for the purpose of preserving the assets and restoring the solvency of these two GSEs. As conservator, FHFA has broad authority to direct the operations of these GSEs. However, these GSEs remain private companies with boards of directors and management responsible for their day-to-day operations. The Budget continues to treat these two GSEs as non-budgetary private entities in conservatorship rather than as Government Agencies. By contrast, CBO treats these GSEs as budgetary Federal Agencies. Both treatments include budgetary and non-budgetary amounts.

While OMB reflects all of the GSEs' transactions with the public as non-budgetary, the payments from the Treasury to the GSEs are recorded as budgetary outlays and dividends received by the Treasury are recorded as budgetary receipts. Under CBO's approach, the subsidy costs of Fannie Mae's and Freddie Mac's past credit activities are treated as having already been recorded in the budget estimates; the subsidy costs of future credit activities will be recorded when the activities occur. Lending and borrowing activities between the GSEs and the public apart from the subsidy costs are treated as non-budgetary by CBO, and Treasury payments to the GSEs are intra-governmental transfers (from Treasury to the GSEs) that net to zero in CBO's budget estimates.

Overall, both the budget's accounting and CBO's accounting present Fannie Mae's and Freddie Mac's gains and losses as Government receipts and outlays, which reduce or increase Government deficits. The two approaches, however, reflect the effect of the gains and losses in the budget at different times.

Other federally created non-budgetary entities.—In addition to the GSEs, the Federal Government has created a number of other entities that are classified as non-budgetary. These include federally funded research and development centers (FFRDCs), non-appropriated fund instrumentalities (NAFIs), and other entities; some of these are non-profit entities and some are for-profit entities.[9]

FFRDCs are entities that conduct agency-specific research under contract or cooperative agreement. Some FFRDCs were created to conduct research for the Department of Defense but are administered by colleges, universities, or other non-profit entities. Despite this non-budgetary classification, many FFRDCs receive direct resource allocation from the Government and are included as budget lines in various agencies. Examples of FFRDCs include the Center for Naval Analysis and the

---

[7] The administrative functions of the Federal Retirement Thrift Investment Board are carried out by Government employees and included in the budget totals.

[8] FHFA is the regulator of Fannie Mae, Freddie Mac, and the Federal Home Loan Banks.

[9] Although most entities created by the Federal Government are budgetary, the Congress and the President have chartered, but not necessarily created, approximately 100 non-profit entities that are non-budgetary. These include patriotic, charitable, and educational organizations under Title 36 of the U.S. Code and foundations and trusts chartered under other titles of the Code. Title 36 corporations include the American Legion, the American National Red Cross, Big Brothers—Big Sisters of America, Boy Scouts of America, Future Farmers of America, Girl Scouts of the United States of America, the National Academy of Public Administration, the National Academies of Sciences, Engineering, and Medicine, and Veterans of Foreign Wars of the United States. Virtually all of the non-profit entities chartered by the Government existed under State law prior to the granting of a Government charter, making the Government charter an honorary rather than governing charter. A major exception to this is the American National Red Cross. Its Government charter requires it to provide disaster relief and to ensure compliance with treaty obligations under the Geneva Convention. Although any Government payments (whether made as direct appropriations or through agency appropriations) to these chartered non-profits, including the Red Cross, would be budgetary, the non-profits themselves are classified as non-budgetary. On April 29, 2015, the Subcommittee on Immigration and Border Security of the Committee on the Judiciary in the U.S. House of Representatives adopted a policy prohibiting the Congress from granting new Federal charters to private, non-profit organizations. This policy has been adopted by every subcommittee with jurisdiction over charters since the 101st Congress.

Jet Propulsion Laboratory.[10] Even though FFRDCs are non-budgetary, Federal payments to the FFRDC are budget outlays. In addition to Federal funding, FFRDCs may receive funding from non-Federal sources.

Non-appropriated fund instrumentalities (NAFIs) are entities that support an agency's current and retired personnel. Nearly all NAFIs are associated with the Departments of Defense, Homeland Security (Coast Guard), and Veterans Affairs. Most NAFIs are located on military bases and include the Armed Forces exchanges (which sell goods to military personnel and their families), recreational facilities, and childcare centers. NAFIs are financed by proceeds from the sale of goods or services and do not receive direct appropriations; thus, they are characterized as non-budgetary but any agency payments to the NAFIs are recorded as budget outlays.

A number of entities created by the Government receive a significant amount of non-Federal funding. Non-Federal individuals or organizations significantly control some of these entities. These entities include Gallaudet University, Howard University, Amtrak, and the Universal Services Administrative Company, among others.[11] Most of these entities receive direct appropriations or other recurring payments from the Government. The appropriations or other payments are budgetary and included in Table 21-1. However, many of these entities are themselves non-budgetary. Generally, entities that receive a significant portion of funding from non-Federal sources but are not controlled by the Government are non-budgetary.

Regulation.—Federal Government regulations often require the private sector or other levels of government to make expenditures for specified purposes that are intended to have public benefits, such as workplace safety and pollution control. Although the budget reflects the Government's cost of conducting regulatory activities, the costs imposed on the private sector as a result of regulation are treated as non-budgetary and not included in the budget. The annual Regulatory Plan and the semi-annual Unified Agenda of Federal Regulatory and Deregulatory Actions describe the Government's regulatory priorities and plans.[12] OMB has published the estimated costs and benefits of Federal regulation annually since 1997.[13]

Monetary policy.—As a fiscal policy tool, the budget is used by elected Government officials to promote economic growth and achieve other public policy objectives. Monetary policy is another tool that governments use to promote economic policy objectives. In the United States, the Federal Reserve System—which is composed of a Board of Governors and 12 regional Federal Reserve Banks—conducts monetary policy. The Federal Reserve Act provides that the goal of monetary policy is to "maintain long-run growth of the monetary and credit aggregates commensurate with the economy's long run potential to increase production, so as to promote effectively the goals of maximum employment, stable prices, and moderate long-term interest rates."[14] The Full Employment and Balanced Growth Act of 1978, also known as the Humphrey-Hawkins Act, reaffirmed the dual goals of full employment and price stability.[15]

By law, the Federal Reserve System is a self-financing entity that is independent of the Executive Branch and subject only to broad oversight by the Congress. Consistent with the recommendations of the Commission, the effects of monetary policy and the actions of the Federal Reserve System are non-budgetary, with exceptions for the transfer to the Treasury of excess income generated through its operations. The Federal Reserve System earns income from a variety of sources including interest on Government securities, foreign currency investments and loans to depository institutions, and fees for services (e.g., check clearing services) provided to depository institutions. The Federal Reserve System remits to Treasury any excess income over expenses annually. For the fiscal year ending September 2020, Treasury recorded $81.9 billion in receipts from the Federal Reserve System. In 2020, the Federal Reserve System also co-invested with the Treasury to establish lending facilities authorized by Section 13(3) of the Federal Reserve Act. The Coronavirus Aid, Relief, and Economic Security (CARES) Act appropriated funds to the Treasury to support Federal Reserve 13(3) lending facilities to provide liquidity to the financial system, including financing for states, tribes, municipalities, eligible businesses, and nonprofit organizations.[16] In addition to remitting excess income to Treasury, current law requires the Federal Reserve to transfer a portion of its excess earnings to the Consumer Financial Protection Bureau (CFPB).[17]

The Board of Governors of the Federal Reserve is a Federal Government Agency, but because of its independent status, its budget is not subject to Executive Branch review and is included in the Budget *Appendix* for informational purposes only. The Federal Reserve Banks are subject to Board oversight and managed by boards of directors chosen by the Board of Governors and member banks, which include all National banks and State banks that choose to become members. The budgets of the regional Banks are subject to approval by the Board of Governors and are not included in the Budget *Appendix*.

---

[10] The National Science Foundation maintains a list of FFRDCs at *www.nsf.gov/statistics/ffrdc.*

[11] Under section 415(b) of the Amtrak Reform and Accountability Act of 1997, (49 U.S.C. 24304 and note), Amtrak was required to redeem all of its outstanding common stock. Once all outstanding common stock is redeemed, Amtrak will be wholly-owned by the Government and, at that point, its non-budgetary status may need to be reassessed.

[12] The most recent Regulatory Plan and introduction to the Unified Agenda issued by the General Services Administration's Regulatory Information Service Center are available at *www.reginfo.gov* and at *www.gpo.gov.*

[13] In the 2018, 2019, and 2020 report, OMB indicates that for the five rules for which monetized costs and benefits were estimated in 2019, the issuing agencies estimated a total of $0.2 to $3.7 billion in annual benefits and up to $0.6 billion in annual costs, in 2018 dollars. These totals include only the benefits and costs for the minority of rules for which both those categories of impacts were estimated. The most recent report is available at *https://www.whitehouse.gov/omb/information-regulatory-affairs/reports/#ORC.*

[14] See 12 U.S.C. 225a.

[15] See 15 U.S.C. 3101 et seq.

[16] See section 4003 of Public Law 116-136.

[17] See section 1011 of Public Law 111-203 (12 U.S.C. 5491).

FEDERAL RECEIPTS

8. GOVERNMENTAL RECEIPTS

This chapter presents the Budget's estimates of taxes and governmental receipts including the effects of tax legislation enacted in 2020 and early 2021, discusses the provisions of those enacted laws, and introduces the Administration's additional receipt proposals.

Table 8–1. RECEIPTS BY SOURCE—SUMMARY
(In billions of dollars)

	2020 Actual	Estimate										
		2021	2022	2023	2024	2025	2026	2027	2028	2029	2030	2031
Individual income taxes	1,608.7	1,704.9	2,038.6	2,242.1	2,287.6	2,435.5	2,676.0	2,895.6	3,044.5	3,194.3	3,353.5	3,526.0
Corporation income taxes	211.8	268.5	371.0	576.6	648.7	672.7	664.2	666.1	678.8	677.5	681.1	692.8
Social insurance and retirement receipts ...	1,310.0	1,296.2	1,462.0	1,527.1	1,590.1	1,646.4	1,711.4	1,775.0	1,858.8	1,929.4	2,009.2	2,088.1
(On-budget)	*(344.5)*	*(352.0)*	*(429.4)*	*(455.5)*	*(472.5)*	*(487.8)*	*(504.6)*	*(522.5)*	*(547.8)*	*(568.0)*	*(592.4)*	*(613.8)*
(Off-budget)	*(965.4)*	*(944.1)*	*(1,032.6)*	*(1,071.6)*	*(1,117.6)*	*(1,158.6)*	*(1,206.8)*	*(1,252.5)*	*(1,311.0)*	*(1,361.4)*	*(1,416.8)*	*(1,474.3)*
Excise taxes	86.8	74.1	84.3	88.7	93.5	93.7	94.8	96.0	96.0	98.4	101.1	101.8
Estate and gift taxes	17.6	17.6	20.8	18.2	19.3	20.1	20.6	32.1	33.0	34.4	36.6	38.9
Customs duties	68.6	84.8	57.4	45.2	45.5	46.5	47.8	49.2	50.8	52.6	54.6	56.8
Miscellaneous receipts	117.7	134.7	140.2	143.1	143.1	122.9	117.3	117.8	126.3	132.0	133.6	139.1
Total, receipts	**3,421.2**	**3,580.8**	**4,174.2**	**4,641.0**	**4,827.8**	**5,037.9**	**5,332.1**	**5,631.7**	**5,888.1**	**6,118.7**	**6,369.8**	**6,643.5**
(On-budget)	*(2,455.7)*	*(2,636.6)*	*(3,141.6)*	*(3,569.4)*	*(3,710.2)*	*(3,879.3)*	*(4,125.3)*	*(4,379.3)*	*(4,577.1)*	*(4,757.2)*	*(4,953.0)*	*(5,169.2)*
(Off-budget)	*(965.4)*	*(944.1)*	*(1,032.6)*	*(1,071.6)*	*(1,117.6)*	*(1,158.6)*	*(1,206.8)*	*(1,252.5)*	*(1,311.0)*	*(1,361.4)*	*(1,416.8)*	*(1,474.3)*
Total receipts as a percentage of GDP ...	16.3	16.3	17.8	18.9	18.9	19.0	19.4	19.7	19.8	19.8	19.8	19.9

ESTIMATES OF GOVERNMENTAL RECEIPTS

Governmental receipts are taxes and other collections from the public that result from the exercise of the Federal Government's sovereign or governmental powers. The difference between governmental receipts and outlays is the surplus or deficit.

The Federal Government also collects income from the public through market-oriented activities. Collections from these activities are subtracted from gross outlays, rather than added to taxes and other governmental receipts, and are discussed in Chapter 9, "Offsetting Collections and Offsetting Receipts," in this volume.

Total governmental receipts (hereafter referred to as "receipts") are estimated to be $3,580.8 billion in 2021, an increase of $159.6 billion or 4.7 percent from 2020. The estimated increase in 2021 is largely due to increases in individual and corporation income taxes. Receipts in 2021 are estimated to be 16.3 percent of Gross Domestic Product (GDP), roughly the same share as in 2020.

Receipts in the 2022 Budget are estimated to rise to $4,174.2 billion in 2022, an increase of $593.4 billion or 16.6 percent relative to 2021. Receipts are projected to grow at an average annual rate of 6.3 percent between 2022 and 2026, rising to $5,332.1 billion. Receipts are projected to rise to $6,643.5 billion in 2031, growing at an average annual rate of 5.3 percent between 2026 and 2031. This growth is largely due to assumed increases in incomes resulting from both real economic growth and inflation, along with tax reforms in the American Jobs Plan and American Families Plan.

As a share of GDP, receipts are projected to increase from 16.3 percent in 2021 to 17.8 percent in 2022, and to steadily increase to 19.9 percent by 2031.

LEGISLATION ENACTED IN 2020 AND 2021 THAT AFFECTS GOVERNMENTAL RECEIPTS

Five laws were enacted during 2020 and early 2021 that affect receipts. The major provisions of these laws that have a significant impact on receipts are described below.[1]

UNITED STATES-MEXICO-CANADA AGREEMENT IMPLEMENTATION ACT (Public Law 116–113)

The Act, which was signed into law on January 29, 2020, provides authority for the trade agreement between the United States, Mexico, and Canada (USMCA), which replaces the North American Free Trade Agreement. The

---

[1] In the discussions of enacted legislation, years referred to are calendar years, unless otherwise noted.

law implements provisions of the USMCA by, among other things, establishing de minimis levels for U.S. exports and providing for cooperation among treaty members to prevent evasion of customs duties.

FAMILIES FIRST CORONAVIRUS RESPONSE ACT (Public Law 116–127)

The Act (FFCRA), which was signed into law on March 18, 2020, responds to the COVID-19 public health emergency by providing paid sick leave tax credits and expanding food assistance and unemployment benefits. The law provides fully refundable credits against payroll taxes to compensate employers (including self-employed individuals) for paid sick leave and family and medical leave that is mandated in the Act.

CORONAVIRUS AID, RELIEF, AND ECONOMIC SECURITY ACT (Public Law 116–136)

The Act, also known as the CARES Act, which was signed into law on March 27, 2020, responds to the COVID-19 public health emergency and its impact on the economy, public health, State and local governments, individuals, and businesses. The law created an Economic Impact Payment which generally provided $1,200 for eligible Americans with $500 for each qualifying child. It also allows employers and self-employed individuals to defer payment of the employer's share of Social Security taxes incurred from March 27, 2020 through December 31, 2020; provides a refundable and advanceable Employee Retention Credit against payroll taxes for employers who kept employees on payroll during mandated shut-downs; permits businesses to offset 100 percent of taxable income for net operating losses incurred over the three-year period from 2018 to 2020 and allows corporations to carry back recently incurred losses for refunds of tax liabilities for the prior five years; and allows taxpayers to use their business losses to offset non-business income for tax years 2018 through 2020, or for farm losses for tax years 2018 through 2025. The Act also waives penalties for certain early withdrawals from retirement accounts in 2020; creates a partial above-the-line deduction for taxpayers who do not itemize deductions in 2020 but make charitable contributions of up to $300 in cash; and excludes from taxation certain employer payments for employees' student loans; among other provisions.

CONSOLIDATED APPROPRIATIONS ACT, 2021 (Public Law 116–260)

The Act, which was signed into law on December 27, 2020, extends by four months the deferral of certain payroll taxes that was enacted in the CARES Act; clarifies the tax treatment of the forgiveness of covered loans and other provisions; excludes from a taxpayer's income any qualified emergency financial aid grants; and extends by three months the CARES Act tax credits for paid sick and family leave; among other provisions. It also created a second round of Economic Impact Payments of $600 for eligible Americans with $600 for each qualifying child.

AMERICAN RESCUE PLAN ACT OF 2021 (Public Law 117-2)

The Act, which was signed into law on March 11, 2021, provides additional relief to address the continued impact of the COVID-19 public health emergency on the economy, public health, State and local governments, individuals, and businesses. Major provisions of the law include:

Promoting economic security.—The Act enhances major tax credits to bolster financial security for families and essential workers during the pandemic. It created a third round of Economic Impact Payments of $1,400 for eligible Americans with $1,400 for each qualifying dependent. It increases the amount of the Child Tax Credit from $2,000 to $3,600 for children under age 6 and $3,000 for other children under 18; expands the credit to cover children aged 17 for 2021; makes available advance payments on a periodic basis through 2021; makes the credit fully refundable; and extends the credit to Puerto Rico and U.S. territories. It increases the maximum Earned Income Tax Credit (EITC) for childless adults from about $540 to just over $1,500; raises the income limit for the credit from about $16,000 to about $21,000; expands eligibility to younger and older workers; expands the EITC by allowing taxpayers with a Social Security number to claim the childless earned income credit when they have qualifying children without Social Security numbers; allows certain separated spouses to claim the EITC; and increases the limitation for individuals with certain disqualified investment income. It also increases the Child and Dependent Care Tax Credit to 50 percent of up to $8,000 for the child care expenses of one child and $16,000 for two or more children, increasing the maximum credit that can be claimed to $4,000 for taxpayers with one child and $8,000 for taxpayers with two or more children; makes the credit refundable; increases the phase-out threshold from $15,000 to $125,000; and increases the excludable amount of employer-provided dependent care assistance. The law extends and expands the tax credit for qualifying paid sick and family leave established under FFCRA through September 30, 2021; extends and modifies the Employee Retention Credit established under the CARES Act through December 21, 2021; provides premium assistance for the full cost of COBRA coverage from April 1 through September 30, 2021 through a refundable tax credit for employers; and modifies the premium tax credit for health insurance purchased through an exchange by eliminating required premium contributions for taxpayers making 100 to 150 percent of the Federal poverty level and lowering the maximum household contribution for all other PTC recipients, for taxable years 2021 and 2022.

Crisis support for unemployed workers.—The Act suspends tax on $10,200 per recipient of unemployment compensation received in 2020 for taxpayers with AGI below $150,000.

Other.—Finally, the law repeals worldwide interest allocation rules, modifies exceptions for reporting third-party network transactions, extends the requirement to apply the limitation on excess business losses of non- corporate taxpayers by one year, and extends certain customs user fees, among other provisions.

BUDGET PROPOSALS

The 2022 Budget, including the American Jobs Plan and the American Families Plan, proposes meaningful tax relief for families and workers while proposing a series of revenue raisers directed at wealthy individuals and large corporations. In addition, the Made in America Tax Plan contained within the American Jobs Plan aims to replace counterproductive tax laws that reward offshoring and profit shifting with provisions that encourage job creation at home and put an end to the worldwide race to the bottom on corporate tax rates. Moreover, the American Families Plan extends key tax cuts in the American Rescue Plan Act that benefit lower- and middle-income workers and families, and includes a set of measures to make sure the wealthiest Americans pay their fair share in taxes while ensuring that no one making $400,000 per year or less will see their taxes rise. These proposals affecting governmental receipts are included in the table that follows. Descriptions of proposals can be found in the Department of the Treasury's *General Explanations of the Administration's Fiscal Year 2022 Revenue Proposals* [2].

[2] Available at this link: *https://home.treasury.gov/policy-issues/tax-policy/revenue-proposals*.

Table 8–2. EFFECT OF BUDGET PROPOSALS
(In millions of dollars)

	2021	2022	2023	2024	2025	2026	2027	2028	2029	2030	2031	2022–2026	2022–2031
American Jobs Plan:													
Reform corporate taxation:													
Increase the domestic corporate tax rate to 28 percent	....	51,127	86,182	88,059	89,385	91,784	92,065	90,730	89,357	88,798	90,330	406,537	857,817
Revise the Global Minimum Tax regime, disallow deductions attributable to exempt income, and limit inversions	....	29,816	51,386	54,192	57,030	55,283	54,699	56,056	56,988	58,223	59,830	247,707	533,503
Reform taxation of foreign fossil fuel income:													
Modify foreign oil and gas extraction income (FOGEI) and foreign oil related income (FORI) rules	....	4,178	7,173	7,468	7,834	8,393	9,055	9,633	10,051	10,358	10,638	35,046	84,781
Modify tax rule for dual capacity taxpayers ...	....	48	123	128	134	143	154	165	173	178	183	576	1,429
Total, reform taxation of foreign fossil fuel income	....	4,226	7,296	7,596	7,968	8,536	9,209	9,798	10,224	10,536	10,821	35,622	86,210
Provide tax incentives for locating jobs and business activity in the United States and remove tax deductions for shipping jobs overseas:													
Provide tax credit for onshoring jobs to the United States	....	–6	–10	–10	–11	–11	–12	–12	–13	–13	–14	–48	–112
Remove tax deductions for shipping jobs overseas	....	6	10	10	11	11	12	12	13	13	14	48	112
Total, provide tax incentives for locating jobs and business activity in the United States and remove tax deductions for shipping jobs overseas	....	....	....	....	....	....	....	....	....	....	....	....	....
Repeal deduction for Foreign Derived Intangible Income (FDII) and provide additional support for research and experimentation expenditures	....	....	....	....	....	....	....	....	....	....	....	....	....
Replace the Base Erosion Anti-Abuse Tax (BEAT) with the Stopping Harmful Inversions and Ending Low-Tax Developments (SHIELD) Rule	....	....	33,244	53,796	51,111	47,655	44,463	41,914	39,425	38,990	39,453	185,806	390,051
Limit foreign tax credits for sales of hybrid entities	....	23	39	41	43	45	47	48	49	50	51	191	436
Restrict deductions of excessive interest of members of financial reporting groups for disproportionate borrowing in the United States	....	2,100	2,334	1,586	1,638	1,690	1,743	1,795	1,846	1,900	1,956	9,348	18,588
Impose 15 percent minimum tax on book earnings of large corporations	....	10,736	15,245	14,588	13,812	14,561	15,203	16,049	16,158	15,775	16,217	68,942	148,344
Total, reform corporate taxation	....	98,028	195,726	219,858	220,987	219,554	217,429	216,390	214,047	214,272	218,658	954,153	2,034,949
Support housing and infrastructure:													

Table 8–2. EFFECT OF BUDGET PROPOSALS—Continued

(In millions of dollars)

	2021	2022	2023	2024	2025	2026	2027	2028	2029	2030	2031	2022–2026	2022–2031
Expand Low-income Housing Tax Credit	....	−35	−212	−707	−1,592	−2,527	−3,427	−4,370	−5,362	−6,339	−7,356	−5,073	−31,927
Provide Neighborhood Homes Investment Tax Credit	....	−10	−99	−398	−944	−1,512	−1,889	−2,063	−2,083	−2,035	−2,001	−2,963	−13,034
Expand New Markets Tax Credit (NMTC) and make permanent	....	....	....	....	....		−97	−280	−492	−736	−1,006	−1,294	−97	−3,905
Provide federally subsidized State and local bonds for infrastructure [1]	....	−291	−767	−1,292	−1,458	−1,439	−1,403	−1,357	−1,308	−1,257	−1,204	−5,247	−11,776
Total, support housing and infrastructure	....	−336	−1,078	−2,397	−3,994	−5,575	−6,999	−8,282	−9,489	−10,637	−11,855	−13,380	−60,642
Prioritize clean energy:													
Eliminate fossil fuel tax preferences:													
Repeal enhanced oil recovery credit	....	158	389	599	808	951	988	980	975	974	976	2,905	7,798
Repeal deduction for tertiary injectants	....	....	....	....	....	....	....	....	....	....	....	....	....
Repeal credit for oil and gas produced from marginal wells	....	39	100	128	116	78	38	14	3	....	....	461	516
Repeal expensing of intangible drilling costs	....	2,182	1,954	1,569	1,174	747	562	586	591	585	536	7,626	10,486
Repeal exemption to passive loss limitation for working interests in oil and natural gas	....	10	10	9	9	9	8	8	8	8	7	47	86
Repeal percentage depletion for oil and natural gas wells	....	678	767	794	831	890	946	996	1,045	1,093	1,132	3,960	9,172
Repeal amortization of air pollution control equipment	....	16	39	60	80	99	117	134	132	119	105	294	901
Increase geological and geophysical amortization period for independent producer	....	38	139	227	247	246	242	233	217	201	195	897	1,985
Repeal expensing of exploration and development costs	....	190	170	136	102	65	49	51	51	51	46	663	911
Repeal percentage depletion for hard mineral fossil fuels	....	97	110	114	119	127	136	142	149	156	161	567	1,311
Repeal capital gains treatment for royalties	....	46	47	48	49	51	52	50	44	37	31	241	455
Treat publicly traded partnerships as C corporations	....	....	....	....	....	....	83	169	216	259	300	....	1,027
Excise tax exemption for Crude Oil derived from bitumen and kerogen-rich rock [2]	....	31	39	39	39	39	40	41	41	42	44	187	395
Total, eliminate fossil fuel tax preferences	....	3,485	3,764	3,723	3,574	3,302	3,261	3,404	3,472	3,525	3,533	17,848	35,043
Extend and enhance renewable and alternative energy incentives:													
Extend and modify the Energy Investment Credit [1]	....	−1,397	−5,767	−26,324	−30,423	−31,149	−35,455	−26,833	−23,061	−18,540	−11,642	−95,060	−210,591
Extend and modify the Renewable Energy Production Tax Credit [1]	....	−2,059	−2,106	−937	−1,429	−1,903	−2,780	−4,606	−6,267	−7,730	−8,802	−8,434	−38,619
Extend and modify the Residential Efficient Property Credit	....	−290	−480	−1,594	−2,256	−2,538	−2,846	−2,425	−1,933	−1,342	−392	−7,158	−16,096
Total, extend and enhance renewable and alternative energy incentives ...	....	−3,746	−8,353	−28,855	−34,108	−35,590	−41,081	−33,864	−31,261	−27,612	−20,836	−110,652	−265,306
Provide tax credit for electricity transmission investments [1]	....	−187	−250	−1,746	−2,280	−2,863	−3,118	−3,239	−3,246	−3,420	−3,447	−7,326	−23,796
Provide allocated credit for electricity generation from existing nuclear power facilities [1]	....	−750	−1,000	−1,000	−1,000	−1,000	−1,000	−1,000	−1,000	−1,000	−1,000	−4,750	−9,750
Establish new tax credits for qualifying advanced energy manufacturing [1]	....	−425	−1,102	−1,492	−988	−824	−940	−1,396	−576	−58	−131	−4,831	−7,932
Establish tax credits for heavy- and medium-duty zero emission vehicles [1]	....	−71	−295	−835	−1,471	−2,692	−4,028	−1,178	−63	−11	....	−5,364	−10,644
Provide tax incentives for sustainable aviation fuel	....	−363	−503	−633	−693	−1,313	−1,696	−743	−376	−199	−117	−3,505	−6,636
Provide a production tax credit for low-carbon hydrogen [1]	....	−14	−53	−156	−358	−548	−979	−1,570	−445	−5	....	−1,129	−4,128
Extend and enhance energy efficiency and electrification incentives:													
Extend and modify the nonbusiness energy property credit	....	−532	−1,806	−2,460	−1,940	−1,056	−634	....	....	....	....	−7,794	−8,428

Table 8–2. EFFECT OF BUDGET PROPOSALS—Continued

(In millions of dollars)

	2021	2022	2023	2024	2025	2026	2027	2028	2029	2030	2031	2022–2026	2022–2031
Extend and increase the tax credit for manufacturing credit for new energy efficient new homes	....	−128	−271	−298	−313	−337	−220	−72	−25	−8	−2	−1,347	−1,674
Extend and increase the commercial buildings deduction	....	−146	−280	−328	−346	−350	−350	−350	−350	−351	−354	−1,450	−3,205
Provide tax credits for the installation of mechanical insulation	....	−317	−606	−736	−867	−1,007	−737	−454	−344	−229	−110	−3,533	−5,407
Total, extend and enhance energy efficiency and electrification incentives	....	−1,123	−2,963	−3,822	−3,466	−2,750	−1,941	−876	−719	−588	−466	−14,124	−18,714
Provide disaster mitigation tax credit	....	−391	−411	−415	−415	−415	−415	−415	−415	−415	−332	−2,047	−4,039
Extend and enhance the Carbon Oxide Sequestration Credit [1]	....	−21	−10	−10	−19	−27	−101	−101	−53	−2,082	−3,634	−87	−6,058
Extend and enhance the electric vehicle charging station credit [1]	....	−236	−432	−848	−1,457	−2,599	−771	−18	26	35	33	−5,572	−6,267
Modify Oil Spill Liability Trust Fund financing [2]	....	38	51	53	53	53	53	53	53	53	53	248	513
Reinstate Superfund excise taxes [2]	....	1,715	2,340	2,406	2,455	2,517	2,560	2,610	2,670	2,723	2,787	11,433	24,783
Total, prioritize clean energy	....	−2,089	−9,217	−33,630	−40,173	−44,749	−50,196	−38,333	−31,933	−29,054	−23,557	−129,858	−302,931
Revenue effect of sparking widespread adoption of EVs [2]	....	−10	−32	−66	−113	−178	−267	−409	−647	−1,022	−1,584	−399	−4,328
Total, American Jobs Plan	**.........**	**95,593**	**185,399**	**183,765**	**176,707**	**169,052**	**159,967**	**169,366**	**171,978**	**173,559**	**181,662**	**810,516**	**1,667,048**
American Families Plan:													
Strengthen taxation of high-income taxpayers:													
Increase top marginal tax rate for high earners	....	19,991	30,594	33,278	36,525	11,532	....	....	....	....	....	131,920	131,920
Reform taxation of capital income	1,241	7,656	25,451	32,906	36,303	33,947	32,252	34,276	36,064	37,937	45,693	136,263	322,485
Rationalize Net Investment Income and Self-Employment Contributions Act (SECA) taxes	....	11,383	19,535	20,779	23,038	24,205	25,464	26,719	27,559	28,416	29,402	98,940	236,500
Total, strengthen taxation of high-income taxpayers	1,241	39,030	75,580	86,963	95,866	69,684	57,716	60,995	63,623	66,353	75,095	367,123	690,905
Support workers, families, and strengthen economic security:													
Extend the American Rescue Plan changes to the Child Credit through 2025 and make permanent full refundability [1]	....	−47,125	−110,999	−108,559	−107,190	−62,060	−2,860	−2,725	−2,611	−2,512	−2,420	−435,933	−449,061
Make permanent the American Rescue Plan expansion to Earned Income Tax Credit for workers without qualifying children [1]	....	−27	−5,589	−11,782	−11,970	−12,145	−12,445	−12,576	−12,745	−12,908	−13,032	−41,513	−105,219
Make permanent the American Rescue Plan changes to the Child and Dependent Care Tax Credit (CDCTC) [1]	....	−3,134	−10,588	−10,588	−10,633	−12,303	−11,032	−11,195	−11,391	−11,573	−11,761	−47,246	−104,198
Increase the employer-provided childcare tax credit for businesses	....	−28	−28	−29	−29	−29	−31	−31	−32	−32	−33	−143	−302
Make permanent the American Rescue Plan expansion of premium tax credits [1]	....	....	−11,490	−15,679	−16,513	−17,215	−18,076	−18,888	−20,149	−21,704	−23,334	−60,897	−163,048
Total, support workers, families, and strengthen economic security	....	−50,314	−138,694	−146,637	−146,335	−103,752	−44,444	−45,415	−46,928	−48,729	−50,580	−585,732	−821,828
Account for CDCTC interaction with new child care program for American families [1,3]	....	982	1,205	1,437	1,680	1,934	2,199	2,474	2,992	3,531	4,093	7,238	22,527
Account for American Opportunity Tax Credit interaction with Free Community College [1]	....	22	455	901	1,354	1,847	2,243	2,662	3,094	3,590	4,031	4,579	20,199
Close loopholes:													
Tax carried (profits) interest as ordinary income	....	100	135	138	141	143	149	155	162	169	176	657	1,468
Repeal deferral of gain from like-kind exchanges	....	676	1,857	1,914	1,971	2,030	2,091	2,154	2,218	2,285	2,354	8,448	19,550
Make permanent excess business loss limitation of noncorporate taxpayers	....	....	....	....	....	....	9,996	11,782	7,627	6,836	6,619	....	42,860
Total, close loopholes	....	776	1,992	2,052	2,112	2,173	12,236	14,091	10,007	9,290	9,149	9,105	63,878
Improve compliance:													
Implement a program integrity allocation adjustment and provide additional resources for tax administration:													

Table 8–2. EFFECT OF BUDGET PROPOSALS—Continued
(In millions of dollars)

	2021	2022	2023	2024	2025	2026	2027	2028	2029	2030	2031	2022–2026	2022–2031
Increase revenues through program integrity allocation adjustment for tax administration	....	334	1,858	3,165	4,055	4,894	5,889	6,595	7,243	7,796	8,451	14,306	50,280
Increase revenues by providing mandatory IRS funding for compliance	....	....	631	3,312	7,562	13,837	22,342	34,081	46,941	62,253	74,937	25,342	265,896
Total, implement a program integrity allocation adjustment and provide additional resources for tax administration	....	334	2,489	6,477	11,617	18,731	28,231	40,676	54,184	70,049	83,388	39,648	316,176
Introduce comprehensive financial account information reporting	....	8,378	32,413	36,551	42,517	46,980	53,032	57,123	61,024	61,886	62,742	166,839	462,646
Total, improve compliance	....	8,712	34,902	43,028	54,134	65,711	81,263	97,799	115,208	131,935	146,130	206,487	778,822
Improve Tax Administration:													
Increase oversight of paid tax return preparers:													
Allow IRS to regulate paid Federal tax return preparers [1]	....	35	52	57	59	58	55	57	61	68	73	261	575
Increase penalties on ghost preparers [1]	....	13	19	21	24	25	26	27	28	29	30	102	242
Total, increase oversight of paid tax return preparers	....	48	71	78	83	83	81	84	89	97	103	363	817
Enhance accuracy of tax information:													
E-file of forms and returns	....	....	....	....	....	....	....	....	....	....	....	....	....
TINs certification for reportable payments	....	36	83	141	193	202	211	221	231	241	252	655	1,811
Total, enhance accuracy of tax information	....	36	83	141	193	202	211	221	231	241	252	655	1,811
Expand broker information reporting with respect to cryptocurrency assets	....	....	....	....	....	....	....	....	....	....	....	....	....
Address taxpayer noncompliance:													
Extend statute of limitation	....	23	52	66	79	77	76	74	73	71	70	297	661
Impose liability on shareholders to collect unpaid income taxes of applicable corporations	....	395	412	428	444	462	479	498	518	539	560	2,141	4,735
Total, address taxpayer noncompliance	....	418	464	494	523	539	555	572	591	610	630	2,438	5,396
Modify tax administration rules:													
Amend centralized partnership audit regime (BBA) to provide for the carryover of non-refundable reporting year amounts that exceed the income tax liability of a partner	....	−5	−5	−5	−5	−6	−6	−7	−7	−7	−7	−26	−60
Modify requisite supervisory approval of penalty included in notice	....	29	254	245	248	222	197	174	173	179	186	998	1,907
Total, modify tax administration rules	....	24	249	240	243	216	191	167	166	172	179	972	1,847
Authorize limited sharing of business tax return information to measure the economy more accurately	....	....	....	....	....	....	....	....	....	....	....	....	....
Total, improve tax administration	....	526	867	953	1,042	1,040	1,038	1,044	1,077	1,120	1,164	4,428	9,871
Increase Low Income Taxpayer Clinic (LITC) grant cap and index it for inflation	....	....	....	....	....	....	....	....	....	....	....	....	....
Total, American Families Plan	**1,241**	**−266**	**−23,693**	**−11,303**	**9,853**	**38,637**	**112,251**	**133,650**	**149,073**	**167,090**	**189,082**	**13,228**	**764,374**
Other:													
Capturing savings to Unemployment Insurance of RESEA allocation adjustment	....	....	−15	−109	−399	−59	−83	−117	−151	−423	−109	−582	−1,465
Total, effect of budget proposals	**1,241**	**95,327**	**161,691**	**172,353**	**186,161**	**207,630**	**272,135**	**302,899**	**320,900**	**340,226**	**370,635**	**823,162**	**2,429,957**

[1] This proposal affects both receipts and outlays for refundable tax credits. Both effects are shown above. The outlay effects included in these estimates are as follows:

	2021	2022	2023	2024	2025	2026	2027	2028	2029	2030	2031	2022–2026	2022–2031
Provide federally subsidized State and local bonds for infrastructure	....	−345	−964	−1,637	−1,880	−1,819	−1,753	−1,686	−1,620	−1,554	−1,488	−6,645	−14,746
Extend and Modify the Energy Investment Credit	....	−3,936	−9,020	−29,234	−33,801	−34,021	−38,010	−29,039	−24,531	−19,430	−12,567	−110,012	−233,589
Extend and Modify the Renewable Energy Production Tax Credit	....	−3,416	−4,582	−4,703	−5,895	−6,530	−7,167	−8,574	−9,749	−10,557	−10,895	−25,126	−72,068
Provide tax credit for electricity transmission investments	....	−203	−270	−1,789	−2,295	−2,801	−2,970	−3,071	−3,105	−3,308	−3,375	−7,358	−23,187

Table 8–2. EFFECT OF BUDGET PROPOSALS—Continued

(In millions of dollars)

	2021	2022	2023	2024	2025	2026	2027	2028	2029	2030	2031	2022–2026	2022–2031
Provide allocated credit for electricity generation from existing nuclear power facilities	....	−675	−900	−900	−900	−900	−900	−900	−900	−900	−900	−4,275	−8,775
Establish new tax credits for qualifying advanced energy manufacturing	....	−385	−1,000	−1,350	−889	−735	−847	−1,261	−518	−39	−117	−4,359	−7,141
Establish tax credits for heavy- and medium-duty zero emission vehicles	....	−66	−272	−768	−1,346	−2,462	−3,673	−992	....	....	....	−4,914	−9,579
Provide a production tax credit for low-carbon hydrogen	....	−11	−42	−128	−313	−469	−839	−1,495	−419	....	....	−963	−3,716
Extend and enhance the Carbon Oxide Sequestration Credit	....	−547	−655	−752	−939	−1,206	−2,063	−2,767	−2,950	−5,018	−6,520	−4,099	−23,417
Extend and enhance the electric vehicle charging station credit	....	−158	−259	−334	−412	−540	−144	....	....	....	....	−1,703	−1,847
Extend the American Rescue Plan changes to the Child Credit make permanent full refundability	....	−80,956	−137,868	−135,741	−134,880	−54,147	−2,851	−2,716	−2,602	−2,503	−2,411	−543,592	−556,675
Make permanent the American Rescue Plan expansion to Earned Income Tax Credit for workers without children	....	....	−5,231	−10,670	−10,839	−10,984	−11,122	−11,018	−11,163	−11,304	−11,409	−37,724	−93,740
Make permanent the American Rescue Plan changes to the Child and Dependent Care Tax Credit (CDCTC)	....	....	−6,442	−6,455	−6,486	−6,554	−4,694	−4,758	−4,835	−4,908	−4,977	−25,937	−50,109
Make permanent the American Rescue Plan expansion of premium tax credits	....	....	−8,620	−11,666	−12,244	−12,327	−12,768	−13,247	−14,073	−15,052	−16,094	−44,857	−116,091
Account for CDCTC interaction with new child care program for American families	....	....	733	876	1,025	1,030	936	1,052	1,270	1,497	1,732	3,664	10,151
Account for American Opportunity Tax Credit interaction with Free Community College	....	....	205	380	579	790	786	940	1,095	1,271	1,459	1,954	7,505
Allow IRS to regulate paid Federal tax return preparers	....	19	34	35	34	30	24	23	24	27	29	152	279
Increase penalties on ghost preparers	....	....	2	2	3	3	3	3	3	3	3	10	25
Total, outlay effects of budget proposals	....	−90,679	−175,151	−204,834	−211,478	−133,642	−88,052	−79,506	−74,073	−71,775	−67,530	−815,784	−1,196,720

[2] Net of income offsets.

[3] Individuals will not be able to claim both the Child and Dependent Care Tax Credit and participate in the new Child Care for American Families program for the same care. This interaction removes costs already included in the Child Care for American Families score.

Table 8–3. RECEIPTS BY SOURCE

(In millions of dollars)

Source	2020 Actual	Estimate										
		2021	2022	2023	2024	2025	2026	2027	2028	2029	2030	2031
Individual income taxes:												
Federal funds	1,608,661	1,703,678	2,005,326	2,173,931	2,209,921	2,346,757	2,645,848	2,851,544	2,986,419	3,127,501	3,274,732	3,431,430
Legislative proposal, not subject to PAYGO	....	....	−29,513	−29,319	−27,255	−24,953	−20,230	−13,050	−5,404	3,302	13,884	21,515
Legislative proposal, subject to PAYGO	....	1,241	62,762	97,500	104,949	113,738	50,362	57,128	63,439	63,526	64,923	73,076
Total, Individual income taxes	**1,608,661**	**1,704,919**	**2,038,575**	**2,242,112**	**2,287,615**	**2,435,542**	**2,675,980**	**2,895,622**	**3,044,454**	**3,194,329**	**3,353,539**	**3,526,021**
Corporation income taxes:												
Federal funds	211,845	268,482	265,878	367,247	412,048	432,265	424,569	423,700	432,917	431,634	433,294	438,463
Legislative proposal, not subject to PAYGO	....	....	−90	56	541	1,274	2,519	4,391	6,640	9,282	12,285	15,390
Legislative proposal, subject to PAYGO	....	....	105,197	209,342	236,113	239,185	237,148	237,967	239,280	236,603	235,557	238,912
Total, Corporation income taxes	**211,845**	**268,482**	**370,985**	**576,645**	**648,702**	**672,724**	**664,236**	**666,058**	**678,837**	**677,519**	**681,136**	**692,765**
Social insurance and retirement receipts (trust funds):												
Employment and general retirement:												
Old-age survivors insurance (off-budget)	825,307	807,033	881,866	912,605	951,590	985,982	1,027,385	1,065,861	1,115,485	1,158,188	1,205,396	1,254,385
Legislative proposal, not subject to PAYGO	....	....	840	3,434	3,810	4,410	4,239	4,801	5,212	5,622	5,751	5,908
Disability insurance (off-budget)	140,121	137,099	149,750	154,971	161,590	167,431	174,461	180,995	189,422	196,674	204,690	213,009
Legislative proposal, not subject to PAYGO	....	....	143	582	646	748	719	814	884	954	975	1,002
Hospital Insurance	291,778	287,149	314,363	326,455	340,511	353,486	368,424	383,054	401,918	418,413	436,698	455,500
Legislative proposal, not subject to PAYGO	....	....	30,567	31,925	33,646	35,993	37,455	38,336	40,953	43,266	45,739	48,431
Legislative proposal, subject to PAYGO	....	....	13,733	24,140	25,742	28,595	29,958	31,650	33,269	34,347	35,365	36,544
Railroad retirement:												
Social security equivalent account	1,728	1,850	2,179	2,269	2,284	2,312	2,345	2,378	2,411	2,445	2,480	2,515
Rail pension & supplemental annuity	2,717	2,725	2,976	3,034	3,093	3,143	3,192	3,386	3,472	3,671	4,211	4,401
Total, Employment and general retirement	1,261,651	1,235,856	1,396,417	1,459,415	1,522,912	1,582,100	1,648,178	1,711,275	1,793,026	1,863,580	1,941,305	2,021,695
On-budget	(296,223)	(291,724)	(363,818)	(387,823)	(405,276)	(423,529)	(441,374)	(458,804)	(482,023)	(502,142)	(524,493)	(547,391)
Off-budget	(965,428)	(944,132)	(1,032,599)	(1,071,592)	(1,117,636)	(1,158,571)	(1,206,804)	(1,252,471)	(1,311,003)	(1,361,438)	(1,416,812)	(1,474,304)
Unemployment insurance:												
Deposits by States [1]	36,863	48,146	52,659	52,779	51,006	46,780	44,571	44,608	45,315	46,053	47,321	48,389
Legislative proposal, not subject to PAYGO	....	....	....	−15	−109	−399	−59	−83	−117	−151	−423	−109
Legislative proposal, subject to PAYGO	....	....	....	....	....	....	....	....	....	....	....	....
Federal unemployment receipts [1]	6,161	6,293	6,503	8,058	9,153	10,419	10,725	10,737	11,593	10,396	10,967	7,552
Railroad unemployment receipts [1]	80	118	289	322	173	64	53	68	106	146	147	126
Total, Unemployment insurance	43,104	54,557	59,451	61,144	60,223	56,864	55,290	55,330	56,897	56,444	58,012	55,958
Other retirement:												
Federal employees retirement - employee share	5,171	5,735	6,114	6,544	6,974	7,420	7,884	8,365	8,852	9,366	9,886	10,432
Non-Federal employees retirement [2]	29	31	31	30	30	30	29	29	28	28	28	28
Total, Other retirement	5,200	5,766	6,145	6,574	7,004	7,450	7,913	8,394	8,880	9,394	9,914	10,460
Total, Social insurance and retirement receipts (trust funds)	**1,309,955**	**1,296,179**	**1,462,013**	**1,527,133**	**1,590,139**	**1,646,414**	**1,711,381**	**1,774,999**	**1,858,803**	**1,929,418**	**2,009,231**	**2,088,113**
On-budget	(344,527)	(352,047)	(429,414)	(455,541)	(472,503)	(487,843)	(504,577)	(522,528)	(547,800)	(567,980)	(592,419)	(613,809)
Off-budget	(965,428)	(944,132)	(1,032,599)	(1,071,592)	(1,117,636)	(1,158,571)	(1,206,804)	(1,252,471)	(1,311,003)	(1,361,438)	(1,416,812)	(1,474,304)

Table 8–3. RECEIPTS BY SOURCE—Continued
(In millions of dollars)

Source	2020 Actual	Estimate										
		2021	2022	2023	2024	2025	2026	2027	2028	2029	2030	2031
Excise taxes:												
Federal funds:												
Alcohol	9,490	9,166	9,204	9,314	9,409	9,470	9,533	9,597	9,658	9,725	9,783	9,845
Tobacco	12,354	11,609	11,465	11,494	11,256	11,142	11,043	10,891	10,770	10,640	10,508	10,373
Transportation fuels	−6,525	−4,890	−3,924	−2,197	−856	−860	−866	−862	−857	−852	−849	−861
Legislative proposal, not subject to PAYGO	....	....	....	1	1	2	5	8	12	19	29	42
Telephone and teletype services	370	315	281	237	201	167	150	119	91	67	46	29
Health insurance providers	15,316	206	....	....	....	....	....	....	....	....	....	....
Indoor tanning services	61	57	56	54	52	50	48	45	43	40	38	35
Medical devices	−4	....	....	....	....	....	....	....	....	....	....	....
Other Federal fund excise taxes	−1,483	3,235	3,339	3,356	3,416	3,513	3,616	3,721	3,828	3,944	4,059	4,180
Legislative proposal, not subject to PAYGO	....	....	....	34	111	224	439	782	1,164	1,635	2,154	2,762
Total, Federal funds	29,579	19,698	20,421	22,293	23,590	23,708	23,968	24,301	24,709	25,218	25,768	26,405
Trust funds:												
Transportation	42,764	39,812	40,928	41,311	41,492	41,801	41,977	42,126	42,264	42,427	43,001	43,991
Legislative proposal, not subject to PAYGO	....	....	−13	−41	−86	−150	−236	−356	−545	−864	−1,364	−2,110
Airport and airway	9,016	9,348	15,293	17,826	18,690	19,628	20,327	21,031	21,763	22,536	23,349	24,217
Sport fish restoration and boating safety	646	599	584	590	596	602	609	615	623	630	638	646
Black lung disability insurance	301	356	230	167	150	135	133	132	131	131	130	128
Inland waterway	112	108	105	102	100	97	95	93	90	88	86	84
Hazardous Substance Superfund	....	....	....	....	....	....	....	....	....	....	....	....
Legislative proposal, subject to PAYGO	....	....	2,287	3,119	3,208	3,274	3,355	3,414	3,481	3,559	3,631	3,716
Oil spill liability	400	630	652	668	681	684	691	687	684	688	685	686
Legislative proposal, subject to PAYGO	....	....	93	122	123	124	124	125	126	126	127	129
Vaccine injury compensation	310	317	323	321	321	323	327	332	337	342	347	352
Leaking underground storage tank	219	177	185	184	185	186	186	185	185	184	186	190
Legislative proposal, not subject to PAYGO	....	....	....	−1	−1	−1	−2	−2	−4	−4	−7	−11
Supplementary medical insurance	3,167	2,677	2,800	1,626	3,974	2,800	2,800	2,800	1,626	2,800	3,974	2,800
Patient-centered outcomes research	266	370	389	409	430	453	477	502	527	555	585	617
Total, Trust funds	57,201	54,394	63,856	66,403	69,863	69,956	70,863	71,684	71,288	73,198	75,368	75,435
Total, Excise taxes	**86,780**	**74,092**	**84,277**	**88,696**	**93,453**	**93,664**	**94,831**	**95,985**	**95,997**	**98,416**	**101,136**	**101,840**
Estate and gift taxes:												
Federal funds	17,624	17,593	20,781	22,268	23,556	24,571	25,099	37,804	38,989	40,689	43,212	45,889
Legislative proposal, subject to PAYGO	....	....	....	−4,037	−4,252	−4,425	−4,524	−5,738	−5,985	−6,249	−6,625	−7,032
Total, Estate and gift taxes	**17,624**	**17,593**	**20,781**	**18,231**	**19,304**	**20,146**	**20,575**	**32,066**	**33,004**	**34,440**	**36,587**	**38,857**
Customs duties and fees:												
Federal funds	67,154	83,165	55,542	43,267	43,555	44,519	45,684	47,003	48,515	50,231	52,155	54,232
Trust funds	1,397	1,669	1,841	1,891	1,943	2,007	2,078	2,154	2,247	2,350	2,456	2,566
Total, Customs duties and fees	**68,551**	**84,834**	**57,383**	**45,158**	**45,498**	**46,526**	**47,762**	**49,157**	**50,762**	**52,581**	**54,611**	**56,798**
Miscellaneous receipts:												
Federal funds:												
Miscellaneous taxes	696	710	694	697	701	702	703	702	701	693	694	694
Deposit of earnings, Federal Reserve System	81,880	97,241	101,604	102,770	99,314	76,615	68,155	65,480	71,443	74,911	74,790	79,067

Table 8–3. RECEIPTS BY SOURCE—Continued

(In millions of dollars)

Source	2020 Actual	Estimate										
		2021	2022	2023	2024	2025	2026	2027	2028	2029	2030	2031
Transfers from the Federal Reserve	537	596	618	637	657	677	698	719	742	765	788	813
Fees for permits and regulatory and judicial services	19,594	20,917	21,969	23,626	26,402	29,048	31,908	35,087	37,481	39,631	41,285	42,435
Fines, penalties, and forfeitures ...	13,294	13,482	13,548	13,894	14,375	14,385	14,451	14,405	14,476	14,541	14,611	14,641
Refunds and recoveries	−129	−37	−37	−37	−37	−37	−37	−37	−37	−37	−37	−37
Total, Federal funds	115,872	132,909	138,396	141,587	141,412	121,390	115,878	116,356	124,806	130,504	132,131	137,613
Trust funds:												
United Mine Workers of America, combined benefit fund	14	9	8	2	2	2	2	6	11	17	21	23
Defense cooperation	512	552	554	193	379	205	188	207	172	175	179	182
Fees for permits and regulatory and judicial services	....	....	40	40	40	40	40	40	40	40	40	40
Fines, penalties, and forfeitures	1,348	1,208	1,185	1,229	1,267	1,250	1,228	1,230	1,240	1,240	1,237	1,233
Total, Trust funds	1,874	1,769	1,787	1,464	1,688	1,497	1,458	1,483	1,463	1,472	1,477	1,478
Total, Miscellaneous receipts	**117,746**	**134,678**	**140,183**	**143,051**	**143,100**	**122,887**	**117,336**	**117,839**	**126,269**	**131,976**	**133,608**	**139,091**
Total, budget receipts	**3,421,162**	**3,580,777**	**4,174,197**	**4,641,026**	**4,827,811**	**5,037,903**	**5,332,101**	**5,631,726**	**5,888,126**	**6,118,679**	**6,369,848**	**6,643,485**
On-budget	(2,455,734)	(2,636,645)	(3,141,598)	(3,569,434)	(3,710,175)	(3,879,332)	(4,125,297)	(4,379,255)	(4,577,123)	(4,757,241)	(4,953,036)	(5,169,181)
Off-budget	(965,428)	(944,132)	(1,032,599)	(1,071,592)	(1,117,636)	(1,158,571)	(1,206,804)	(1,252,471)	(1,311,003)	(1,361,438)	(1,416,812)	(1,474,304)

[1] Deposits by States cover the benefit part of the program. Federal unemployment receipts cover administrative costs at both the Federal and State levels. Railroad unemployment receipts cover both the benefits and administrative costs of the program for the railroads.

[2] Represents employer and employee contributions to the civil service retirement and disability fund for covered employees of Government-sponsored, privately owned enterprises and the District of Columbia municipal government.

9. OFFSETTING COLLECTIONS AND OFFSETTING RECEIPTS

I. INTRODUCTION AND BACKGROUND

The Government records money collected in one of two ways. It is either recorded as a governmental receipt and included in the amount reported on the receipts side of the budget or it is recorded as an offsetting collection or offsetting receipt, which reduces (or "offsets") the amount reported on the outlay side of the budget. Governmental receipts are discussed in the previous chapter, "Governmental Receipts." The first section of this chapter broadly discusses offsetting collections and offsetting receipts. The second section discusses user charges, which consist of a subset of offsetting collections and offsetting receipts and a small share of governmental receipts. The third section describes the user charge proposals in the 2022 Budget.

Offsetting collections and offsetting receipts are recorded as offsets to spending so that the budget totals for receipts and (net) outlays reflect the amount of resources allocated by the Government through collective political choice, rather than through the marketplace.[1] This practice ensures that the budget totals measure the transactions of the Government with the public, and avoids the double counting that would otherwise result when one account makes a payment to another account and the receiving account then spends the proceeds. Offsetting receipts and offsetting collections are recorded in the budget in one of two ways, based on interpretation of laws and longstanding budget concepts and practice. They are offsetting collections when the collections are authorized to be credited to expenditure accounts. Otherwise, they are deposited in receipt accounts and called offsetting receipts.

There are two sources of offsetting receipts and offsetting collections: from the public and from other budget accounts. Like governmental receipts, offsetting receipts and offsetting collections from the public reduce the deficit or increase the surplus. In contrast, offsetting receipts and offsetting collections resulting from transactions with other budget accounts, called intragovernmental transactions, exactly offset the payments made by these accounts, with no net impact on the deficit or surplus.[2] In 2020, offsetting receipts and offsetting collections from the public were $625 billion, while receipts and collections from intragovernmental transactions were $1,314 billion, for a total of $1,939 billion Government-wide.

As described above, intragovernmental transactions are responsible for the majority of offsetting collections and offsetting receipts, when measured by the magnitude of the dollars collected. Examples of intragovernmental transactions include interest payments to funds that hold Government securities (such as the Social Security trust funds), general fund transfers to civilian and military retirement pension and health benefits funds, and agency payments to funds for employee health insurance and retirement benefits. Although receipts and collections from intragovernmental collections exactly offset the payments themselves, with no effect on the deficit or surplus, it is important to record these transactions in the budget to show how much the Government is allocating to fund various programs. For example, in the case of civilian retirement pensions, Government agencies make accrual payments to the Civil Service Retirement and Disability Fund on behalf of current employees to fund their future retirement benefits; the receipt of these payments to the Fund is shown in a single receipt account. Recording the receipt of these payments is important because it demonstrates the total cost to the Government today of providing this future benefit.

Offsetting receipts and collections from the public comprise approximately one-third of total offsetting collections and offsetting receipts, when measured by the magnitude of the dollars collected. Most of the funds collected through offsetting collections and offsetting receipts from the public arise from business-like transactions with the public. Unlike governmental receipts, which are derived from the Government's exercise of its sovereign power, these offsetting collections and offsetting receipts arise primarily from voluntary payments from the public for goods or services provided by the Government. They are classified as offsets to outlays for the cost of producing the goods or services for sale, rather than as governmental receipts. These activities include the sale of postage stamps, land, timber, and electricity; charging fees for services provided to the public (e.g., admission to National parks); and collecting premiums for healthcare benefits (e.g., Medicare Parts B and D). As described above, treating offsetting collections and offsetting receipts as offsets to outlays ensures the budgetary totals represent governmental rather than market activity.

A relatively small portion ($20.1 billion in 2020) of offsetting collections and offsetting receipts from the public is derived from the Government's exercise of its sovereign power. From a conceptual standpoint, these should be classified as governmental receipts. However, they are classified as offsetting rather than governmental receipts either because this classification has been specified in law or because these collections have traditionally been classi-

---

[1] Showing collections from business-type transactions as offsets on the spending side of the budget follows the concept recommended by the Report of the President's Commission on Budget Concepts in 1967 and is discussed in Chapter 6 of this volume, "Budget Concepts."

[2] For the purposes of this discussion, "collections from the public" include collections from non-budgetary Government accounts, such as credit financing accounts and deposit funds. For more information on these non-budgetary accounts, see Chapter 7, "Coverage of the Budget."

fied as offsets to outlays. Most of the offsetting collections and offsetting receipts in this category derive from fees from Government regulatory services or Government licenses, and include, for example, charges for regulating the nuclear energy industry, bankruptcy filing fees, and immigration fees.[3]

The final source of offsetting collections and offsetting receipts from the public is gifts. Gifts are voluntary contributions to the Government to support particular purposes or reduce the amount of Government debt held by the public.

The spending associated with the activities that generate offsetting collections and offsetting receipts from the public is included in total or "gross outlays." Offsetting collections and offsetting receipts from the public are subtracted from gross outlays to the public to yield "net outlays," which is the most common measure of outlays cited and generally referred to as simply "outlays."[4] For 2020, gross outlays to the public were $7,176 billion, or 34.2 percent of GDP and offsetting collections and offsetting receipts from the public were $625 billion, or 3.0 percent of GDP, resulting in net outlays of $6,550 billion or 31.2 percent of GDP. Government-wide net outlays reflect the Government's net disbursements to the public and are subtracted from governmental receipts to derive the Government's deficit or surplus. For 2020, governmental receipts were $3,421 billion, or 16.3 percent of GDP, and the deficit was $3,129 billion, or 14.9 percent of GDP.

Although both offsetting collections and offsetting receipts are subtracted from gross outlays to derive net outlays, they are treated differently when it comes to accounting for specific programs and agencies. Offsetting collections are usually authorized to be spent for the purposes of an expenditure account and are generally available for use when collected, without further action by the Congress. Therefore, offsetting collections are recorded as offsets to spending within expenditure accounts, so that the account total highlights the net flow of funds.

Like governmental receipts, offsetting receipts are credited to receipt accounts, and any spending of the receipts is recorded in separate expenditure accounts. As a result, the budget separately displays the flow of funds into and out of the Government. Offsetting receipts may or may not be designated for a specific purpose, depending on the legislation that authorizes their collection. If designated for a particular purpose, the offsetting receipts may, in some cases, be spent without further action by the Congress. When not designated for a particular purpose, offsetting receipts are credited to the general fund, which contains all funds not otherwise allocated and which is used to finance Government spending that is not financed out of dedicated funds. In some cases where the receipts are designated for a particular purpose, offsetting receipts are reported in a particular agency and reduce or offset the outlays reported for that agency. In other cases, the offsetting receipts are "undistributed," which means they reduce total Government outlays, but not the outlays of any particular agency.

Table 9–1 summarizes offsetting collections and offsetting receipts from the public. The amounts shown in the table are not evident in the commonly cited budget measure of outlays, which is already net of these collections and receipts. For 2022, the table shows that total offsetting collections and offsetting receipts from the public are estimated to be $590.1 billion or 2.5 percent of GDP. Of these, an estimated $243.8 billion are offsetting collections and an estimated $346.3 billion are offsetting receipts. Table 9–1 also identifies those offsetting collections and offsetting receipts that are considered user charges, as defined and discussed below.

As shown in the table, major offsetting collections from the public include proceeds from Postal Service sales, electrical power sales, loan repayments to the Commodity Credit Corporation for loans made prior to enactment of the Federal Credit Reform Act, and Federal employee payments for health insurance. As also shown in the table, major offsetting receipts from the public include premiums for Medicare Parts B and D, proceeds from military assistance program sales, rents and royalties from Outer Continental Shelf oil extraction, and interest income.

Tables 9–2 and 9–3 provide further detail about offsetting receipts, including both offsetting receipts from the public (as summarized in Table 9–1) and intragovernmental transactions. Table 9–5, "Offsetting Receipts by Type," and Table 9–6, "Offsetting Collections and Offsetting Receipts, Detail—FY 2022 Budget," which is a complete listing by account, are available at *https://www.whitehouse.gov/omb/analytical-perspectives/*. In total, offsetting receipts are estimated to be $1,291.2 billion in 2022; $944.9 billion are from intragovernmental transactions and $346.3 billion are from the public. The offsetting receipts from the public consist of proprietary receipts ($333.2 billion), which are those resulting from business-like transactions such as the sale of goods or services, and offsetting governmental receipts, which, as discussed above, are derived from the exercise of the Government's sovereign power and, absent a specification in law or a long-standing practice, would be classified on the receipts side of the budget ($13.1 billion).

---

[3] This category of receipts is known as "offsetting governmental receipts." Some argue that regulatory or licensing fees should be viewed as payments for a particular service or for the right to engage in a particular type of business. However, these fees are conceptually much more similar to taxes because they are compulsory, and they fund activities that are intended to provide broadly dispersed benefits, such as protecting the health of the public. Reclassifying these fees as governmental receipts could require a change in law, and because of conventions for scoring appropriations bills, would make it impossible for fees that are controlled through annual appropriations acts to be scored as offsets to discretionary spending.

[4] Gross outlays to the public are derived by subtracting intragovernmental outlays from gross outlays. For 2020, gross outlays were $8,489 billion and intragovernmental outlays were $1,314 billion.

Table 9–1. OFFSETTING COLLECTIONS AND OFFSETTING RECEIPTS FROM THE PUBLIC

(In billions of dollars)

	Actual	Estimate	
	2020	2021	2022
Offsetting collections (credited to expenditure accounts):			
User charges:			
Postal Service stamps and other Postal Service fees (off-budget)	75.7	69.4	67.3
Sale of energy:			
Tennessee Valley Authority	55.3	55.9	54.1
Bonneville Power Administration	3.6	3.8	3.8
Employee contributions for employees and retired employees health benefits funds	17.1	17.8	18.6
Deposit Insurance	7.3	7.9	19.5
Pension Benefit Guaranty Corporation fund	11.2	10.8	11.6
Federal Crop Insurance Corporation Fund	3.9	6.0	4.0
Defense Commissary Agency	4.5	4.6	4.7
All other user charges	44.2	40.8	43.5
Subtotal, user charges	222.9	216.9	227.2
Other collections credited to expenditure accounts:			
Commodity Credit Corporation fund	8.1	9.5	9.0
Supplemental Security Income (collections from the States)	2.5	2.6	2.8
Other collections	73.9	16.8	4.9
Subtotal, other collections	84.6	28.9	16.7
Subtotal, offsetting collections	307.5	245.8	243.8
Offsetting receipts (deposited in receipt accounts):			
User charges:			
Medicare premiums	116.8	124.6	138.7
Spectrum auction, relocation, and licenses	2.7	90.1	21.0
Immigration fees	4.4	4.4	4.7
Outer Continental Shelf rents, bonuses, and royalties	3.6	3.8	5.0
All other user charges	24.1	23.6	25.6
Subtotal, user charges deposited in receipt accounts	151.6	246.5	195.1
Other collections deposited in receipt accounts:			
Interest received from credit financing accounts	55.5	58.7	50.0
Military assistance program sales	39.6	54.1	51.5
Student loan receipt of negative subsidy and downward reestimates	12.2	5.5	3.9
All other collections deposited in receipt accounts	58.9	98.9	45.8
Subtotal, other collections deposited in receipt accounts	166.2	217.2	151.2
Subtotal, offsetting receipts	317.8	463.8	346.3
Total, offsetting collections and offsetting receipts from the public	**625.3**	**709.5**	**590.1**
Total, offsetting collections and offsetting receipts excluding off-budget	549.4	640.0	522.7
ADDENDUM:			
User charges that are offsetting collections and offsetting receipts [1]	374.5	463.4	422.3
Other offsetting collections and offsetting receipts from the public	250.8	246.1	167.8

[1] Excludes user charges that are classified on the receipts side of the budget. For total user charges, see Table 9-3.

User charges or user fees[5] refer generally to those monies that the Government receives from the public for market-oriented activities and regulatory activities. In combination with budget concepts, laws that authorize user charges determine whether a user charge is classified as an offsetting collection, an offsetting receipt, or a governmental receipt. Almost all user charges, as defined below, are classified as offsetting collections or offsetting receipts; for 2022, only an estimated 1.1 percent of user charges are classified as governmental receipts. As summarized in Table 9–3, total user charges for 2022 are estimated to be $427.1 billion with $422.3 billion being offsetting collections or offsetting receipts, and account-

_____

[5] In this chapter, the term "user charge" is generally used and has the same meaning as the term "user fee." The term "user charge" is the one used in OMB Circular No. A–11, "Preparation, Submission, and Execution of the Budget"; OMB Circular No. A–25, "User Charges"; and Chapter 6 of this volume, "Budget Concepts." In common usage, the terms "user charge" and "user fee" are often used interchangeably, and in A Glossary of Terms Used in the Federal Budget Process, GAO provides the same definition for both terms.

Table 9–2. SUMMARY OF OFFSETTING RECEIPTS BY TYPE

(In millions of dollars)

Receipt Type	Actual 2020	Estimate					
		2021	2022	2023	2024	2025	2026
Intragovernmental	932,528	1,187,035	944,891	983,443	1,030,794	1,079,325	1,135,822
Receipts from non-Federal sources:							
Proprietary	303,363	366,321	333,202	346,143	360,638	375,676	385,943
Offsetting governmental	14,455	97,438	13,065	14,866	15,173	15,416	15,533
Total, receipts from non-Federal sources	317,818	463,759	346,267	361,009	375,811	391,092	401,476
Total, offsetting receipts	1,250,346	1,650,794	1,291,158	1,344,452	1,406,605	1,470,417	1,537,298

ing for more than two-thirds of all offsetting collections and offsetting receipts from the public.[6]

Definition. In this chapter, user charges refer to fees, charges, and assessments levied on individuals or organizations directly benefiting from or subject to regulation by a Government program or activity, where the payers do not represent a broad segment of the public such as those who pay income taxes.

Examples of business-type or market-oriented user charges and regulatory and licensing user charges include those charges listed in Table 9-1 for offsetting collections and offsetting receipts. User charges exclude certain offsetting collections and offsetting receipts from the public, such as payments received from credit programs, and interest, and also exclude payments from one part of the Federal Government to another. In addition, user charges do not include dedicated taxes (such as taxes paid to social insurance programs or excise taxes on gasoline) or customs duties, fines, penalties, or forfeitures.

Alternative definitions. The definition for user charges used in this chapter follows the definition used in OMB Circular No. A–25, "User Charges," which provides policy guidance to Executive Branch Agencies on setting the amount for user charges. Alternative definitions may be used for other purposes. Much of the discussion of user charges below—their purpose, when they should be levied, and how the amount should be set—applies to these alternative definitions as well.

A narrower definition of user charges could be limited to proceeds from the sale of goods and services, excluding the proceeds from the sale of assets, and to proceeds that are dedicated to financing the goods and services being provided. This definition is similar to one the House of Representatives uses as a guide for purposes of committee jurisdiction. (See the Congressional Record, January 3, 1991, p. H31, item 8.) The definition of user charges could be even narrower by excluding regulatory fees and focusing solely on business-type transactions. Alternatively, the user charge definition could be broader than the one

used in this chapter by including beneficiary- or liability-based excise taxes.[7]

What is the purpose of user charges? User charges are intended to improve the efficiency and equity of financing certain Government activities. Charging users for activities that benefit a relatively limited number of people reduces the burden on the general taxpayer, as does charging regulated parties for regulatory activities in a particular sector.

User charges that are set to cover the costs of production of goods and services can result in more efficient resource allocation within the economy. When buyers are charged the cost of providing goods and services, they make better cost-benefit calculations regarding the size of their purchase, which in turn signals to the Government how much of the goods or services it should provide. Prices in private, competitive markets serve the same purposes. User charges for goods and services that do not have special social or distributional benefits may also improve equity or fairness by requiring those who benefit from an activity to pay for it and by not requiring those who do not benefit from an activity to pay for it.

When should the Government impose a charge? Discussions of whether to finance spending with a tax or a fee often focus on whether the benefits of the activity accrue to the public in general or to a limited group of people. In general, if the benefits of spending accrue broadly to the public or include special social or distributional benefits, then the program should be financed by taxes paid by the public. In contrast, if the benefits accrue to a limited number of private individuals or organizations and do not include special social or distributional benefits, then the program should be financed by charges paid by the private beneficiaries. For Federal programs where the benefits are entirely public or entirely private, applying this principle can be relatively easy. For example, the benefits from national defense accrue to the public in general, and according to this principle should be (and are) financed by taxes. In contrast, the benefits of electricity

---

[6] User charge totals presented in this chapter include collections from accounts classified as containing user fee data. OMB accounts are classified as containing user fee data if more than half of collections are estimated to include user charges. Consequently, totals may include collections that are not user charges in accounts that meet the threshold and exclude user charges in accounts that do not meet the threshold.

[7] Beneficiary- and liability-based taxes are terms taken from the Congressional Budget Office, The Growth of Federal User Charges, August 1993, and updated in October 1995. Gasoline taxes are an example of beneficiary-based taxes. An example of a liability-based tax is the excise tax that formerly helped fund the hazardous substance superfund in the Environmental Protection Agency. This tax was paid by industry groups to finance environmental cleanup activities related to the industry activity but not necessarily caused by the payer of the fee.

Table 9–3.   GROSS OUTLAYS, USER CHARGES, OTHER OFFSETTING COLLECTIONS AND OFFSETTING RECEIPTS FROM THE PUBLIC, AND NET OUTLAYS

(In billions of dollars)

	Actual 2020	Estimate	
		2021	2022
Gross outlays to the public	7,175.7	7,959.0	6,601.2
Offsetting collections and offsetting receipts from the public:			
User charges [1]	374.5	463.4	422.3
Other	250.8	246.1	167.8
Subtotal, offsetting collections and offsetting receipts from the public	625.3	709.5	590.1
Net outlays	6,550.4	7,249.5	6,011.1

[1] $4.4 billion of the total user charges for 2020 were classified as governmental receipts, and the remainder were classified as offsetting collections and offsetting receipts. $4.2 billion and $4.8 billion of the total user charges for 2021 and 2022 are classified as governmental receipts, respectively.

sold by the Tennessee Valley Authority accrue primarily to those using the electricity, and should be (and predominantly are) financed by user charges.

In many cases, however, an activity has benefits that accrue to both public and private groups, and it may be difficult to identify how much of the benefits accrue to each. Because of this, it can be difficult to know how much of the program should be financed by taxes and how much by fees. For example, the benefits from recreation areas are mixed. Fees for visitors to these areas are appropriate because the visitors benefit directly from their visit, but the public in general also benefits because these areas protect the Nation's natural and historic heritage now and for posterity. For this reason, visitor recreation fees generally cover only part of the cost to the Government of maintaining the recreation property. Where a fee may be appropriate to finance all or part of an activity, the extent to which a fee can be easily administered must be considered. For example, if fees are charged for entering or using Government-owned land then there must be clear points of entry onto the land and attendants patrolling and monitoring the land's use.

What amount should be charged? When the Government is acting in its capacity as sovereign and where user charges are appropriate, such as for some regulatory activities, current policy supports setting fees equal to the full cost to the Government, including both direct and indirect costs. When the Government is not acting in its capacity as sovereign and engages in a purely business-type transaction (such as leasing or selling goods, services, or resources), market price is generally the basis for establishing the fee.[8] If the Government is engaged in a purely business-type transaction and economic resources are allocated efficiently, then this market price should be equal to or greater than the Government's full cost of production.

Classification of user charges in the budget. As shown in the note to Table 9–3, most user charges are classified as offsets to outlays on the spending side of the budget, but a few are classified on the receipts side of the budget. An estimated $4.8 billion in 2022 of user charges are classified on the receipts side and are included in the governmental receipts totals described in the previous chapter, "Governmental Receipts." They are classified as receipts because they are regulatory charges collected by the Federal Government by the exercise of its sovereign powers. Examples include filing fees in the United States courts and agricultural quarantine inspection fees.

The remaining user charges, an estimated $422.3 billion in 2022, are classified as offsetting collections and offsetting receipts on the spending side of the Budget. As discussed above in the context of all offsetting collections and offsetting receipts, some of these user charges are collected by the Federal Government by the exercise of its sovereign powers and conceptually should appear on the receipts side of the budget, but they are required by law or a long-standing practice to be classified on the spending side.

---

[8] Policies for setting user charges are promulgated in OMB Circular No. A–25: "User Charges" (July 8, 1993).

III. USER CHARGE PROPOSALS

As shown in Table 9–1, an estimated $227.2 billion of user charges for 2022 will be credited directly to expenditure accounts and will generally be available for expenditure when they are collected, without further action by the Congress. An estimated $195.1 billion of user charges for 2022 will be deposited in offsetting receipt accounts and will be available to be spent only according to the legislation that established the charges.

As shown in Table 9–4, the Administration is proposing new or increased user charges that would, in the aggregate, increase collections by an estimated $616 million in 2022 and an average of $655 million per year from 2023 through 2031. These estimates reflect only the amounts to be collected; they do not include related spending. Proposals are classified as either discretionary or mandatory, as those terms are defined in the Balanced Budget and Emergency Deficit Control Act of 1985, as amended. All user charge proposals in the 2022 Budget are classified as discretionary. "Discretionary" refers to user charges controlled through annual appropriations acts and generally under the jurisdiction of the appropriations committees in the Congress. "Mandatory" refers to user

Table 9–4. USER CHARGE PROPOSALS IN THE FY 2022 BUDGET[1]

(Estimated collections in millions of dollars)

	2022	2023	2024	2025	2026	2027	2028	2029	2030	2031	2022-2026	2022-2031
OFFSETTING COLLECTIONS AND OFFSETTING RECEIPTS												
DISCRETIONARY:												
Offsetting collections												
Department of Health and Human Services												
Food and Drug Administration (FDA): Increase export certification user fee cap	4	4	4	4	4	4	4	4	4	4	20	40
FDA: Increase tobacco product user fee	100	103	105	108	110	113	116	119	122	125	526	1,121
Department of State												
Establish The National Museum of American Diplomacy rental fee	*	*	*	*	*	*	*	*	*	*	*	*
Commodity Futures Trading Commission (CFTC)												
Establish CFTC user fee	116	121	126	131	136	141	146	152	158	164	630	1,391
Offsetting receipts												
Department of State												
Extend Western Hemisphere Travel Initiative surcharge	385	385	385	385	385	385	385	385	385	385	1,925	3,850
Increase Border Crossing Card fee	11	11	11	11	11	11	11	11	11	11	55	110
Subtotal, discretionary user charge proposals	616	624	631	639	646	654	662	671	680	689	3,156	6,512
Total, user charge proposals	**616**	**624**	**631**	**639**	**646**	**654**	**662**	**671**	**680**	**689**	**3,156**	**6,512**

[1] A positive sign indicates an increase in collections.

* $500,000 or less

charges controlled by permanent laws and under the jurisdiction of the authorizing committees. These and other terms are discussed further in this volume in Chapter 6, "Budget Concepts."

Discretionary User Charge Proposals

1. Offsetting collections

Department of Health and Human Services

Food and Drug Administration (FDA): Increase export certification user fee cap. Firms exporting products from the United States are often asked by foreign customers or foreign governments to supply a "certificate" for products regulated by the FDA to document the product's regulatory or marketing status. The proposal increases the maximum user fee cap from $175 per export certification to $600 to meet FDA's true cost of issuing export certificates and to ensure better and faster service for American companies that request the service.

FDA: Increase tobacco product user fee. Currently, FDA's regulation of all tobacco products is financed through user fees collected from six product categories: cigarettes, roll your own tobacco, snuff, chewing tobacco, cigars, and pipe tobacco. This proposal would expand FDA's tobacco user fees and include user fee assessments on e-cigarettes and other electronic nicotine delivery systems (ENDS) manufacturers, which currently do not pay user fees, and increase the current limitation on total tobacco user fee collections by $100 million in 2022. To ensure that resources keep up with new tobacco products, the proposal would also index future collections to inflation. The expansion of tobacco user fees will strengthen FDA's ability to respond to the growth of newer products such as e-cigarettes through investments in regulatory science, enforcement, and premarket review of product applications.

Department of State

Establish The National Museum of American Diplomacy rental fee. This new user fee will enable the Department of State to provide support, on a cost-recovery basis, to outside organizations for programs and conference activities held at The National Museum of American Diplomacy.

Commodity Futures Trading Commission (CFTC)

Establish CFTC user fee. The Budget proposes an amendment to the Commodity Exchange Act authorizing the CFTC to collect user fees to fund the Commission's activities, like other Federal financial and banking regulators. Fee funding would shift the costs of services provided by CFTC from the general taxpayer to the primary beneficiaries of CFTC oversight. Contingent upon enactment of legislation authorizing the CFTC to collect fees, the Administration proposes that collections begin in 2022 to offset a portion of CFTC's annual appropriation.

2. *Offsetting receipts*

Department of State

Extend Western Hemisphere Travel Initiative surcharge. The Administration proposes to permanently extend the authority for the Department of State to collect the Western Hemisphere Travel Initiative surcharge. The surcharge was initially enacted by the Passport Services Enhancement Act of 2005 (P.L. 109–167) to cover the Department's costs of meeting increased demand for passports, which resulted from the implementation of the Western Hemisphere Travel Initiative.

Increase Border Crossing Card (BCC) fee. The Budget includes a proposal to allow the fee charged for BCC minor applicants to be set administratively, rather than statutorily, at one-half the fee charged for processing an adult border crossing card. Administrative fee setting will allow the fee to better reflect the associated cost of service, consistent with other fees charged for consular services. As a result of this change, annual BCC fee collections beginning in 2022 are projected to increase by $11 million (from $3 million to $14 million).

10. TAX EXPENDITURES

The Congressional Budget Act of 1974 (Public Law 93–344) requires that a list of "tax expenditures" be included in the budget. Tax expenditures are defined in the law as "revenue losses attributable to provisions of the Federal tax laws which allow a special exclusion, exemption, or deduction from gross income or which provide a special credit, a preferential rate of tax, or a deferral of tax liability." These exceptions may be viewed as alternatives to other policy instruments, such as spending or regulatory programs.

Identification and measurement of tax expenditures depends crucially on the baseline tax system against which the actual tax system is compared. The tax expenditure estimates presented in this document are patterned on a comprehensive income tax, which defines income as the sum of consumption and the change in net wealth in a given period of time.

An important assumption underlying each tax expenditure estimate reported below is that other parts of the Tax Code remain unchanged. The estimates would be different if tax expenditures were changed simultaneously because of potential interactions among provisions. For that reason, this document does not present a grand total for the estimated tax expenditures.

Tax expenditures relating to the individual and corporate income taxes are estimated for fiscal years 2020–2030 using two methods of accounting: current tax receipt effects and present value effects. The present value approach provides estimates of the receipt effects for tax expenditures that generally involve deferrals of tax payments into the future.

TAX EXPENDITURES IN THE INCOME TAX

Tax Expenditure Estimates

All tax expenditure estimates and descriptions presented here are based upon current tax law enacted as of December 31, 2020, and reflect the economic assumptions from the 2022 Budget. In some cases, expired or repealed provisions are listed if their tax receipt effects occur in fiscal year 2020 or later.

The total receipt effects for tax expenditures for fiscal years 2020–2030 are displayed according to the Budget's functional categories in Table 10–1. Descriptions of the specific tax expenditure provisions follow the discussion of general features of the tax expenditure concept.

Two baseline concepts—the normal tax baseline and the reference tax law baseline—are used to identify and estimate tax expenditures.[1] For the most part, the two concepts coincide. However, items treated as tax expenditures under the normal tax baseline, but not the reference tax law baseline, are indicated by the designation "normal tax method" in the tables. The receipt effects for these items are zero using the reference tax law. The alternative baseline concepts are discussed in detail below.

Tables 10–2A and 10–2B report separately the respective portions of the total receipt effects that arise under the individual and corporate income taxes. The location of the estimates under the individual and corporate headings does not imply that these categories of filers benefit

from the special tax provisions in proportion to the respective tax expenditure amounts shown. Rather, these breakdowns show the form of tax liability that the various provisions affect. The ultimate beneficiaries of corporate tax expenditures could be shareholders, employees, customers, or other providers of capital, depending on economic forces.

Table 10–3 ranks the major tax expenditures by the size of their 2021–2030 receipt effect. The first column provides the number of the provision in order to cross reference this table to Tables 10–1, 10–2A, and 10–2B, as well as to the descriptions below.

Interpreting Tax Expenditure Estimates

The estimates shown for individual tax expenditures in Tables 10–1 through 10–3 do not necessarily equal the increase in Federal receipts (or the change in the budget balance) that would result from repealing these special provisions, for the following reasons.

First, eliminating a tax expenditure may have incentive effects that alter economic behavior. These incentives can affect the resulting magnitudes of the activity, or the consequences of other tax provisions or Government programs. For example, if capital gains were taxed at higher ordinary income tax rates, capital gain realizations would be expected to decline, which could result in lower tax receipts depending on the elasticity of the capital gains tax rates. Such behavioral effects are not reflected in the estimates.

Second, tax expenditures are interdependent even without incentive effects. Repeal of a tax expenditure

---

[1] These baseline concepts are thoroughly discussed in Special Analysis G of the 1985 Budget, where the former is referred to as the pre-1983 method and the latter the post-1982 method.

provision can increase or decrease the tax receipts associated with other provisions. For example, even if behavior does not change, repeal of an itemized deduction could increase the receipt costs from other deductions because some taxpayers would be moved into higher tax brackets. Alternatively, repeal of an itemized deduction could lower the receipt cost from other deductions if taxpayers are led to claim the standard deduction instead of itemizing. Similarly, if two provisions were repealed simultaneously, the increase in tax liability could be greater or less than the sum of the two separate tax expenditures, because each is estimated assuming that the other remains in force. In addition, the estimates reported in Table 10–1 are the totals of individual and corporate income tax receipt effects reported in Tables 10–2A and 10–2B, and do not reflect any possible interactions between individual and corporate income tax receipts. For this reason, the estimates in Table 10–1 should be regarded as approximations.

Present-Value Estimates

The annual value of tax expenditures for tax deferrals is reported on a cash basis in all tables except Table 10–4. Cash-based estimates reflect the difference between taxes deferred in the current year and incoming receipts that are received due to deferrals of taxes from prior years. Although such estimates are useful as a measure of cash flows into the Government, they do not accurately reflect the true economic cost of these provisions. For example, for a provision where activity levels have changed over time, so that incoming tax receipts from past deferrals are greater than deferred receipts from new activity, the cash-basis tax expenditure estimate can be negative, despite the fact that in present-value terms current deferrals have a real cost to the Government (i.e., taxpayers). Alternatively, in the case of a newly enacted deferral provision, a cash-based estimate can overstate the real effect on receipts to the Government because the newly deferred taxes will ultimately be received.

Discounted present-value estimates of receipt effects are presented in Table 10–4 for certain provisions that involve tax deferrals or other long-term receipt effects. These estimates complement the cash-based tax expenditure estimates presented in the other tables.

The present-value estimates represent the receipt effects, net of future tax payments that follow from activities undertaken during calendar year 2020 which cause the deferrals or other long-term receipt effects. For instance, a pension contribution in 2020 would cause a deferral of tax payments on wages in 2020 and on pension fund earnings on this contribution (e.g., interest) in later years. In some future year, however, the 2020 pension contribution and accrued earnings will be paid out and taxes will be due; these receipts are included in the present-value estimate. In general, this conceptual approach is similar to the one used for reporting the budgetary effects of credit programs, where direct loans and guarantees in a given year affect future cash flows.

Tax Expenditure Baselines

A tax expenditure is an exception to baseline provisions of the tax structure that usually results in a reduction in the amount of tax owed. The 1974 Congressional Budget Act, which mandated the tax expenditure budget, did not specify the baseline provisions of the tax law. As noted previously, deciding whether provisions are exceptions, therefore, is a matter of judgment. As in prior years, most of this year's tax expenditure estimates are presented using two baselines: the normal tax baseline and the reference tax law baseline. Tax expenditures may take the form of credits, deductions, special exceptions and allowances.

The normal tax baseline is patterned on a practical variant of a comprehensive income tax, which defines income as the sum of consumption and the change in net wealth in a given period of time. The normal tax baseline allows personal exemptions, a standard deduction, and deduction of expenses incurred in earning income. It is not limited to a particular structure of tax rates, or by a specific definition of the taxpaying unit.

The reference tax law baseline is also patterned on a comprehensive income tax, but it is closer to existing law. Reference tax law tax expenditures are limited to special exceptions from a generally provided tax rule that serves programmatic functions in a way that is analogous to spending programs. Provisions under the reference tax law baseline are generally tax expenditures under the normal tax baseline, but the reverse is not always true.

Both the normal tax and reference tax law baselines allow several major departures from a pure comprehensive income tax. For example, under the normal tax and reference tax law baselines:

- Income is taxable only when it is realized in exchange. Thus, the deferral of tax on unrealized capital gains is not regarded as a tax expenditure. Accrued income would be taxed under a comprehensive income tax.

- There is a separate corporate income tax.

- Tax rates on noncorporate business income vary by level of income.

- Individual tax rates, including brackets, standard deduction, and personal exemptions, are allowed to vary with marital status.

- Values of assets and debt are not generally adjusted for inflation. A comprehensive income tax would adjust the cost basis of capital assets and debt for changes in the general price level. Thus, under a comprehensive income tax baseline, the failure to take account of inflation in measuring depreciation, capital gains, and interest income would be regarded as a negative tax expenditure (i.e., a tax penalty), and failure to take account of inflation in measuring interest costs would be regarded as a positive tax expenditure (i.e., a tax subsidy).

- The base erosion and anti-abuse tax (BEAT) for multinational corporations is treated as a minimum tax and considered part of the rate structure.

Although the reference tax law and normal tax baselines are generally similar, areas of difference include:

Tax rates. The separate schedules applying to the various taxpaying units and the Alternative Minimum Tax are treated as part of the baseline rate structure under both the reference tax law and normal tax methods.

Income subject to the tax. Income subject to tax is defined as gross income less the costs of earning that income. Under the reference tax law, gross income does not include gifts defined as receipts of money or property that are not consideration in an exchange nor does gross income include most transfer payments from the Government.[2] The normal tax baseline also excludes gifts between individuals from gross income. Under the normal tax baseline, however, all cash transfer payments from the Government to private individuals are counted in gross income, and exemptions of such transfers from tax are identified as tax expenditures. The costs of earning income are generally deductible in determining taxable income under both the reference tax law and normal tax baselines.[3]

Capital recovery. Under the reference tax law baseline no tax expenditures arise from accelerated depreciation. Under the normal tax baseline, the depreciation allowance for property is computed using estimates of economic depreciation.

Descriptions of Income Tax Provisions

Descriptions of the individual and corporate income tax expenditures reported on in this document follow. These descriptions relate to current law as of December 31, 2020. Legislation enacted in 2020 expanded the scope and size of tax expenditures. The Families First Coronavirus Response Act created a tax credit for qualified sick leave and family leave equivalent amounts for self-employed individuals. The Coronavirus Aid, Relief, and Economic Security (CARES) Act introduced a recovery rebate tax credit for eligible individuals and an exclusion for certain loans received under the "Paycheck Protection Program" and subsequently forgiven. CARES also modified a number of tax expenditures. It created an exception to the

10-percent early withdrawal tax for "coronavirus related distributions" from a qualified retirement plan or IRA, and another exception to the required minimum distribution rules. It introduced a partial above-the-line deduction for charitable deductions, and expanded the limits on deductions for charitable contributions. It also included over-the-counter medicines and drugs and menstrual care products as qualified medical expenses for HSAs, Archer MSAs, health FSAs, and HRAs. It also modified a number of other provisions in the tax Code. The Consolidated Appropriations Act (CAA) created another rebate and adjusted several provisions in CARES.

National Defense

1. ***Exclusion of benefits and allowances to armed forces personnel.***—Under the baseline tax system, all compensation, including dedicated payments and in-kind benefits, should be included in taxable income because they represent accretions to wealth that do not materially differ from cash wages. As an example, a rental voucher of $100 is (approximately) equal in value to $100 of cash income. In contrast to this treatment, certain housing and meals, in addition to other benefits provided military personnel, either in cash or in kind, as well as certain amounts of pay related to combat service, are excluded from income subject to tax.

International Affairs

2. ***Exclusion of income earned abroad by U.S. citizens.***—Under the baseline tax system, all compensation received by U.S. citizens and residents is properly included in their taxable income. It makes no difference whether the compensation is a result of working abroad or whether it is labeled as a housing allowance. In contrast to this treatment, U.S. tax law allows U.S. citizens and residents who live abroad, work in the private sector, and satisfy a foreign residency requirement to exclude up to $80,000, plus adjustments for inflation since 2004, in foreign earned income from U.S. taxes. In addition, if these taxpayers are provided housing by their employers, then they may also exclude the cost of such housing from their income to the extent that it exceeds 16 percent of the earned income exclusion limit. This housing exclusion is capped at 30 percent of the earned income exclusion limit, with geographical adjustments. If taxpayers do not receive a specific allowance for housing expenses, they may deduct housing expenses up to the amount by which foreign earned income exceeds their foreign earned income exclusion.

3. ***Exclusion of certain allowances for Federal employees abroad.***—In general, all compensation received by U.S. citizens and residents is properly included in their taxable income. It makes no difference whether the compensation is a result of working abroad or whether it is labeled as an allowance for the high cost of living abroad. In contrast to this treatment, U.S. Federal civilian employees and Peace Corps members who work outside the continental United States are allowed to exclude

---

[2] Gross income does, however, include transfer payments associated with past employment, such as Social Security benefits.

[3] In the case of individuals who hold "passive" equity interests in businesses, the pro-rata shares of sales and expense deductions reportable in a year are limited. A passive business activity is defined generally to be one in which the holder of the interest, usually a partnership interest, does not actively perform managerial or other participatory functions. The taxpayer may generally report no larger deductions for a year than will reduce taxable income from such activities to zero. Deductions in excess of the limitation may be taken in subsequent years, or when the interest is liquidated. In addition, costs of earning income may be limited under the Alternative Minimum Tax.

Table 10–1. ESTIMATES OF TOTAL INCOME TAX EXPENDITURES FOR FISCAL YEARS 2020–2030

(In millions of dollars)

		Total from corporations and individuals											
		2020	2021	2022	2023	2024	2025	2026	2027	2028	2029	2030	2021–2030
National Defense													
1	Exclusion of benefits and allowances to armed forces personnel	12,910	13,940	14,460	15,010	13,770	13,890	14,380	14,990	15,660	16,390	17,160	149,650
International affairs:													
2	Exclusion of income earned abroad by U.S. citizens	6,160	6,470	6,790	7,130	7,490	7,860	8,260	8,670	9,100	9,560	10,040	81,370
3	Exclusion of certain allowances for Federal employees abroad	270	280	290	310	320	340	360	370	390	410	430	3,500
4	Reduced tax rate on active income of controlled foreign corporations (normal tax method)	27,570	29,780	32,240	33,980	35,730	37,550	29,390	30,580	30,890	31,370	32,040	323,560
5	Deduction for foreign-derived intangible income dervied from trade or business within the United States	9,450	10,200	11,050	11,650	12,250	12,870	7,620	7,930	8,010	8,140	8,310	98,030
6	Interest Charge Domestic International Sales Corporations (IC-DISCs)	890	1,370	1,440	1,510	1,590	1,690	2,010	2,280	2,410	2,520	2,600	19,420
General science, space, and technology:													
7	Expensing of research and experimentation expenditures (normal tax method)	5,420	3,980	−17,100	−29,140	−22,200	−13,600	−4,180	0	0	0	0	−82,240
8	Credit for increasing research activities	16,940	18,300	19,910	21,360	22,720	24,060	25,420	26,790	28,170	29,600	31,070	247,400
Energy:													
9	Expensing of exploration and development costs, fuels	40	−40	90	230	380	430	460	480	490	500	490	3,510
10	Excess of percentage over cost depletion, fuels	590	600	720	790	830	870	950	1,020	1,090	1,150	1,210	9,230
11	Exception from passive loss limitation for working interests in oil and gas properties	20	20	10	20	20	20	20	20	20	20	20	190
12	Capital gains treatment of royalties on coal	100	70	50	50	50	50	60	60	60	70	70	590
13	Exclusion of interest on energy facility bonds	0	10	10	10	10	10	10	10	10	10	10	100
14	Enhanced oil recovery credit	470	500	560	660	880	1,080	1,190	1,250	1,310	1,360	1,400	10,190
15	Energy production credit [1]	5,020	5,280	5,180	5,420	5,770	6,010	5,740	5,570	5,260	4,870	4,280	53,380
16	Marginal wells credit	150	250	310	280	210	140	90	40	20	0	0	1,340
17	Energy investment credit [1]	6,070	6,330	7,050	6,780	7,380	7,540	6,970	6,880	5,520	4,450	3,180	62,080
18	Alcohol fuel credits [2]	0	10	0	0	0	0	0	0	0	0	0	10
19	Bio-Diesel and small agri-biodiesel producer tax credits [3]	30	40	40	20	0	0	0	0	0	0	0	100
20	Tax credits for clean-fuel burning vehicles and refueling property	570	440	480	440	380	360	330	270	240	230	230	3,400
21	Exclusion of utility conservation subsidies	60	60	50	50	50	40	40	40	30	30	30	420
22	Credit for holding clean renewable energy bonds [4]	70	70	70	70	70	70	70	70	70	70	70	700
23	Credit for investment in clean coal facilities	30	30	20	10	30	30	30	30	40	30	30	280
24	Amortize all geological and geophysical expenditures over 2 years	80	80	90	100	110	110	110	110	110	100	100	1,020
25	Allowance of deduction for certain energy efficient commercial building property	160	190	130	110	110	110	110	110	110	110	110	1,200
26	Credit for construction of new energy efficient homes	320	370	280	260	250	260	270	170	60	20	0	1,940
27	Credit for energy efficiency improvements to existing homes	240	240	120	0	0	0	0	0	0	0	0	360
28	Credit for residential energy efficient property	2,370	2,390	1,980	1,450	420	120	0	0	0	0	0	6,360
29	Qualified energy conservation bonds [5]	30	30	30	30	30	30	30	30	30	30	30	300
30	Advanced Energy Property Credit	10	10	10	10	10	10	10	10	10	10	10	100
31	Advanced nuclear power production credit	0	0	80	180	220	240	270	280	280	270	180	2,000
32	Reduced tax rate for nuclear decommissioning funds	100	110	110	120	120	130	130	140	150	150	160	1,320
Natural resources and environment:													
33	Expensing of exploration and development costs, nonfuel minerals	0	0	10	20	40	40	40	40	50	50	50	340

Table 10–1. ESTIMATES OF TOTAL INCOME TAX EXPENDITURES FOR FISCAL YEARS 2020–2030—Continued

(In millions of dollars)

		Total from corporations and individuals											
		2020	2021	2022	2023	2024	2025	2026	2027	2028	2029	2030	2021–2030
34	Excess of percentage over cost depletion, nonfuel minerals	110	100	120	140	140	160	160	180	200	200	220	1,620
35	Exclusion of interest on bonds for water, sewage, and hazardous waste facilities	270	330	350	350	350	360	370	390	400	430	420	3,750
36	Capital gains treatment of certain timber income	130	130	140	140	150	150	170	190	200	210	220	1,700
37	Expensing of multiperiod timber growing costs	50	60	60	70	70	70	80	80	90	80	80	740
38	Tax incentives for preservation of historic structures	660	610	590	670	820	930	1,000	1,030	1,060	1,070	1,090	8,870
39	Carbon oxide sequestration credit	14	123	277	449	646	873	1,111	1,319	1,511	1,694	1,905	9,908
40	Deduction for endangered species recovery expenditures	30	30	30	30	40	40	40	60	60	60	70	460
Agriculture:													
41	Expensing of certain capital outlays	80	120	160	160	170	180	220	240	250	260	270	2,030
42	Expensing of certain multiperiod production costs	560	370	340	360	370	390	480	540	560	580	600	4,590
43	Treatment of loans forgiven for solvent farmers	50	50	60	60	60	60	70	70	70	70	70	640
44	Capital gains treatment of certain agriculture income	1,330	1,340	1,370	1,410	1,470	1,540	1,720	1,900	1,990	2,090	2,190	17,020
45	Income averaging for farmers	170	180	200	200	210	220	230	230	230	230	230	2,160
46	Deferral of gain on sale of farm refiners	15	15	15	15	15	20	20	20	20	20	20	180
47	Expensing of reforestation expenditures	50	60	60	70	70	70	80	80	90	80	80	740
Commerce and housing:													
	Financial institutions and insurance:												
48	Exemption of credit union income	2,140	2,080	2,120	2,170	2,350	2,410	2,450	2,650	2,740	2,790	2,830	24,564
49	Exclusion of life insurance death benefits	11,690	11,560	12,060	12,440	12,870	13,400	14,210	15,160	15,700	16,100	16,580	140,080
50	Exemption or special alternative tax for small property and casualty insurance companies	110	120	120	130	130	130	140	140	150	150	160	1,370
51	Tax exemption of insurance income earned by tax-exempt organizations	320	320	340	350	350	360	360	370	380	380	390	3,600
52	Exclusion of interest spread of financial institutions	4,230	3,110	2,030	2,080	2,150	2,240	2,380	2,500	2,580	2,660	2,740	24,470
	Housing:												
53	Exclusion of interest on owner-occupied mortgage subsidy bonds	710	850	920	900	910	920	980	1,020	1,050	1,110	1,100	9,760
54	Exclusion of interest on rental housing bonds	1,200	1,430	1,550	1,530	1,530	1,560	1,640	1,720	1,770	1,870	1,870	16,470
55	Deductibility of mortgage interest on owner-occupied homes	24,730	25,440	26,170	26,920	28,340	30,250	67,330	89,630	95,150	100,420	106,330	595,980
56	Deductibility of State and local property tax on owner-occupied homes [17]	6,450	6,370	6,450	6,620	6,860	7,130	35,890	52,340	55,090	57,590	60,260	294,600
57	Deferral of income from installment sales	1,480	1,470	1,460	1,510	1,550	1,610	1,670	1,730	1,800	1,870	1,950	16,620
58	Capital gains exclusion on home sales	39,450	40,610	41,800	43,030	44,730	46,340	51,480	55,060	57,070	59,170	61,370	500,660
59	Exclusion of net imputed rental income	123,210	130,590	139,290	148,090	153,210	154,180	176,960	180,390	183,950	187,880	191,440	1,645,980
60	Exception from passive loss rules for $25,000 of rental loss	5,700	5,540	5,870	6,210	6,460	6,860	7,490	7,600	7,700	7,770	7,850	69,350
61	Credit for low-income housing investments	6,310	8,900	11,280	10,540	10,390	10,360	10,430	10,710	10,980	11,270	11,570	106,430
62	Accelerated depreciation on rental housing (normal tax method)	4,250	4,660	4,900	5,060	5,300	5,510	6,250	6,740	6,890	7,040	7,200	59,550
	Commerce:												
63	Discharge of business indebtedness	40	30	40	20	20	10	30	30	30	30	40	280
64	Exceptions from imputed interest rules	60	60	70	70	70	80	80	90	90	100	100	810
65	Treatment of qualified dividends	29,450	30,760	32,130	33,560	34,710	36,250	39,120	42,250	44,290	46,140	48,030	387,240
66	Capital gains (except agriculture, timber, iron ore, and coal)	99,210	99,890	101,950	105,290	109,710	114,910	128,090	141,870	148,780	156,060	163,700	1,270,250
67	Capital gains exclusion of small corporation stock	1,410	1,530	1,640	1,750	1,850	1,930	2,000	2,080	2,160	2,250	2,350	19,540
68	Step-up basis of capital gains at death	35,460	37,780	40,260	42,910	45,510	48,050	50,350	54,840	58,340	61,790	65,620	505,450

Table 10–1.   ESTIMATES OF TOTAL INCOME TAX EXPENDITURES FOR FISCAL YEARS 2020–2030—Continued

(In millions of dollars)

		Total from corporations and individuals											
		2020	2021	2022	2023	2024	2025	2026	2027	2028	2029	2030	2021–2030
69	Carryover basis of capital gains on gifts	2,610	3,050	3,560	3,820	4,070	4,090	4,750	5,430	5,270	5,210	5,300	44,550
70	Ordinary income treatment of loss from small business corporation stock sale	70	70	70	70	80	80	80	80	90	90	90	800
71	Deferral of gains from like-kind exchanges	3,030	3,200	3,350	3,520	3,690	3,870	4,070	4,260	4,480	4,710	4,940	40,090
72	Depreciation of buildings other than rental housing (normal tax method)	6,010	4,090	3,990	3,660	3,350	3,120	3,130	2,940	2,830	2,940	3,060	33,110
73	Accelerated depreciation of machinery and equipment (normal tax method)	32,800	31,320	26,390	12,170	–2,370	–14,870	–26,700	–38,830	–30,520	–16,000	–7,310	–66,720
74	Expensing of certain small investments (normal tax method)	–300	–1,630	–830	3,710	7,660	10,170	13,700	17,220	15,710	12,860	11,400	89,970
75	Exclusion of interest on small issue bonds	80	90	90	90	90	90	100	110	110	120	120	1,010
76	Special rules for certain film and TV production	–190	–50	0	100	200	260	–420	–570	–270	–130	–50	–930
77	Allow 20-percent deduction to certain pass-through income	29,195	50,518	52,668	54,406	56,904	60,728	25,001	0	0	0	0	300,225
Transportation:													
78	Tonnage tax	140	140	140	140	140	140	140	140	140	140	140	1,400
79	Deferral of tax on shipping companies	10	10	10	10	10	10	10	10	10	10	10	100
80	Exclusion of reimbursed employee parking expenses	1,686	1,759	1,861	2,006	2,063	2,130	2,238	2,343	2,448	2,565	2,740	22,153
81	Exclusion for employer-provided transit passes ..	341	363	397	442	463	487	530	565	609	653	741	5,250
82	Tax credit for certain expenditures for maintaining railroad tracks	140	170	170	130	80	60	40	30	30	20	10	740
83	Exclusion of interest on bonds for Highway Projects and rail-truck transfer facilities	170	160	160	140	140	130	130	120	110	110	100	1,300
Community and regional development:													
84	Investment credit for rehabilitation of structures (other than historic)	10	0	0	0	0	0	0	0	0	0	0	0
85	Exclusion of interest for airport, dock, and similar bonds	720	850	930	910	920	930	990	1,030	1,060	1,120	1,120	9,860
86	Exemption of certain mutuals' and cooperatives' income	90	90	100	100	100	100	100	110	110	110	110	1,030
87	Empowerment zones	160	130	90	100	110	110	90	60	40	20	20	770
88	New markets tax credit	1,280	1,290	1,320	1,280	1,170	1,110	1,130	1,100	970	780	560	10,710
89	Credit to holders of Gulf Tax Credit Bonds	100	110	120	100	90	90	80	80	70	70	60	870
90	Recovery Zone Bonds [6]	90	90	100	90	80	80	80	70	60	60	50	760
91	Tribal Economic Development Bonds	10	10	10	10	10	10	10	10	10	10	10	100
92	Opportunity Zones	3,770	2,680	2,850	1,960	2,000	1,920	–6,080	–9,170	540	730	900	–1,670
93	Employee retention credit	230	160	140	90	60	60	50	40	40	30	30	700
Education, training, employment, and social services:													
	Education:												
94	Exclusion of scholarship and fellowship income (normal tax method)	3,510	3,660	3,910	4,180	4,440	4,710	5,270	6,140	6,500	6,870	7,280	52,960
95	Tax credits and deductions for postsecondary education expenses [7]	10,730	10,070	14,140	14,450	14,450	14,310	14,180	14,350	14,130	13,930	13,710	137,720
96	Deductibility of student-loan interest	2,170	2,030	2,150	2,230	2,250	2,340	2,380	2,820	2,970	2,960	3,040	25,170
97	Qualified tuition programs (includes Education IRA)	2,420	2,670	2,950	3,280	3,680	4,160	5,130	6,160	7,320	8,830	10,840	55,020
98	Exclusion of interest on student-loan bonds	140	160	180	180	180	180	190	200	200	220	220	1,910
99	Exclusion of interest on bonds for private nonprofit educational facilities	1,910	2,280	2,480	2,430	2,440	2,480	2,610	2,740	2,810	2,970	2,970	26,210
100	Credit for holders of zone academy bonds [8]	150	130	110	90	80	60	50	50	40	40	40	690
101	Exclusion of interest on savings bonds redeemed to finance educational expenses	30	40	40	40	40	40	50	50	50	50	50	450
102	Parental personal exemption for students age 19 or over	0	0	0	0	0	0	3,570	5,270	5,180	5,090	5,000	24,110

Table 10-1.   ESTIMATES OF TOTAL INCOME TAX EXPENDITURES FOR FISCAL YEARS 2020-2030—Continued

(In millions of dollars)

		Total from corporations and individuals											
		2020	2021	2022	2023	2024	2025	2026	2027	2028	2029	2030	2021–2030
103	Deductibility of charitable contributions (education)	4,530	4,880	5,190	5,510	5,820	6,130	7,290	9,370	9,800	10,260	10,430	74,680
104	Exclusion of employer-provided educational assistance	1,190	1,390	1,500	1,620	1,730	1,850	1,640	1,560	1,640	1,720	1,800	16,450
105	Special deduction for teacher expenses	170	170	170	170	170	170	180	210	210	210	220	1,880
106	Discharge of student loan indebtedness	80	80	90	100	110	120	150	170	190	220	240	1,470
107	Qualified school construction bonds [9]	570	540	520	490	470	440	410	390	360	330	320	4,270
	Training, employment, and social services:												
108	Work opportunity tax credit	1,650	1,690	1,780	1,830	1,890	1,950	1,300	530	370	280	200	11,820
109	Employer provided child care exclusion	580	570	570	610	650	690	920	1,060	1,120	1,190	1,260	8,640
110	Employer-provided child care credit	20	20	20	20	20	20	20	20	20	30	30	220
111	Assistance for adopted foster children	620	660	700	750	800	850	900	960	1,020	1,080	1,150	8,870
112	Adoption credit and exclusion	770	790	850	870	900	920	930	940	950	960	970	9,080
113	Exclusion of employee meals and lodging (other than military)	3,290	4,320	6,430	6,100	5,610	5,900	6,940	7,530	7,750	8,030	8,360	66,970
114	Credit for child and dependent care expenses	3,190	3,080	3,300	3,440	3,530	3,580	3,700	3,880	3,970	4,060	4,160	36,700
115	Credit for disabled access expenditures	10	10	10	10	10	10	10	10	10	10	10	100
116	Deductibility of charitable contributions, other than education and health	40,320	43,610	46,410	49,220	52,050	54,810	66,080	86,500	90,570	94,830	99,300	683,380
117	Exclusion of certain foster care payments	490	510	510	520	530	540	540	540	540	560	580	5,370
118	Exclusion of parsonage allowances	900	950	1,000	1,050	1,110	1,170	1,230	1,300	1,370	1,440	1,510	12,130
119	Indian employment credit	70	70	50	30	30	30	20	20	20	10	10	290
120	Credit for employer differential wage payments	0	0	0	0	0	0	10	10	10	20	20	70
Health:													
121	Exclusion of employer contributions for medical insurance premiums and medical care [10]	191,350	197,530	211,550	224,320	235,050	248,420	290,960	322,500	340,250	358,670	377,880	2,807,130
122	Self-employed medical insurance premiums	7,430	7,740	8,150	8,720	9,290	9,930	11,330	12,450	13,140	13,820	14,550	109,120
123	Medical Savings Accounts / Health Savings Accounts	5,330	4,540	4,680	4,890	5,080	5,260	5,970	6,440	6,660	6,890	7,130	57,540
124	Deductibility of medical expenses	7,100	7,960	8,480	9,250	10,050	10,900	16,800	20,970	22,760	24,630	26,610	158,410
125	Exclusion of interest on hospital construction bonds	2,730	3,250	3,540	3,470	3,480	3,540	3,740	3,920	4,010	4,260	4,250	37,460
126	Refundable Premium Assistance Tax Credit [11]	7,960	6,220	6,180	6,380	6,670	6,590	7,520	7,710	8,060	8,390	8,800	72,520
127	Credit for employee health insurance expenses of small business [12]	40	40	30	10	10	0	0	0	0	0	0	90
128	Deductibility of charitable contributions (health)	8,230	8,820	9,350	9,870	10,400	10,910	12,390	14,870	15,560	16,260	16,990	125,420
129	Tax credit for orphan drug research	1,720	2,080	2,500	3,010	3,620	4,380	5,270	6,360	7,660	9,240	11,140	55,260
130	Special Blue Cross/Blue Shield tax benefits	140	190	250	280	300	320	340	360	380	410	440	3,270
131	Tax credit for health insurance purchased by certain displaced and retired individuals [13]	0	0	0	0	0	0	0	0	0	0	0	0
132	Distributions from retirement plans for premiums for health and long-term care insurance	430	450	460	470	490	500	590	630	650	660	670	5,570
133	Credit for family and sick leave taken by self-employed individuals [14]	500	590	90	0	0	0	0	0	0	0	0	680
Income security:													
134	Child credit [15]	70,170	73,320	74,420	76,760	77,170	77,690	55,090	21,160	20,960	20,780	20,570	517,920
135	Exclusion of railroad retirement (Social Security equivalent) benefits	310	290	270	250	240	220	220	210	180	160	140	2,180
136	Exclusion of workers' compensation benefits	9,160	9,200	9,250	9,290	9,330	9,370	9,420	9,460	9,500	9,550	9,590	93,960
137	Exclusion of public assistance benefits (normal tax method)	580	600	620	640	670	680	690	710	720	720	710	6,760
138	Exclusion of special benefits for disabled coal miners	20	30	20	20	20	20	20	20	10	10	10	180
139	Exclusion of military disability pensions	160	160	170	170	170	180	200	210	220	220	220	1,920
	Net exclusion of pension contributions and earnings:												

Table 10–1.   ESTIMATES OF TOTAL INCOME TAX EXPENDITURES FOR FISCAL YEARS 2020–2030—Continued

(In millions of dollars)

		Total from corporations and individuals											
		2020	2021	2022	2023	2024	2025	2026	2027	2028	2029	2030	2021–2030
140	Defined benefit employer plans	65,920	67,960	70,030	71,000	73,290	74,470	82,290	82,660	83,330	80,490	77,360	762,880
141	Defined contribution employer plans	80,690	87,610	93,380	98,720	101,970	106,200	126,010	130,550	135,700	141,480	147,230	1,168,850
142	Individual Retirement Accounts	16,510	17,360	17,880	18,940	20,000	20,660	24,770	26,070	27,510	28,820	30,330	232,340
143	Low and moderate income savers credit	1,220	1,220	1,260	1,300	1,270	1,270	1,440	1,410	1,400	1,400	1,390	13,360
144	Self-Employed plans	25,680	28,260	30,120	31,840	32,890	34,260	40,650	42,110	43,770	45,640	47,490	377,030
	Exclusion of other employee benefits:												
145	Premiums on group term life insurance	2,160	2,990	3,160	3,300	3,420	3,530	4,030	4,290	4,430	4,570	4,720	38,440
146	Premiums on accident and disability insurance	330	340	340	340	350	350	350	350	350	350	350	3,470
147	Income of trusts to finance supplementary unemployment benefits	20	10	20	20	30	30	40	50	50	60	60	370
148	Income of trusts to finance voluntary employee benefits associations	1,090	1,070	1,120	1,170	1,230	1,300	1,440	1,510	1,590	1,680	1,760	13,870
149	Special ESOP rules	210	210	220	220	220	230	230	240	240	260	260	2,330
150	Additional deduction for the blind	30	40	40	40	40	40	40	50	50	50	50	440
151	Additional deduction for the elderly	5,680	5,810	5,950	8,390	6,630	7,150	6,060	6,540	6,960	7,320	7,830	68,640
152	Deductibility of casualty losses	0	0	0	0	0	0	623	959	993	1,019	1,048	4,641
153	Earned income tax credit [16]	2,660	700	700	800	850	900	940	2,410	2,530	2,670	2,800	15,300
154	Recovery rebate credits [17]	0	9,110	1,012	0	0	0	0	0	0	0	0	10,122
Social Security:													
	Exclusion of social security benefits:												
155	Social Security benefits for retired and disabled workers and spouses, dependents and survivors	27,050	27,180	27,970	30,300	31,180	31,520	35,890	41,750	43,880	46,290	48,940	364,900
156	Credit for certain employer contributions to social security	720	990	1,360	1,490	1,590	1,690	1,790	1,890	1,990	2,090	2,190	17,070
Veterans benefits and services:													
157	Exclusion of veterans death benefits and disability compensation	8,230	9,210	9,520	9,870	10,220	10,590	11,450	12,990	13,480	13,980	14,510	115,820
158	Exclusion of veterans pensions	210	220	220	220	220	220	230	250	250	260	260	2,350
159	Exclusion of GI bill benefits	1,460	1,580	1,590	1,650	1,720	1,780	1,930	2,200	2,290	2,380	2,480	19,600
160	Exclusion of interest on veterans housing bonds	70	80	80	90	80	90	90	100	100	100	110	920
General purpose fiscal assistance:													
161	Exclusion of interest on public purpose State and local bonds	24,310	28,980	31,500	30,920	31,020	31,500	33,290	34,950	35,730	37,890	37,830	333,610
162	Build America Bonds [18]	0	0	0	0	0	0	0	0	0	0	0	0
163	Deductibility of nonbusiness State and local taxes other than on owner-occupied homes [19]	7,060	6,890	6,990	7,140	7,330	7,520	76,740	107,610	108,740	113,500	118,550	561,020
Interest:													
164	Deferral of interest on U.S. savings bonds	910	840	830	820	810	800	800	790	780	770	760	8,000
Addendum: Aid to State and local governments:													
	Deductibility of:												
	Property taxes on owner-occupied homes	6,450	6,370	6,450	6,620	6,860	7,130	35,890	52,340	55,090	57,590	60,260	294,600
	Nonbusiness State and local taxes other than on owner-occupied homes	7,060	6,890	6,990	7,140	7,330	7,520	76,740	107,610	108,740	113,500	118,550	561,020
	Exclusion of interest on State and local bonds for:												
	Public purposes	24,310	28,980	31,500	30,920	31,020	31,500	33,290	34,950	35,730	37,890	37,830	333,610
	Energy facilities	0	10	10	10	10	10	10	10	10	10	10	100
	Water, sewage, and hazardous waste disposal facilities	270	330	350	350	350	360	370	390	400	430	420	3,750
	Small-issues	80	90	90	90	90	90	100	110	110	120	120	1,010
	Owner-occupied mortgage subsidies	710	850	920	900	910	920	980	1,020	1,050	1,110	1,100	9,760

Table 10–1. ESTIMATES OF TOTAL INCOME TAX EXPENDITURES FOR FISCAL YEARS 2020–2030—Continued

(In millions of dollars)

	Total from corporations and individuals											
	2020	2021	2022	2023	2024	2025	2026	2027	2028	2029	2030	2021–2030
Rental housing	1,200	1,430	1,550	1,530	1,530	1,560	1,640	1,720	1,770	1,870	1,870	16,470
Airports, docks, and similar facilities	720	850	930	910	920	930	990	1,030	1,060	1,120	1,120	9,860
Student loans	140	160	180	180	180	180	190	200	200	220	220	1,910
Private nonprofit educational facilities	1,910	2,280	2,480	2,430	2,440	2,480	2,610	2,740	2,810	2,970	2,970	26,210
Hospital construction	2,730	3,250	3,540	3,470	3,480	3,540	3,740	3,920	4,010	4,260	4,250	37,460
Veterans' housing	70	80	80	90	80	90	90	100	100	100	110	920

[1] Firms can take an energy grant in lieu of the energy production credit or the energy investment credit for facilities whose construction began in 2009, 2010, or 2011. The effect of the grant on outlays (in millions of dollars) is as follows: $0 in 2019 and thereafter.

[2] The alternative fuel mixture credit results in a reduction in excise tax receipts (in millions of dollars) as follows: 2020 $550; 2021 $1,020; 2022 $330 and $0 thereafter.

[3] In addition, the biodiesel producer tax credit results in a reduction in excise tax receipts (in millions of dollars) as follows: 2020 $5,090; 2021 $3,000; 2022 $2,720; 2023 $1,340 and $0 thereafter.

[4] In addition, the credit for holding clean renewable energy bonds has outlay effects of (in millions of dollars): 2020 $30; 2021 $40; 2022 $40; 2023 $40; 2024 $40; 2025 $40; 2026, $40; 2027 $40; 2028 $40; 2029 $40, and 2030 $40.

[5] In addition, the qualified energy conservation bonds have outlay effects of (in millions of dollars): 2020 $30; 2021 $40; 2022 $40; 2023 $40; 2024 $40; 2025 $40; 2026, $40; 2027 $40; 2028 $40; 2029 $40, and 2030 $40.

[6] In addition, recovery zone bonds have outlay effects (in millions of dollars) as follows: 2020 $90; 2021 $120; 2022 $120; 2023 $120; 2024 $110; 2025 $110; 2026, $110; 2027 $110; 2028 $110; 2029 $110, and 2030 $100.

[7] In addition, the tax credits for postsecondary education expenses have outlay effects of (in millions of dollars): 2020 $2810; 2021 $2950; 2022 $2980; 2023 $3020; 2024 $3010; 2025 $2980; 2026 $2950; 2027 $2920; 2028 $2880; 2029 $2850; and 2030 $2810

[8] In addition, the credit for holders of zone academy bonds has outlay effects of (in millions of dollars): 2020 $30; 2021 $40; 2022 $40; 2023 $40; 2024 $40; 2025 $40; 2026 $40; 2027 $40; 2028 $40; 2029 $40, and 2030 $40.

[9] In addition, the provision for school construction bonds has outlay effects of (in millions of dollars): 2020 $460; 2021 $570; 2022 $560; 2023 $560; 2024 $560; 2025 $550; 2026 $550; 2027 $550; 2028 $540; 2029 $540, and 2030 $540.

[10] In addition, the employer contributions for health have effects on payroll tax receipts (in millions of dollars) as follows: 2020 $120,580; 2021 $131,100; 2022 $140,480; 2023 $147,030; 2024 $153,530; 2025 $161,600; 2026 $170,340; 2027 $179,460; 2028 $189,000; 2029 $198,890; and 2030 $209,140.

[11] In addition, the premium assistance credit provision has outlay effects of (in millions of dollars) as follows: 2020 $44,550; 2021 $43,440; 2022 $35,290; 2023 $33,700; 2024 $34,770; 2025 $35,610; 2026 $36,290; 2027 $37,330; 2028 $39,380; 2029 $41,790; and 2030 $43,890.

[12] In addition, the small business credit provision has outlay effects (in millions of dollars) as follows: The outlays round down to zero.

[13] In addition, the effect of the health coverage tax credit on receipts has outlay effects of (in millions of dollars) $10 in 2020 and $0 thereafter.

[14] In addition, the credit for sick and family leave taken by self-employed individuals has outlay effects of (in millions of dollars):

[15] In addition, the effect of the child tax credit on receipts has outlay effects of (in millions of dollars): The child tax credit line also includes the credit for other dependents (in millions of dollars):

[16] In addition, the earned income tax credit on receipts has outlay effects of (in millions of dollars):

[17] In addition, the recovery rebate credits have outlay effects of (in millions of dollars):

[18] In addition, the Build America Bonds have outlay effects of (in millions of dollars):

[19] Because of interactions with the $10,000 cap on state and local tax deductions for the years 2018 through 2025, these estimates understate the combined effects of repealing deductions for both property taxes on owner occupied housing and other non-business taxes. The estimate of repealing both is (in millions of dollars):

Table 10–2A.   ESTIMATES OF TOTAL CORPORATE INCOME TAX EXPENDITURES FOR FISCAL YEARS 2020–2030

(In millions of dollars)

	Total from corporations											
	2020	2021	2022	2023	2024	2025	2026	2027	2028	2029	2030	2021–2030
National Defense												
1 Exclusion of benefits and allowances to armed forces personnel	0	0	0	0	0	0	0	0	0	0	0	0
International affairs:												
2 Exclusion of income earned abroad by U.S. citizens	0	0	0	0	0	0	0	0	0	0	0	0
3 Exclusion of certain allowances for Federal employees abroad	0	0	0	0	0	0	0	0	0	0	0	0
4 Reduced tax rate on active income of controlled foreign corporations (normal tax method)	27,390	29,580	32,020	33,760	35,500	37,300	29,190	30,380	30,690	31,160	31,830	321,410
5 Deduction for foreign-derived intangible income dervied from trade or business within the United States	9,450	10,200	11,050	11,650	12,250	12,870	7,620	7,930	8,010	8,140	8,310	98,030
6 Interest Charge Domestic International Sales Corporations (IC-DISCs)	0	0	0	0	0	0	0	0	0	0	0	0
General science, space, and technology:												
7 Expensing of research and experimentation expenditures (normal tax method)	4,240	3,490	−15,250	−23,930	−17,150	−10,250	−3,000	0	0	0	0	−66,090
8 Credit for increasing research activities	15,150	16,370	17,820	19,120	20,340	21,540	22,750	23,960	25,180	26,430	27,710	221,220
Energy:												
9 Expensing of exploration and development costs, fuels	10	−10	20	50	80	90	90	90	90	90	90	680
10 Excess of percentage over cost depletion, fuels ...	370	360	420	460	480	500	530	560	600	630	670	5,210
11 Exception from passive loss limitation for working interests in oil and gas properties	0	0	0	0	0	0	0	0	0	0	0	0
12 Capital gains treatment of royalties on coal	0	0	0	0	0	0	0	0	0	0	0	0
13 Exclusion of interest on energy facility bonds	0	0	0	0	0	0	0	0	0	0	0	0
14 Enhanced oil recovery credit	450	480	530	630	830	1,030	1,130	1,190	1,240	1,290	1,330	9,680
15 Energy production credit [1]	4,520	4,750	4,660	4,880	5,190	5,410	5,170	5,010	4,730	4,380	3,850	48,030
16 Marginal wells credit	130	210	260	240	180	120	80	30	20	0	0	1,140
17 Energy investment credit [1]	5,560	5,800	6,470	6,220	6,770	6,910	6,390	6,310	5,070	4,100	2,940	56,980
18 Alcohol fuel credits [2]	0	0	0	0	0	0	0	0	0	0	0	0
19 Bio-Diesel and small agri-biodiesel producer tax credits [3]	10	20	20	10	0	0	0	0	0	0	0	50
20 Tax credits for clean-fuel burning vehicles and refueling property	170	140	150	130	110	100	90	70	60	60	70	980
21 Exclusion of utility conservation subsidies	0	0	0	0	0	0	0	0	0	0	0	0
22 Credit for holding clean renewable energy bonds [4] ...	20	20	20	20	20	20	20	20	20	20	20	200
23 Credit for investment in clean coal facilities	30	30	20	10	30	30	30	30	40	30	30	280
24 Amortize all geological and geophysical expenditures over 2 years	30	30	30	40	40	40	40	40	40	30	30	360
25 Allowance of deduction for certain energy efficient commercial building property	10	40	20	20	20	20	20	20	20	20	20	220
26 Credit for construction of new energy efficient homes	210	230	160	160	150	160	170	110	40	10	0	1,190
27 Credit for energy efficiency improvements to existing homes	0	0	0	0	0	0	0	0	0	0	0	0
28 Credit for residential energy efficient property	0	0	0	0	0	0	0	0	0	0	0	0
29 Qualified energy conservation bonds [5]	10	10	10	10	10	10	10	10	10	10	10	100
30 Advanced Energy Property Credit	10	10	10	10	10	10	10	10	10	10	10	100
31 Advanced nuclear power production credit	0	0	80	180	220	240	270	280	280	270	180	2,000
32 Reduced tax rate for nuclear decommissioning funds	100	110	110	120	120	130	130	140	150	150	160	1,320
Natural resources and environment:												
33 Expensing of exploration and development costs, nonfuel minerals	0	0	0	0	10	10	10	10	10	10	10	70
34 Excess of percentage over cost depletion, nonfuel minerals	70	60	70	80	80	90	90	100	110	110	120	910

Table 10–2A. ESTIMATES OF TOTAL CORPORATE INCOME TAX EXPENDITURES FOR FISCAL YEARS 2020–2030—Continued

(In millions of dollars)

		Total from corporations											
		2020	2021	2022	2023	2024	2025	2026	2027	2028	2029	2030	2021–2030
35	Exclusion of interest on bonds for water, sewage, and hazardous waste facilities	30	50	50	40	40	50	50	60	70	80	70	560
36	Capital gains treatment of certain timber income	0	0	0	0	0	0	0	0	0	0	0	0
37	Expensing of multiperiod timber growing costs ...	10	10	10	10	10	10	10	10	10	10	10	100
38	Tax incentives for preservation of historic structures	520	480	470	540	660	740	800	820	840	850	870	7,070
39	Carbon oxide sequestration credit	14	123	277	449	646	873	1,111	1,319	1,511	1,694	1,905	9,908
40	Deduction for endangered species recovery expenditures	10	10	10	10	10	10	10	20	20	20	20	140
Agriculture:													
41	Expensing of certain capital outlays	0	0	10	10	10	10	10	10	10	10	10	90
42	Expensing of certain multiperiod production costs	20	10	10	10	10	10	10	20	20	20	20	140
43	Treatment of loans forgiven for solvent farmers ...	0	0	0	0	0	0	0	0	0	0	0	0
44	Capital gains treatment of certain agriculture income	0	0	0	0	0	0	0	0	0	0	0	0
45	Income averaging for farmers	0	0	0	0	0	0	0	0	0	0	0	0
46	Deferral of gain on sale of farm refiners	0	0	0	0	0	0	0	0	0	0	0	0
47	Expensing of reforestation expenditures	10	10	10	10	10	10	10	10	10	10	10	100
Commerce and housing:													
	Financial institutions and insurance:												
48	Exemption of credit union income	2,135	2,076	2,118	2,173	2,353	2,406	2,446	2,645	2,737	2,785	2,825	24,564
49	Exclusion of life insurance death benefits	1,180	1,190	1,240	1,280	1,310	1,330	1,360	1,380	1,410	1,430	1,460	13,390
50	Exemption or special alternative tax for small property and casualty insurance companies	930	1,000	1,080	1,110	1,140	1,160	1,210	1,240	1,270	1,300	1,350	11,860
51	Tax exemption of insurance income earned by tax-exempt organizations	320	320	340	350	350	360	360	370	380	380	390	3,600
52	Exclusion of interest spread of financial institutions	0	0	0	0	0	0	0	0	0	0	0	0
	Housing:												
53	Exclusion of interest on owner-occupied mortgage subsidy bonds	80	120	130	100	110	120	140	160	180	200	190	1,450
54	Exclusion of interest on rental housing bonds .	140	210	220	180	180	210	230	270	300	340	330	2,470
55	Deductibility of mortgage interest on owner-occupied homes	0	0	0	0	0	0	0	0	0	0	0	0
56	Deductibility of State and local property tax on owner-occupied homes	0	0	0	0	0	0	0	0	0	0	0	0
57	Deferral of income from installment sales	0	0	0	0	0	0	0	0	0	0	0	0
58	Capital gains exclusion on home sales	0	0	0	0	0	0	0	0	0	0	0	0
59	Exclusion of net imputed rental income	0	0	0	0	0	0	0	0	0	0	0	0
60	Exception from passive loss rules for $25,000 of rental loss	0	0	0	0	0	0	0	0	0	0	0	0
61	Credit for low-income housing investments	6,010	8,430	10,720	10,020	9,870	9,840	9,910	10,170	10,430	10,710	10,990	101,090
62	Accelerated depreciation on rental housing (normal tax method)	60	60	60	60	70	80	90	80	90	90	100	780
	Commerce:												
63	Discharge of business indebtedness	0	0	0	0	0	0	0	0	0	0	0	0
64	Exceptions from imputed interest rules	0	0	0	0	0	0	0	0	0	0	0	0
65	Treatment of qualified dividends	0	0	0	0	0	0	0	0	0	0	0	0
66	Capital gains (except agriculture, timber, iron ore, and coal)	0	0	0	0	0	0	0	0	0	0	0	0
67	Capital gains exclusion of small corporation stock	0	0	0	0	0	0	0	0	0	0	0	0
68	Step-up basis of capital gains at death	0	0	0	0	0	0	0	0	0	0	0	0
69	Carryover basis of capital gains on gifts	0	0	0	0	0	0	0	0	0	0	0	0
70	Ordinary income treatment of loss from small business corporation stock sale	0	0	0	0	0	0	0	0	0	0	0	0
71	Deferral of gains from like-kind exchanges	1,060	1,120	1,170	1,230	1,290	1,350	1,420	1,480	1,560	1,640	1,720	13,980

Table 10–2A.   ESTIMATES OF TOTAL CORPORATE INCOME TAX EXPENDITURES FOR FISCAL YEARS 2020–2030—Continued

(In millions of dollars)

		Total from corporations										
		2020	2021	2022	2023	2024	2025	2026	2027	2028	2029	2030	2021–2030
72	Depreciation of buildings other than rental housing (normal tax method)	1,210	720	590	500	440	390	360	310	320	380	440	4,450
73	Accelerated depreciation of machinery and equipment (normal tax method)	15,970	13,630	9,520	4,610	–2,030	–9,120	–14,500	–18,770	–14,760	–8,380	–4,440	–44,240
74	Expensing of certain small investments (normal tax method)	370	–20	20	110	360	620	800	940	810	600	480	4,720
75	Exclusion of interest on small issue bonds	10	10	10	10	10	10	10	20	20	20	20	140
76	Special rules for certain film and TV production	–110	–30	0	60	110	150	–230	–310	–150	–70	–30	–500
77	Allow 20-percent deduction to certain pass-through income	0	0	0	0	0	0	0	0	0	0	0	0
Transportation:													
78	Tonnage tax	140	140	140	140	140	140	140	140	140	140	140	1,400
79	Deferral of tax on shipping companies	10	10	10	10	10	10	10	10	10	10	10	100
80	Exclusion of reimbursed employee parking expenses	–1,208	–1,255	–1,328	–1,368	–1,419	–1,486	–1,553	–1,621	–1,697	–1,778	–1,814	–15,319
81	Exclusion for employer-provided transit passes	–407	–435	–472	–498	–529	–569	–608	–653	–699	–750	–765	–5,978
82	Tax credit for certain expenditures for maintaining railroad tracks	90	110	110	80	50	40	30	20	20	10	10	480
83	Exclusion of interest on bonds for Highway Projects and rail-truck transfer facilities	40	40	40	30	30	30	30	30	20	20	20	290
Community and regional development:													
84	Investment credit for rehabilitation of structures (other than historic)	10	0	0	0	0	0	0	0	0	0	0	0
85	Exclusion of interest for airport, dock, and similar bonds	90	120	130	100	110	120	140	160	180	200	200	1,460
86	Exemption of certain mutuals' and cooperatives' income	90	90	100	100	100	100	100	110	110	110	110	1,030
87	Empowerment zones	90	80	70	70	80	80	60	40	30	20	20	550
88	New markets tax credit	1,250	1,260	1,290	1,250	1,140	1,080	1,100	1,070	940	760	540	10,430
89	Credit to holders of Gulf Tax Credit Bonds	10	20	20	10	10	10	10	10	10	10	10	120
90	Recovery Zone Bonds [6]	10	10	10	10	10	10	10	10	10	10	10	100
91	Tribal Economic Development Bonds	0	0	0	0	0	0	0	0	0	0	0	0
92	Opportunity Zones	1,260	1,150	990	780	760	760	–3,560	–2,470	220	300	350	–720
93	Employee retention credit	190	130	110	70	50	50	40	30	30	20	20	550
Education, training, employment, and social services:													
	Education:												
94	Exclusion of scholarship and fellowship income (normal tax method)	0	0	0	0	0	0	0	0	0	0	0	0
95	Tax credits and deductions for postsecondary education expenses [7]	0	0	0	0	0	0	0	0	0	0	0	0
96	Deductibility of student-loan interest	0	0	0	0	0	0	0	0	0	0	0	0
97	Qualified tuition programs (includes Education IRA)	0	0	0	0	0	0	0	0	0	0	0	0
98	Exclusion of interest on student-loan bonds	20	20	30	20	20	20	30	30	30	40	40	280
99	Exclusion of interest on bonds for private nonprofit educational facilities	230	330	360	280	290	330	370	430	470	540	520	3,920
100	Credit for holders of zone academy bonds [8]	150	130	110	90	80	60	50	50	40	40	40	690
101	Exclusion of interest on savings bonds redeemed to finance educational expenses	0	0	0	0	0	0	0	0	0	0	0	0
102	Parental personal exemption for students age 19 or over	0	0	0	0	0	0	0	0	0	0	0	0
103	Deductibility of charitable contributions (education)	610	630	670	700	740	770	810	840	870	900	940	7,870
104	Exclusion of employer-provided educational assistance	0	0	0	0	0	0	0	0	0	0	0	0
105	Special deduction for teacher expenses	0	0	0	0	0	0	0	0	0	0	0	0
106	Discharge of student loan indebtedness	0	0	0	0	0	0	0	0	0	0	0	0
107	Qualified school construction bonds [9]	140	130	130	120	120	110	100	100	90	80	80	1,060

Table 10–2A. ESTIMATES OF TOTAL CORPORATE INCOME TAX EXPENDITURES FOR FISCAL YEARS 2020–2030—Continued

(In millions of dollars)

		Total from corporations											
		2020	2021	2022	2023	2024	2025	2026	2027	2028	2029	2030	2021–2030
	Training, employment, and social services:												
108	Work opportunity tax credit	1,240	1,280	1,340	1,380	1,430	1,470	920	410	290	220	160	8,900
109	Employer provided child care exclusion	0	0	0	0	0	0	0	0	0	0	0	0
110	Employer-provided child care credit	20	20	20	20	20	20	20	20	20	30	30	220
111	Assistance for adopted foster children	0	0	0	0	0	0	0	0	0	0	0	0
112	Adoption credit and exclusion	0	0	0	0	0	0	0	0	0	0	0	0
113	Exclusion of employee meals and lodging (other than military)	−490	−210	−140	−560	−840	−870	−910	−940	−980	−1,020	−1,060	−7,530
114	Credit for child and dependent care expenses	0	0	0	0	0	0	0	0	0	0	0	0
115	Credit for disabled access expenditures	0	0	0	0	0	0	0	0	0	0	0	0
116	Deductibility of charitable contributions, other than education and health	1,230	1,270	1,320	1,370	1,420	1,480	1,550	1,610	1,670	1,730	1,800	15,220
117	Exclusion of certain foster care payments	0	0	0	0	0	0	0	0	0	0	0	0
118	Exclusion of parsonage allowances	0	0	0	0	0	0	0	0	0	0	0	0
119	Indian employment credit	40	40	30	10	10	10	10	10	10	0	0	130
120	Credit for employer differential wage payments	0	0	0	0	0	0	10	10	10	10	10	50
Health:													
121	Exclusion of employer contributions for medical insurance premiums and medical care [10]	0	0	0	0	0	0	0	0	0	0	0	0
122	Self-employed medical insurance premiums	0	0	0	0	0	0	0	0	0	0	0	0
123	Medical Savings Accounts / Health Savings Accounts	0	0	0	0	0	0	0	0	0	0	0	0
124	Deductibility of medical expenses	0	0	0	0	0	0	0	0	0	0	0	0
125	Exclusion of interest on hospital construction bonds	330	470	510	400	420	470	530	620	670	780	750	5,620
126	Refundable Premium Assistance Tax Credit [11]	0	0	0	0	0	0	0	0	0	0	0	0
127	Credit for employee health insurance expenses of small business [12]	10	10	10	0	0	0	0	0	0	0	0	20
128	Deductibility of charitable contributions (health)	3,880	4,110	4,330	4,540	4,760	4,980	5,200	5,420	5,660	5,890	6,130	51,020
129	Tax credit for orphan drug research	1,710	2,070	2,490	3,000	3,610	4,360	5,250	6,340	7,640	9,220	11,120	55,100
130	Special Blue Cross/Blue Shield tax benefits	140	190	250	280	300	320	340	360	380	410	440	3,270
131	Tax credit for health insurance purchased by certain displaced and retired individuals [13]	0	0	0	0	0	0	0	0	0	0	0	0
132	Distributions from retirement plans for premiums for health and long-term care insurance	0	0	0	0	0	0	0	0	0	0	0	0
133	Credit for family and sick leave taken by self-employed individuals [14]	0	0	0	0	0	0	0	0	0	0	0	0
Income security:													
134	Child credit [14]	0	0	0	0	0	0	0	0	0	0	0	0
135	Exclusion of railroad retirement (Social Security equivalent) benefits	0	0	0	0	0	0	0	0	0	0	0	0
136	Exclusion of workers' compensation benefits	0	0	0	0	0	0	0	0	0	0	0	0
137	Exclusion of public assistance benefits (normal tax method)	0	0	0	0	0	0	0	0	0	0	0	0
138	Exclusion of special benefits for disabled coal miners	0	0	0	0	0	0	0	0	0	0	0	0
139	Exclusion of military disability pensions	0	0	0	0	0	0	0	0	0	0	0	0
	Net exclusion of pension contributions and earnings:												
140	Defined benefit employer plans	0	0	0	0	0	0	0	0	0	0	0	0
141	Defined contribution employer plans	0	0	0	0	0	0	0	0	0	0	0	0
142	Individual Retirement Accounts	0	0	0	0	0	0	0	0	0	0	0	0
143	Low and moderate income savers credit	0	0	0	0	0	0	0	0	0	0	0	0
144	Self-Employed plans	0	0	0	0	0	0	0	0	0	0	0	0
	Exclusion of other employee benefits:												
145	Premiums on group term life insurance	0	0	0	0	0	0	0	0	0	0	0	0
146	Premiums on accident and disability insurance	0	0	0	0	0	0	0	0	0	0	0	0

Table 10–2A. ESTIMATES OF TOTAL CORPORATE INCOME TAX EXPENDITURES FOR FISCAL YEARS 2020–2030—Continued

(In millions of dollars)

	Total from corporations											
	2020	2021	2022	2023	2024	2025	2026	2027	2028	2029	2030	2021–2030
147 Income of trusts to finance supplementary unemployment benefits	0	0	0	0	0	0	0	0	0	0	0	0
148 Income of trusts to finance voluntary employee benefits associations	1,090	1,070	1,120	1,170	1,230	1,300	1,440	1,510	1,590	1,680	1,760	13,870
149 Special ESOP rules	180	180	190	190	190	200	200	210	210	220	220	2,010
150 Additional deduction for the blind	0	0	0	0	0	0	0	0	0	0	0	0
151 Additional deduction for the elderly	0	0	0	0	0	0	0	0	0	0	0	0
152 Deductibility of casualty losses	0	0	0	0	0	0	0	0	0	0	0	0
153 Earned income tax credit [15]	0	0	0	0	0	0	0	0	0	0	0	0
154 Recovery rebate credits [16]	0	0	0	0	0	0	0	0	0	0	0	0
Social Security:												
Exclusion of social security benefits:												
155 Social Security benefits for retired and disabled workers and spouses, dependents and survivors	0	0	0	0	0	0	0	0	0	0	0	0
156 Credit for certain employer contributions to social security	150	210	290	320	340	360	380	400	420	440	460	3,620
Veterans benefits and services:												
157 Exclusion of veterans death benefits and disability compensation	0	0	0	0	0	0	0	0	0	0	0	0
158 Exclusion of veterans pensions	0	0	0	0	0	0	0	0	0	0	0	0
159 Exclusion of GI bill benefits	0	0	0	0	0	0	0	0	0	0	0	0
160 Exclusion of interest on veterans housing bonds	10	10	10	10	10	10	10	20	20	20	20	140
General purpose fiscal assistance:												
161 Exclusion of interest on public purpose State and local bonds	2,900	4,210	4,520	3,540	3,710	4,160	4,720	5,520	5,990	6,910	6,650	49,930
162 Build America Bonds [16]	0	0	0	0	0	0	0	0	0	0	0	0
163 Deductibility of nonbusiness State and local taxes other than on owner-occupied homes	0	0	0	0	0	0	0	0	0	0	0	0
Interest:												
164 Deferral of interest on U.S. savings bonds	0	0	0	0	0	0	0	0	0	0	0	0
Addendum: Aid to State and local governments:												
Deductibility of:												
Property taxes on owner-occupied homes	0	0	0	0	0	0	0	0	0	0	0	0
Nonbusiness State and local taxes other than on owner-occupied homes	0	0	0	0	0	0	0	0	0	0	0	0
Exclusion of interest on State and local bonds for:												
Public purposes	2,900	4,210	4,520	3,540	3,710	4,160	4,720	5,520	5,990	6,910	6,650	49,930
Energy facilities	0	0	0	0	0	0	0	0	0	0	0	0
Water, sewage, and hazardous waste disposal facilities	30	50	50	40	40	50	50	60	70	80	70	560
Small-issues	10	10	10	10	10	10	10	20	20	20	20	140
Owner-occupied mortgage subsidies	80	120	130	100	110	120	140	160	180	200	190	1,450
Rental housing	140	210	220	180	180	210	230	270	300	340	330	2,470
Airports, docks, and similar facilities	90	120	130	100	110	120	140	160	180	200	200	1,460
Student loans	20	20	30	20	20	20	30	30	30	40	40	280
Private nonprofit educational facilities	230	330	360	280	290	330	370	430	470	540	520	3,920
Hospital construction	330	470	510	400	420	470	530	620	670	780	750	5,620
Veterans' housing	10	10	10	10	10	10	10	20	20	20	20	140

See Table 10–1 footnotes for specific table information

Table 10–2B.   ESTIMATES OF TOTAL INDIVIDUAL INCOME TAX EXPENDITURES FOR FISCAL YEARS 2020–2030

(In millions of dollars)

	Total from individuals											
	2020	2021	2022	2023	2024	2025	2026	2027	2028	2029	2030	2021–2030
National Defense												
1 Exclusion of benefits and allowances to armed forces personnel	12,910	13,940	14,460	15,010	13,770	13,890	14,380	14,990	15,660	16,390	17,160	149,650
International affairs:												
2 Exclusion of income earned abroad by U.S. citizens	6,160	6,470	6,790	7,130	7,490	7,860	8,260	8,670	9,100	9,560	10,040	81,370
3 Exclusion of certain allowances for Federal employees abroad	270	280	290	310	320	340	360	370	390	410	430	3,500
4 Reduced tax rate on active income of controlled foreign corporations (normal tax method)	180	200	210	230	240	250	200	200	210	210	210	2,150
5 Deduction for foreign-derived intangible income dervied from trade or business within the United States	0	0	0	0	0	0	0	0	0	0	0	0
6 Interest Charge Domestic International Sales Corporations (IC-DISCs)	890	1,370	1,440	1,510	1,590	1,690	2,010	2,280	2,410	2,520	2,600	19,420
General science, space, and technology:												
7 Expensing of research and experimentation expenditures (normal tax method)	1,180	490	−1,850	−5,210	−5,050	−3,350	−1,180	0	0	0	0	−16,150
8 Credit for increasing research activities	1,790	1,930	2,090	2,240	2,380	2,520	2,670	2,830	2,990	3,170	3,360	26,180
Energy:												
9 Expensing of exploration and development costs, fuels	30	−30	70	180	300	340	370	390	400	410	400	2,830
10 Excess of percentage over cost depletion, fuels .	220	240	300	330	350	370	420	460	490	520	540	4,020
11 Exception from passive loss limitation for working interests in oil and gas properties	20	20	10	20	20	20	20	20	20	20	20	190
12 Capital gains treatment of royalties on coal	100	70	50	50	50	50	60	60	60	70	70	590
13 Exclusion of interest on energy facility bonds	0	10	10	10	10	10	10	10	10	10	10	100
14 Enhanced oil recovery credit	20	20	30	30	50	50	60	60	70	70	70	510
15 Energy production credit [1]	500	530	520	540	580	600	570	560	530	490	430	5,350
16 Marginal wells credit	20	40	50	40	30	20	10	10	0	0	0	200
17 Energy investment credit [1]	510	530	580	560	610	630	580	570	450	350	240	5,100
18 Alcohol fuel credits [2]	0	10	0	0	0	0	0	0	0	0	0	10
19 Bio-Diesel and small agri-biodiesel producer tax credits [3]	20	20	20	10	0	0	0	0	0	0	0	50
20 Tax credits for clean-fuel burning vehicles and refueling property	400	300	330	310	270	260	240	200	180	170	160	2,420
21 Exclusion of utility conservation subsidies	60	60	50	50	50	40	40	40	30	30	30	420
22 Credit for holding clean renewable energy bonds [4]	50	50	50	50	50	50	50	50	50	50	50	500
23 Credit for investment in clean coal facilities	0	0	0	0	0	0	0	0	0	0	0	0
24 Amortize all geological and geophysical expenditures over 2 years	50	50	60	60	70	70	70	70	70	70	70	660
25 Allowance of deduction for certain energy efficient commercial building property	150	150	110	90	90	90	90	90	90	90	90	980
26 Credit for construction of new energy efficient homes	110	140	120	100	100	100	100	60	20	10	0	750
27 Credit for energy efficiency improvements to existing homes	240	240	120	0	0	0	0	0	0	0	0	360
28 Credit for residential energy efficient property	2,370	2,390	1,980	1,450	420	120	0	0	0	0	0	6,360
29 Qualified energy conservation bonds [5]	20	20	20	20	20	20	20	20	20	20	20	200
30 Advanced Energy Property Credit	0	0	0	0	0	0	0	0	0	0	0	0
31 Advanced nuclear power production credit	0	0	0	0	0	0	0	0	0	0	0	0
32 Reduced tax rate for nuclear decommissioning funds	0	0	0	0	0	0	0	0	0	0	0	0
Natural resources and environment:												
33 Expensing of exploration and development costs, nonfuel minerals	0	0	10	20	30	30	30	30	40	40	40	270
34 Excess of percentage over cost depletion, nonfuel minerals	40	40	50	60	60	70	70	80	90	90	100	710

Table 10–2B. ESTIMATES OF TOTAL INDIVIDUAL INCOME TAX EXPENDITURES FOR FISCAL YEARS 2020–2030—Continued

(In millions of dollars)

		Total from individuals										
		2020	2021	2022	2023	2024	2025	2026	2027	2028	2029	2030	2021–2030
35	Exclusion of interest on bonds for water, sewage, and hazardous waste facilities	240	280	300	310	310	310	320	330	330	350	350	3,190
36	Capital gains treatment of certain timber income	130	130	140	140	150	150	170	190	200	210	220	1,700
37	Expensing of multiperiod timber growing costs ...	40	50	50	60	60	60	70	70	80	70	70	640
38	Tax incentives for preservation of historic structures	140	130	120	130	160	190	200	210	220	220	220	1,800
39	Carbon oxide sequestration credit	0	0	0	0	0	0	0	0	0	0	0	0
40	Deduction for endangered species recovery expenditures	20	20	20	20	30	30	30	40	40	40	50	320
Agriculture:													
41	Expensing of certain capital outlays	80	120	150	150	160	170	210	230	240	250	260	1,940
42	Expensing of certain multiperiod production costs	540	360	330	350	360	380	470	520	540	560	580	4,450
43	Treatment of loans forgiven for solvent farmers ...	50	50	60	60	60	60	70	70	70	70	70	640
44	Capital gains treatment of certain agriculture income	1,330	1,340	1,370	1,410	1,470	1,540	1,720	1,900	1,990	2,090	2,190	17,020
45	Income averaging for farmers	170	180	200	200	210	220	230	230	230	230	230	2,160
46	Deferral of gain on sale of farm refiners	15	15	15	15	15	20	20	20	20	20	20	180
47	Expensing of reforestation expenditures	40	50	50	60	60	60	70	70	80	70	70	640
Commerce and housing:													
	Financial institutions and insurance:												
48	Exemption of credit union income	0	0	0	0	0	0	0	0	0	0	0	0
49	Exclusion of life insurance death benefits	10,510	10,370	10,820	11,160	11,560	12,070	12,850	13,780	14,290	14,670	15,120	126,690
50	Exemption or special alternative tax for small property and casualty insurance companies	0	0	0	0	0	0	0	0	0	0	0	0
51	Tax exemption of insurance income earned by tax-exempt organizations	0	0	0	0	0	0	0	0	0	0	0	0
52	Exclusion of interest spread of financial institutions	4,230	3,110	2,030	2,080	2,150	2,240	2,380	2,500	2,580	2,660	2,740	24,470
	Housing:												
53	Exclusion of interest on owner-occupied mortgage subsidy bonds	630	730	790	800	800	800	840	860	870	910	910	8,310
54	Exclusion of interest on rental housing bonds .	1,060	1,220	1,330	1,350	1,350	1,350	1,410	1,450	1,470	1,530	1,540	14,000
55	Deductibility of mortgage interest on owner-occupied homes	24,730	25,440	26,170	26,920	28,340	30,250	67,330	89,630	95,150	100,420	106,330	595,980
56	Deductibility of State and local property tax on owner-occupied homes	6,450	6,370	6,450	6,620	6,860	7,130	35,890	52,340	55,090	57,590	60,260	294,600
57	Deferral of income from installment sales	1,480	1,470	1,460	1,510	1,550	1,610	1,670	1,730	1,800	1,870	1,950	16,620
58	Capital gains exclusion on home sales	39,450	40,610	41,800	43,030	44,730	46,340	51,480	55,060	57,070	59,170	61,370	500,660
59	Exclusion of net imputed rental income	123,210	130,590	139,290	148,090	153,210	154,180	176,960	180,390	183,950	187,880	191,440	1,645,980
60	Exception from passive loss rules for $25,000 of rental loss	5,700	5,540	5,870	6,210	6,460	6,860	7,490	7,600	7,700	7,770	7,850	69,350
61	Credit for low-income housing investments	300	470	560	520	520	520	520	540	550	560	580	5,340
62	Accelerated depreciation on rental housing (normal tax method)	4,190	4,600	4,840	5,000	5,230	5,430	6,160	6,660	6,800	6,950	7,100	58,770
	Commerce:												
63	Discharge of business indebtedness	40	30	40	20	20	10	30	30	30	30	40	280
64	Exceptions from imputed interest rules	60	60	70	70	70	80	80	90	90	100	100	810
65	Treatment of qualified dividends	29,450	30,760	32,130	33,560	34,710	36,250	39,120	42,250	44,290	46,140	48,030	387,240
66	Capital gains (except agriculture, timber, iron ore, and coal)	99,210	99,890	101,950	105,290	109,710	114,910	128,090	141,870	148,780	156,060	163,700	1,270,250
67	Capital gains exclusion of small corporation stock	1,410	1,530	1,640	1,750	1,850	1,930	2,000	2,080	2,160	2,250	2,350	19,540
68	Step-up basis of capital gains at death	35,460	37,780	40,260	42,910	45,510	48,050	50,350	54,840	58,340	61,790	65,620	505,450
69	Carryover basis of capital gains on gifts	2,610	3,050	3,560	3,820	4,070	4,090	4,750	5,430	5,270	5,210	5,300	44,550
70	Ordinary income treatment of loss from small business corporation stock sale	70	70	70	70	80	80	80	80	90	90	90	800
71	Deferral of gains from like-kind exchanges	1,970	2,080	2,180	2,290	2,400	2,520	2,650	2,780	2,920	3,070	3,220	26,110

Table 10–2B.   ESTIMATES OF TOTAL INDIVIDUAL INCOME TAX EXPENDITURES FOR FISCAL YEARS 2020–2030—Continued

(In millions of dollars)

		Total from individuals											
		2020	2021	2022	2023	2024	2025	2026	2027	2028	2029	2030	2021–2030
72	Depreciation of buildings other than rental housing (normal tax method)	4,800	3,370	3,400	3,160	2,910	2,730	2,770	2,630	2,510	2,560	2,620	28,660
73	Accelerated depreciation of machinery and equipment (normal tax method)	16,830	17,690	16,870	7,560	−340	−5,750	−12,200	−20,060	−15,760	−7,620	−2,870	−22,480
74	Expensing of certain small investments (normal tax method)	−670	−1,610	−850	3,600	7,300	9,550	12,900	16,280	14,900	12,260	10,920	85,250
75	Exclusion of interest on small issue bonds	70	80	80	80	80	80	90	90	90	100	100	870
76	Special rules for certain film and TV production	−80	−20	0	40	90	110	−190	−260	−120	−60	−20	−430
77	Allow 20-percent deduction to certain pass-through income	29,195	50,518	52,668	54,406	56,904	60,728	25,001	0	0	0	0	300,225
Transportation:													
78	Tonnage tax	0	0	0	0	0	0	0	0	0	0	0	0
79	Deferral of tax on shipping companies	0	0	0	0	0	0	0	0	0	0	0	0
80	Exclusion of reimbursed employee parking expenses	2,894	3,014	3,189	3,374	3,482	3,616	3,791	3,964	4,145	4,343	4,554	37,472
81	Exclusion for employer-provided transit passes	748	798	869	940	992	1,056	1,138	1,218	1,308	1,403	1,506	11,228
82	Tax credit for certain expenditures for maintaining railroad tracks	50	60	60	50	30	20	10	10	10	10	0	260
83	Exclusion of interest on bonds for Highway Projects and rail-truck transfer facilities	130	120	120	110	110	100	100	90	90	90	80	1,010
Community and regional development:													
84	Investment credit for rehabilitation of structures (other than historic)	0	0	0	0	0	0	0	0	0	0	0	0
85	Exclusion of interest for airport, dock, and similar bonds	630	730	800	810	810	810	850	870	880	920	920	8,400
86	Exemption of certain mutuals' and cooperatives' income	0	0	0	0	0	0	0	0	0	0	0	0
87	Empowerment zones	70	50	20	30	30	30	30	20	10	0	0	220
88	New markets tax credit	30	30	30	30	30	30	30	30	30	20	20	280
89	Credit to holders of Gulf Tax Credit Bonds	90	90	100	90	80	80	70	70	60	60	50	750
90	Recovery Zone Bonds [6]	80	80	90	80	70	70	70	60	50	50	40	660
91	Tribal Economic Development Bonds	10	10	10	10	10	10	10	10	10	10	10	100
92	Opportunity Zones	2,510	1,530	1,860	1,180	1,240	1,160	−2,520	−6,700	320	430	550	−950
93	Employee retention credit	40	30	30	20	10	10	10	10	10	10	10	150
Education, training, employment, and social services:													
	Education:													
94	Exclusion of scholarship and fellowship income (normal tax method)	3,510	3,660	3,910	4,180	4,440	4,710	5,270	6,140	6,500	6,870	7,280	52,960
95	Tax credits and deductions for postsecondary education expenses [7]	10,730	10,070	14,140	14,450	14,450	14,310	14,180	14,350	14,130	13,930	13,710	137,720
96	Deductibility of student-loan interest	2,170	2,030	2,150	2,230	2,250	2,340	2,380	2,820	2,970	2,960	3,040	25,170
97	Qualified tuition programs (includes Education IRA)	2,420	2,670	2,950	3,280	3,680	4,160	5,130	6,160	7,320	8,830	10,840	55,020
98	Exclusion of interest on student-loan bonds	120	140	150	160	160	160	160	170	170	180	180	1,630
99	Exclusion of interest on bonds for private nonprofit educational facilities	1,680	1,950	2,120	2,150	2,150	2,150	2,240	2,310	2,340	2,430	2,450	22,290
100	Credit for holders of zone academy bonds [8]	0	0	0	0	0	0	0	0	0	0	0	0
101	Exclusion of interest on savings bonds redeemed to finance educational expenses	30	40	40	40	40	40	50	50	50	50	50	450
102	Parental personal exemption for students age 19 or over	0	0	0	0	0	0	3,570	5,270	5,180	5,090	5,000	24,106
103	Deductibility of charitable contributions (education)	3,920	4,250	4,520	4,810	5,080	5,360	6,480	8,530	8,930	9,360	9,490	66,810
104	Exclusion of employer-provided educational assistance	1,190	1,390	1,500	1,620	1,730	1,850	1,640	1,560	1,640	1,720	1,800	16,450
105	Special deduction for teacher expenses	170	170	170	170	170	170	180	210	210	210	220	1,880
106	Discharge of student loan indebtedness	80	80	90	100	110	120	150	170	190	220	240	1,470

Table 10–2B.   ESTIMATES OF TOTAL INDIVIDUAL INCOME TAX EXPENDITURES FOR FISCAL YEARS 2020–2030—Continued

(In millions of dollars)

		Total from individuals										
		2020	2021	2022	2023	2024	2025	2026	2027	2028	2029	2030	2021–2030
107	Qualified school construction bonds [9]	430	410	390	370	350	330	310	290	270	250	240	3,210
	Training, employment, and social services:											
108	Work opportunity tax credit	410	410	440	450	460	480	380	120	80	60	40	2,920
109	Employer provided child care exclusion	580	570	570	610	650	690	920	1,060	1,120	1,190	1,260	8,640
110	Employer-provided child care credit	0	0	0	0	0	0	0	0	0	0	0	0
111	Assistance for adopted foster children	620	660	700	750	800	850	900	960	1,020	1,080	1,150	8,870
112	Adoption credit and exclusion	770	790	850	870	900	920	930	940	950	960	970	9,080
113	Exclusion of employee meals and lodging (other than military)	3,780	4,530	6,570	6,660	6,450	6,770	7,850	8,470	8,730	9,050	9,420	74,500
114	Credit for child and dependent care expenses	3,190	3,080	3,300	3,440	3,530	3,580	3,700	3,880	3,970	4,060	4,160	36,700
115	Credit for disabled access expenditures	10	10	10	10	10	10	10	10	10	10	10	100
116	Deductibility of charitable contributions, other than education and health	39,090	42,340	45,090	47,850	50,630	53,330	64,530	84,890	88,900	93,100	97,500	668,160
117	Exclusion of certain foster care payments	490	510	510	520	530	540	540	540	540	560	580	5,370
118	Exclusion of parsonage allowances	900	950	1,000	1,050	1,110	1,170	1,230	1,300	1,370	1,440	1,510	12,130
119	Indian employment credit	30	30	20	20	20	20	10	10	10	10	10	160
120	Credit for employer differential wage payments	0	0	0	0	0	0	0	0	0	10	10	20
Health:													
121	Exclusion of employer contributions for medical insurance premiums and medical care [10]	191,350	197,530	211,550	224,320	235,050	248,420	290,960	322,500	340,250	358,670	377,880	2,807,130
122	Self-employed medical insurance premiums	7,430	7,740	8,150	8,720	9,290	9,930	11,330	12,450	13,140	13,820	14,550	109,120
123	Medical Savings Accounts / Health Savings Accounts	5,330	4,540	4,680	4,890	5,080	5,260	5,970	6,440	6,660	6,890	7,130	57,540
124	Deductibility of medical expenses	7,100	7,960	8,480	9,250	10,050	10,900	16,800	20,970	22,760	24,630	26,610	158,410
125	Exclusion of interest on hospital construction bonds	2,400	2,780	3,030	3,070	3,060	3,070	3,210	3,300	3,340	3,480	3,500	31,840
126	Refundable Premium Assistance Tax Credit [11]	7,960	6,220	6,180	6,380	6,670	6,590	7,520	7,710	8,060	8,390	8,800	72,520
127	Credit for employee health insurance expenses of small business [12]	30	30	20	10	10	0	0	0	0	0	0	70
128	Deductibility of charitable contributions (health)	4,350	4,710	5,020	5,330	5,640	5,930	7,190	9,450	9,900	10,370	10,860	74,400
129	Tax credit for orphan drug research	10	10	10	10	10	20	20	20	20	20	20	160
130	Special Blue Cross/Blue Shield tax benefits	0	0	0	0	0	0	0	0	0	0	0	0
131	Tax credit for health insurance purchased by certain displaced and retired individuals [13]	0	0	0	0	0	0	0	0	0	0	0	0
132	Distributions from retirement plans for premiums for health and long-term care insurance	430	450	460	470	490	500	590	630	650	660	670	5,570
133	Credit for family and sick leave taken by self-employed individuals [14]	500	590	90	0	0	0	0	0	0	0	0	680
Income security:													
134	Child credit [14]	70,170	73,320	74,420	76,760	77,170	77,690	55,090	21,160	20,960	20,780	20,570	517,920
135	Exclusion of railroad retirement (Social Security equivalent) benefits	310	290	270	250	240	220	220	210	180	160	140	2,180
136	Exclusion of workers' compensation benefits	9,160	9,200	9,250	9,290	9,330	9,370	9,420	9,460	9,500	9,550	9,590	93,960
137	Exclusion of public assistance benefits (normal tax method)	580	600	620	640	670	680	690	710	720	720	710	6,760
138	Exclusion of special benefits for disabled coal miners	20	30	20	20	20	20	20	20	10	10	10	180
139	Exclusion of military disability pensions	160	160	170	170	170	180	200	210	220	220	220	1,920
	Net exclusion of pension contributions and earnings:	0	0	0	0	0	0	0	0	0	0	0	0
140	Defined benefit employer plans	65,920	67,960	70,030	71,000	73,290	74,470	82,290	82,660	83,330	80,490	77,360	762,880
141	Defined contribution employer plans	80,690	87,610	93,380	98,720	101,970	106,200	126,010	130,550	135,700	141,480	147,230	1,168,850
142	Individual Retirement Accounts	16,510	17,360	17,880	18,940	20,000	20,660	24,770	26,070	27,510	28,820	30,330	232,340
143	Low and moderate income savers credit	1,220	1,220	1,260	1,300	1,270	1,270	1,440	1,410	1,400	1,400	1,390	13,360
144	Self-Employed plans	25,680	28,260	30,120	31,840	32,890	34,260	40,650	42,110	43,770	45,640	47,490	377,030
	Exclusion of other employee benefits:	0	0	0	0	0	0	0	0	0	0	0	0
145	Premiums on group term life insurance	2,160	2,990	3,160	3,300	3,420	3,530	4,030	4,290	4,430	4,570	4,720	38,440

Table 10–2B. ESTIMATES OF TOTAL INDIVIDUAL INCOME TAX EXPENDITURES FOR FISCAL YEARS 2020–2030—Continued

(In millions of dollars)

		Total from individuals											
		2020	2021	2022	2023	2024	2025	2026	2027	2028	2029	2030	2021–2030
146	Premiums on accident and disability insurance ...	330	340	340	340	350	350	350	350	350	350	350	3,470
147	Income of trusts to finance supplementary unemployment benefits	20	10	20	20	30	30	40	50	50	60	60	370
148	Income of trusts to finance voluntary employee benefits associations	0	0	0	0	0	0	0	0	0	0	0	0
149	Special ESOP rules	30	30	30	30	30	30	30	30	30	40	40	320
150	Additional deduction for the blind	30	40	40	40	40	40	40	50	50	50	50	440
151	Additional deduction for the elderly	5,680	5,810	5,950	8,390	6,630	7,150	6,060	6,540	6,960	7,320	7,830	68,640
152	Deductibility of casualty losses	0	0	0	0	0	0	620	960	990	1,020	1,050	4,640
153	Earned income tax credit [15]	2,660	700	700	800	850	900	940	2,410	2,530	2,670	2,800	15,300
154	Recovery rebate credits [16]	0	9,110	1,012	0	0	0	0	0	0	0	0	10,122
Social Security:													
	Exclusion of social security benefits:												
155	Social Security benefits for retired and disabled workers and spouses, dependents and survivors	27,050	27,180	27,970	30,300	31,180	31,520	35,890	41,750	43,880	46,290	48,940	364,900
156	Credit for certain employer contributions to social security	570	780	1,070	1,170	1,250	1,330	1,410	1,490	1,570	1,650	1,730	13,450
Veterans benefits and services:													
157	Exclusion of veterans death benefits and disability compensation	8,230	9,210	9,520	9,870	10,220	10,590	11,450	12,990	13,480	13,980	14,510	115,820
158	Exclusion of veterans pensions	210	220	220	220	220	220	230	250	250	260	260	2,350
159	Exclusion of GI bill benefits	1,460	1,580	1,590	1,650	1,720	1,780	1,930	2,200	2,290	2,380	2,480	19,600
160	Exclusion of interest on veterans housing bonds	60	70	70	80	70	80	80	80	80	80	90	780
General purpose fiscal assistance:													
161	Exclusion of interest on public purpose State and local bonds	21,410	24,770	26,980	27,380	27,310	27,340	28,570	29,430	29,740	30,980	31,180	283,680
162	Build America Bonds [16]	0	0	0	0	0	0	0	0	0	0	0	0
163	Deductibility of nonbusiness State and local taxes other than on owner-occupied homes [17]	7,060	6,890	6,990	7,140	7,330	7,520	76,740	107,610	108,740	113,500	118,550	561,020
Interest:													
164	Deferral of interest on U.S. savings bonds	910	840	830	820	810	800	800	790	780	770	760	8,000
Addendum: Aid to State and local governments:													
	Deductibility of:												
	Property taxes on owner-occupied homes	6,450	6,370	6,450	6,620	6,860	7,130	35,890	52,340	55,090	57,590	60,260	294,600
	Nonbusiness State and local taxes other than on owner-occupied homes	7,060	6,890	6,990	7,140	7,330	7,520	76,740	107,610	108,740	113,500	118,550	561,020
	Exclusion of interest on State and local bonds for:												
	Public purposes	21,410	24,770	26,980	27,380	27,310	27,340	28,570	29,430	29,740	30,980	31,180	283,680
	Energy facilities	0	10	10	10	10	10	10	10	10	10	10	100
	Water, sewage, and hazardous waste disposal facilities	240	280	300	310	310	310	320	330	330	350	350	3,190
	Small-issues	70	80	80	80	80	80	90	90	90	100	100	870
	Owner-occupied mortgage subsidies	630	730	790	800	800	800	840	860	870	910	910	8,310
	Rental housing	1,060	1,220	1,330	1,350	1,350	1,350	1,410	1,450	1,470	1,530	1,540	14,000
	Airports, docks, and similar facilities	630	730	800	810	810	810	850	870	880	920	920	8,400
	Student loans	120	140	150	160	160	160	160	170	170	180	180	1,630
	Private nonprofit educational facilities	1,680	1,950	2,120	2,150	2,150	2,150	2,240	2,310	2,340	2,430	2,450	22,290
	Hospital construction	2,400	2,780	3,030	3,070	3,060	3,070	3,210	3,300	3,340	3,480	3,500	31,840
	Veterans' housing	60	70	70	80	70	80	80	80	80	80	90	780

See Table 10–1 footnotes for specific table information

Table 10–3.　INCOME TAX EXPENDITURES RANKED BY TOTAL FISCAL YEAR 2021–2030 PROJECTED REVENUE EFFECT

(In millions of dollars)

	Provision	2020	2021	2021–2030
121	Exclusion of employer contributions for medical insurance premiums and medical care [10]	191,350	197,530	2,807,130
59	Exclusion of net imputed rental income	123,210	130,590	1,645,980
66	Capital gains (except agriculture, timber, iron ore, and coal)	99,210	99,890	1,270,250
141	Defined contribution employer plans	80,690	87,610	1,168,850
140	Defined benefit employer plans	65,920	67,960	762,880
116	Deductibility of charitable contributions, other than education and health	40,320	43,610	683,380
55	Deductibility of mortgage interest on owner-occupied homes	24,730	25,440	595,980
163	Deductibility of nonbusiness State and local taxes other than on owner-occupied homes [19]	7,060	6,890	561,020
134	Child credit [15]	70,170	73,320	517,920
68	Step-up basis of capital gains at death	35,460	37,780	505,450
58	Capital gains exclusion on home sales	39,450	40,610	500,660
65	Treatment of qualified dividends	29,450	30,760	387,240
144	Self-Employed plans	25,680	28,260	377,030
155	Social Security benefits for retired and disabled workers and spouses, dependents and survivors	27,050	27,180	364,900
161	Exclusion of interest on public purpose State and local bonds	24,310	28,980	333,610
4	Reduced tax rate on active income of controlled foreign corporations (normal tax method)	27,570	29,780	323,560
77	Allow 20-percent deduction to certain pass-through income	29,195	50,518	300,225
56	Deductibility of State and local property tax on owner-occupied homes [17]	6,450	6,370	294,600
8	Credit for increasing research activities	16,940	18,300	247,400
142	Individual Retirement Accounts	16,510	17,360	232,340
124	Deductibility of medical expenses	7,100	7,960	158,410
1	Exclusion of benefits and allowances to armed forces personnel	12,910	13,940	149,650
49	Exclusion of life insurance death benefits	11,690	11,560	140,080
95	Tax credits and deductions for postsecondary education expenses [7]	10,730	10,070	137,720
128	Deductibility of charitable contributions (health)	8,230	8,820	125,420
157	Exclusion of veterans death benefits and disability compensation	8,230	9,210	115,820
122	Self-employed medical insurance premiums	7,430	7,740	109,120
61	Credit for low-income housing investments	6,310	8,900	106,430
5	Deduction for foreign-derived intangible income dervied from trade or business within the United States	9,450	10,200	98,030
136	Exclusion of workers' compensation benefits	9,160	9,200	93,960
74	Expensing of certain small investments (normal tax method)	−300	−1,630	89,970
2	Exclusion of income earned abroad by U.S. citizens	6,160	6,470	81,370
103	Deductibility of charitable contributions (education)	4,530	4,880	74,680
126	Refundable Premium Assistance Tax Credit [11]	7,960	6,220	72,520
60	Exception from passive loss rules for $25,000 of rental loss	5,700	5,540	69,350
151	Additional deduction for the elderly	5,680	5,810	68,640
113	Exclusion of employee meals and lodging (other than military)	3,290	4,320	66,970
17	Energy investment credit [1]	6,070	6,330	62,080
62	Accelerated depreciation on rental housing (normal tax method)	4,250	4,660	59,550
123	Medical Savings Accounts / Health Savings Accounts	5,330	4,540	57,540
129	Tax credit for orphan drug research	1,720	2,080	55,260
97	Qualified tuition programs (includes Education IRA)	2,420	2,670	55,020
15	Energy production credit [1]	5,020	5,280	53,380
94	Exclusion of scholarship and fellowship income (normal tax method)	3,510	3,660	52,960
69	Carryover basis of capital gains on gifts	2,610	3,050	44,550
71	Deferral of gains from like-kind exchanges	3,030	3,200	40,090
145	Premiums on group term life insurance	2,160	2,990	38,440
125	Exclusion of interest on hospital construction bonds	2,730	3,250	37,460
114	Credit for child and dependent care expenses	3,190	3,080	36,700
72	Depreciation of buildings other than rental housing (normal tax method)	6,010	4,090	33,110
99	Exclusion of interest on bonds for private nonprofit educational facilities	1,910	2,280	26,210
96	Deductibility of student-loan interest	2,170	2,030	25,170
48	Exemption of credit union income	2,140	2,080	24,564
52	Exclusion of interest spread of financial institutions	4,230	3,110	24,470
102	Parental personal exemption for students age 19 or over	0	0	24,110

Table 10–3.   INCOME TAX EXPENDITURES RANKED BY TOTAL FISCAL YEAR 2021–2030 PROJECTED REVENUE EFFECT—Continued

(In millions of dollars)

	Provision	2020	2021	2021–2030
80	Exclusion of reimbursed employee parking expenses	1,686	1,759	22,153
159	Exclusion of GI bill benefits	1,460	1,580	19,600
67	Capital gains exclusion of small corporation stock	1,410	1,530	19,540
6	Interest Charge Domestic International Sales Corporations (IC-DISCs)	890	1,370	19,420
156	Credit for certain employer contributions to social security	720	990	17,070
44	Capital gains treatment of certain agriculture income	1,330	1,340	17,020
57	Deferral of income from installment sales	1,480	1,470	16,620
54	Exclusion of interest on rental housing bonds	1,200	1,430	16,470
104	Exclusion of employer-provided educational assistance	1,190	1,390	16,450
153	Earned income tax credit [16]	2,660	700	15,300
148	Income of trusts to finance voluntary employee benefits associations	1,090	1,070	13,870
143	Low and moderate income savers credit	1,220	1,220	13,360
118	Exclusion of parsonage allowances	900	950	12,130
108	Work opportunity tax credit	1,650	1,690	11,820
88	New markets tax credit	1,280	1,290	10,710
14	Enhanced oil recovery credit	470	500	10,190
154	Recovery rebate credits [17]	0	9,110	10,122
39	Carbon oxide sequestration credit	14	123	9,908
85	Exclusion of interest for airport, dock, and similar bonds	720	850	9,860
53	Exclusion of interest on owner-occupied mortgage subsidy bonds	710	850	9,760
10	Excess of percentage over cost depletion, fuels	590	600	9,230
112	Adoption credit and exclusion	770	790	9,080
38	Tax incentives for preservation of historic structures	660	610	8,870
111	Assistance for adopted foster children	620	660	8,870
109	Employer provided child care exclusion	580	570	8,640
164	Deferral of interest on U.S. savings bonds	910	840	8,000
137	Exclusion of public assistance benefits (normal tax method)	580	600	6,760
28	Credit for residential energy efficient property	2,370	2,390	6,360
132	Distributions from retirement plans for premiums for health and long-term care insurance	430	450	5,570
117	Exclusion of certain foster care payments	490	510	5,370
81	Exclusion for employer-provided transit passes	341	363	5,250
152	Deductibility of casualty losses	0	0	4,641
42	Expensing of certain multiperiod production costs	560	370	4,590
107	Qualified school construction bonds [9]	570	540	4,270
35	Exclusion of interest on bonds for water, sewage, and hazardous waste facilities	270	330	3,750
51	Tax exemption of insurance income earned by tax-exempt organizations	320	320	3,600
9	Expensing of exploration and development costs, fuels	40	–40	3,510
3	Exclusion of certain allowances for Federal employees abroad	270	280	3,500
146	Premiums on accident and disability insurance	330	340	3,470
20	Tax credits for clean-fuel burning vehicles and refueling property	570	440	3,400
130	Special Blue Cross/Blue Shield tax benefits	140	190	3,270
158	Exclusion of veterans pensions	210	220	2,350
149	Special ESOP rules	210	210	2,330
135	Exclusion of railroad retirement (Social Security equivalent) benefits	310	290	2,180
45	Income averaging for farmers	170	180	2,160
41	Expensing of certain capital outlays	80	120	2,030
31	Advanced nuclear power production credit	0	0	2,000
26	Credit for construction of new energy efficient homes	320	370	1,940
139	Exclusion of military disability pensions	160	160	1,920
98	Exclusion of interest on student-loan bonds	140	160	1,910
105	Special deduction for teacher expenses	170	170	1,880
36	Capital gains treatment of certain timber income	130	130	1,700
34	Excess of percentage over cost depletion, nonfuel minerals	110	100	1,620
106	Discharge of student loan indebtedness	80	80	1,470
78	Tonnage tax	140	140	1,400

Table 10–3. INCOME TAX EXPENDITURES RANKED BY TOTAL FISCAL YEAR 2021–2030 PROJECTED REVENUE EFFECT—Continued

(In millions of dollars)

	Provision	2020	2021	2021–2030
50	Exemption or special alternative tax for small property and casualty insurance companies	110	120	1,370
16	Marginal wells credit	150	250	1,340
32	Reduced tax rate for nuclear decommissioning funds	100	110	1,320
83	Exclusion of interest on bonds for Highway Projects and rail-truck transfer facilities	170	160	1,300
25	Allowance of deduction for certain energy efficient commercial building property	160	190	1,200
86	Exemption of certain mutuals' and cooperatives' income	90	90	1,030
24	Amortize all geological and geophysical expenditures over 2 years	80	80	1,020
75	Exclusion of interest on small issue bonds	80	90	1,010
160	Exclusion of interest on veterans housing bonds	70	80	920
89	Credit to holders of Gulf Tax Credit Bonds.	100	110	870
64	Exceptions from imputed interest rules	60	60	810
70	Ordinary income treatment of loss from small business corporation stock sale	70	70	800
87	Empowerment zones	160	130	770
90	Recovery Zone Bonds [6]	90	90	760
37	Expensing of multiperiod timber growing costs	50	60	740
47	Expensing of reforestation expenditures	50	60	740
82	Tax credit for certain expenditures for maintaining railroad tracks	140	170	740
22	Credit for holding clean renewable energy bonds [4]	70	70	700
93	Employee retention credit	230	160	700
100	Credit for holders of zone academy bonds [8]	150	130	690
133	Credit for family and sick leave taken by self-employed individuals [14]	500	590	680
43	Treatment of loans forgiven for solvent farmers	50	50	640
12	Capital gains treatment of royalties on coal	100	70	590
40	Deduction for endangered species recovery expenditures	30	30	460
101	Exclusion of interest on savings bonds redeemed to finance educational expenses	30	40	450
150	Additional deduction for the blind	30	40	440
21	Exclusion of utility conservation subsidies	60	60	420
147	Income of trusts to finance supplementary unemployment benefits	20	10	370
27	Credit for energy efficiency improvements to existing homes	240	240	360
33	Expensing of exploration and development costs, nonfuel minerals	0	0	340
29	Qualified energy conservation bonds [5]	30	30	300
119	Indian employment credit	70	70	290
23	Credit for investment in clean coal facilities	30	30	280
63	Discharge of business indebtedness	40	30	280
110	Employer-provided child care credit	20	20	220
11	Exception from passive loss limitation for working interests in oil and gas properties	20	20	190
46	Deferral of gain on sale of farm refiners	15	15	180
138	Exclusion of special benefits for disabled coal miners	20	30	180
13	Exclusion of interest on energy facility bonds	0	10	100
19	Bio-Diesel and small agri-biodiesel producer tax credits [3]	30	40	100
30	Advanced Energy Property Credit	10	10	100
79	Deferral of tax on shipping companies	10	10	100
91	Tribal Economic Development Bonds	10	10	100
115	Credit for disabled access expenditures	10	10	100
127	Credit for employee health insurance expenses of small business [12]	40	40	90
120	Credit for employer differential wage payments	0	0	70
18	Alcohol fuel credits [2]	0	10	10
84	Investment credit for rehabilitation of structures (other than historic)	10	0	0
131	Tax credit for health insurance purchased by certain displaced and retired individuals [13]	0	0	0
162	Build America Bonds [18]	0	0	0
76	Special rules for certain film and TV production	−190	−50	−930
92	Opportunity Zones	3,770	2,680	−1,670
73	Accelerated depreciation of machinery and equipment (normal tax method)	32,800	31,320	−66,720
7	Expensing of research and experimentation expenditures (normal tax method)	5,420	3,980	−82,240

See Table 10–1 footnotes for specific table information

Table 10–4. PRESENT VALUE OF SELECTED TAX EXPENDITURES FOR ACTIVITY IN CALENDAR YEAR 2020

(In millions of dollars)

	Provision	2020 Present Value of Revenue Loss
7	Expensing of research and experimentation expenditures (normal tax method)	740
22	Credit for holding clean renewable energy bonds	0
9	Expensing of exploration and development costs - fuels	140
33	Expensing of exploration and development costs - nonfuels	10
37	Expensing of multiperiod timber growing costs	60
42	Expensing of certain multiperiod production costs - agriculture	−260
41	Expensing of certain capital outlays - agriculture	−110
47	Expensing of reforestation expenditures	20
62	Accelerated depreciation on rental housing	−4,860
72	Depreciation of buildings other than rental	−1,250
73	Accelerated depreciation of machinery and equipment	−23,620
74	Expensing of certain small investments (normal tax method)	0
100	Credit for holders of zone academy bonds	0
61	Credit for low-income housing investments	8,680
97	Qualified tuition programs	5,720
140	Defined benefit employer plans	46,030
141	Defined contribution employer plans	120,610
142	Exclusion of IRA contributions and earnings	2,870
142	Exclusion of Roth earnings and distributions	6,620
142	Exclusion of non-deductible IRA earnings	790
144	Exclusion of contributions and earnings for Self-Employed plans	7,630
162	Exclusion of interest on public-purpose bonds	11,140
	Exclusion of interest on non-public purpose bonds [1]	4,450
165	Deferral of interest on U.S. savings bonds	70

[1] Includes all components, other than public purpose, listed under 'Exclusion of interest on State and local bonds' in the Addendum to Table 10–1.

from U.S. taxable income certain special allowances they receive to compensate them for the relatively high costs associated with living overseas. The allowances supplement wage income and cover expenses such as rent, education, and the cost of travel to and from the United States.

4. *Reduced tax rate on active income of controlled foreign corporations (normal tax method).*—Under the baseline tax system, worldwide income forms the tax base of U.S. corporations. In contrast, U.S. tax law exempts or preferentially taxes certain portions of this income. Prior to the passage of the Tax Cuts and Jobs Act TCJA (effective January 1, 2018), active foreign income was generally taxed only upon repatriation. TCJA changed these rules, so that certain active income (called "global intangible low tax income" or "GILTI") is taxed currently, even if it is not distributed. However, U.S. corporations generally receive a 50 percent deduction from U.S. tax on their GILTI (the deduction decreases to 37.5 percent in 2026), resulting in a substantially reduced rate of tax. In addition, some active income is excluded from tax, and distributions out of active income are no longer taxed upon repatriation. These reductions and exemptions from U.S. taxation are considered tax expenditures. However, U.S. shareholders of specified foreign corpora-

tions must include their pro rata share of accumulated post-1986 deferred foreign income (as of the last taxable year before January 1, 2018) in U.S. taxable income, and this inclusion acts as an offset to the reduced tax rate on CFC income in the years in which the payments are received.

5. *Deduction for foreign-derived intangible income derived from a trade or business within the United States.*—Under the baseline tax system, the United States taxes income earned by U.S. corporations from serving foreign markets (e.g., exports and royalties) at the full U.S. rate. After the passage of TCJA, domestic corporations are allowed a deduction equal to 37.5 percent of "foreign-derived intangible income," which is essentially income from serving foreign markets (defined on a formulaic basis). The deduction falls to 21.875 percent in 2026.

6. *Interest Charge Domestic International Sales Corporations (IC-DISCs).*—Under the baseline tax system, taxpayer earnings are subject to tax using the regular tax rates applied to all taxpayers. In contrast, IC-DISCs allow a portion of income from exports to be taxed at the qualified dividend rate which is no higher than 20 percent (plus a 3.8 percent surtax for high-income taxpayers).

General Science, Space, and Technology

7. *Expensing of research and experimentation expenditures (normal tax method).*—The baseline tax system allows a deduction for the cost of producing income. It requires taxpayers to capitalize the costs associated with investments over time to better match the streams of income and associated costs. Research and experimentation (R&E) projects can be viewed as investments because, if successful, their benefits accrue for several years. It is often difficult, however, to identify whether a specific R&E project is successful and, if successful, what its expected life will be. Because of this ambiguity, the reference tax law baseline system would allow expensing of R&E expenditures. In contrast, under the normal tax method, the expensing of R&E expenditures is viewed as a tax expenditure. The baseline assumed for the normal tax method is that all R&E expenditures are successful and have an expected life of five years. Current law requires R&E expenditures paid or incurred in taxable years beginning after December 31, 2021, to be capitalized and amortized over 5 years, while allowing R&E expenditures paid or incurred in prior taxable years to be expensed.

8. *Credit for increasing research activities.*— The baseline tax system would uniformly tax all returns to investments and not allow credits for particular activities, investments, or industries. In contrast, the Tax Code allows an R&E credit of up to 20 percent of qualified research expenditures in excess of a base amount. The base amount of the credit is generally determined by multiplying a "fixed-base percentage" by the average amount of the company's gross receipts for the prior four years. The taxpayer's fixed base percentage generally is the ratio of its research expenses to gross receipts for 1984 through 1988. Taxpayers can elect the alternative simplified credit regime, which equals 14 percent of qualified research expenses that exceed 50 percent of the average qualified research expenses for the three preceding taxable years.

Energy

9. *Expensing of exploration and development costs, fuels.*—Under the baseline tax system, the costs of exploring and developing oil and gas wells and coal mines or other natural fuel deposits would be capitalized and then amortized (or depreciated) over an estimate of the economic life of the property. This insures that the net income from the well or mine is measured appropriately each year. In contrast to this treatment, current law allows immediate deduction, i.e., expensing, of intangible drilling costs for successful investments in domestic oil and gas wells (such as wages, the cost of using machinery for grading and drilling, and the cost of unsalvageable materials used in constructing wells). Current law also allows immediate deduction of eligible exploration and development costs for domestic coal mines and other natural fuel deposits. Because expensing allows recovery of costs sooner, it is more advantageous to the taxpayer than amortization. Expensing provisions for exploration expenditures apply only to properties for which a deduc-

tion for percentage depletion is allowable. For oil and gas wells, integrated oil companies may expense only 70 percent of intangible drilling costs and must amortize the remaining 30 percent over five years. Non-integrated oil companies may expense all such costs.

10. *Excess of percentage over cost depletion, fuels.*—The baseline tax system would allow recovery of the costs of developing certain oil, gas, and mineral fuel properties using cost depletion. Cost depletion is similar in concept to depreciation, in that the costs of developing or acquiring the asset are capitalized and then gradually reduced over an estimate of the asset's economic life, as is appropriate for measuring net income. In contrast, the Tax Code generally allows independent fuel producers and royalty owners to take percentage depletion deductions rather than cost depletion on limited quantities of output. Under percentage depletion, taxpayers deduct a percentage of gross income from fossil fuel production. In certain cases the deduction is limited to a fraction of the asset's net income. Over the life of an investment, percentage depletion deductions can exceed the cost of the investment. Consequently, percentage depletion may provide more advantageous tax treatment than would cost depletion, which limits deductions to an investment's cost.

11. *Exception from passive loss limitation for working interests in oil and gas properties.*—The baseline tax system accepts current law's general rule limiting taxpayers' ability to deduct losses from passive activities against nonpassive income (e.g., wages, interest, and dividends). Passive activities generally are defined as those in which the taxpayer does not materially participate, though there are numerous additional considerations brought to bear on the determination of which activities are passive for a given taxpayer. Losses are limited in an attempt to limit tax sheltering activities. Passive losses that are unused may be carried forward and applied against future passive income. An exception from the passive loss limitation is provided for a working interest in an oil or gas property that the taxpayer holds directly or through an entity that does not limit the liability of the taxpayer with respect to the interest. Thus, taxpayers can deduct losses from such working interests against nonpassive income without regard to whether they materially participate in the activity.

12. *Capital gains treatment of royalties on coal.*—The baseline tax system generally would tax all income under the regular tax rate schedule. It would not allow preferentially low tax rates to apply to certain types or sources of income. For individuals, tax rates on regular income vary from 10 percent to 39.6 percent in the budget window (plus a 3.8 percent surtax on high income taxpayers), depending on the taxpayer's income. In contrast, current law allows capital gains realized by individuals to be taxed at a preferentially low rate that is no higher than 20 percent (plus the 3.8 percent surtax). Certain sales of coal under royalty contracts qualify for taxation as capital gains rather than ordinary income, and so benefit from the preferentially low 20 percent maximum tax rate on capital gains.

13. ***Exclusion of interest on energy facility bonds.***—The baseline tax system generally would tax all income under the regular tax rate schedule. It would not allow preferentially low (or zero) tax rates to apply to certain types or sources of income. In contrast, the Tax Code allows interest earned on State and local bonds used to finance construction of certain energy facilities to be exempt from tax. These bonds are generally subject to the State private-activity-bond annual volume cap.

14. ***Enhanced oil recovery credit.***—A credit is provided equal to 15 percent of the taxpayer's costs for enhanced oil recovery on U.S. projects. The credit is reduced in proportion to the ratio of the reference price of oil for the previous calendar year minus $28 (adjusted for inflation from 1990) to $6.

15. ***Energy production credit.***—The baseline tax system would not allow credits for particular activities, investments, or industries. Instead, it generally would seek to tax uniformly all returns from investment-like activities. In contrast, the Tax Code provides a credit for certain electricity produced from wind energy, biomass, geothermal energy, solar energy, small irrigation power, municipal solid waste, or qualified hydropower and sold to an unrelated party. Wind facilities must have begun construction before January 1, 2022. Facilities that begin construction in 2017 receive 80 percent of the credit, facilities that begin construction in 2018 receive 60 percent of the credit, facilities that begin construction in 2019 receive 40 percent of the credit, and facilities that begin construction in 2020-2021 receive 60 percent of the credit. Qualified facilities producing electricity from sources other than wind must begin construction before January 1, 2022. In addition to the electricity production credit, a ten-year income tax credit is allowed for the production of refined coal for facilities placed in service before January 1, 2012. The Tax Code also provided an income tax credit for Indian coal facilities. The Indian coal facilities credit expires on December 31, 2021.

16. ***Marginal wells credit.***—A credit is provided for crude oil and natural gas produced from a qualified marginal well. A marginal well is one that does not produce more than 1,095 barrel-of-oil equivalents per year, with this limit adjusted proportionally for the number of days the well is in production. The credit is no more than $3.00 per barrel of qualified crude oil production and $0.50 per thousand cubic feet of qualified natural gas production. The credit for natural gas is reduced in proportion to the amount by which the reference price of natural gas at the wellhead for the previous calendar year exceeds $1.67 per thousand cubic feet and is zero for a reference price that exceeds $2.00. The credit for crude oil is reduced in proportion to the amount by which the reference price of oil for the previous calendar year exceeds $15.00 per barrel and is zero for a reference price that exceeds $18.00. All dollar amounts are adjusted for inflation from 2004.

17. ***Energy investment credit.***—The baseline tax system would not allow credits for particular activities, investments, or industries. Instead, it generally would seek to tax uniformly all returns from investment-like activities. However, the Tax Code provides credits for investments in solar and geothermal energy property, qualified fuel cell power plants, stationary microturbine power plants, geothermal heat pumps, waste energy recovery property, small wind property, offshore wind, and combined heat and power property. The credit is 30 percent for property that begins construction before 2020, 26 percent for property that begins construction in 2020-2022, and 22 percent for property that begins construction in 2023 and in all cases that is placed in service before January 1, 2026. The credit for offshore wind is 30 percent for facilities placed in service before January 1, 2026. A 10 percent credit is available for geothermal or qualified solar property placed in service after December 31, 2025. Owners of renewable power facilities that qualify for the energy production credit may instead elect to take an energy investment credit at a rate specified by law.

18. ***Alcohol fuel credits.***—The baseline tax system would not allow credits for particular activities, investments, or industries. Instead, it generally would seek to tax uniformly all returns from investment-like activities. In contrast, the Tax Code provides an income tax credit for qualified cellulosic biofuel production which was renamed the Second generation biofuel producer credit. This provision expires on December 31, 2021.

19. ***Bio-diesel and small agri-biodiesel producer tax credits.***—The baseline tax system would not allow credits for particular activities, investments, or industries. Instead, it generally would seek to tax uniformly all returns from investment-like activities. However, the Tax Code allows an income tax credit for Bio-diesel and for Bio-diesel derived from virgin sources. In lieu of the Bio-diesel credit, the taxpayer could claim a refundable excise tax credit. In addition, small agri-biodiesel producers were eligible for a separate income tax credit for biodiesel production, and a separate credit was available for qualified renewable diesel fuel mixtures. This provision expires on December 31, 2022.

20. ***Tax credits for clean-fuel burning vehicles and refueling property.***—The baseline tax system would not allow credits for particular activities, investments, or industries. Instead, it generally would seek to tax uniformly all returns from investment-like activities. In contrast, the Tax Code allows credits for plug-in electric-drive motor vehicles, alternative fuel vehicle refueling property, two-wheeled plug-in electric vehicles, and fuel cell motor vehicles. These provisions, except for the plug-in electric-drive motor vehicle credit, expired after December 31, 2017.

21. ***Exclusion of utility conservation subsidies.***—The baseline tax system generally takes a comprehensive view of taxable income that includes a wide variety of (measurable) accretions to wealth. In certain circumstances, public utilities offer rate subsidies to non-business customers who invest in energy conservation measures. These rate subsidies are equivalent to payments from the utility to its customer, and so represent accretions to wealth, income that would be taxable to the customer under the baseline tax system. In contrast, the Tax Code exempts these subsidies from the non-business customer's gross income.

22. *Credit for holding clean renewable energy bonds.*—The baseline tax system would uniformly tax all returns to investments and not allow credits for particular activities, investments, or industries. In contrast, the Tax Code provides for the issuance of Clean Renewable Energy Bonds that entitle the bond holder to a Federal income tax credit in lieu of interest. As of March 2010, issuers of the unused authorization of such bonds could opt to receive direct payment with the yield becoming fully taxable.

23. *Credit for investment in clean coal facilities.*—The baseline tax system would uniformly tax all returns to investments and not allow credits for particular activities, investments, or industries. In contrast, the Tax Code provides investment tax credits for clean coal facilities producing electricity and for industrial gasification combined cycle projects.

24. *Amortize all geological and geophysical expenditures over two years.*—The baseline tax system allows taxpayers to deduct the decline in the economic value of an investment over its economic life. However, the Tax Code allows geological and geophysical expenditures incurred in connection with oil and gas exploration in the United States to be amortized over two years for non-integrated oil companies, a span of time that is generally shorter than the economic life of the assets.

25. *Allowance of deduction for certain energy efficient commercial building property.*—The baseline tax system would not allow deductions in lieu of normal depreciation allowances for particular investments in particular industries. Instead, it generally would seek to tax uniformly all returns from investment-like activities. In contrast, the Tax Code allows a deduction for certain energy efficient commercial building property. The basis of such property is reduced by the amount of the deduction. Starting in 2021, the maximum deduction amount per square foot will be increased by a cost-of -living adjustment.

26. *Credit for construction of new energy efficient homes.*—The baseline tax system would not allow credits for particular activities, investments, or industries. Instead, it generally would seek to tax uniformly all returns from investment-like activities. However, the Tax Code allowed contractors a tax credit of $2,000 for the construction of a qualified new energy-efficient home that had an annual level of heating and cooling energy consumption at least 50 percent below the annual consumption under the 2006 International Energy Conservation Code. The credit equaled $1,000 in the case of a new manufactured home that met a 30 percent standard or requirements for EPA's Energy Star homes. This provision expired on December 31, 2017.

27. *Credit for energy efficiency improvements to existing homes.*—The baseline tax system would not allow credits for particular activities, investments, or industries. However, the Tax Code provided an investment tax credit for expenditures made on insulation, exterior windows, and doors that improved the energy efficiency of homes and met certain standards. The Tax Code also provided a credit for purchases of advanced main air circulating fans, natural gas, propane, or oil furnaces or hot water boilers, and other qualified energy efficient property. This provision expired on December 31, 2017. But legislation enacted in 2020 allowed taxpayers to claim tax credits retroactively for three years.

28. *Credit for residential energy efficient property.*—The baseline tax system would uniformly tax all returns to investments and not allow credits for particular activities, investments, or industries. However, the Tax Code provides a credit for the purchase of a qualified photovoltaic property and solar water heating property, as well as for fuel cell power plants, geothermal heat pumps, and small wind property used in or placed on a residence. The credit is 30 percent for property placed in service before January 1, 2020, 26 percent for property placed in service in 2020- 2022, and 22 percent for property placed in service in 2023.

29. *Credit for qualified energy conservation bonds.*—The baseline tax system would uniformly tax all returns to investments and not allow credits for particular activities, investments, or industries. However, the Tax Code provides for the issuance of energy conservation bonds which entitle the bond holder to a Federal income tax credit in lieu of interest. As of March 2010, issuers of the unused authorization of such bonds could opt to receive direct payment with the yield becoming fully taxable.

30. *Advanced energy property credit.*—The baseline tax system would not allow credits for particular activities, investments, or industries. However, the Tax Code provides a 30 percent investment credit for property used in a qualified advanced energy manufacturing project. The Treasury Department may award up to $2.3 billion in tax credits for qualified investments.

31. *Advanced nuclear power facilities production credit.*—The baseline tax system would not allow credits or deductions for particular activities, investments, or industries. Instead, it generally would seek to tax uniformly all returns from investment-like activities. In contrast, the Tax Code allows a tax credit equal to 1.8 cents times the number of kilowatt hours of electricity produced at a qualifying advanced nuclear power facility. A taxpayer may claim no more than $125 million per 1,000 megawatts of capacity. The Treasury Department may allocate up to 6,000 megawatts of credit-eligible capacity. Any unutilized national capacity limitation shall be allocated after December 31, 2020, according to prioritization rules set forth by statute.

32. *Reduced tax rate for nuclear decommissioning funds.*—The baseline tax system would uniformly tax all returns to investments and not allow special rates for particular activities, investments, or industries. In contrast, the Tax Code provides a special 20 percent tax rate for investments made by Nuclear Decommissioning Reserve Funds.

Natural Resources and Environment

33. *Expensing of exploration and development costs, nonfuel minerals.*—The baseline tax system

allows the taxpayer to deduct the depreciation of an asset according to the decline in its economic value over time. However, certain capital outlays associated with exploration and development of nonfuel minerals may be expensed rather than depreciated over the life of the asset.

34. *Excess of percentage over cost depletion, nonfuel minerals.* —The baseline tax system allows the taxpayer to deduct the decline in the economic value of an investment over time. Under current law, however, most nonfuel mineral extractors may use percentage depletion (whereby the deduction is fixed as a percentage of receipts) rather than cost depletion, with percentage depletion rates ranging from 22 percent for sulfur to 5 percent for sand and gravel. Over the life of an investment, percentage depletion deductions can exceed the cost of the investment. Consequently, percentage depletion may provide more advantageous tax treatment than would cost depletion, which limits deductions to an investment's cost.

35. *Exclusion of interest on bonds for water, sewage, and hazardous waste facilities.* —The baseline tax system generally would tax all income under the regular tax rate schedule. It would not allow preferentially low (or zero) tax rates to apply to certain types or sources of income. In contrast, the Tax Code allows interest earned on State and local bonds used to finance construction of sewage, water, or hazardous waste facilities to be exempt from tax. These bonds are generally subject to the State private-activity bond annual volume cap.

36. *Capital gains treatment of certain timber.* —The baseline tax system generally would tax all income under the regular tax rate schedule. It would not allow preferentially low tax rates to apply to certain types or sources of income. However, under current law certain timber sales can be treated as a capital gain rather than ordinary income and therefore subject to the lower capital-gains tax rate. For individuals, tax rates on regular income vary from 10 percent to 39.6 percent in the budget window (plus a 3.8 percent surtax on high income taxpayers), depending on the taxpayer's income. In contrast, current law allows capital gains to be taxed at a preferentially low rate that is no higher than 20 percent (plus the 3.8 percent surtax).

37. *Expensing of multi-period timber growing costs.* —The baseline tax system requires the taxpayer to capitalize costs associated with investment property. However, most of the production costs of growing timber may be expensed under current law rather than capitalized and deducted when the timber is sold, thereby accelerating cost recovery.

38. *Tax incentives for preservation of historic structures.* —The baseline tax system would not allow credits for particular activities, investments, or industries. However, expenditures to preserve and restore certified historic structures qualify for an investment tax credit of 20 percent for certified rehabilitation activities. The taxpayer's recoverable basis must be reduced by the amount of the credit. The credit must be claimed ratably over the five years after the property is placed in service, for property placed in service after December 31, 2017.

39. *Carbon oxide sequestration credit.* —The baseline tax system would uniformly tax all returns to investments and not allow credits for particular activities, investments, or industries. In contrast, the Tax Code allows a credit for qualified carbon oxide captured at a qualified facility and disposed of in secure geological storage. In addition, the provision allows a credit for qualified carbon oxide that is captured at a qualified facility and used as a tertiary injectant in a qualified enhanced oil or natural gas recovery project. The credit differs according to whether the carbon was captured using equipment which was originally placed in service before February 9, 2018, or thereafter.

40. *Deduction for endangered species recovery expenditures.* —The baseline tax system would not allow deductions in addition to normal depreciation allowances for particular investments in particular industries. Instead, it generally would seek to tax uniformly all returns from investment-like activities. In contrast, under current law farmers can deduct up to 25 percent of their gross income for expenses incurred as a result of site and habitat improvement activities that will benefit endangered species on their farm land, in accordance with site specific management actions included in species recovery plans approved pursuant to the Endangered Species Act of 1973.

Agriculture

41. *Expensing of certain capital outlays.* —The baseline tax system requires the taxpayer to capitalize costs associated with investment property. However, farmers may expense certain expenditures for feed and fertilizer, for soil and water conservation measures, and certain other capital improvements under current law.

42. *Expensing of certain multiperiod production costs.* —The baseline tax system requires the taxpayer to capitalize costs associated with an investment over time. However, the production of livestock and crops with a production period greater than two years is exempt from the uniform cost capitalization rules (e.g., for costs for establishing orchards or structure improvements), thereby accelerating cost recovery.

43. *Treatment of loans forgiven for solvent farmers.* —Because loan forgiveness increases a debtors net worth the baseline tax system requires debtors to include the amount of loan forgiveness as income or else reduce their recoverable basis in the property related to the loan. If the amount of forgiveness exceeds the basis, the excess forgiveness is taxable if the taxpayer is not insolvent. For bankrupt debtors, the amount of loan forgiveness reduces carryover losses, unused credits, and then basis, with the remainder of the forgiven debt excluded from taxation. Qualified farm debt that is forgiven, however, is excluded from income even when the taxpayer is solvent.

44. *Capital gains treatment of certain agriculture income.* —For individuals, tax rates on regular income vary from 10 percent to 39.6 percent in the budget window (plus a 3.8 percent surtax on high income taxpayers), depending on the taxpayer's income. The baseline tax system generally would tax all income under the regular tax rate schedule. It would not allow preferentially low tax rates to apply to certain types or sources of income. In contrast, current law allows capital gains to be taxed at a preferentially low rate that is no higher than 20 percent (plus the 3.8 percent surtax). Certain agricultural income, such as unharvested crops, qualify for taxation as capital gains rather than ordinary income, and so benefit from the preferentially low 20 percent maximum tax rate on capital gains.

45. *Income averaging for farmers.*—The baseline tax system generally taxes all earned income each year at the rate determined by the income tax. However, taxpayers may average their taxable income from farming and fishing over the previous three years.

46. *Deferral of gain on sales of farm refiners.*—The baseline tax system generally subjects capital gains to taxes the year that they are realized. However, the Tax Code allows a taxpayer who sells stock in a farm refiner to a farmers' cooperative to defer recognition of the gain if the proceeds are re-invested in a qualified replacement property.

47. *Expensing of reforestation expenditures.*—The baseline tax system requires the taxpayer to capitalize costs associated with an investment over time. In contrast, the Tax Code provides for the expensing of the first $10,000 in reforestation expenditures with 7-year amortization of the remaining expenses.

Commerce and Housing

This category includes a number of tax expenditure provisions that also affect economic activity in other functional categories. For example, provisions related to investment, such as accelerated depreciation, could be classified under the energy, natural resources and environment, agriculture, or transportation categories.

48. *Exemption of credit union income.*—Under the baseline tax system, corporations pay taxes on their profits under the regular tax rate schedule. However, in the Tax Code the earnings of credit unions not distributed to members as interest or dividends are exempt from the income tax.

49. *Exclusion of life insurance death benefits.*—Under the baseline tax system, individuals and corporations would pay taxes on their income when it is (actually or constructively) received or accrued. Nevertheless, current law generally excludes from tax amounts received under life insurance contracts if such amounts are paid by reason of the death of the insured.

50. *Exclusion or special alternative tax for small property and casualty insurance companies.*—The baseline tax system would require corporations to pay taxes on their profits under the regular tax rate schedule. It would not allow preferentially low (or zero) tax rates to apply to certain types or sources of income. Under current law, however, stock non-life insurance companies are generally exempt from tax if their gross receipts for the taxable year do not exceed $600,000 and more than 50 percent of such gross receipts consist of premiums. Mutual non-life insurance companies are generally tax-exempt if their annual gross receipts do not exceed $150,000 and more than 35 percent of gross receipts consist of premiums. Also, non-life insurance companies with no more than a specified level of annual net written premiums generally may elect to pay tax only on their taxable investment income provided certain ownership diversification requirements are met. The underwriting income (premiums, less insurance losses and expenses) of electing companies is excluded from tax. The specified premium limit is indexed for inflation; for 2021, the premium limit is $2.4 million.

51. *Tax exemption of insurance income earned by tax-exempt organizations.*—Under the baseline tax system, corporations pay taxes on their profits under the regular tax rate schedule. The baseline tax system would not allow preferentially low (or zero) tax rates to apply to certain types or sources of income. Generally the income generated by life and property and casualty insurance companies is subject to tax, albeit under special rules. However, income from insurance operations conducted by certain tax-exempt organizations, such as fraternal societies, voluntary employee benefit associations, and others are exempt from tax.

52. *Exclusion of interest spread of financial institutions.*—The baseline tax system generally would tax all income under the regular tax rate schedule. It would not allow preferentially low (or zero) tax rates to apply to certain types or sources of income. Consumers pay for some deposit-linked services, such as check cashing, by accepting a below-market interest rate on their demand deposits. If they received a market rate of interest on those deposits and paid explicit fees for the associated services, they would pay taxes on the full market rate and (unlike businesses) could not deduct the fees. The Government thus foregoes tax on the difference between the risk-free market interest rate and below-market interest rates on demand deposits, which under competitive conditions should equal the value of deposit services.

53. *Exclusion of interest on owner-occupied mortgage subsidy bonds.*—The baseline tax system generally would tax all income under the regular tax rate schedule. It would not allow preferentially low (or zero) tax rates to apply to certain types or sources of income. In contrast, the Tax Code allows interest earned on State and local bonds used to finance homes purchased by first-time, low-to-moderate-income buyers to be exempt from tax. These bonds are generally subject to the State private-activity-bond annual volume cap.

54. *Exclusion of interest on rental housing bonds.*—The baseline tax system generally would tax all income under the regular tax rate schedule. It would not allow preferentially low (or zero) tax rates to apply to certain types or sources of income. In contrast, the Tax Code allows interest earned on State and local government bonds used to finance multifamily rental housing projects to be tax-exempt.

55. *Mortgage interest expense on owner-occupied residences.*—Under the baseline tax system, expenses incurred in earning income would be deductible. However, such expenses would not be deductible when the income or the return on an investment is not taxed. In contrast, the Tax Code allows an exclusion from a taxpayer's taxable income for the value of owner-occupied housing services and also allows the owner-occupant to deduct mortgage interest paid on his or her primary residence and one secondary residence as an itemized non-business deduction. In general, the mortgage interest deduction is limited to interest on debt no greater than the owner's basis in the residence, and is also limited to interest on debt of no more than $1 million. Interest on up to $100,000 of other debt secured by a lien on a principal or second residence is also deductible, irrespective of the purpose of borrowing, provided the total debt does not exceed the fair market value of the residence. As an alternative to the deduction, holders of qualified Mortgage Credit Certificates issued by State or local governmental units or agencies may claim a tax credit equal to a proportion of their interest expense. In the case of taxable years beginning after December 31, 2017, and before January 1, 2026, (1) the $1 million limit is reduced to $750,000 for indebtedness incurred after December 15, 2017, and (2) the deduction for interest on home equity indebtedness is disallowed.

56. *Deductibility of State and local property tax on owner-occupied homes.*—Under the baseline tax system, expenses incurred in earning income would be deductible. However, such expenses would not be deductible when the income or the return on an investment is not taxed. In contrast, the Tax Code allows an exclusion from a taxpayer's taxable income for the value of owner-occupied housing services and also allows the owner-occupant to deduct property taxes paid on real property. In the case of taxable years beginning after December 31, 2017, and before January 1, 2026, (1) the deduction for foreign real property taxes paid is disallowed and (2) the deduction for taxes paid in any taxable year, which includes the deduction for property taxes on real property, is limited to $10,000 ($5,000 in the case of a married individual filing a separate return).

57. *Deferral of income from installment sales.*—The baseline tax system generally would tax all income under the regular tax rate schedule. It would not allow preferentially low (or zero) tax rates, or deferral of tax, to apply to certain types or sources of income. Dealers in real and personal property (i.e., sellers who regularly hold property for sale or resale) cannot defer taxable income from installment sales until the receipt of the loan repayment. Nondealers (i.e., sellers of real property used in their business) are required to pay interest on deferred taxes attributable to their total installment obligations in excess of $5 million. Only properties with sales prices exceeding $150,000 are includable in the total. The payment of a market rate of interest eliminates the benefit of the tax deferral. The tax exemption for nondealers with total installment obligations of less than $5 million is, therefore, a tax expenditure.

58. *Capital gains exclusion on home sales.*—The baseline tax system would not allow deductions and exemptions for certain types of income. In contrast, the Tax Code allows homeowners to exclude from gross income up to $250,000 ($500,000 in the case of a married couple filing a joint return) of the capital gains from the sale of a principal residence. To qualify, the taxpayer must have owned and used the property as the taxpayer's principal residence for a total of at least two of the five years preceding the date of sale. In addition, the exclusion may not be used more than once every two years.

59. *Exclusion of net imputed rental income.*—Under the baseline tax system, the taxable income of a taxpayer who is an owner-occupant would include the implicit value of gross rental income on housing services earned on the investment in owner-occupied housing and would allow a deduction for expenses, such as interest, depreciation, property taxes, and other costs, associated with earning such rental income. In contrast, the Tax Code allows an exclusion from taxable income for the implicit gross rental income on housing services, while in certain circumstances allows a deduction for some costs associated with such income, such as for mortgage interest and property taxes.

60. *Exception from passive loss rules for $25,000 of rental loss.*—The baseline tax system accepts current law's general rule limiting taxpayers' ability to deduct losses from passive activities against nonpassive income (e.g., wages, interest, and dividends). Passive activities generally are defined as those in which the taxpayer does not materially participate, and there are numerous additional considerations brought to bear on the determination of which activities are passive for a given taxpayer. Losses are limited in an attempt to limit tax sheltering activities. Passive losses that are unused may be carried forward and applied against future passive income. In contrast to the general restrictions on passive losses, the Tax Code exempts certain owners of rental real estate activities from "passive income" limitations. The exemption is limited to $25,000 in losses and phases out for taxpayers with income between $100,000 and $150,000.

61. *Credit for low-income housing investments.*—The baseline tax system would uniformly tax all returns to investments and not allow credits for particular activities, investments, or industries. However, under current law taxpayers who invest in certain low-income housing are eligible for a tax credit. The credit rate is set so that the present value of the credit is equal to at least 70 percent of the building's qualified basis for new construction and 30 percent for (1) housing receiving other Federal benefits (such as tax-exempt bond financing) or (2) substantially rehabilitated existing housing. The credit can exceed these levels in certain statutorily defined and State designated areas where project development costs are higher. The credit is allowed in equal amounts over 10 years and is generally subject to a volume cap.

62. *Accelerated depreciation on rental housing (normal tax method).*—Under a comprehensive economic income tax, the costs of acquiring a building are capitalized and depreciated over time in accordance with the decline in the property's economic value due to wear and tear or obsolescence. This insures that the net income from the rental property is measured appropriately each year. Current law allows depreciation that is accelerated relative to economic depreciation. However, the depreciation provisions of the Tax Code are part of the reference tax law, and thus do not give rise to tax expenditures under reference tax law. Under normal tax baseline, in contrast, depreciation allowances reflect estimates of economic depreciation.

63. ***Discharge of business indebtedness.***—Under the baseline tax system, all income would generally be taxed under the regular tax rate schedule. The baseline tax system would not allow preferentially low (or zero) tax rates to apply to certain types or sources of income. In contrast, the Tax Code allows an exclusion from a taxpayer's taxable income for any discharge of qualified real property business indebtedness by taxpayers other than a C corporation. If the canceled debt is not reported as current income, however, the basis of the underlying property must be reduced by the amount canceled.

64. ***Exceptions from imputed interest rules.***— Under the baseline tax system, holders (issuers) of debt instruments are generally required to report interest earned (paid) in the period it accrues, not when received. In addition, the amount of interest accrued is determined by the actual price paid, not by the stated principal and interest stipulated in the instrument. But under current law, any debt associated with the sale of property worth less than $250,000 is exempted from the general interest accounting rules. This general $250,000 exception is not a tax expenditure under reference tax law but is under normal tax baseline. Current law also includes exceptions for certain property worth more than $250,000. These are tax expenditure under reference tax law and normal tax baselines. These exceptions include, sales of personal residences worth more than $250,000, and sales of farms and small businesses worth between $250,000 and $1 million.

65. ***Treatment of qualified dividends.***—The baseline tax system generally would tax all income under the regular tax rate schedule. It would not allow preferentially low tax rates to apply to certain types or sources of income. For individuals, tax rates on regular income vary from 10 percent to 39.6 percent in the budget window (plus a 3.8 percent surtax on high income taxpayers), depending on the taxpayer's income. In contrast, under current law, qualified dividends are taxed at a preferentially low rate that is no higher than 20 percent (plus the 3.8 percent surtax).

66. ***Capital gains (except agriculture, timber, iron ore, and coal).***—The baseline tax system generally would tax all income under the regular tax rate schedule. It would not allow preferentially low tax rates to apply to certain types or sources of income. For individuals, tax rates on regular income vary from 10 percent to 39.6 percent in the budget window (plus a 3.8 percent surtax on high income taxpayers), depending on the taxpayer's income. In contrast, under current law, capital gains on assets held for more than one year are taxed at a prefer-

entially low rate that is no higher than 20 percent (plus the 3.8 percent surtax).

67. ***Capital gains exclusion of small corporation stock.***—The baseline tax system would not allow deductions and exemptions or provide preferential treatment of certain sources of income or types of activities. In contrast, the Tax Code provided an exclusion of 50 percent, applied to ordinary rates with a maximum of a 28 percent tax rate, for capital gains from qualified small business stock held by individuals for more than 5 years; 75 percent for stock issued after February 17, 2009 and before September 28, 2010; and 100 percent for stock issued after September 27, 2010. A qualified small business is a corporation whose gross assets do not exceed $50 million as of the date of issuance of the stock.

68. ***Step-up basis of capital gains at death.***— Under the baseline tax system, unrealized capital gains would be taxed when assets are transferred at death. It would not allow for exempting gains upon transfer of the underlying assets to the heirs. In contrast, capital gains on assets held at the owner's death are not subject to capital gains tax under current law. The cost basis of the appreciated assets is adjusted to the market value at the owner's date of death which becomes the basis for the heirs.

69. ***Carryover basis of capital gains on gifts.***— Under the baseline tax system, unrealized capital gains would be taxed when assets are transferred by gift. In contrast, when a gift of appreciated asset is made under current law, the donor's basis in the transferred property (the cost that was incurred when the transferred property was first acquired) carries over to the donee. The carryover of the donor's basis allows a continued deferral of unrealized capital gains.

70. ***Ordinary income treatment of loss from small business corporation stock sale.***—The baseline tax system limits to $3,000 the write-off of losses from capital assets, with carryover of the excess to future years. In contrast, the Tax Code allows up to $100,000 in losses from the sale of small business corporate stock (capitalization less than $1 million) to be treated as ordinary losses and fully deducted.

71. ***Deferral of capital gains from like-kind exchanges.***—The baseline tax system generally would tax all income under the regular tax rate schedule. It would not allow preferentially low (or zero) tax rates, or deferral of tax, to apply to certain types or sources of income. In contrast, current law allows the deferral of accrued gains on assets transferred in qualified like-kind exchanges.

72. ***Depreciation of buildings other than rental housing (normal tax method).***—Under a comprehensive economic income tax, the costs of acquiring a building are capitalized and depreciated over time in accordance with the decline in the property's economic value due to wear and tear or obsolescence. This insures that the net income from the property is measured appropriately each year. Current law allows depreciation deductions that differ from those under economic depreciation. However, the depreciation provisions of the Tax Code are part of the reference tax law, and thus do not give rise to tax expenditures under reference tax law. Under normal tax baseline,

in contrast, depreciation allowances reflect estimates of economic depreciation.

73. Accelerated depreciation of machinery and equipment (normal tax method).—Under a comprehensive economic income tax, the costs of acquiring machinery and equipment are capitalized and depreciated over time in accordance with the decline in the property's economic value due to wear and tear or obsolescence. This insures that the net income from the property is measured appropriately each year. Current law allows depreciation deductions that are accelerated relative to economic depreciation. In particular, through 2022, 100 percent of the purchase cost of qualified property is eligible to be expensed immediately; this percentage phases out to zero through 2027. The depreciation provisions of the Tax Code are part of the reference tax law, and thus do not give rise to tax expenditures under reference tax law. Under the normal tax baseline, in contrast, depreciation allowances reflect estimates of economic depreciation.

74. Expensing of certain small investments (normal tax method).—Under the reference tax law baseline, the costs of acquiring tangible property and computer software would be depreciated using the Tax Code's depreciation provisions. Under the normal tax baseline, depreciation allowances are estimates of economic depreciation. However, subject to investment limitations, the Tax Code allows up to $1 million (indexed for inflation) in qualifying investments in tangible property and certain computer software to be expensed rather than depreciated over time.

75. Exclusion of interest on small issue bonds.—The baseline tax system generally would tax all income under the regular tax rate schedule. It would not allow preferentially low (or zero) tax rates to apply to certain types or sources of income. In contrast, the Tax Code allows interest earned on small issue industrial development bonds (IDBs) issued by State and local governments to finance manufacturing facilities to be tax exempt. Depreciable property financed with small issue IDBs must be depreciated, however, using the straight-line method. The annual volume of small issue IDBs is subject to the unified volume cap discussed in the mortgage housing bond section above.

76. Special rules for certain film and TV production.—The baseline tax system generally would tax all income under the regular tax rate schedule. It would not allow deductions and exemptions or preferentially low (or zero) tax rates to apply to certain types or sources of income. In contrast, the Tax Code allowed taxpayers to deduct up to $15 million per production ($20 million in certain distressed areas) in non-capital expenditures incurred during the year. This provision is scheduled to expire at the end of 2025.

77. Allow 20-percent deduction to certain pass-through income.—The baseline tax system generally would tax all income under the regular tax rate schedule. It would not allow deductions and exemptions or preferentially low (or zero) tax rates to apply to certain types or sources of income. In contrast, for tax years 2018 to 2025, the Tax Code allows for a deduction equal to up to 20 percent of income attributable to domestic pass-through businesses, subject to certain limitations.

Transportation

78. Tonnage tax.—The baseline tax system generally would tax all profits and income under the regular tax rate schedule. U.S. shipping companies may choose to be subject to a tonnage tax based on gross shipping weight in lieu of an income tax, in which case profits would not be subject to tax under the regular tax rate schedule.

79. Deferral of tax on shipping companies.—The baseline tax system generally would tax all profits and income under the regular tax rate schedule. It would not allow preferentially low (or zero) tax rates to apply to certain types or sources of income. In contrast, the Tax Code allows certain companies that operate U.S. flag vessels to defer income taxes on that portion of their income used for shipping purposes (e.g., primarily construction, modernization and major repairs to ships, and repayment of loans to finance these investments).

80. Exclusion of reimbursed employee parking expenses.—Under the baseline tax system, all compensation, including dedicated payments and in-kind benefits, would be included in taxable income. Dedicated payments and in-kind benefits represent accretions to wealth that do not differ materially from cash wages. In contrast, the Tax Code allows an exclusion from taxable income for employee parking expenses that are paid for by the employer or that are received by the employee in lieu of wages. In 2021, the maximum amount of the parking exclusion is $270 per month. The tax expenditure estimate does not include any subsidy provided through employer-owned parking facilities. However, beginning in 2018, parking expenses are no longer deductible to employers (except government).

81. Exclusion for employer-provided transit passes.—Under the baseline tax system, all compensation, including dedicated payments and in-kind benefits, would be included in taxable income. Dedicated payments and in-kind benefits represent accretions to wealth that do not differ materially from cash wages. In contrast, the Tax Code allows an exclusion from a taxpayer's taxable income for passes, tokens, fare cards, and vanpool expenses that are paid for by an employer or that are received by the employee in lieu of wages to defray an employee's commuting costs. Due to a parity to parking provision, the maximum amount of the transit exclusion is $270 per month in 2021. However, beginning in 2018, transit expenses are no longer deductible to employers (except government).

82. Tax credit for certain expenditures for maintaining railroad tracks.—The baseline tax system would not allow credits for particular activities, investments, or industries. However, the Tax Code allowed eligible taxpayers to claim a credit equal to the lesser of 50 percent of maintenance expenditures and the product of $3,500 and the number of miles of railroad track owned or leased. This provision applies to maintenance expenditures in taxable years beginning before January 1, 2017.

83. *Exclusion of interest on bonds for Highway Projects and rail-truck transfer facilities.* —The baseline tax system generally would tax all income under the regular tax rate schedule. It would not allow preferentially low (or zero) tax rates to apply to certain types or sources of income. In contrast, the Tax Code provides for $15 billion of tax-exempt bond authority to finance qualified highway or surface freight transfer facilities.

Community and Regional Development

84. *Investment credit for rehabilitation of structures (other than historic).* —The baseline tax system would uniformly tax all returns to investments and not allow credits for particular activities, investments, or industries. Under prior law, the Tax Code allowed a 10 percent investment tax credit for the rehabilitation of buildings that are used for business or productive activities and that were erected before 1936 for other than residential purposes. The taxpayer's recoverable basis must be reduced by the amount of the credit. The credit is repealed for rehabilitation expenditures incurred after December 31, 2017.

85. *Exclusion of interest for airport, dock, and similar bonds.* —The baseline tax system generally would tax all income under the regular tax rate schedule. It would not allow preferentially low (or zero) tax rates to apply to certain types or sources of income. In contrast, the Tax Code allows interest earned on State and local bonds issued to finance high-speed rail facilities and Government-owned airports, docks, wharves, and sport and convention facilities to be tax-exempt. These bonds are not subject to a volume cap.

86. *Exemption of certain mutuals' and cooperatives' income.* —Under the baseline tax system, corporations pay taxes on their profits under the regular tax rate schedule. In contrast, the Tax Code provides for the incomes of mutual and cooperative telephone and electric companies to be exempt from tax if at least 85 percent of their receipts are derived from patron service charges.

87. *Empowerment zones.* —The baseline tax system generally would tax all income under the regular tax rate schedule. It would not allow preferentially low tax rates to apply to certain types or sources of income, tax credits, and write-offs faster than economic depreciation. In contrast, the Tax Code allows qualifying businesses in designated economically depressed areas to receive tax benefits such as an employment credit and special tax-exempt financing. A taxpayer's ability to accrue new tax benefits for empowerment zones expires on December 31, 2025.

88. *New markets tax credit.* —The baseline tax system would not allow credits for particular activities, investments, or industries. However, the Tax Code allows taxpayers who make qualified equity investments in a community development entity (CDE), which then make qualified investments in low-income communities, to be eligible for a tax credit that is received over 7 years. The total equity investment available for the credit across all CDEs is generally $5 billion for each calendar year 2020 through 2025, the last year for which credit allocations are authorized.

89. *Credit to holders of Gulf and Midwest Tax Credit Bonds.* —The baseline tax system would not allow credits for particular activities, investments, or industries. Instead, under current law taxpayers that own Gulf and Midwest Tax Credit bonds receive a non-refundable tax credit rather than interest. The credit is included in gross income.

90. *Recovery Zone Bonds.* —The baseline tax system would not allow credits for particular activities, investments, or industries. In addition, it would tax all income under the regular tax rate schedule. It would not allow preferentially low (or zero) tax rates to apply to certain types or sources of income. In contrast, the Tax Code allowed local governments to issue up $10 billion in taxable Recovery Zone Economic Development Bonds in 2009 and 2010 and receive a direct payment from Treasury equal to 45 percent of interest expenses. In addition, local governments could issue up to $15 billion in tax exempt Recovery Zone Facility Bonds. These bonds financed certain kinds of business development in areas of economic distress.

91. *Tribal Economic Development Bonds.* —The baseline tax system generally would tax all income under the regular tax rate schedule. It would not allow preferentially low (or zero) tax rates to apply to certain types or sources of income. In contrast, the Tax Code was modified in 2009 to allow Indian tribal governments to issue tax exempt "tribal economic development bonds." There is a national bond limitation of $2 billion on such bonds.

92. *Opportunity Zones.* —The baseline tax system generally would tax all income under the regular tax rate schedule. It would not allow deferral or exclusion from income for investments made within certain geographic regions. In contrast, the Tax Code allows the temporary deferral of the recognition of capital gain if reinvested prior to December 31, 2026, in a qualifying opportunity fund which in turn invests in qualifying low-income communities designated as opportunity zones. For qualifying investments held at least 5 years, 10 percent of the deferred gain is excluded from income; this exclusion increases to 15 percent for investments held for at least 7 years. In addition, capital gains from the sale or exchange of an investment in a qualified opportunity fund held for at least 10 years are excluded from gross income.

93. *Disaster Employee Retention Credit.* —The baseline tax system would not allow credits for particular activities, investments, or industries. In contrast, the Tax Code provides employers located in certain presidentially declared disaster areas during the years 2017 through 2020 a 40 percent credit for up to $6,000 in wages paid to each eligible employee while the business was inoperable as a result of the disaster. Only wages paid after the disaster occurred and within 150 days of the last day of the incident period are eligible for the credit. Employers must reduce their deduction for wages paid by the amount of the credit claimed.

Education, Training, Employment, and Social Services

94. *Exclusion of scholarship and fellowship income (normal tax method).*—Scholarships and fellowships are excluded from taxable income to the extent they pay for tuition and course-related expenses of the grantee. Similarly, tuition reductions for employees of educational institutions and their families are not included in taxable income. From an economic point of view, scholarships and fellowships are either gifts not conditioned on the performance of services, or they are rebates of educational costs. Thus, under the baseline tax system of the reference tax law method, this exclusion is not a tax expenditure because this method does not include either gifts or price reductions in a taxpayer's gross income. The exclusion, however, is considered a tax expenditure under the normal tax method, which includes gift-like transfers of Government funds in gross income. (Many scholarships are derived directly or indirectly from Government funding.)

95. *Tax credits for post-secondary education expenses.*—The baseline tax system would not allow credits for particular activities, investments, or industries. Under current law in 2020, however, there are two credits for certain post-secondary education expenses. The American Opportunity Tax Credit allows a partially refundable credit of up to $2,500 per eligible student for qualified tuition and related expenses paid during each of the first four years of the student's post-secondary education. The credit is phased out for taxpayers with modified adjusted gross income between $160,000 and $180,000 if married filing jointly ($80,000 and $90,000 for other taxpayers), not indexed. The Lifetime Learning Credit allows a non-refundable credit for 20 percent of an eligible student's qualified tuition and fees, up to a maximum credit per return of $2,000. In Tax Year 2020, the credit is phased out ratably for taxpayers with modified AGI between $118,000 and $138,000 if married filing jointly ($59,000 and $69,000 for other taxpayers). Beginning with Tax Year 2021, the phaseout ranges for the Lifetime Learning credit are raised to conform to the ranges for the American Opportunity Tax Credit and indexing is eliminated. The Lifetime Learning credit can be claimed in any year in which post-secondary education expenses are incurred. Only one credit can be claimed per qualifying student. Married individuals filing separate returns cannot claim either credit. For tax years ending before December 31, 2020, certain taxpayers could choose to claim an above the line deduction for qualified tuition and related expenses rather than either of the two credits.

96. *Deductibility of student loan interest.*—The baseline tax system accepts current law's general rule limiting taxpayers' ability to deduct non-business interest expenses. In contrast, taxpayers may claim an above-the-line deduction of up to $2,500 on interest paid on an education loan. In Tax Year 2020, the maximum deduction is phased down ratably for taxpayers with modified AGI between $140,000 and $170,000 if married filing jointly ($70,000 and $85,000 for other taxpayers).

Married individuals filing separate returns cannot claim the deduction.

97. *Qualified tuition programs (includes Education IRA).*—The baseline tax system generally would tax all income under the regular tax rate schedule. It would not allow preferentially low (or zero) tax rates to apply to certain types or sources of income. Some States have adopted prepaid tuition plans, prepaid room and board plans, and college savings plans, which allow persons to pay in advance or save for college expenses for designated beneficiaries. Under current law, investment income, or the return on prepayments, is not taxed when earned, and is tax-exempt when withdrawn to pay for qualified expenses. Beginning in 2018, the definition of a qualified expense was expanded to include up to $10,000 per child per year of expenses for primary or secondary education, including tuition at religious schools.

98. *Exclusion of interest on student-loan bonds.*—The baseline tax system generally would tax all income under the regular tax rate schedule. It would not allow preferentially low (or zero) tax rates to apply to certain types or sources of income. In contrast, interest earned on State and local bonds issued to finance student loans is tax-exempt under current law. The volume of all such private activity bonds that each State may issue annually is limited.

99. *Exclusion of interest on bonds for private nonprofit educational facilities.*—The baseline tax system generally would tax all income under the regular tax rate schedule. It would not allow preferentially low (or zero) tax rates to apply to certain types or sources of income. In contrast, under current law interest earned on State and local Government bonds issued to finance the construction of facilities used by private nonprofit educational institutions is not taxed.

100. *Credit for holders of zone academy bonds.*—The baseline tax system would not allow credits for particular activities, investments, or industries. Under current law, however, financial institutions that own zone academy bonds receive a non-refundable tax credit rather than interest. The credit is included in gross income. Proceeds from zone academy bonds may only be used to renovate, but not construct, qualifying schools and for certain other school purposes. The total amount of zone academy bonds that may be issued was limited to $1.4 billion in 2009 and 2010. As of March 2010, issuers of the unused authorization of such bonds could opt to receive direct payment with the yield becoming fully taxable. An additional $0.4 billion of these bonds with a tax credit was authorized to be issued each year in 2011 through 2016.

101. *Exclusion of interest on savings bonds redeemed to finance educational expenses.*—The baseline tax system generally would tax all income under the regular tax rate schedule. It would not allow preferentially low (or zero) tax rates to apply to certain types or sources of income. Under current law, however, interest earned on U.S. savings bonds issued after December 31, 1989, is tax-exempt if the bonds are transferred to an educational institution to pay for educational expenses. The tax exemption is phased out for taxpayers with AGI between \$123,550 and \$153,550 if married filing jointly (\$82,350 and \$97,350 for other taxpayers) in 2020.

102. *Parental personal exemption for students age 19 or over.*—Under the baseline tax system, a personal exemption would be allowed for the taxpayer, as well as for the taxpayer's spouse and dependents who do not claim a personal exemption on their own tax returns. These exemptions are repealed for taxable years beginning after December 31, 2017, and before January 1, 2026. However, the definitions regarding eligibility for dependent exemptions for children (and qualifying relatives), which determine eligibility for a number of family-related provisions, remain in place. These provisions include the new \$500 credit for dependents other than qualifying children (Other Dependent Credit, or ODP). In general, to be considered a dependent child, a child would have to be under age 19. In contrast, the Tax Code allows taxpayers to consider their children aged 19 to 23 as dependents, as long as the children are full-time students and reside with the taxpayer for over half the year (with exceptions for temporary absences from home, such as for school attendance). Absent this provision, children over 18 would need to meet the more stringent rules for qualified relatives in order to qualify the taxpayer for certain benefits, including the ODP.

103. *Charitable contributions to educational institutions.*—The baseline tax system would not allow a deduction for personal expenditures. In contrast, the Tax Code provides taxpayers a deduction for contributions to nonprofit educational institutions that are similar to personal expenditures. Moreover, taxpayers who donate capital assets to educational institutions can deduct the asset's current value without being taxed on any appreciation in value. An individual's total charitable contribution generally may not exceed 50 percent (60 percent for tax years 2018 and 2025) of adjusted gross income; a corporation's total charitable contributions generally may not exceed 10 percent of pre-tax income.

104. *Exclusion of employer-provided educational assistance.*—Under the baseline tax system, all compensation, including dedicated payments and in-kind benefits, should be included in taxable income because it represents accretions to wealth that do not materially differ from cash wages. Under current law, however, employer-provided educational assistance is excluded from an employee's gross income, even though the employer's costs for this assistance are a deductible business expense. The maximum exclusion is \$5,250 per taxpayer. From March 2020 through December 31, 2025 employer-provided student loan payments are considered eligible educational assistance.

105. *Special deduction for teacher expenses.*— The baseline tax system would not allow a deduction for personal expenditures. In contrast, the Tax Code allowed educators in both public and private elementary and secondary schools, who worked at least 900 hours during a school year as a teacher, instructor, counselor, principal or aide, to subtract up to \$250 of qualified expenses, indexed to 2014, when determining their adjusted gross income (AGI).

106. *Discharge of student loan indebtedness.*— Under the baseline tax system, all compensation, including dedicated payments and in-kind benefits, should be included in taxable income. In contrast, the Tax Code allows certain professionals who perform in underserved areas or specific fields, and as a consequence have their student loans discharged, not to recognize such discharge as income.

107. *Qualified school construction bonds.*—The baseline tax system would not allow credits for particular activities, investments, or industries. Instead, it generally would seek to tax uniformly all returns from investment-like activities. In contrast, the Tax Code was modified in 2009 to provide a tax credit in lieu of interest to holders of qualified school construction bonds. The national volume limit is \$22.4 billion over 2009 and 2010. As of March 2010, issuers of such bonds could opt to receive direct payment with the yield becoming fully taxable.

108. *Work opportunity tax credit.*—The baseline tax system would not allow credits for particular activities, investments, or industries. Instead, it generally would seek to tax uniformly all returns from investment-like activities. In contrast, the Tax Code provides employers with a tax credit for qualified wages paid to individuals. The credit applies to employees who began work on or before December 31, 2025 and who are certified as members of various targeted groups. The amount of the credit that can be claimed is 25 percent of qualified wages for employment less than 400 hours and 40 percent for employment of 400 hours or more. Generally, the maximum credit per employee is \$2,400 and can only be claimed on the first year of wages an individual earns from an employer. However, the credit for long-term welfare recipients can be claimed on second year wages as well and has a \$9,000 maximum. Also, certain categories of veterans are eligible for a higher maximum credit of up to \$9,600. Employers must reduce their deduction for wages paid by the amount of the credit claimed.

109. *Employer-provided child care exclusion.*—Under the baseline tax system, all compensation, including dedicated payments and in-kind benefits, should be included in taxable income. In contrast, in Taxable Year 2020 up to \$5,000 of employer-provided child care is excluded from an employee's gross income even though the employer's costs for the child care are a deductible business expense.

110. *Employer-provided child care credit.*—The baseline tax system would not allow credits for particular activities, investments, or industries. In contrast, current law provides a credit equal to 25 percent of qualified expenses for employee child care and 10 percent of qualified expenses for child care resource and referral services. Employer deductions for such expenses are reduced by the amount of the credit. The maximum total credit is limited to \$150,000 per taxable year.

111. *Assistance for adopted foster children.*— Under the baseline tax system, all compensation, including dedicated payments and in-kind benefits, should be included in taxable income. Taxpayers who adopt eligible children from the public foster care system can receive

monthly payments for the children's significant and varied needs and a reimbursement of up to $2,000 for nonrecurring adoption expenses; special needs adoptions receive the maximum benefit even if that amount is not spent. These payments are excluded from gross income under current law.

112. ***Adoption credit and exclusion.***—The baseline tax system would not allow credits for particular activities. In contrast, taxpayers can receive a tax credit for qualified adoption expenses under current law. Taxpayers may also exclude qualified adoption expenses provided or reimbursed by an employer from income, subject to the same maximum amounts and phase-out as the credit. The same expenses cannot qualify for tax benefits under both programs; however, a taxpayer may use the benefits of the exclusion and the tax credit for different expenses.

113. ***Exclusion of employee meals and lodging (other than military).***—Under the baseline tax system, all compensation, including dedicated payments and in-kind benefits, should be included in taxable income. Furthermore, all compensation would generally be deductible by the employer. In contrast, under current law employer-provided meals and lodging are excluded from an employee's gross income. Additionally, beginning in 2018, employers are allowed a deduction for only 50 percent of the expenses of employer-provided meals, except that in 2021 and 2022, employers are eligible for a full deduction on restaurant meals provided to employees. Employer-provided lodging is fully deductible by the employer, in general.

114. ***Credit for child and dependent care expenses.***—The baseline tax system would not allow credits for particular activities or targeted at specific groups. In contrast, the Tax Code provides a tax credit to parents who work or attend school and who have child and dependent care expenses. In taxable year 2020 expenditures up to a maximum $3,000 for one dependent and $6,000 for two or more dependents are eligible for the credit. The credit is equal to 35 percent of qualified expenditures for taxpayers with incomes of up to $15,000. The credit is reduced to a minimum of 20 percent by one percentage point for each $2,000 of income in excess of $15,000.

115. ***Credit for disabled access expenditures.***—The baseline tax system would not allow credits for particular activities, investments, or industries. In contrast, the Tax Code provides small businesses (less than $1 million in gross receipts or fewer than 31 full-time employees) a 50 percent credit for expenditures in excess of $250 to remove access barriers for disabled persons. The credit is limited to $5,000.

116. ***Deductibility of charitable contributions, other than education and health.***—The baseline tax system would not allow a deduction for personal expenditures including charitable contributions. In contrast, the Tax Code provides taxpayers a deduction for contributions to charitable, religious, and certain other nonprofit organizations. Taxpayers who donate capital assets to charitable organizations can deduct the assets' current value without being taxed on any appreciation in value. An individual's total charitable contribution generally may not exceed 50 percent (60 percent between 2018 and 2025) of adjusted gross income; a corporation's total charitable contributions generally may not exceed 10 percent of pre-tax income.

117. ***Exclusion of certain foster care payments.***—The baseline tax system generally would tax all income under the regular tax rate schedule. It would not allow preferentially low (or zero) tax rates to apply to certain types or sources of income. Foster parents provide a home and care for children who are wards of the State, under contract with the State. Under current law, compensation received for this service is excluded from the gross incomes of foster parents; the expenses they incur are nondeductible.

118. ***Exclusion of parsonage allowances.***—Under the baseline tax system, all compensation, including dedicated payments and in-kind benefits, would be included in taxable income. Dedicated payments and in-kind benefits represent accretions to wealth that do not differ materially from cash wages. In contrast, the Tax Code allows an exclusion from a clergyman's taxable income for the value of the clergyman's housing allowance or the rental value of the clergyman's parsonage.

119. ***Indian employment credit.***—The baseline tax system would not allow credits for particular activities, investments, or industries. Instead, it generally would seek to tax uniformly all returns from investment-like activities. In contrast, the Tax Code provides employers with a tax credit for qualified wages paid to employees who are enrolled members of Indian tribes. The amount of the credit that could be claimed is 20 percent of the excess of qualified wages and health insurance costs paid by the employer in the current tax year over the amount of such wages and costs paid by the employer in 1993. Qualified wages and health insurance costs with respect to any employee for the taxable year could not exceed $20,000. Employees have to live on or near the reservation where they work to be eligible for the credit. Employers must reduce their deduction for wages paid by the amount of the credit claimed. The credit does not apply to taxable years beginning after December 31, 2021.

120. ***Credit for employer differential wage payments.***—The baseline tax system would not allow credits for particular activities, investments, or industries. In contrast, the Tax Code provides employers with a 20 percent tax credit for eligible differential wages paid to employees who are members of the uniformed services while on active duty for more than 30 days. The amount of eligible differential wage payments made to a qualified employee in a taxable year is capped at $20,000. Employers must reduce their deduction for wages paid by the amount of the credit claimed.

Health

121. ***Exclusion of employer contributions for medical insurance premiums and medical care.***—Under the baseline tax system, all compensation, including dedicated payments and in-kind benefits,

should be included in taxable income. In contrast, under current law, employer-paid health insurance premiums and other medical expenses (including long-term care or Health Reimbursement Accounts) are not included in employee gross income even though they are deducted as a business expense by the employee.

122. **Self-employed medical insurance premiums.**—Under the baseline tax system, all compensation and remuneration, including dedicated payments and in-kind benefits, should be included in taxable income. In contrast, under current law self-employed taxpayers may deduct their family health insurance premiums. Taxpayers without self-employment income are not eligible for this special deduction. The deduction is not available for any month in which the self-employed individual is eligible to participate in an employer-subsidized health plan and the deduction may not exceed the self-employed individual's earned income from self-employment.

123. **Medical Savings Accounts and Health Savings Accounts.**—Under the baseline tax system, all compensation, including dedicated payments and in-kind benefits, should be included in taxable income. Also, the baseline tax system would not allow a deduction for personal expenditures and generally would tax investment earnings. In contrast, individual contributions to Archer Medical Savings Accounts (Archer MSAs) and Health Savings Accounts (HSAs) are allowed as a deduction in determining adjusted gross income whether or not the individual itemizes deductions. Employer contributions to Archer MSAs and HSAs are excluded from income and employment taxes. Archer MSAs and HSAs require that the individual have coverage by a qualifying high deductible health plan. Earnings from the accounts are excluded from taxable income. Distributions from the accounts used for medical expenses are not taxable. The rules for HSAs are generally more flexible than for Archer MSAs and the deductible contribution amounts are greater (in 2019, $3,500 for taxpayers with individual coverage and $7,000 for taxpayers with family coverage). Thus, HSAs have largely replaced MSAs.

124. **Deductibility of medical expenses.**—The baseline tax system would not allow a deduction for personal expenditures. In contrast, under current law personal expenditures for medical care (including the costs of prescription drugs) exceeding 7.5 percent of the taxpayer's adjusted gross income are deductible. For tax years beginning after 2012, only medical expenditures exceeding 10 percent of the taxpayer's adjusted gross income are deductible. However, for the years 2013, 2014, 2015 and 2016, if either the taxpayer or the taxpayer's spouse turned 65 before the end of the taxable year, the threshold remained at 7.5 percent of adjusted income. Beginning in 2017, the 10 percent threshold applied to all taxpayers, including those over 65.

125. **Exclusion of interest on hospital construction bonds.**—The baseline tax system generally would tax all income under the regular tax rate schedule. It would not allow preferentially low (or zero) tax rates to apply to certain types or sources of income. In contrast, under current law interest earned on State and local government debt issued to finance hospital construction is excluded from income subject to tax.

126. **Refundable Premium Assistance Tax Credit.**—The baseline tax system would not allow credits for particular activities or targeted at specific groups. In contrast, for taxable years ending after 2013, the Tax Code provides a premium assistance credit to any eligible taxpayer for any qualified health insurance purchased through a Health Insurance Exchange. In general, an eligible taxpayer is a taxpayer with annual household income between 100 percent and 400 percent of the federal poverty level for a family of the taxpayer's size and that does not have access to affordable minimum essential health care coverage. The amount of the credit equals the lesser of (1) the actual premiums paid by the taxpayer for such coverage or (2) the difference between the cost of a statutorily-identified benchmark plan offered on the exchange and a required payment by the taxpayer that increases with income. The American Rescue Plan Act of 2021 (P.L. 117-2) temporarily increased the Premium Tax Credit in three ways. For 2021 and 2022, the legislation increased the Premium Tax Credit for currently eligible individuals and families, providing access to free plans for those earning 100 to 150 percent of the federal poverty level, and expanded eligibility to newly include individuals and families with income above 400 percent of the federal poverty level. The legislation also expanded eligibility in 2021 to individuals who receive unemployment insurance for any week in 2021. The legislation also eliminated the requirement for individuals to repay any excess advance payments of the Premium Tax Credit for 2020.

127. **Credit for employee health insurance expenses of small business.**—The baseline tax system would not allow credits for particular activities or targeted at specific groups. In contrast, the Tax Code provides a tax credit to qualified small employers that make a certain level of non-elective contributions towards the purchase of certain health insurance coverage for its employees. To receive a credit, an employer must have fewer than 25 full-time-equivalent employees whose average annual full-time-equivalent wages from the employer are less than $50,000 (indexed for taxable years after 2013). However, to receive a full credit, an employer must have no more than 10 full-time employees, and the average wage paid to these employees must be no more than $25,000 (indexed for taxable years after 2013). A qualifying employer may claim the credit for any taxable year beginning in 2010, 2011, 2012, and 2013 and for up to two years for insurance purchased through a Health Insurance Exchange thereafter. For taxable years beginning in 2010, 2011, 2012, and 2013, the maximum credit is 35 percent of premiums paid by qualified taxable employers and 25 percent of premiums paid by qualified tax-exempt organizations. For taxable years beginning in 2014 and later years, the maximum tax credit increases to 50 percent of premiums paid by qualified taxable employers and 35 percent of premiums paid by qualified tax-exempt organizations.

128. **Deductibility of charitable contributions to health institutions.**—The baseline tax system would

not allow a deduction for personal expenditures including charitable contributions. In contrast, the Tax Code provides individuals and corporations a deduction for contributions to nonprofit health institutions. Tax expenditures resulting from the deductibility of contributions to other charitable institutions are listed under the education, training, employment, and social services function.

129. *Tax credit for orphan drug research.*—The baseline tax system would not allow credits for particular activities, investments, or industries. In contrast, under current law drug firms can claim a tax credit of 50 percent of the costs for clinical testing required by the Food and Drug Administration for drugs that treat rare physical conditions or rare diseases. This rate is modified to 25 percent by TCJA for expenditures incurred or paid in tax years beginning after December 31, 2017.

130. *Special Blue Cross/Blue Shield tax benefits.*—The baseline tax system generally would tax all profits under the regular tax rate schedule using broadly applicable measures of baseline income. It would not allow preferentially low tax rates to apply to certain types or sources of income. In contrast, certain Blue Cross and Blue Shield (BC/BS) health insurance providers and certain other health insurers are provided with special tax benefits, provided that their percentage of total premium revenue expended on reimbursement for clinical services provided to enrollees or for activities that improve health care quality is not less than 85 percent for the taxable year. A qualifying insurer may take as a deduction 100 percent of any net increase in its unearned premium reserves, instead of the 80 percent allowed other insurers. A qualifying insurer is also allowed a special deduction equal to the amount by which 25 percent of its health-claim expenses exceeds its beginning-of-the-year accounting surplus. The deduction is limited to the insurer's taxable income determined without the special deduction.

131. *Tax credit for health insurance purchased by certain displaced and retired individuals.*—The baseline tax system would not allow credits for particular activities, investments, or industries. In contrast, the Tax Code provides a refundable tax credit of 72.5 percent for the purchase of health insurance coverage by individuals eligible for Trade Adjustment Assistance and certain Pension Benefit Guarantee Corporation pension recipients. This provision will expire on December 31, 2019.

132. *Distributions from retirement plans for premiums for health and long-term care insurance.*—Under the baseline tax system, all compensation, including dedicated and deferred payments, should be included in taxable income. In contrast, the Tax Code provides for tax-free distributions of up to $3,000 from governmental retirement plans for premiums for health and long term care premiums of public safety officers.

133. *Credit for family and sick leave taken by self-employed individuals.*—The baseline tax system would not allow credits for particular activities or targeted as specific groups. Under current law, however, self-employed individuals are allowed a refundable credit equal for certain family or sick leave taken. In general, the sick leave credit is equal to 100% of daily self-employment

income (equal to self-employment income divided by 260) during a period of qualified sick leave, up to $511 per day for 10 days. The family leave credit is equal to two thirds of daily self-employment income (but no greater than two thirds of $200) during a period of qualified family leave for up to 10 weeks. Under current law, the credit applies to leave taken prior to April 1, 2021.

Income Security

134. *Child credit.*—The baseline tax system would not allow credits for particular activities or targeted at specific groups. Under current law, however, taxpayers with children under age 17 can qualify for a $2,000 per child partially refundable child credit. Up to $1,400 per child of unclaimed credit due to insufficient tax liability may be refundable—taxpayers may claim a refund for 15 percent of earnings in excess of a $2,500 floor, up to the lesser of the amount of unused credit or $1,400 per child. To be eligible for the child credit, the child must have a Social Security Number (SSN). A taxpayer may also claim a nonrefundable credit of $500 for each qualifying child not eligible for the $2,000 credit (those over sixteen and those without SSNs) and for each dependent relative. The total combined child and other dependent credit is phased out for taxpayers at the rate of $50 per $1,000 of modified AGI above $400,000 ($200,000 for single or head of household filers and $200,000 for married taxpayers filing separately). For tax years beginning after December 31, 2025, the credit returns to its pre-TCJA value of $1,000. At that time, up to the full value of the credit (subject to a phase-in of 15 percent of earnings in excess of $3,000) will be refundable and the $500 other dependent credit will expire. The credit will once again phase out at the rate of $50 per $1,000 of modified AGI above $110,000 ($75,000 for single or head of household filers and $55,000 for married taxpayers filing separately). The social security requirement will remain in place.

135. *Exclusion of railroad Social Security equivalent benefits.*—Under the baseline tax system, all compensation, including dedicated and deferred payments, should be included in taxable income. In contrast, the Social Security Equivalent Benefit paid to railroad retirees is not generally subject to the income tax unless the recipient's gross income reaches a certain threshold under current law. See provision number 156, Social Security benefits for retired workers, for discussion of the threshold.

136. *Exclusion of workers' compensation benefits.*—Under the baseline tax system, all compensation, including dedicated payments and in-kind benefits, should be included in taxable income. However, workers compensation is not subject to the income tax under current law.

137. *Exclusion of public assistance benefits (normal tax method).*—Under the reference tax law baseline, gifts and transfers are not treated as income to the recipients. In contrast, the normal tax method considers cash transfers from the Government as part of the recipients' income, and thus, treats the exclusion

for public assistance benefits under current law as a tax expenditure.

138. *Exclusion of special benefits for disabled coal miners.*—Under the baseline tax system, all compensation, including dedicated payments and in-kind benefits, should be included in taxable income. However, disability payments to former coal miners out of the Black Lung Trust Fund, although income to the recipient, are not subject to the income tax.

139. *Exclusion of military disability pensions.*—Under the baseline tax system, all compensation, including dedicated payments and in-kind benefits, should be included in taxable income. In contrast, most of the military disability pension income received by current disabled military retirees is excluded from their income subject to tax.

140. *Defined benefit employer plans.*—Under the baseline tax system, all compensation, including deferred and dedicated payments, should be included in taxable income. In addition, investment income would be taxed as earned. In contrast, under current law certain contributions to defined benefit pension plans are excluded from an employee's gross income even though employers can deduct their contributions. In addition, the tax on the investment income earned by defined benefit pension plans is deferred until the money is withdrawn.

141. *Defined contribution employer plans.*—Under the baseline tax system, all compensation, including deferred and dedicated payments, should be included in taxable income. In addition, investment income would be taxed as earned. In contrast, under current law individual taxpayers and employers can make tax-preferred contributions to employer-provided 401(k) and similar plans (e.g. 403(b) plans and the Federal Government's Thrift Savings Plan). In 2020, an employee could exclude up to $19,500 of wages from AGI under a qualified arrangement with an employer's 401(k) plan. Employees age 50 or over could exclude up to $26,000 in contributions. The defined contribution plan limit, including both employee and employer contributions, is $57,000 in 2020. The tax on contributions made by both employees and employers and the investment income earned by these plans is deferred until withdrawn.

142. *Individual Retirement Accounts (IRAs).*—Under the baseline tax system, all compensation, including deferred and dedicated payments, should be included in taxable income. In addition, investment income would be taxed as earned. In contrast, under current law individual taxpayers can take advantage of traditional and Roth IRAs to defer or otherwise reduce the tax on the return to their retirement savings. The IRA contribution limit is $6,000 in 2020; taxpayers age 50 or over are allowed to make additional "catch-up" contributions of $1,000. Contributions to a traditional IRA are generally deductible but the deduction is phased out for workers with incomes above certain levels if the workers or their spouses are active participants in an employer-provided retirement plan. Contributions and account earnings are includible in income when withdrawn from traditional IRAs. Roth IRA contributions are not deductible, but earnings and withdrawals are exempt from taxation. Income limits also apply to Roth IRA contributions.

143. *Low and moderate-income savers' credit.*—The baseline tax system would not allow credits for particular activities or targeted at specific groups. In contrast, the Tax Code provides an additional incentive for lower-income taxpayers to save through a nonrefundable credit of up to 50 percent on IRA and other retirement contributions of up to $2,000. This credit is in addition to any deduction or exclusion. The credit is completely phased out by $65,000 for joint filers, $48,750 for head of household filers, and $32,500 for other filers in 2020.

144. *Self-employed plans.*—Under the baseline tax system, all compensation, including deferred and dedicated payments, should be included in taxable income. In addition, investment income would be taxed as earned. In contrast, under current law self-employed individuals can make deductible contributions to their own retirement plans equal to 25 percent of their income, up to a maximum of $57,000 in 2020. Total plan contributions are limited to 25 percent of a firm's total wages. The tax on the investment income earned by self-employed SEP, SIMPLE, and qualified plans is deferred until withdrawn.

145. *Premiums on group term life insurance.*—Under the baseline tax system, all compensation, including deferred and dedicated payments, should be included in taxable income. In contrast, under current law employer-provided life insurance benefits are excluded from an employee's gross income (to the extent that the employer's share of the total costs does not exceed the cost of $50,000 of such insurance) even though the employer's costs for the insurance are a deductible business expense.

146. *Premiums on accident and disability insurance.*—Under the baseline tax system, all compensation, including dedicated payments and in-kind benefits, should be included in taxable income. In contrast, under current law employer-provided accident and disability benefits are excluded from an employee's gross income even though the employer's costs for the benefits are a deductible business expense.

147. *Exclusion of investment income from Supplementary Unemployment Benefit Trusts.*—Under the baseline tax system, all compensation, including dedicated payments and in-kind benefits, should be included in taxable income. In addition, investment income would be taxed as earned. Under current law, employers may establish trusts to pay supplemental unemployment benefits to employees separated from employment. Investment income earned by such trusts is exempt from taxation.

148. *Exclusion of investment income from Voluntary Employee Benefit Associations trusts.*—Under the baseline tax system, all compensation, including dedicated payments and in-kind benefits, should be included in taxable income. Under current law, employers may establish associations, or VEBAs, to pay employee benefits, which may include health benefit plans, life insurance, and disability insurance, among other employee benefits. Investment income earned by such trusts is exempt from taxation.

149. ***Special Employee Stock Ownership Plan (ESOP) rules.***— Under the baseline tax system, all compensation, including dedicated payments and in-kind benefits, should be included in taxable income. In addition, investment income would be taxed as earned. In contrast, employer-paid contributions (the value of stock issued to the ESOP) are deductible by the employer as part of employee compensation costs. They are not included in the employees' gross income for tax purposes, however, until they are paid out as benefits. In addition, the following special income tax provisions for ESOPs are intended to increase ownership of corporations by their employees: (1) annual employer contributions are subject to less restrictive limitations than other qualified retirement plans; (2) ESOPs may borrow to purchase employer stock, guaranteed by their agreement with the employer that the debt will be serviced by the payment (deductible by firm) of a portion of wages (excludable by the employees) to service the loan; (3) employees who sell appreciated company stock to the ESOP may defer any taxes due until they withdraw benefits; (4) dividends paid to ESOP-held stock are deductible by the employer; and (5) earnings are not taxed as they accrue.

150. ***Additional deduction for the blind.***—Under the baseline tax system, the standard deduction is allowed. An additional standard deduction for a targeted group within a given filing status would not be allowed. In contrast, the Tax Code allows taxpayers who are blind to claim an additional $1,700 standard deduction if single, or $1,350 if married in 2019.

151. ***Additional deduction for the elderly.***— Under the baseline tax system, the standard deduction is allowed. An additional standard deduction for a targeted group within a given filing status would not be allowed. In contrast, the Tax Code allows taxpayers who are 65 years or older to claim an additional $1,700 standard deduction if single, or $1,350 if married in 2020.

152. ***Deductibility of casualty losses.***—Under the baseline tax system, neither the purchase of property nor insurance premiums to protect the property's value are deductible as costs of earning income. Therefore, reimbursement for insured loss of such property is not included as a part of gross income, and uninsured losses are not deductible. In contrast, the Tax Code provides a deduction for uninsured casualty and theft losses of more than $100 each, to the extent that total losses during the year exceed 10 percent of the taxpayer's adjusted gross income. In the case of taxable years beginning after December 31, 2017, and before January 1, 2026, personal casualty losses are deductible only to the extent they are attributable to a Federally declared disaster area.

153. ***Earned income tax credit (EITC).***—The baseline tax system would not allow credits for particular activities or targeted at specific groups. In contrast, the Tax Code provides an EITC to low-income workers at a maximum rate of 45 percent of income. In 2020, for a family with one qualifying child, the credit is 34 percent of the first $10,540 of earned income. The credit is 40 percent of the first $14,800 of income for a family with two qualifying children, and it is 45 percent of the first $14,800 of income for a family with three or more qualifying children. Low-income workers with no qualifying children are eligible for a 7.65 percent credit on the first $7,030 of earned income. The credit plateaus and then phases out with the greater of AGI or earnings at income levels and rates which depend upon how many qualifying children are eligible and marital status. In 2020, the phase-down for married filers begins at incomes $5,890 ($5,800 for filers without children) greater than for otherwise similar unmarried filers. Earned income tax credits in excess of tax liabilities owed through the individual income tax system are refundable to individuals. Beginning in 2018, the parameters of the EITC are indexed by the chained CPI, which results in a smaller inflation adjustment than previously. This change is permanent.

154. ***Recovery rebate credits.***—The baseline tax system would not allow credits for particular activities or targeted at specific groups. In contrast, the Coronavirus Aid, Relief, and Economic Security (CARES) Act provided rebates of $1,200 ($2,400 for married couples filing jointly) and 500 per child. The total rebate amount begins phasing out at adjusted gross income over $75,000 ($150,000 for married couples filing jointly, $112,500 heads of household). This was followed by the Consolidated Appropriations Act which provided rebates of $600 per eligible taxpayer ($1,200 for married couples filing jointly) plus an additional $600 per child, with phase out features similar to CARES.

Social Security

155. ***Social Security benefits for retired and disabled workers and spouses, dependents, and survivors.***—The baseline tax system would tax Social Security benefits to the extent that contributions to Social Security were not previously taxed. Thus, the portion of Social Security benefits that is attributable to employer contributions and to earnings on employer and employee contributions (and not attributable to employee contributions which are taxed at the time of contribution) would be subject to tax. In contrast, the Tax Code may not tax all of the Social Security benefits that exceed the beneficiary's contributions from previously taxed income. Actuarially, previously taxed contributions generally do not exceed 15 percent of benefits, even for retirees receiving the highest levels of benefits. Therefore, up to 85 percent of recipients' Social Security and Railroad Social Security Equivalent retirement benefits are included in (phased into) the income tax base if the recipient's provisional income exceeds certain base amounts. (Provisional income is equal to other items included in adjusted gross income plus foreign or U.S. possession income, tax-exempt interest, and one half of Social Security and Railroad Social Security Equivalent retirement benefits.) The untaxed portion of the benefits received by taxpayers who are below the income amounts at which 85 percent of the benefits are taxable is counted as a tax expenditure. Benefits paid to disabled workers and to spouses, dependents, and survivors are treated in a similar manner. Railroad Social Security Equivalent benefits are treated like Social Security benefits. See

also provision number 136, Exclusion of railroad Social Security equivalent benefits.

156. ***Credit for certain employer social security contributions.***—Under the baseline tax system, employer contributions to Social Security represent labor cost and are deductible expenses. Under current law, however, certain employers are allowed a tax credit, instead of a deduction, against taxes paid on tips received from customers in connection with the providing, delivering, or serving of food or beverages for consumption. The tip credit equals the full amount of the employer's share of FICA taxes paid on the portion of tips, when added to the employee's non-tip wages, in excess of $5.15 per hour. The credit is available only with respect to FICA taxes paid on tips.

Veterans Benefits and Services

157. ***Exclusion of veterans death benefits and disability compensation.***—Under the baseline tax system, all compensation, including dedicated payments and in-kind benefits, should be included in taxable income because they represent accretions to wealth that do not materially differ from cash wages. In contrast, all compensation due to death or disability paid by the Veterans Administration is excluded from taxable income under current law.

158. ***Exclusion of veterans pensions.***—Under the baseline tax system, all compensation, including dedicated payments and in-kind benefits, should be included in taxable income because they represent accretions to wealth that do not materially differ from cash wages. Under current law, however, pension payments made by the Veterans Administration are excluded from gross income.

159. ***Exclusion of G.I. Bill benefits.***—Under the baseline tax system, all compensation, including dedicated payments and in-kind benefits, should be included in taxable income because they represent accretions to wealth that do not materially differ from cash wages. Under current law, however, G.I. Bill benefits paid by the Veterans Administration are excluded from gross income.

160. ***Exclusion of interest on veterans housing bonds.***—The baseline tax system generally would tax all income under the regular tax rate schedule. It would not allow preferentially low (or zero) tax rates to apply to certain types or sources of income. In contrast, under current law, interest earned on general obligation bonds issued by State and local governments to finance housing for veterans is excluded from taxable income.

General Government

161. ***Exclusion of interest on public purpose State and local bonds.***—The baseline tax system generally would tax all income under the regular tax rate schedule. It would not allow preferentially low (or zero) tax rates to apply to certain types or sources of income. In contrast, under current law interest earned on State and local government bonds issued to finance public-purpose construction (e.g., schools, roads, sewers), equipment acquisition, and other public purposes is tax-exempt. Interest on bonds issued by Indian tribal governments for essential governmental purposes is also tax-exempt.

162. ***Build America Bonds.***—The baseline tax system would not allow credits for particular activities or targeted at specific groups. In contrast, the Tax Code in 2009 allowed State and local governments to issue taxable bonds through 2010 and receive a direct payment from Treasury equal to 35 percent of interest expenses. Alternatively, State and local governments could issue taxable bonds and the private lenders receive the 35 percent credit which is included in taxable income.

163. ***Deductibility of nonbusiness State and local taxes other than on owner-occupied homes.***—Under the baseline tax system, a deduction for personal consumption expenditures would not be allowed. In contrast, the Tax Code allows taxpayers who itemize their deductions to claim a deduction for State and local income taxes (or, at the taxpayer's election, State and local sales taxes) and property taxes, even though these taxes primarily pay for services that, if purchased directly by taxpayers, would not be deductible. (The estimates for this tax expenditure do not include the estimates for the deductibility of State and local property tax on owner-occupied homes. See item 57.) In the case of taxable years beginning after December 31, 2017, and before January 1, 2026, (1) the deduction for foreign real property taxes paid is disallowed and (2) the deduction for taxes paid in any taxable year, which includes the deduction for property taxes on real property, is limited to $10,000 ($5,000 in the case of a married individual filing a separate return).

Interest

164. ***Deferral of interest on U.S. savings bonds.***—The baseline tax system would uniformly tax all returns to investments and not allow an exemption or deferral for particular activities, investments, or industries. In contrast, taxpayers may defer paying tax on interest earned on U.S. savings bonds until the bonds are redeemed.

APPENDIX

Performance Measures and the Economic Effects of Tax Expenditures

The Government Performance and Results Act of 1993 (GPRA) directs Federal agencies to develop annual and strategic plans for their programs and activities. These plans set out performance objectives to be achieved over a specific time period. Most of these objectives are achieved through direct expenditure programs. Tax expenditures—spending programs implemented through the tax code by reducing tax obligations for certain activities—contribute to achieving these goals in a manner similar to direct expenditure programs.

Tax expenditures by definition work through the tax system and, particularly, the income tax. Thus, they may be relatively advantageous policy approaches when the benefit or incentive is related to income and is intended to be widely available. Because there is an existing public administrative and private compliance structure for the tax system, income-based programs that require little oversight might be efficiently run through the tax system. In addition, some tax expenditures actually simplify the operation of the tax system. Tax expenditures also implicitly subsidize certain activities in a manner similar to direct expenditures. For example, exempting employer-sponsored health insurance from income taxation is equivalent to a direct spending subsidy equal to the forgone tax obligations for this type of compensation. Spending, regulatory or tax-disincentive policies can also modify behavior, but may have different economic effects. Finally, a variety of tax expenditure tools can be used, e.g., deductions, credits, exemptions, deferrals, floors, ceilings, phase-ins, phase-outs, and these can be dependent on income, expenses, or demographic characteristics (age, number of family members, etc.). This wide range of policy instruments means that tax expenditures can be flexible and can have very different economic effects.

Tax expenditures also have limitations. In many cases they add to the complexity of the tax system, which raises both administrative and compliance costs. For example, exemptions, deductions, credits, and phase-outs can complicate filing and decision-making. The income tax system may have little or no contact with persons who have no or very low incomes, and does not require information on certain characteristics of individuals used in some spending programs, such as wealth or duration of employment. These features may reduce the effectiveness of tax expenditures for addressing socioeconomic disparities. Tax expenditures also generally do not enable the same degree of agency discretion as an outlay program. For example, grant or direct Federal service delivery programs can prioritize activities to be addressed with specific resources in a way that is difficult to emulate with tax expenditures.

Outlay programs have advantages where the direct provision of government services is particularly warranted, such as equipping and maintaining the armed forces or administering the system of justice. Outlay programs may also be specifically designed to meet the needs of low-income families who would not otherwise be subject to income taxes or need to file a tax return. Outlay programs may also receive more year-to-year oversight and fine tuning through the legislative and executive budget process. In addition, many different types of spending programs include direct Government provision; credit programs; and payments to State and local governments, the private sector, or individuals in the form of grants or contracts, which provide flexibility for policy design. On the other hand, certain outlay programs may rely less directly on economic incentives and private-market provision than tax incentives, thereby reducing the relative efficiency of spending programs for some goals. Finally,

spending programs, particularly on the discretionary side, may respond less rapidly to changing activity levels and economic conditions than tax expenditures.

Regulations may have more direct and immediate effects than outlay and tax-expenditure programs because regulations apply directly and immediately to the regulated party (i.e., the intended actor), generally in the private sector. Regulations can also be fine-tuned more quickly than tax expenditures because they can often be changed as needed by the Executive Branch without legislation. Like tax expenditures, regulations often rely largely on voluntary compliance, rather than detailed inspections and policing. As such, the public administrative costs tend to be modest relative to the private resource costs associated with modifying activities. Historically, regulations have tended to rely on proscriptive measures, as opposed to economic incentives. This reliance can diminish their economic efficiency, although this feature can also promote full compliance where (as in certain safety-related cases) policymakers believe that trade-offs with economic considerations are not of paramount importance. Also, regulations generally do not directly affect Federal outlays or receipts. Thus, like tax expenditures, they may escape the degree of scrutiny that outlay programs receive.

A Framework for Evaluating the Effectiveness of Tax Expenditures

Across all major budgetary categories—from housing and health to space, technology, agriculture, and national defense—tax expenditures make up a significant portion of Federal activity and affect every area of the economy. For these reasons, a comprehensive evaluation framework that examines incentives, direct results, and spillover effects will benefit the budgetary process by informing decisions on tax expenditure policy.

As described above, tax expenditures, like spending and regulatory programs, have a variety of objectives and economic effects. These include encouraging certain types of activities (e.g., saving for retirement or investing in certain sectors); increasing certain types of after-tax income (e.g., favorable tax treatment of Social Security income); and reducing private compliance costs and Government administrative costs (e.g., the exclusion for up to $500,000 of capital gains on home sales). Some of these objectives are well-suited to quantitative measurement and evaluation, while others are less well-suited.

Performance measurement is generally concerned with inputs, outputs, and outcomes. In the case of tax expenditures, the principal input is usually the revenue effect. Outputs are quantitative or qualitative measures of goods and services, or changes in income and investment, directly produced by these inputs. Outcomes, in turn, represent the changes in the economy, society, or environment that are the ultimate goals of programs. Evaluations assess whether programs are meeting intended goals, but may also encompass analyzing whether initiatives are superior to other policy alternatives.

Similar to prior years, the Administration is working towards examining the objectives and effects of the wide range of tax expenditures in the President's Budget, despite challenges related to data availability, measurement, and analysis. Evaluations include an assessment of whether tax expenditures are achieving intended policy results in an efficient manner, with minimal burdens on individual taxpayers, consumers, and firms, and an examination of possible unintended effects and their consequences.

As an illustration of how evaluations can inform budgetary decisions, consider education, and research investment credits.

Education. There are millions of individuals taking advantage of tax credits designed to help pay for educational expenses. There are a number of different credits available as well as other important forms of Federal support for higher education such as subsidized student loans and grants. An evaluation would explore the possible relationships between use of the credits and the use of student loans and grants, seeking to answer, for example, whether the use of credits reduces or increases the likelihood of students applying for loans. Such an evaluation would allow stakeholders to determine the need for programs—whether they involve tax credits, subsidized loans, or grants.

Investment. A series of tax expenditures reduce the cost of investment, both in specific activities such as research and experimentation, extractive industries, and certain financial activities, and more generally throughout the economy, through accelerated depreciation for plant and equipment. These provisions can be evaluated along a number of dimensions. For example, it is useful to consider the strength of the incentives by measuring their effects on the cost of capital (the return which investments must yield to cover their costs) and effective tax rates. The impact of these provisions on the amount of corresponding forms of investment (e.g., research spending, exploration activity, equipment) might also be estimated. In some cases, such as research, there is evidence that this private investment can provide significant positive externalities—that is, economic benefits that are not reflected in the market transactions between private parties. It could be useful to quantify these externalities and compare them with the size of tax expenditures. Measures could also indicate the effects on production from these investments such as numbers or values of patents, en-

ergy production and reserves, and industrial production. Issues to be considered include the extent to which the preferences increase production (as opposed to benefiting existing output) and their cost-effectiveness relative to other policies. Analysis could also consider objectives that are more difficult to measure but could be ultimate goals, such as promoting energy security or economic growth. Such an assessment is likely to involve tax analysis as well as consideration of non-tax matters such as market structure, scientific, and other information.

The tax proposals subject to these analyses include items that indirectly affect the estimated value of tax expenditures (such as changes in income tax rates), proposals that make reforms to improve tax compliance and administration, as well as proposals which would change, add, or delete tax expenditures.

Barriers to Evaluation. Developing a framework that is sufficiently comprehensive, accurate, and flexible is a significant challenge. Evaluations are constrained by the availability of appropriate data and challenges in economic modeling:

- Data availability—Data may not exist, or may not exist in an analytically appropriate form, to conduct rigorous evaluations of certain types of expenditures. For example, measuring the effects of tax expenditures designed to achieve tax neutrality for individuals and firms earning income abroad, and foreign firms could require data from foreign governments or firms which are not readily available.

- Analytical constraints—Evaluations of tax expenditures face analytical constraints even when data are available. For example, individuals might have access to several tax expenditures and programs aimed at improving the same outcome. Isolating the effect of a single tax credit is challenging absent a well-specified research design.

- Resources—Tax expenditure analyses are seriously constrained by staffing considerations. Evaluations typically require expert analysts who are often engaged in other areas of work related to the budget.

The Executive Branch is focused on addressing these challenges to lay the foundation for the analysis of tax expenditures comprehensively, alongside evaluations of the effectiveness of direct spending initiatives.

SPECIAL TOPICS

11. AID TO STATE AND LOCAL GOVERNMENTS

The analysis in this chapter focuses on Federal spending that is provided to State and local governments, U.S. territories, and American Indian Tribal governments to help fund programs administered by those entities. This type of Federal spending is known as Federal financial assistance, primarily administered as grants.

In 2020 the Federal Government spent $829 billion on aid to State, local, tribal and territorial governments. Spending on grants was 4 percent of GDP in 2020. These funds support activities that touch every American, such as education, transportation infrastructure, workforce initiatives, community development, and homeland security.

The Budget provides $1.1 trillion in outlays for aid to State, local, tribal and territorial governments in 2022, an increase of 7 percent from spending in 2021, which is estimated to be $1 trillion. Total Federal grant spending to State and local governments is estimated to be 5 percent of GDP in 2022.

Background and Analysis

Federal grants are authorized by the Congress in statute, which then establishes the purpose of the grant and how it is awarded. Most often Federal grants are awarded as direct cash assistance, but Federal grants can also include in-kind assistance—non-monetary aid, such as commodities purchased for the National School Lunch Program—and Federal revenues or assets shared with State and local governments.

In its 2020 State Expenditure Report, the National Association of State Budget Officers (NASBO) reports that 14 percent of total State spending, which is estimated to be about $2.26 trillion[1] in State fiscal year[2] 2020 came from Federal funds. "Overall, total state expenditures (including general funds, other state funds, bonds and federal funds) increased 3.2 percent in 2018, 5.1 percent in fiscal 2019 and are estimated to have grown 7.7 percent in fiscal 2020."[3]

Table 11-1, below, shows Federal grants spending by decade, actual spending in 2020, and estimated spending in 2021 and 2022. Table 11-2 shows the Budget's funding level for grants in every Budget account, organized by functional category, BEA category, and by Federal Agency.

The Federal budget classifies grants by general area or function. Of the total proposed grant spending in

2022, 56 percent is for health programs, with most of the funding for Medicaid. Beyond health programs, 15 percent of Federal aid is estimated to go to income security programs; 8 percent to transportation programs; 12 percent to education, training, and social services; and 9 percent for all other functions.

The Federal budget also classifies grant spending by BEA category—discretionary or mandatory.[4] Funding for discretionary grant programs is determined annually through appropriations acts. Outlays for discretionary grant programs account for 31 percent of total grant spending in 2020. Funding for mandatory programs is provided directly in authorizing legislation that establishes eligibility criteria or benefit formulas; funding for mandatory programs usually is not limited by the annual appropriations process. Outlays for mandatory grant programs account for 69 percent of total grant spending in 2020. Section B of Table 11-1 shows the distribution of grants between mandatory and discretionary spending.

Since much of this budget authority will outlay in future fiscal years, the increase in outlays in 2022 is considerably smaller then will increase over the next couple years. In 2022, grants provided from discretionary funding are estimated to have outlays of $360 billion, an increase of roughly one percent from 2021. The three largest discretionary programs in 2022 are estimated to be Federal-aid Highways programs, with outlays of $46 billion; Tenant Based Rental Assistance, with outlays of $30 billion; and Education for the Disadvantaged (Title 1), with outlays of $56 billion.[5]

In 2022, outlays for mandatory grant programs are estimated to be $751 billion, an increase of 8 percent from spending in 2021, which is estimated to be $695 billion. Medicaid is by far the largest mandatory grant program with estimated outlays of $571 billion in 2022. After Medicaid, the three largest mandatory grant programs by outlays in 2022 are: Child Nutrition programs, which include the School Breakfast Program, the National School Lunch Program and others, $32 billion; the Temporary Assistance for Needy Families program, $17 billion; and the Children's Health Insurance Program, $17 billion.[6]

Federal spending by State for major grants, including the programs mentioned above, may be found on the OMB website at *www.whitehouse.gov/omb/Analytical-Perspectives/*. This supplemental material includes two

---

[1] "2020 State Expenditure Report." National Association of State Budget Officers, 2020. p. 1.

[2] According to "The Fiscal Survey of States" published by the National Association of State Budget Officers (Fall 2019, p. VI), "Forty-six States begin their fiscal years in July and end them in June. The exceptions are New York, which starts its fiscal year on April 1; Texas, with a September 1 start date; and Alabama and Michigan, which start their fiscal years on October 1."

[3] "2020 State Expenditure Report." National Association of State Budget Officers, 2010. p. 2.

[4] For more information on these categories, see Chapter 6, "Budget Concepts," in this volume.

[5] Obligation data by State for programs in each of these budget accounts may be found in the State-by-State tables included with other Budget materials on the OMB website.

[6] Obligation data by State for programs in each of these budget accounts may be found in the State-by-State tables included with other budget materials on the OMB web site.[7] https://www.cfo.gov/wp-content/uploads/2021/Managing-for-Results-Performance-Management-Playbook-for-Federal-Awarding-Agencies.pdf.

tables that summarize State-by-State spending for major grant programs, one summarizing obligations for each program by agency and bureau, and another summarizing total obligation across all programs for each State, followed by 45 individual tables showing State-by-State obligation data for each grant program. The programs shown in these State-by-State tables cover 95 percent of total grants to State and local governments.

In 2020 and 2021, the Federal government provided significant financial assistance to State, local, tribal and territorial governments to help them respond to the health and economic crises caused by the COVID-19 pandemic. Most recently, the American Rescue Plan Act of 2021 (ARP) included funding to set up community vaccination sites, scale up testing and tracing, eliminate supply shortage problems, invest in high-quality treatments, and address disparities in obtaining quality healthcare.

The Administration is committed to effective implementation and strong stewardship of these ARP funds. To support this effort, on March 19 OMB issued M-21-20 to provide guidance to Federal agencies on the equity and accountability requirements for the Federal assistance programs in the Act. OMB has also worked to provide temporary emergency administrative relief to Federal agencies and recipients for the administration of grants and cooperative agreements. Going forward, the Administration will continue to take proactive steps to foster accountability, performance, and public trust in these ARP programs, while implementing sound financial management of these resources.

OTHER SOURCES OF INFORMATION ON FEDERAL GRANTS

A number of other sources provide State-by-State spending data and other information on Federal grants, but may use a broader definition of grants beyond what is included in this chapter.

The website *Grants.gov* is a primary source of information for communities wishing to apply for grants and other financial assistance. *Grants.gov* hosts all competitive open notices of opportunities to apply for Federal grants.

The *System for Award Management* hosted by the General Services Administration contains detailed Assistance Listings (formerly known as the Catalog of Federal Domestic Assistance) of grant and other assistance programs; discussions of eligibility criteria, application procedures, and estimated obligations; and related information. The *Assistance Listings* are available on the internet at *https://beta.sam.gov*.

Current and updated grant receipt information by State and local governments and other non-Federal entities can be found on *USASpending.gov*. This public website includes additional detail on Federal spending, including contract and loan information.

The Federal Audit Clearinghouse maintains an online database *(https://harvester.census.gov/facweb/)* that provides public access to audit reports conducted under OMB guidance located at 2 CFR part 200, Uniform Administrative Requirements, Cost Principles, and Audit Requirements for Federal Awards. Information is available for each audited entity, including the amount of Federal money expended by program and whether there were audit findings.

The Bureau of Economic Analysis, in the Department of Commerce, produces the monthly *Survey of Current Business*, which provides data on the National income and product accounts (NIPA), a broad statistical concept encompassing the entire economy. These accounts, which are available at *bea.gov/national*, include data on Federal grants to State and local governments.

In addition, information on grants and awards can be found through individual Federal Agencies' websites:[7]

---

[7] *https://www.cfo.gov/wp-content/uploads/2021/Managing-for-Results-Performance-Management-Playbook-for-Federal-Awarding-Agencies.pdf*.

- USDA Current Research Information System, *https://cris.nifa.usda.gov/*DOD Medical Research Programs, *https://cdmrp.army.mil/search.aspx*

- Department of Education, Institute of Education Sciences, Funded Research Grants and Contracts, *https://www2.ed.gov/fund/grants-apply.html*

- Department of Health and Human Services (HHS) Grants, *https://www.hhs.gov/grants/grants/index.html*

- HHS Tracking Accountability in Government Grants System (TAGGS), *https://taggs.hhs.gov/AdvancedSearch.cfm*

- National Institutes of Health (NIH) Grants and Funding, *https://grants.nih.gov/funding/index.htm*

- Department of Housing and Urban Development Grants, *https://www.hud.gov/program_offices/spm/gmomgmt/grantsinfo*

- Department of Justice Grants, *https://www.justice.gov/grants*

- Department of Labor Employment and Training Administration (ETA), Grants Awarded, *https://www.doleta.gov/grants/grants_awarded.cfm*

- Department of Transportation Grants, *https://www.transportation.gov/grants*

- Environmental Protection Agency (EPA), *https://www.epa.gov/grants*

- National Library of Medicine (NLM), Health Services Research Projects in Progress (HSRProj), *https://wwwcf.nlm.nih.gov/hsr_project/home_proj.cfm*

- National Science Foundation (NSF) Awards, *https://www.nsf.gov/awardsearch/*

- Small Business Innovation Research (SBIR) and Small Business Technology Transfer (STTR) Awards, *https://www.sbir.gov/sbirsearch/award/all*

Table 11–1. TRENDS IN FEDERAL GRANTS TO STATE AND LOCAL GOVERNMENTS
(Outlays in billions of dollars)

	Actual									Estimate	
	1960	1970	1980	1990	2000	2005	2010	2015	2020	2021	2022
A. Distribution of grants by function:											
Natural resources and environment	0.1	0.4	5.4	3.7	4.6	5.9	9.1	7.0	7.2	6.7	20.7
Agriculture	0.2	0.6	0.6	1.1	0.7	0.9	0.8	0.7	0.8	0.8	1.5
Transportation	3.0	4.6	13.0	19.2	32.2	43.4	61.0	60.8	69.3	73.9	87.8
Community and regional development	0.1	1.8	6.5	5.0	8.7	20.2	18.9	14.4	52.5	80.3	46.6
Education, training, employment, and social services	0.5	6.4	21.9	21.8	36.7	57.2	97.6	60.5	67.9	99.5	133.5
Health	0.2	3.8	15.8	43.9	124.8	197.8	290.2	368.0	493.4	582.9	625.7
Income security	2.6	5.8	18.5	36.9	68.7	90.9	115.2	101.1	118.2	166.9	168.2
Administration of justice	....	0.0	0.5	0.6	5.3	4.8	5.1	3.7	9.4	10.7	8.6
General government	0.2	0.5	8.6	2.3	2.1	4.4	5.2	3.8	4.3	3.7	3.7
Other	0.0	0.1	0.7	0.8	2.1	2.6	5.3	4.3	6.1	14.1	15.0
Total	**7.0**	**24.1**	**91.4**	**135.3**	**285.9**	**428.0**	**608.4**	**624.4**	**829.1**	**1,039.5**	**1,111.2**
B. Distribution of grants by BEA category:											
Discretionary	N/A	10.2	53.4	63.5	116.7	182.3	247.4	189.6	259.4	344.1	360.2
Mandatory	N/A	13.9	38.0	71.9	169.2	245.7	361.0	434.7	569.7	695.4	751.0
Total	**7.0**	**24.1**	**91.4**	**135.3**	**285.9**	**428.0**	**608.4**	**624.4**	**829.1**	**1,039.5**	**1,111.2**
C. Composition:											
Current dollars:											
Payments for individuals	2.6	9.1	20.5	77.4	186.5	278.8	391.4	463.4	608.6	711.0	773.4
Physical capital [1]	3.3	7.1	13.5	27.2	48.7	60.8	93.3	77.2	85.3	96.0	122.8
Other grants	1.1	7.9	25.0	30.7	50.7	88.4	123.7	83.7	135.2	232.5	215.0
Total	**7.0**	**24.1**	**91.4**	**135.3**	**285.9**	**428.0**	**608.4**	**624.4**	**829.1**	**1,039.5**	**1,111.2**
Percentage of total grants:											
Payments for individuals [1]	37.4%	37.7%	22.5%	57.2%	65.3%	65.1%	64.3%	74.2%	73.4%	68.4%	69.6%
Physical capital [1]	47.3%	29.3%	14.8%	20.1%	17.0%	14.2%	15.3%	12.4%	10.3%	9.2%	11.1%
Other grants	15.3%	33.0%	27.4%	22.7%	17.7%	20.7%	20.3%	13.4%	16.3%	22.4%	19.4%
Total	**100.0%**	**100.0%**	**64.7%**	**100.0%**	**100.0%**	**100.0%**	**100.0%**	**100.0%**	**100.0%**	**100.0%**	**100.0%**
Constant (FY 2012) dollars:											
Payments for individuals [1]	16.0	44.0	69.9	123.4	239.6	322.6	408.5	447.9	546.6	625.8	667.0
Physical capital [1]	25.1	40.1	45.8	48.0	71.9	77.8	98.5	73.4	73.0	80.4	100.0
Other grants	13.7	67.6	139.0	67.5	77.6	111.1	130.5	78.4	115.2	193.7	174.2
Total	**54.8**	**151.7**	**254.7**	**238.9**	**389.1**	**511.6**	**637.6**	**599.7**	**734.9**	**899.8**	**941.2**
D. Total grants as a percent of:											
Federal outlays:											
Total	7.6%	12.3%	15.5%	10.8%	16.0%	17.3%	17.6%	16.9%	12.7%	14.3%	18.5%
Domestic programs [2]	18.0%	23.2%	22.2%	17.1%	22.0%	23.5%	23.4%	21.2%	15.0%	16.4%	22.1%
State and local expenditures	14.2%	19.4%	26.4%	18.0%	21.0%	22.9%	25.6%	23.9%	27.0%	N/A	N/A
Gross domestic product	1.3%	2.3%	3.3%	2.3%	2.8%	3.3%	4.1%	3.4%	3.9%	4.7%	4.7%
E. As a share of total State and local gross investments:											
Federal capital grants	24.1%	24.6%	20.7%	21.0%	21.3%	21.2%	26.8%	21.9%	19.1%	N/A	N/A
State and local own-source financing	75.9%	75.4%	79.3%	79.0%	78.7%	78.8%	73.2%	78.1%	80.9%	N/A	N/A
Total	**100.0%**	**100.0%**	**100.0%**	**100.0%**	**100.0%**	**100.0%**	**100.0%**	**100.0%**	**100.0%**		

N/A: Not available at publishing.

[1] Grants that are both payments for individuals and capital investment are shown under capital investment.

[2] Excludes national defense, international affairs, net interest, and undistributed offsetting receipts.

Table 11–2. FEDERAL GRANTS TO STATE AND LOCAL GOVERNMENTS—BUDGET AUTHORITY AND OUTLAYS

(In millions of dollars)

Function, Category, Agency and Program	Budget Authority			Outlays		
	2020 Actual	2021 Estimate	2022 Estimate	2020 Actual	2021 Estimate	2022 Estimate
Energy						
Discretionary:						
Department of Energy:						
Energy Programs:						
Energy Efficiency and Renewable Energy	387	404	863	296	325	511
Mandatory:						
Department of Energy:						
Energy Programs:						
Energy Efficiency and Renewable Energy	....	....	17,300	....	....	5,790
Tennessee Valley Authority:						
Tennessee Valley Authority Fund	528	508	492	528	508	492
Total, mandatory	528	508	17,792	528	508	6,282
Total, Energy	915	912	18,655	824	833	6,793
Natural Resources and Environment						
Discretionary:						
Department of Agriculture:						
Farm Service Agency:						
Grassroots Source Water Protection Program	7	7	7	7	7	7
Natural Resources Conservation Service:						
Watershed Rehabilitation Program	11	41	....	16	46	51
Watershed and Flood Prevention Operations	294	726	148	174	428	88
Forest Service:						
State and Private Forestry	222	219	255	211	420	471
Department of Commerce:						
National Oceanic and Atmospheric Administration:						
Operations, Research, and Facilities	109	107	151	107	105	148
Pacific Coastal Salmon Recovery	65	65	65	62	92	80
Department of the Interior:						
Office of Surface Mining Reclamation and Enforcement:						
Regulation and Technology	69	43	65	64	58	63
Abandoned Mine Reclamation Fund	115	115	165	50	90	106
United States Geological Survey:						
Surveys, Investigations, and Research	7	8	8	7	7	8
United States Fish and Wildlife Service:						
Cooperative Endangered Species Conservation Fund	36	30	43	66	32	44
State Wildlife Grants	68	72	82	62	67	78
National Park Service:						
National Recreation and Preservation	71	74	75	61	85	81
Land Acquisition and State Assistance	140	−23	....	35	90	139
Historic Preservation Fund	119	144	152	82	152	218
Department-Wide Programs:						
Energy Community Revitalization Program	....	....	169	....	....	17
Environmental Protection Agency:						
State and Tribal Assistance Grants	4,546	4,344	5,130	4,019	2,842	3,649
Hazardous Substance Superfund	250	250	250	244	244	254
Leaking Underground Storage Tank Trust Fund	83	84	83	88	76	79
Total, discretionary	6,212	6,306	6,848	5,355	4,841	5,581
Mandatory:						
Department of Agriculture:						
Farm Service Agency:						
Grassroots Source Water Protection Program	....	....	....	5	....	....
Department of Commerce:						

154

ANALYTICAL PERSPECTIVES

Table 11–2. FEDERAL GRANTS TO STATE AND LOCAL GOVERNMENTS—BUDGET AUTHORITY AND OUTLAYS—Continued

(In millions of dollars)

Function, Category, Agency and Program	Budget Authority			Outlays		
	2020 Actual	2021 Estimate	2022 Estimate	2020 Actual	2021 Estimate	2022 Estimate
National Oceanic and Atmospheric Administration:						
Gulf Coast Ecosystem Restoration Science, Observation, Monitoring, and Technology	6	6	6	6	6	6
Department of the Interior:						
Bureau of Land Management:						
Miscellaneous Permanent Payment Accounts	59	28	48	58	25	35
Office of Surface Mining Reclamation and Enforcement:						
Payments to States in Lieu of Coal Fee Receipts	....	....	....	....	10	7
Abandoned Mine Reclamation Fund	129	115	112	148	143	131
United States Fish and Wildlife Service:						
Federal Aid in Wildlife Restoration	672	725	847	751	775	810
Cooperative Endangered Species Conservation Fund	66	86	90	66	78	84
Coastal Impact Assistance	....	....	....	....	1	1
Sport Fish Restoration	458	513	498	421	469	504
National Park Service:						
Land Acquisition and State Assistance	115	507	519	8	55	137
Departmental Offices:						
National Forests Fund, Payment to States	4	4	5	4	4	5
Leases of Lands Acquired for Flood Control, Navigation, and Allied Purpos es	35	28	30	35	28	30
States Share from Certain Gulf of Mexico Leases	353	249	363	353	249	363
Corps of Engineers--Civil Works:						
South Dakota Terrestrial Wildlife Habitat Restoration Trust Fund	2	2	3	1	2	2
Environmental Protection Agency:						
State and Tribal Assistance Grants	....	....	25,400	....	....	12,700
Environmental Programs and Management	....	43	540	....	3	282
Total, mandatory	1,899	2,306	28,461	1,856	1,848	15,097
Total, Natural Resources and Environment	8,111	8,612	35,309	7,211	6,689	20,678
Agriculture						
Discretionary:						
Department of Agriculture:						
National Institute of Food and Agriculture:						
Extension Activities	446	562	....	429	380	492
National Institute of Food and Agriculture	....	....	979	....	....	536
Research and Education Activities	373	389	....	292	328	333
Agricultural Marketing Service:						
Payments to States and Possessions	1	6	....	1	6	....
Farm Service Agency:						
State Mediation Grants	6	7	7	5	7	7
Total, discretionary	826	964	986	727	721	1,368
Mandatory:						
Department of Agriculture:						
Agricultural Marketing Service:						
Payments to States and Possessions	80	185	85	77	92	85
Total, Agriculture	906	1,149	1,071	804	813	1,453
Commerce and Housing Credit						
Discretionary:						
Department of Commerce:						
National Oceanic and Atmospheric Administration:						
Fisheries Disaster Assistance	300	300	....	85	390	380
Mandatory:						
Department of Commerce:						
National Telecommunications and Information Administration:						

Table 11–2. FEDERAL GRANTS TO STATE AND LOCAL GOVERNMENTS—BUDGET AUTHORITY AND OUTLAYS—Continued

(In millions of dollars)

Function, Category, Agency and Program	Budget Authority			Outlays		
	2020 Actual	2021 Estimate	2022 Estimate	2020 Actual	2021 Estimate	2022 Estimate
State and Local Implementation Fund	....	....	....	8	11	2
Department of the Treasury:						
Departmental Offices:						
State Small Business Credit Initiative	....	10,000	....	....	7,372	2,472
Federal Communications Commission:						
Universal Service Fund	1,744	2,235	2,104	2,141	1,951	2,085
Total, mandatory	**1,744**	**12,235**	**2,104**	**2,149**	**9,334**	**4,559**
Total, Commerce and Housing Credit	**2,044**	**12,535**	**2,104**	**2,234**	**9,724**	**4,939**
Transportation						
Discretionary:						
Department of Transportation:						
Office of the Secretary:						
National Infrastructure Investments	975	980	980	482	1,223	942
Federal Aviation Administration:						
Grants for Airports (Airport and Airway Trust Fund)	....	....	....	3,289	3,382	3,482
Grants for Airports (Airport and Airway Trust Fund) (non-add obligati on limitations) [1]	*3,350*	*3,350*	*3,350*	....	....	....
Federal Highway Administration:						
Emergency Relief Program	....	....	....	973	888	608
Highway Infrastructure Programs	2,166	12,000	....	1,013	2,093	5,726
Appalachian Development Highway System	....	....	....	3	9	6
Federal-aid Highways	....	....	....	45,596	45,827	45,888
Federal-aid Highways (non-add obligation limitations) [1]	*45,035*	*44,839*	*45,030*	....	....	....
Miscellaneous Appropriations	−19	....	....	5	13	12
Miscellaneous Highway Trust Funds	....	....	....	3	12	11
Federal Motor Carrier Safety Administration:						
Motor Carrier Safety Grants	....	....	....	357	470	365
Motor Carrier Safety Grants (non-add obligation limitations) [1]	*391*	*420*	*388*	....	....	....
National Highway Traffic Safety Administration:						
Highway Traffic Safety Grants	....	....	....	575	736	782
Highway Traffic Safety Grants (non-add obligation limitations) [1]	*724*	*728*	*623*	....	....	....
Federal Railroad Administration:						
Northeast Corridor Improvement Program	....	....	....	2	8	9
Capital and Debt Service Grants to the National Railroad Passenger Corp oration	....	....	....	1	....	....
Restoration and Enhancement Grants	2	5	....	....	....	1
Magnetic Levitation Technology Deployment Program	2	2	....	....	....	2
Rail Safety Technology Program	....	−1	....	....	....	1
Railroad Safety Grants	....	....	....	10	16	7
Grants to the National Railroad Passenger Corporation	....	....	....	....	4	11
Intercity Passenger Rail Grant Program	....	−10	....	1	5	5
Rail Line Relocation and Improvement Program	....	−13	....	....	....	1
Capital Assistance for High Speed Rail Corridors and Intercity Passenger Rail Service	....	....	....	8	88	56
Next Generation High-speed Rail	....	−3	....	....	....	1
Pennsylvania Station Redevelopment Project	....	....	....	4	1	....
Northeast Corridor Grants to the National Railroad Passenger Corporation	1,188	1,351	1,293	1,190	1,352	1,299
National Network Grants to the National Railroad Passenger Corporation	1,819	1,637	1,393	1,819	1,638	1,396
Federal-State Partnership for State of Good Repair	198	198	....	....	24	113
Consolidated Rail Infrastructure and Safety Improvements	322	371	368	40	147	205
Federal Transit Administration:						
Job Access and Reverse Commute Grants	....	....	....	....	1	....
Washington Metropolitan Area Transit Authority	150	150	150	178	144	144
Formula Grants	....	−2	....	15	34	....
Capital Investment Grants	1,978	2,014	2,473	2,134	2,349	3,216
Public Transportation Emergency Relief Program	....	....	....	802	1,202	1,083

Table 11–2. FEDERAL GRANTS TO STATE AND LOCAL GOVERNMENTS—BUDGET AUTHORITY AND OUTLAYS—Continued

(In millions of dollars)

Function, Category, Agency and Program	Budget Authority			Outlays		
	2020 Actual	2021 Estimate	2022 Estimate	2020 Actual	2021 Estimate	2022 Estimate
Discretionary Grants (Highway Trust Fund, Mass Transit Account)	....	....	....	....	15	....
Transit Formula Grants	....	....	....	9,909	9,601	9,962
Transit Formula Grants (non-add obligation limitations) [1]	*11,372*	*11,450*	*11,450*	....	....	....
Pipeline and Hazardous Materials Safety Administration:						
Pipeline Safety	56	58	56	56	77	69
Trust Fund Share of Pipeline Safety	8	8	11	8	8	11
Total, discretionary	**8,845**	**18,745**	**6,724**	**68,473**	**71,367**	**75,414**
Total, obligation limitations (non-add) [1]	*60,872*	*60,787*	*60,841*	....	....	....
Mandatory:						
Department of Homeland Security:						
United States Coast Guard:						
Boat Safety	112	126	119	105	119	119
Department of Transportation:						
American Jobs Plan Funding for Transportation Infrastructure	....	....	75,740		....	11,576
Federal Aviation Administration:						
Grants for Airports (Airport and Airway Trust Fund)	3,579	5,575	3,168	....	....	....
Federal Highway Administration:						
Federal-aid Highways	45,350	45,283	45,343	731	742	726
Miscellaneous Appropriations	–1	....	....	....	....	....
Federal Motor Carrier Safety Administration:						
Motor Carrier Safety Grants	388	388	388	....	....	....
National Highway Traffic Safety Administration:						
Highway Traffic Safety Grants	661	665	560	....	....	....
Federal Railroad Administration:						
Northeast Corridor Grants to the National Railroad Passenger Corporation	....	969	....	....	969	....
National Network Grants to the National Railroad Passenger Corporation	....	729	....	....	729	....
Federal Transit Administration:						
Transit Formula Grants	11,344	11,422	11,422	....	....	....
Total, mandatory	**61,433**	**65,157**	**136,740**	**836**	**2,559**	**12,421**
Total, Transportation	**70,278**	**83,902**	**143,464**	**69,309**	**73,926**	**87,835**
Community and Regional Development						
Discretionary:						
Department of Agriculture:						
Rural Utilities Service:						
Distance Learning, Telemedicine, and Broadband Program	470	555	672	72	447	566
Rural Water and Waste Disposal Program Account	657	617	717	614	741	802
Rural Housing Service:						
Rural Community Facilities Program Account	86	60	60	61	65	53
Rural Business-Cooperative Service:						
Rural Business Program Account	92	61	81	58	78	84
Department of Commerce:						
Economic Development Administration:						
Economic Development Assistance Programs	1,763	3,296	359	302	1,046	1,748
Department of Homeland Security:						
Federal Emergency Management Agency:						
Federal Assistance	3,025	2,915	2,905	2,023	2,047	2,872
State and Local Programs	....	....	....	273	131	....
Disaster Relief Fund	62,546	18,892	19,299	43,317	40,738	12,503
Department of Housing and Urban Development:						
Community Planning and Development:						
Community Development Fund	8,425	3,475	3,770	5,235	9,196	9,676
Brownfields Redevelopment	....	....	....	....	2	1
Office of Lead Hazard Control and Healthy Homes:						

Table 11–2. FEDERAL GRANTS TO STATE AND LOCAL GOVERNMENTS—BUDGET AUTHORITY AND OUTLAYS—Continued

(In millions of dollars)

Function, Category, Agency and Program	Budget Authority			Outlays		
	2020 Actual	2021 Estimate	2022 Estimate	2020 Actual	2021 Estimate	2022 Estimate
Lead Hazard Reduction	290	360	400	81	232	283
Department of the Interior:						
Bureau of Indian Affairs:						
Operation of Indian Programs	178	178	178	178	180	176
Indian Guaranteed Loan Program Account	12	12	12	6	3	7
Delta Regional Authority	15	15	15	10	16	21
Denali Commission	15	15	15	36	22	22
Total, discretionary	77,574	30,451	28,483	52,266	54,944	28,814
Mandatory:						
Department of Commerce:						
Economic Development Administration:						
Economic Development Assistance Programs	....	....	1,500	....	....	227
Regional Innovation Hubs	....	....	10,000	....	....	3,500
Department of Homeland Security:						
Federal Emergency Management Agency:						
Federal Assistance	....	400	300	....	4	129
Disaster Relief Fund	....	50,000	....	....	25,000	13,593
Department of Housing and Urban Development:						
Community Planning and Development:						
Community Development Fund	....	....	500	....	....	5
Main Street Grants	....	....	250	....	....	....
Community Development Loan Guarantees Program Account	....	2	....	....	2	....
Neighborhood Stabilization Program	....	....	....	19	18	17
Department of the Interior:						
Bureau of Indian Affairs:						
Indian Guaranteed Loan Program Account	35	14	....	35	15	....
Department of the Treasury:						
Fiscal Service:						
Gulf Coast Restoration Trust Fund	335	319	320	179	292	292
Total, mandatory	370	50,735	12,870	233	25,331	17,763
Total, Community and Regional Development	77,944	81,186	41,353	52,499	80,275	46,577
Education, Training, Employment, and Social Services						
Discretionary:						
Department of Education:						
Office of Elementary and Secondary Education:						
Indian Education	176	193	178	163	225	192
Impact Aid	1,481	1,496	1,536	1,464	1,391	1,575
Safe Schools and Citizenship Education	310	217	650	164	279	241
Education Stabilization Fund	16,644	185,149	....	2,107	24,663	56,816
Education for the Disadvantaged	16,946	17,176	37,176	15,810	18,746	17,502
School Improvement Programs	5,261	5,296	6,401	4,591	5,862	5,431
Office of Innovation and Improvement:						
Innovation and Improvement	988	999	1,163	775	1,484	1,122
Office of English Language Acquisition:						
English Language Acquisition	736	745	848	634	827	748
Office of Special Education and Rehabilitative Services:						
Special Education	13,674	16,886	16,810	12,741	14,313	14,149
Rehabilitation Services	86	87	110	78	86	101
Office of Career, Technical, and Adult Education:						
Career, Technical and Adult Education	1,938	2,010	2,031	1,687	2,083	2,019
Office of Postsecondary Education:						
Higher Education	365	368	408	335	428	223
Institute of Education Sciences	27	27	27	21	43	34

Table 11–2.   FEDERAL GRANTS TO STATE AND LOCAL GOVERNMENTS—BUDGET AUTHORITY AND OUTLAYS—Continued

(In millions of dollars)

Function, Category, Agency and Program	Budget Authority			Outlays		
	2020 Actual	2021 Estimate	2022 Estimate	2020 Actual	2021 Estimate	2022 Estimate
Disaster Education Recovery	....	....	....	279	586	550
Department of Health and Human Services:						
Administration for Children and Families:						
Promoting Safe and Stable Families	93	83	106	86	77	88
Children and Families Services Programs	14,393	15,891	14,545	11,892	13,510	14,743
Administration for Community Living:						
Aging and Disability Services Programs	3,038	3,853	1,963	2,291	2,502	4,093
Department of the Interior:						
Bureau of Indian Affairs:						
Operation of Indian Programs	....	....	....	68	2	....
Bureau of Indian Education:						
Operation of Indian Education Programs	94	94	94	38	66	93
Department of Labor:						
Employment and Training Administration:						
Training and Employment Services	3,433	3,125	3,685	2,782	3,430	3,516
State Unemployment Insurance and Employment Service Operations	84	81	81	88	84	76
Unemployment Trust Fund	4,098	1,124	1,192	3,275	1,128	1,161
Corporation for National and Community Service:						
Operating Expenses	15	15	15	270	133	66
Corporation for Public Broadcasting	540	640	485	540	640	485
District of Columbia:						
District of Columbia General and Special Payments:						
Federal Payment for Resident Tuition Support	40	40	40	40	40	40
Federal Payment for School Improvement	53	53	53	53	53	53
Institute of Museum and Library Services:						
Office of Museum and Library Services: Grants and Administration	284	436	240	216	208	407
National Endowment for the Arts:						
Grants and Administration	82	68	80	77	76	70
National Endowment for the Humanities:						
Grants and Administration	....	53	....	....	42	....
Total, discretionary	**84,879**	**256,205**	**89,917**	**62,565**	**93,007**	**125,594**
Mandatory:						
Department of Education:						
Office of Elementary and Secondary Education:						
Infrastructure	....	....	12,400	....	....	1,240
Office of Innovation and Improvement:						
Innovation and Improvement	....	....	1,800	....	....	36
Office of Special Education and Rehabilitative Services:						
Special Education	....	....	90	....	....	4
Rehabilitation Services	3,397	3,466	3,507	2,961	3,920	3,483
Office of Career, Technical, and Adult Education:						
Career, Technical and Adult Education	....	....	1,100	....	....	55
Office of Postsecondary Education:						
Higher Education	....	....	6,200	....	....	186
Office of Federal Student Aid:						
Free Community College	....	....	14,312	....	....	429
Department of Health and Human Services:						
Administration for Children and Families:						
Promoting Safe and Stable Families	975	560	475	462	727	601
Social Services Block Grant	1,685	1,607	1,603	1,727	1,583	1,640
Department of Labor:						
Employment and Training Administration:						
Federal Unemployment Benefits and Allowances	410	371	235	175	154	201
National Endowment for the Arts:						
Grants and Administration	....	52	....	....	14	38

Table 11–2. FEDERAL GRANTS TO STATE AND LOCAL GOVERNMENTS—BUDGET AUTHORITY AND OUTLAYS—Continued

(In millions of dollars)

Function, Category, Agency and Program	Budget Authority			Outlays		
	2020 Actual	2021 Estimate	2022 Estimate	2020 Actual	2021 Estimate	2022 Estimate
National Endowment for the Humanities:						
Grants and Administration	....	52	....	....	50	6
Total, mandatory	6,467	6,108	41,722	5,325	6,448	7,919
Total, Education, Training, Employment, and Social Services	91,346	262,313	131,639	67,890	99,455	133,513
Health						
Discretionary:						
Department of Agriculture:						
Food Safety and Inspection Service:						
Salaries and Expenses	56	57	58	55	57	58
Department of Health and Human Services:						
Health Resources and Services Administration:						
Health Resources and Services	3,031	2,972	3,037	2,926	2,970	3,037
Indian Health Service:						
Payments for Tribal Leases	....	101	150	....	101	150
Contract Support Costs	909	916	1,142	839	1,039	1,142
Centers for Disease Control and Prevention:						
CDC-wide Activities and Program Support	4,197	4,870	4,870	1,649	1,727	1,689
Substance Abuse and Mental Health Services Administration	5,332	12,622	8,757	4,322	5,698	7,998
Departmental Management:						
Public Health and Social Services Emergency Fund	276	58,761	292	247	22,540	13,961
Department of Labor:						
Occupational Safety and Health Administration:						
Salaries and Expenses	180	183	170	180	183	171
Mine Safety and Health Administration:						
Salaries and Expenses	11	11	11	11	11	11
Total, discretionary	13,992	80,493	18,487	10,229	34,326	28,217
Mandatory:						
Department of Health and Human Services:						
Health Resources and Services Administration:						
Maternal, Infant, and Early Childhood Home Visiting Programs	376	527	377	389	407	430
Centers for Medicare and Medicaid Services:						
Rate Review Grants	....	....	....	7	5	5
Affordable Insurance Exchange Grants	....	20	....	....	15	5
Cost-sharing Reductions	....	1,307	1,307	....	1,307	1,326
Grants to States for Medicaid	467,569	519,918	570,375	458,468	521,127	570,687
Children's Health Insurance Fund	20,515	19,801	20,601	16,880	17,220	17,142
State Grants and Demonstrations	422	526	511	333	307	364
Child Enrollment Contingency Fund	4,913	60	184	2	294	....
Departmental Management:						
Pregnancy Assistance Fund	....	....	....	20	6	....
Department of the Treasury:						
Internal Revenue Service:						
Refundable Premium Tax Credit	7,730	7,875	7,485	7,072	7,875	7,485
Total, mandatory	501,525	550,034	600,840	483,171	548,563	597,444
Total, Health	515,517	630,527	619,327	493,400	582,889	625,661
Income Security						
Discretionary:						
Department of Agriculture:						
Food and Nutrition Service:						
Commodity Assistance Program	1,195	841	442	652	1,492	440
Special Supplemental Nutrition Program for Women, Infants, and Children (WIC)	5,500	4,750	6,000	5,011	4,283	5,886
Department of Health and Human Services:						
Administration for Children and Families:						

Table 11–2. FEDERAL GRANTS TO STATE AND LOCAL GOVERNMENTS—BUDGET AUTHORITY AND OUTLAYS—Continued

(In millions of dollars)

Function, Category, Agency and Program	Budget Authority			Outlays		
	2020 Actual	2021 Estimate	2022 Estimate	2020 Actual	2021 Estimate	2022 Estimate
Low Income Home Energy Assistance	4,640	8,250	3,850	3,812	7,178	5,260
Refugee and Entrant Assistance	524	535	1,500	496	2,000	1,925
Payments to States for the Child Care and Development Block Grant	9,314	54,899	7,365	7,021	18,299	26,351
Department of Homeland Security:						
Federal Emergency Management Agency:						
Federal Assistance	325	130	130	251	299	131
Emergency Food and Shelter	....	....	....	2	....	....
Department of Housing and Urban Development:						
Public and Indian Housing Programs:						
Public Housing Operating Fund	5,171	....	....	4,580	1,833	....
Revitalization of Severely Distressed Public Housing (HOPE VI)	....	....	....	4	4	4
Native Hawaiian Housing Block Grant	2	2	7	1	3	5
Tenant Based Rental Assistance	25,171	30,821	30,519	24,632	26,101	30,436
Public Housing Capital Fund	2,839	....	....	2,220	2,553	1,823
Native American Programs	1,124	825	1,000	627	922	946
Housing Certificate Fund	....	....	....	20	27	15
Choice Neighborhoods Initiative	175	200	250	124	144	185
Self-Sufficiency Programs	130	155	175	77	105	134
Public Housing Fund	....	7,687	8,424	....	3,729	5,753
Community Planning and Development:						
Homeless Assistance Grants	5,481	1,600	1,867	1,216	2,485	2,574
Home Investment Partnership Program	1,350	1,350	1,850	827	1,161	1,267
Housing Opportunities for Persons with AIDS	475	430	450	317	439	459
Permanent Supportive Housing	....	....	....	....	5	....
Housing Programs:						
Project-based Rental Assistance	345	350	355	272	277	282
Department of Labor:						
Employment and Training Administration:						
Unemployment Trust Fund	1,118	3,316	3,249	964	3,864	3,480
Total, discretionary	64,879	116,141	67,433	53,126	77,203	87,356
Mandatory:						
Department of Agriculture:						
Agricultural Marketing Service:						
Funds for Strengthening Markets, Income, and Supply (section 32)	1,167	1,191	1,219	947	1,421	1,245
Food and Nutrition Service:						
Supplemental Nutrition Assistance Program	8,121	10,320	8,559	8,006	10,173	8,717
Commodity Assistance Program	24	61	24	16	57	33
Special Supplemental Nutrition Program for Women, Infants, and Children (WIC)	....	881	....	....	471	177
Child Nutrition Programs	32,587	26,573	28,257	22,709	31,928	32,178
Department of Health and Human Services:						
Administration for Children and Families:						
Payments to States for Child Support Enforcement and Family Support Pr ograms	4,566	4,439	4,194	4,424	4,388	4,157
Contingency Fund	608	608	608	628	608	608
Payments for Foster Care and Permanency	9,108	10,415	9,965	8,836	10,764	10,242
Child Care Entitlement to States	2,917	3,550	3,550	2,979	3,187	3,447
Temporary Assistance for Needy Families	16,736	17,736	16,736	16,551	16,667	17,267
Department of Homeland Security:						
Federal Emergency Management Agency:						
Federal Assistance	....	510	....	....	....	352
Department of Housing and Urban Development:						
Public and Indian Housing Programs:						
Native Hawaiian Housing Block Grant	....	5	....	....	1	3
Native American Programs	....	740	400	....	101	483
Public Housing Fund	....	....	40,000	....	....	1,200
Community Planning and Development:						

Table 11–2.   FEDERAL GRANTS TO STATE AND LOCAL GOVERNMENTS—BUDGET AUTHORITY AND OUTLAYS—Continued

(In millions of dollars)

Function, Category, Agency and Program	Budget Authority			Outlays		
	2020 Actual	2021 Estimate	2022 Estimate	2020 Actual	2021 Estimate	2022 Estimate
Home Investment Partnership Program	....	4,950	7,000	....	1	679
Department of the Treasury:						
Departmental Offices:						
Homeowner Assistance Fund	....	9,958	....	....	9,923	11
Total, mandatory	75,834	91,937	120,512	65,096	89,690	80,799
Total, Income Security	140,713	208,078	187,945	118,222	166,893	168,155
Social Security						
Mandatory:						
Social Security Administration:						
Federal Disability Insurance Trust Fund	3	7	2	14	10	7
Veterans Benefits and Services						
Discretionary:						
Department of Veterans Affairs:						
Veterans Health Administration:						
Medical Community Care	1,424	1,991	1,766	1,424	1,991	1,766
Medical Services	1,297	1,012	705	1,297	1,012	705
Departmental Administration:						
Grants for Construction of State Extended Care Facilities	240	590	....	214	405	230
Grants for Construction of Veterans Cemeteries	45	45	45	44	93	45
Total, discretionary	3,006	3,638	2,516	2,979	3,501	2,746
Mandatory:						
Department of Veterans Affairs:						
Veterans Health Administration:						
Veterans Medical Care and Health Fund	....	538	....	....	....	538
Total, Veterans Benefits and Services	3,006	4,176	2,516	2,979	3,501	3,284
Administration of Justice						
Discretionary:						
Department of Housing and Urban Development:						
Fair Housing and Equal Opportunity:						
Fair Housing Activities	73	73	85	65	71	77
Department of Justice:						
Legal Activities and U.S. Marshals:						
Assets Forfeiture Fund	21	21	21	15	20	20
Office of Justice Programs:						
Research, Evaluation, and Statistics	17	17	17	4	4	4
State and Local Law Enforcement Assistance	605	605	605	918	1,305	1,269
Juvenile Justice Programs	301	320	772	224	319	483
Community Oriented Policing Services	288	331	596	150	384	523
Violence against Women Prevention and Prosecution Programs	500	510	981	427	514	493
Equal Employment Opportunity Commission:						
Salaries and Expenses	31	28	32	46	40	42
Federal Drug Control Programs:						
High Intensity Drug Trafficking Areas Program	264	290	294	252	358	248
State Justice Institute:						
Salaries and Expenses	7	7	8	7	7	12
Total, discretionary	2,107	2,202	3,411	2,108	3,022	3,171
Mandatory:						
Department of Housing and Urban Development:						
Fair Housing and Equal Opportunity:						
Fair Housing Activities	....	19	....	....	....	8
Department of Justice:						
Legal Activities and U.S. Marshals:						

Table 11–2. FEDERAL GRANTS TO STATE AND LOCAL GOVERNMENTS—BUDGET AUTHORITY AND OUTLAYS—Continued

(In millions of dollars)

Function, Category, Agency and Program	Budget Authority			Outlays		
	2020 Actual	2021 Estimate	2022 Estimate	2020 Actual	2021 Estimate	2022 Estimate
Assets Forfeiture Fund	556	225	250	640	273	289
Office of Justice Programs:						
Crime Victims Fund	7,166	5,860	5,860	6,533	7,340	5,020
Department of the Treasury:						
Departmental Offices:						
Treasury Forfeiture Fund	101	109	132	87	102	108
Total, mandatory	7,823	6,213	6,242	7,260	7,715	5,425
Total, Administration of Justice	9,930	8,415	9,653	9,368	10,737	8,596
General Government						
Discretionary:						
Department of the Interior:						
United States Fish and Wildlife Service:						
National Wildlife Refuge Fund	13	13	....	13	13	....
Insular Affairs:						
Assistance to Territories	130	79	86	66	122	99
Department-Wide Programs:						
Payments in Lieu of Taxes	....	....	525	....	....	525
District of Columbia:						
District of Columbia Courts:						
Federal Payment to the District of Columbia Courts	251	250	274	259	253	271
Federal Payment for Defender Services in District of Columbia Courts	46	46	46	34	50	52
District of Columbia General and Special Payments:						
Federal Support for Economic Development and Management Reforms in the District	15	15	16	15	15	16
Election Assistance Commission:						
Election Security Grants	825	....	100	822	3	100
Total, discretionary	1,280	403	1,047	1,209	456	1,063
Mandatory:						
Department of Agriculture:						
Forest Service:						
Forest Service Permanent Appropriations	201	240	95	267	288	120
Department of Energy:						
Energy Programs:						
Payments to States under Federal Power Act	3	6	6	4	9	6
Department of the Interior:						
Office of Surface Mining Reclamation and Enforcement:						
Payments to States in Lieu of Coal Fee Receipts	42	38	35	72	125	103
United States Fish and Wildlife Service:						
National Wildlife Refuge Fund	7	8	8	8	8	8
Departmental Offices:						
Mineral Leasing and Associated Payments	1,400	1,488	1,581	1,400	1,488	1,581
National Petroleum Reserve, Alaska	13	12	14	13	12	14
Payment to Alaska, Arctic National Wildlife Refuge	....	8	2	....	8	2
Geothermal Lease Revenues, Payment to Counties	4	5	5	4	5	5
Insular Affairs:						
Assistance to Territories	28	28	28	22	21	22
Payments to the United States Territories, Fiscal Assistance	343	302	331	343	302	331
Department-Wide Programs:						
Payments in Lieu of Taxes	517	525	....	517	525	....
Department of the Treasury:						
Alcohol and Tobacco Tax and Trade Bureau:						
Internal Revenue Collections for Puerto Rico	471	476	481	471	476	481
District of Columbia:						
District of Columbia Courts:						

Table 11–2. FEDERAL GRANTS TO STATE AND LOCAL GOVERNMENTS—BUDGET AUTHORITY AND OUTLAYS—Continued

(In millions of dollars)

Function, Category, Agency and Program	Budget Authority			Outlays		
	2020 Actual	2021 Estimate	2022 Estimate	2020 Actual	2021 Estimate	2022 Estimate
District of Columbia Crime Victims Compensation Fund	6	6	6	9	6	6
Total, mandatory	3,035	3,142	2,592	3,130	3,273	2,679
Total, General Government	4,315	3,545	3,639	4,339	3,729	3,742
Total, Grants [2]	925,028	1,305,357	1,196,677	829,093	1,039,474	1,111,233
Discretionary	264,287	516,252	226,715	259,418	344,103	360,215
Transportation obligation limitations (non-add) [1]	*60,872*	*60,787*	*60,841*	....	....	....
Mandatory	660,741	789,105	969,962	569,675	695,371	751,018

[1] Mandatory contract authority provides budget authority for these programs, but program levels are set by discretionary obligation limitations in appropriations bills and outlays are recorded as discretionary. This table shows the obligation limitations as non-additive items to avoid double counting.

[2] Amounts reflected in 2021 and 2022 may understate total grants funding because some American Jobs Plan initiatives and certain American Rescue Plan Act programs cover a range of activities (including, but not solely, grants to states and localities).

12. INFORMATION TECHNOLOGY AND CYBERSECURITY FUNDING

Federal Information Technology (IT) provides Americans with important services and information, and is the foundation of how Government serves the public in the digital age. The President proposes spending $58.4 billion on IT at civilian agencies in FY 2022[1], which will be used to deliver critical citizen services, keep sensitive data and systems secure, and further the vision of digital Government. The Budget also supports the implementation of Federal laws that enable agency technology planning, oversight, funding, and accountability practices and Office of Management and Budget (OMB) guidance to agencies on the strategic use of IT to enable mission outcomes. It supports the modernization of antiquated and often unsecured IT; agency migration to secure, cost-effective commercial cloud solutions and shared services; the recruitment, retention, and reskilling of the Federal technology and cybersecurity workforce to ensure higher value service delivery; and the reduction of cybersecurity risk across the Federal enterprise.

Cybersecurity is an important component of the Administration's IT modernization efforts, and the President remains dedicated to securing the Federal enterprise from cyber-related threats. The President's Budget includes approximately $9.8 billion for civilian cybersecurity funding, which supports the protection of Federal IT and our Nation's most valuable information including the personal information of the American public. These investments will, in alignment with the Administration's priorities, focus on addressing root cause structural issues, promoting stronger collaboration and coordination among Federal agencies, and addressing capability challenges that have impeded the Government's technology vision.

Federal Spending on IT and Cybersecurity

As shown in Table 12-1, the Federal Government Budget for IT at civilian Federal agencies is estimated to be $58.4 billion in 2022. This figure is a 2.4 percent increase from the estimate reported for 2021. Chart 12-1 shows trending information for Federal civilian IT spending from 2020 forward.[2] The 2022 Budget includes funding for 4,531 investments at 25 agencies. These investments support the three IT Portfolio areas shown in Chart 12-2.

Of those 4,531 IT investments, 546 are considered major IT investments. As outlined in OMB Circular A-11 and FY 2022 Capital Planning and Investment Control (CPIC) Guidance, agencies determine if an IT investment

is classified as major based on whether the associated investment: has significant program or policy implications; has high executive visibility; has high development, operating, or maintenance costs; or requires special management attention because of its importance to the mission or function of the agency. For all major IT investments, agencies are required to submit Business Cases, which provide additional transparency regarding the cost, schedule, risk, and performance data related to its spending. OMB requires that agency Chief Information Officers (CIOs) provide risk ratings for all major IT investments on the IT Dashboard website on a continuous basis and assess how risks for major development efforts are being addressed and mitigated.

Cybersecurity is a top priority for this Administration, and recent events, such as the SolarWinds cyber incident, have shown that adversaries continue to target Federal systems. Recognizing that this is a critical issue that must be prioritized, the President's Budget includes approximately $9.8 billion of budget authority for civilian cybersecurity-related activities. This figure is a 14 percent increase from the estimate reported for 2021. Cybersecurity budgetary priorities will continue to seek to reduce the risk and impact of cyber incidents (e.g. SolarWinds), based on data-driven, risk-based assessments of the threat environment and the current Federal cybersecurity posture. Table 12-2 provides an agency level view of cybersecurity spending. Table 12-3 provides an overview of civilian Chief Financial Officers (CFO) Act Agency cybersecurity spending as aligned to the National Institute of Standards and Technology (NIST) Cybersecurity Framework functions: Identify, Protect, Detect, Respond, and Recover.

The remainder of this chapter describes important aspects of the latest initiatives undertaken with respect to Federal IT policies and projects, as well as cybersecurity policy and spending.

IT Modernization

Agencies prioritize the modernization of Federal IT systems to better deliver their mission and services to the American public in an effective, efficient, and secure manner. Agencies are continuing to deploy standards-based platforms and systems, leveraging commercial capabilities that replace highly-customized government technology. The Federal Government has been focused on enhancing Federal IT and digital services, reducing cybersecurity risks to the Federal mission, and building a modern IT and cybersecurity workforce. Federal agencies' ongoing efforts to modernize their IT will enhance mission effectiveness and reduce mission risks through a series of complementary initiatives that will drive sus-

---

[1] The scope of the analysis in this chapter refers to agencies represented on the IT Dashboard, located at *https://www.itdashboard.gov/*. This analysis excludes the Department of Defense

[2] Note that as of the 2020 CPIC guidance, IT related grants made to State and local governments are no longer included in agency IT investment submissions.

Chart 12-1. Trends in Federal Civilian IT Spending

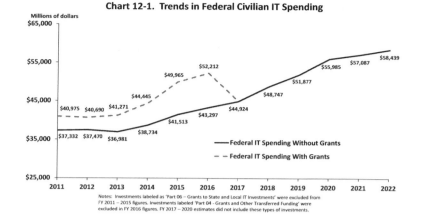

Notes: Investments labeled as 'Part 06 – Grants to State and Local IT Investments' were excluded from FY 2011 – 2015 figures. Investments labeled 'Part 04 - Grants and Other Transferred Funding' were excluded in FY 2016 figures. FY 2017 – 2020 estimates did not include these types of investments.

tained change in Federal technology, deployment, security, and service delivery.

Notable IT Modernization efforts include Cloud Adoption, Shared Services, and IPv6, among other efforts. The Federal Government will continue to accelerate the adoption of cloud technologies to improve the efficiency of Government business and communications. Cloud Adoption positioned Federal agencies to convert to maximum telework during the COVID-19 pandemic, rapidly and proficiently enabling the continuity of their missions. Shared Services include the Government-wide identification and creation of centralized capabilities, shared governance, and performance expectations that are current for common functions across government. These will lead the way to transform the Federal Government by enabling the delivery of innovative, flexible, and competitive solutions and services that improve mission support service quality and decrease the total cost of services across the Federal enterprise. The Federal Government is also continuing its transition to Internet Protocol 6 (IPv6), replacing IPv4. The global demand for IP addresses has grown exponentially with the ever-increasing number of users, devices, and virtual entities connecting to the Internet, resulting in the exhaustion of readily available IPv4 addresses in all regions of the world. While stop-gap measures have served to extend IPv4's viability thus far, it is imperative that IPv6, with its vastly larger address space, sees widespread adoption in the near future. This will accommodate Internet growth and innovation, giving

better support to mobility, security, and virtualized network services.

Technology Modernization Fund

The Budget includes $500 million for the Technology Modernization Fund (TMF), building on the $1 billion provided in the American Rescue Plan, to strengthen Federal cybersecurity and retire antiquated technology systems. With the continuously evolving IT and cyber landscape, these investments are an important down payment on delivering modern and secure services to the American public, and continued investment in IT will be necessary to ensure the United States meets the accelerated pace of modernization. The funding provided to TMF through the American Rescue Plan recognizes the critical need to provide funding to address urgent IT modernization challenges, bolster cybersecurity defenses following the SolarWinds incident, and improve the delivery of COVID-19 relief. The Administration will prioritize projects that focus on high-priority systems modernization, cybersecurity, public-facing digital services, and cross-government services and infrastructure. To implement the TMF funding provided through the American Rescue Plan, the TMF model has been updated to include repayment flexibilities that may accelerate modernization efforts to better serve the American public.

The TMF is an innovative funding vehicle that gives agencies additional ways to deliver services to the

Chart 12-2. 2022 Federal Civilian IT Investment Portfolio Summary

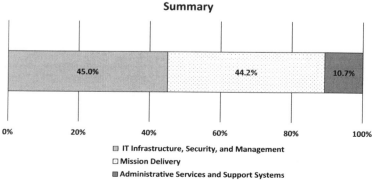

Table 12–1. ESTIMATED FY 2022 CIVILIAN FEDERAL IT SPENDING AND PERCENTAGE BY AGENCY

(In millions of dollars)

Agency	FY 2022	Percent of Total
Department of Veterans Affairs	$8,495	14.5%
Department of Homeland Security	$8,150	13.9%
Department of Health and Human Services	$6,956	11.9%
Department of the Treasury	$5,967	10.2%
Department of Transportation	$3,694	6.3%
Department of Justice	$3,475	5.9%
Department of Energy	$3,245	5.6%
Department of Agriculture	$2,762	4.7%
Department of State	$2,756	4.7%
Department of Commerce	$2,598	4.4%
Social Security Administration	$2,157	3.7%
National Aeronautics and Space Administration	$2,145	3.7%
Department of the Interior	$1,502	2.6%
Department of Education	$982	1.7%
Department of Labor	$819	1.4%
General Services Administration	$702	1.2%
Department of Housing and Urban Development	$437	0.7%
Environmental Protection Agency	$370	0.6%
U.S. Army Corps of Engineers	$269	0.5%
U.S. Agency for International Development	$263	0.4%
National Science Foundation	$165	0.3%
Nuclear Regulatory Commission	$152	0.3%
Office of Personnel Management	$141	0.2%
National Archives and Records Administration	$127	0.2%
Small Business Administration	$109	0.2%
Total	**$58,439**	**100.0%**

This analysis excludes the Department of Defense

American public more quickly, to better secure sensitive systems and data, and to use taxpayer dollars more efficiently.[3] The mission of the TMF is to enable agencies to accelerate transformation of the way they use technology to deliver their mission and services to the American public in an effective, efficient, and secure manner. Agencies must apply and compete for TMF funds. The TMF awards are levers to accelerate modernization across the Government in a manner that demonstrates efficient management of taxpayer resources.

Since its start in March 2019, the TMF Board has awarded ten initiatives a total of approximately $79.4 million. In 2020, the TMF Board awarded $15 million for one new modernization project – the Automated Commercial Environment Collections Module (ACE). This project serves to update the Customs and Border Protection's (CPB's) 30-year old collection tool, the Automated Commercial System (ACS), to meet the demands of the CBP mission and provide the agency with a flexible secure platform to support the growing complexities of global trade and CBP enforcement.

Improving the IT and Cyber Workforce

Maintaining and securing Federal IT requires a large, highly capable IT and Cyber workforce. A current focus for policies guiding the strengthening of the Federal IT workforce is the direction given to Federal agencies to build a workforce able to leverage data as a strategic asset to support economic growth, increase the effectiveness of the Federal Government, facilitate oversight, and promote transparency.

To accomplish this goal, agencies need a workforce that is highly trained and equipped with modern-day technical skills in areas such as data science, cybersecurity, and artificial intelligence. As technology is a rapidly-changing field, the Administration is committed to investing in the Federal workforce to ensure they are equipped to adapt and develop their skills. To date, the Government has taken steps to expand the IT workforce, and provide training and other professional development opportunities to build skillsets and capacity Government-wide.

The President's Budget continues to invest in the IT and Cyber workforce, to make the Government an attractive employer for top-tier talent, improve our ability to oversee and administer Government-wide programs, and better deliver services to the American people. For example, a highly skilled IT workforce is essential for the Government's ability to innovate in artificial intelligence and machine learning. Agencies need staff who understand these technologies, both to generate the foundational data needed for them to operate, as well as to manage the automated services to ensure they are accurate, fair, and aligned to the needs of the Government and the American people. Agencies also need cross-functional professionals who can work in areas like financial management, acquisition, and privacy protections, to drive value across a range of Government domains. Ultimately, a strong cadre of cybersecurity and IT professionals will allow the Government to run more efficiently and effectively, and drive more user-centric services to the American people.

United States Digital Service

Americans expect and deserve their interactions with the Federal Government to be simple, fast, and responsive. The United States Digital Service (USDS) is enhancing the Federal Government's most critical public-facing digital services through design and technology expertise. USDS recruits some of the country's top technical talent and partners directly with Federal Agencies to ensure that critical services reach the public. USDS projects not only provide the public with better digital services, but also help streamline agency processes and save taxpayer dollars. Recognizing this, the Administration requested and Congress appropriated $200 million through the American Rescue Plan for USDS that is being used to increase the number of USDS personnel. This will allow USDS to quickly address technology emergencies, ensure access and equity are integrated into products and processes, and help agencies modernize their systems for long-term stability.

---

[3] See *https://tmf.cio.gov/*

Table 12–2. ESTIMATED CIVILIAN FEDERAL CYBERSECURITY SPENDING BY AGENCY

(In millions of dollars)

Organization	FY 2020	FY 2021	FY 2022
Civilian CFO Act Agencies	**$7,383**	**$8,184**	**$9,402**
Department of Agriculture	$223	$223	$239
Department of Commerce	$701	$472	$422
Department of Education	$123	$165	$225
Department of Energy	$590	$711	$793
Department of Health and Human Services	$544	$598	$715
Department of Homeland Security	$1,613	$2,097	$2,409
Department of Housing and Urban Development	$73	$81	$76
Department of Justice	$903	$934	$1,241
Department of Labor	$101	$109	$105
Department of State	$284	$320	$447
Department of the Interior	$106	$124	$144
Department of the Treasury	$556	$653	$829
Department of Transportation	$267	$334	$345
Department of Veterans Affairs	$426	$472	$450
Environmental Protection Agency	$29	$28	$29
General Services Administration	$77	$80	$78
National Aeronautics and Space Administration	$162	$155	$187
National Science Foundation	$241	$244	$256
Nuclear Regulatory Commission	$28	$27	$25
Office of Personnel Management	$47	$44	$44
Small Business Administration	$16	$17	$17
Social Security Administration	$216	$243	$266
U.S. Agency for International Development	$57.7	$54.2	$58.1
Non-CFO Act Agencies	**$442.2**	**$466.4**	**$452.1**
Access Board	$0.6	$0.6	$0.6
American Battle Monuments Commission	$0.8	$1.3	$1.3
Armed Forces Retirement Home	*	*	*
U.S. Agency for Global Media	$7.6	$7.8	$8.0
Chemical Safety and Hazard Investigation Board	$0.8	$2.7	$2.6
Commission on Civil Rights	$0.5	$0.5	$0.8
Commodity Futures Trading Commission	$8.7	$9.2	$9.6
Consumer Product Safety Commission	$3.5	$3.1	$3.2
Corporation for National and Community Service	$2.5	$4.8	$4.8
Council of the Inspectors General on Integrity and Efficiency	$0.6	$0.6	$0.6
Court Services and Offender Supervision Agency for the District	$4.0	$4.0	$4.0
Defense Nuclear Facilities Safety Board	$2.1	$2.8	$2.6
Equal Employment Opportunity Commission	$4.8	$5.4	$5.5
Export-Import Bank of the United States	$4.2	$4.6	$3.9
Farm Credit Administration	$3.2	$3.6	$3.8
Federal Communications Commission	$20.0	$26.0	$27.0
Federal Deposit Insurance Corporation	$109.8	$109.8	$109.8
Federal Election Commission	$1.0	$1.0	$1.0
Federal Financial Institutions Examination Council	*	*	*
Federal Labor Relations Authority	*	*	*
Federal Maritime Commission	*	*	$0.9
Federal Retirement Thrift Investment Board	$84.3	$85.5	$67.3
Federal Trade Commission	$12.5	$12.6	$12.8
Gulf Coast Ecosystem Restoration Council	*	*	*
Institute of Museum and Library Services	*	*	*
African Development Foundation	$1.0	$1.0	$1.0
Inter-American Foundation	*	*	*
Millennium Challenge Corporation	$1.7	$1.5	$1.5
Peace Corps	$8.0	$9.4	$10.8
Trade and Development Agency	$1.3	$1.3	$1.3
International Trade Commission	$3.13	$3.36	$3.67

Table 12–2. ESTIMATED CIVILIAN FEDERAL CYBERSECURITY SPENDING BY AGENCY—Continued

(In millions of dollars)

Organization	FY 2020	FY 2021	FY 2022
Marine Mammal Commission	*	*	*
Merit Systems Protection Board	$1.0	$0.7	$0.6
Morris K. Udall and Stewart L. Udall Foundation	*	*	*
National Archives and Records Administration	$7.7	$7.8	$7.8
National Credit Union Administration	$7.4	$7.3	$7.3
National Endowment for the Arts	$1.3	$1.2	$1.2
National Endowment for the Humanities	$1.0	$1.2	$1.2
National Labor Relations Board	$2.2	$2.3	$3.3
National Transportation Safety Board	$1.5	$1.7	$1.8
Nuclear Waste Technical Review Board	*	*	*
Occupational Safety and Health Review Commission	$1.0	$1.0	$1.1
Office of Government Ethics	*	*	*
Office of Special Counsel	*	*	*
Presidio Trust	*	*	*
Privacy and Civil Liberties Oversight Board	$1.4	$1.4	$1.4
Securities and Exchange Commission	$52.8	$44.3	$52.1
Selective Service System	*	$2.0	$5.0
Smithsonian Institution	$8.4	$9.9	$12.8
Surface Transportation Board	$2.3	$1.5	$1.4
Tennessee Valley Authority	$41.4	$53.5	$37.8
U.S. Army Corps of Engineers	$18.8	$20.3	$20.4
United States Holocaust Memorial Museum	$1.6	$1.7	$2.2
United States Institute of Peace	*	*	*
National Gallery of Art	$2.1	$2.1	$2.1
Postal Regulatory Commission	*	*	*
Total	$7,825.6	$8,650.1	$9,854.5

* $500,000 or less

Federal Data Strategy

OMB released the Federal Data Strategy (FDS) in 2019 as a foundational document for enabling agencies to use and manage Federal data to serve the American people. The FDS provides a consistent framework of Principles and Practices that are intended to guide agencies as they continue to implement existing and future data initiatives. It lays out an overarching and iterative plan on how the Federal Government will accelerate the use of data to deliver on mission and serve the public while promoting data accountability and transparency over the next ten years. Agency progress can be viewed at *https://strategy.data.gov/progress/*.

Table 12–3. NIST FRAMEWORK FUNCTION CIVILIAN CFO ACT AGENCY FUNDING TOTALS

(In millions of dollars)

NIST Framework Function	FY 2022
Identify	$2,894
Protect	$3,622
Detect	$1,108
Respond	$1,488
Recover	$290
Total	**$9,402**

This analysis excludes Department of Defense spending.

Cybersecurity

The President's Budget supports the Administration's commitment to secure Federal networks, protect our Nation's infrastructure, and support efforts to share information, standards, and best practices with our critical infrastructure partners and American businesses. The COVID-19 pandemic and recent cybersecurity incidents continue to highlight the urgent need to modernize and secure Federal technology, and the President's Budget includes resources for Federal civilian agencies to protect their networks and safeguard citizens' sensitive information. This includes critical government-wide protections provided by DHS through the Continuous Diagnostics and Mitigation (CDM) Program. The Budget also fully supports the Department of Defense (DOD) cyber efforts, which include safeguarding DOD's networks, information, and systems; supporting military commander objectives; and defending the nation against cyber threats. In addition to approximately $9.8 billion for civilian cybersecurity funding, the Budget includes $20 million for a new Cyber Response and Recovery Fund to improve national critical infrastructure cybersecurity response.

Assessments of the Federal Government's overall cybersecurity risk continue to find the Federal enterprise to be vulnerable, and the President's Budget provides resources to agencies to continue to implement key cybersecurity hygiene capabilities which are necessary to defend against cyber criminals and nation-state actors. This section addresses various areas of cybersecurity, including supply chain risk management, Coordinated Vulnerability Disclosure (CVD), and data methodology for assessing the threat environment and the current Federal cybersecurity posture.

With the passage of the SECURE Technology Act in 2018, agencies are required to assess the risks to their respective information and communications technology supply chains. In addition to agency Supply Chain Risk Management (SCRM) programs, enterprise wide risk is evaluated through the Federal Acquisition Security Council (FASC). The FASC will make recommendations on potential exclusion and removal orders to the Secretaries of Defense and Homeland Security as well as the Director of National Intelligence to address risk to each of their enterprises. These critical steps help agencies safeguard information and communication technology from emerging threats and support the need to establish standards for the acquisition community around SCRM.

Among the most effective methods for obtaining new insights to improve agency information-security programs, CVD enables agencies to coordinate with cybersecurity talent from outside the government to resolve and disclose cybersecurity vulnerabilities in affected products and services, while providing protection for those who uncover these vulnerabilities through good-faith security research. In Fiscal Year 2020, OMB, in coordination with the Department of Homeland Security (DHS), issued memorandum M-20-32, Improving Vulnerability Identification, Management, and Remediation, providing guidance for agencies on management of vulnerability research and CVD programs, as well as Binding Operational Directive 20-01 (BOD-20-01), Develop and Publish a Vulnerability Disclosure Policy, which directed agencies to develop implementation plans providing timelines and milestones for CVD to cover all Federal information systems by May 2, 2021.

Section 630 of the Consolidated Appropriations Act, 2017 (P. L. 115–31) as amended 31 U.S.C. § 1105 (a) (35) to require that an analysis of Federal cybersecurity funding be incorporated into the President's Budget. The Federal spending estimates in this analysis utilize funding and programmatic information collected on the Executive Branch's cybersecurity activities that protect agency information systems, and also on activities that broadly involve cybersecurity such as the development of standards, research and development, and the investigation of cybercrimes. Agencies provide funding data at a level of detail sufficient to consolidate information to determine total governmental spending on cybersecurity. Within each agency, FY 2020 actual levels reflect the actual budgetary resources available in the prior year, FY 2021 estimates reflect the estimated budgetary resources available in the current year, and FY 2022 levels are to reflect levels consistent with the President's Budget.

13. FEDERAL INVESTMENT

Federal investment is the portion of Federal spending of taxpayer money intended to yield long-term benefits for the economy and the Nation that would be greater than if that money had been allocated in the private sector. It promotes improved efficiency within Federal agencies, as well as growth in the national economy by increasing the overall stock of capital. Investment spending can take the form of direct Federal spending or grants to State, local, tribal and territorial governments.[1] It can be designated for physical capital—a tangible asset or the improvement of that asset—that increases production over a period of years or increases value to the Government. It can also be for research and development, education, or training, all of which are intangible, but can still increase income in the future or provide other long-term benefits.

Most presentations in the *Analytical Perspectives* volume combine investment spending with spending intended for current use. In contrast, this chapter focuses solely on Federal and federally financed investment, providing a comprehensive picture of Federal spending for physical capital, research and development, and education and training. Because the analysis in this chapter excludes spending for non-investment activities, it gives only a partial picture of Federal support for specific national needs, such as defense.

Total Federal investment spending was $712 billion in 2020. It is expected to increase by 11 percent in 2021 to $791 billion. The Budget proposes a 0.7 percent increase from 2021 for a total of $796 billion in 2022.

DESCRIPTION OF FEDERAL INVESTMENT

The budget uses a relatively broad definition of investment. It defines Federal investment as encompassing spending for research, development, education, and training as well as physical assets such as land, structures, infrastructure, and major equipment. It also includes spending regardless of the ultimate ownership of the resulting asset, or the purpose it serves. For the purposes of this definition, however, Federal investment does not include "social investment" items like healthcare or social services where it is difficult to separate out the degree to which the spending provides current versus future benefits. The distinction between investment spending and current outlays is a matter of judgment, but the definition used for the purposes of this analysis has remained consistent over time and is useful for historical comparisons.[2]

Investment in physical assets can be for the construction or improvement of buildings, structures, and infrastructure or for the development or acquisition of major equipment. The broader research and development category include spending on the facilities in which these activities occur, major equipment for the conduct of research and development, as well as spending for basic and applied research, and experimental development.[3] Investment in education and training includes vocational rehabilitation, programs for veterans, funding for school systems and higher education, and agricultural extension services. This category excludes training for military personnel or other individuals in Government service.

The budget further classifies investments as either grants to State, local, tribal and territorial governments (e.g. for highways or education), or "direct Federal programs." This "direct Federal" category consists primarily of spending for assets owned by the Federal Government, such as weapons systems and buildings, but also includes grants to private organizations and individuals for investment, such as capital grants to Amtrak, Pell Grants, and higher education loans to individuals. For grants made to State and local governments, it is the recipient jurisdiction, not the Federal Government that ultimately determines whether the money is used to finance investment or for current use. This analysis classifies outlays based on the category in which the recipient jurisdictions are expected to spend a majority of the money. General purpose fiscal assistance is classified as current spending, although in practice, some may be spent by recipient jurisdictions on investment.

Additionally, in this analysis, Federal investment includes credit programs that are for investment purposes. When direct loans and loan guarantees are used to fund investment, the subsidy value is included as investment. The subsidies are classified according to their program purpose, such as construction, or education and training.

This discussion presents spending for gross investment, without adjusting for depreciation.

Composition of Federal Investment Outlays

Major Federal Investment

The composition of major Federal investment outlays is summarized in Table 13–1. The categories include major public physical investment, the conduct of research and development, and the conduct of education and training. Total major Federal investment outlays were $710 billion in 2020. They are estimated to increase 11 percent to

---

[1] For more information on Federal grants to State and local governments see Chapter 11, "Aid to State and Local Governments," in this volume.

[2] Historical figures on investment outlays beginning in 1940 may be found in the Budget's *Historical Tables*. The *Historical Tables* are available at *https://www.whitehouse.gov/omb/historical-tables/*.

[3] A more thorough discussion of research and development funding may be found in Chapter 14, "Research and Development," in this volume.

$788 billion in 2021, and increase by 0.7 percent to $793 billion in 2022.[4] For 2020 through 2022, defense investment outlays comprise about 30 percent of total major Federal investment while non-defense investment comprises around 70 percent. In 2021, defense investment outlays are expected to increase by $4 billion, 2 percent, while non-defense investment outlays are expected to increase by $74 billion, 16 percent. In 2022, the Budget projects a defense investment decrease of $4 billion, or 2 percent, over 2021 and an increase in non-defense investment of $9 billion, or 2 percent.

Major Federal investment outlays will comprise an estimated 13.2 percent of total Federal outlays in 2022 and 3.4 percent of the Nation's gross domestic product. Budget authority and outlays for major Federal investment by subcategory may be found in Table 13–2 at the end of this chapter.

Miscellaneous Physical Investment

In addition to the categories of major Federal investment, several miscellaneous categories of investment outlays are shown at the bottom of Table 13–1. These items, all for physical investment, are generally unrelated to improving Government operations or enhancing economic activity.

Outlays for commodity inventories are for the purchase or sale of agricultural products pursuant to farm price support programs and other commodities. Sales are estimated to exceed purchases by $0.8 billion in 2022.

Outlays for other miscellaneous physical investment are estimated to be $3.4 billion in 2022. This category consists entirely of direct Federal outlays and includes primarily conservation programs.

Detailed Table on Investment Spending

Table 13-2 provides data on budget authority as well as outlays for major Federal investment, divided according to grants to State and local governments and direct Federal spending. Miscellaneous investment is not included because it is generally unrelated to improving Government operations or enhancing economic activity.

---

[4]Amounts shown in FY 2022 may understate total investment funding because some American Jobs Plan initiatives cover a range of activities (including, but not solely, investment). Additionally, the 2020 and 2021 amounts present funding provided to address the pandemic emergency.

Table 13–1. COMPOSITION OF FEDERAL INVESTMENT OUTLAYS
(In billions of dollars)

Federal Investment	Actual	Estimate	
	2020	2021	2022
Major public physical capital investment:			
Direct Federal:			
National defense	183.6	181.8	176.8
Nondefense	54.8	80.0	74.9
Subtotal, direct major public physical capital investment	238.3	261.8	251.7
Grants to State and local governments	85.3	96.0	122.8
Subtotal, major public physical capital investment	323.6	357.8	374.5
Conduct of research and development:			
National defense	63.1	68.9	70.1
Nondefense	70.5	78.1	89.2
Subtotal, conduct of research and development	133.6	146.9	159.3
Conduct of education and training:			
Grants to State and local governments	60.8	95.0	128.4
Direct Federal	192.3	188.4	131.3
Subtotal, conduct of education and training	253.0	283.4	259.7
Total, major Federal investment outlays	**710.2**	**788.2**	**793.5**
MEMORANDUM			
Major Federal investment outlays:			
National defense	246.6	250.7	246.9
Nondefense	463.5	537.5	546.6
Total, major Federal investment outlays	710.2	788.2	793.5
Miscellaneous physical investment:			
Commodity inventories	−0.6	−0.5	−0.8
Other physical investment (direct)	2.4	3.2	3.4
Total, miscellaneous physical investment	1.9	2.8	2.6
Total, Federal investment outlays, including miscellaneous physical investment	712.0	790.9	796.1

Table 13–2. FEDERAL INVESTMENT BUDGET AUTHORITY AND OUTLAYS: GRANT AND DIRECT FEDERAL PROGRAMS

(In millions of dollars)

Description	Budget Authority			Outlays		
	2020 Actual	2021 Estimate	2022 Estimate	2020 Actual	2021 Estimate	2022 Estimate
GRANTS TO STATE AND LOCAL GOVERNMENTS						
Major public physical investment:						
Construction and rehabilitation:						
Transportation:						
Highways	47,282	57,069	45,131	48,305	49,565	52,958
Mass transportation	13,472	13,584	14,045	13,038	13,346	14,405
Rail transportation	3,529	5,230	3,054	3,075	4,981	3,106
Air and other transportation	4,554	6,555	79,888	3,771	4,605	16,000
Subtotal, transportation	68,837	82,438	142,118	68,189	72,497	86,469
Other construction and rehabilitation:						
Pollution control and abatement	4,161	3,975	4,616	3,660	2,652	3,282
Community and regional development	11,343	7,901	17,667	6,416	11,418	16,439
Housing assistance	5,490	8,072	50,507	3,803	4,895	6,595
Other	1,593	2,300	18,159	1,280	1,849	6,949
Subtotal, other construction and rehabilitation	22,587	22,248	90,949	15,159	20,814	33,265
Subtotal, construction and rehabilitation	91,424	104,686	233,067	83,348	93,311	119,734
Other physical assets	2,511	2,935	3,291	1,911	2,687	3,078
Subtotal, major public physical investment	93,935	107,621	236,358	85,259	95,998	122,812
Conduct of research and development:						
Agriculture	373	389	438	292	328	611
Other	199	224	271	53	53	61
Subtotal, conduct of research and development	572	613	709	345	381	672
Conduct of education and training:						
Elementary, secondary, and vocational education	58,284	230,273	82,242	40,554	70,562	101,802
Higher education	405	408	20,960	375	468	878
Research and general education aids	933	1,328	832	854	1,073	1,040
Training and employment	3,843	3,496	3,920	2,957	3,584	3,717
Social services	16,418	17,986	16,704	13,228	15,829	16,683
Agriculture	446	562	541	429	380	750
Other	1,966	2,459	3,543	2,353	3,124	3,523
Subtotal, conduct of education and training	82,295	256,512	128,742	60,750	95,020	128,393
Subtotal, grants for investment	176,802	364,746	365,809	146,354	191,399	251,877
DIRECT FEDERAL PROGRAMS						
Major public physical investment:						
Construction and rehabilitation:						
National defense:						
Military construction and family housing	16,471	6,804	8,227	8,638	7,319	10,370
Atomic energy defense activities and other	1,936	3,166	2,469	1,679	2,645	2,291
Subtotal, national defense	18,407	9,970	10,696	10,317	9,964	12,661
Nondefense:						
International affairs	1,090	1,329	1,044	1,097	1,440	1,413
General science, space, and technology	2,078	2,062	1,940	1,510	2,065	2,019
Water resources projects	4,590	4,592	4,299	3,565	3,856	4,492
Other natural resources and environment	1,466	2,773	2,817	1,398	1,555	2,186
Energy	2,150	653	10,556	2,177	3,056	5,509
Postal service	763	1,006	964	856	658	897
Transportation	25,579	45,044	1,240	12,281	24,846	15,942
Veterans hospitals and other health facilities	5,094	7,894	23,099	4,210	4,663	7,644
Administration of justice	3,265	2,989	−125	1,985	3,536	894
GSA real property activities	1,224	807	7,142	1,963	1,899	2,176
Other construction	3,337	6,717	29,721	3,248	6,510	6,433
Subtotal, nondefense	50,636	75,866	82,697	34,290	54,084	49,605

Table 13–2. FEDERAL INVESTMENT BUDGET AUTHORITY AND OUTLAYS: GRANT AND DIRECT FEDERAL PROGRAMS—Continued

(In millions of dollars)

Description	Budget Authority			Outlays		
	2020 Actual	2021 Estimate	2022 Estimate	2020 Actual	2021 Estimate	2022 Estimate
Subtotal, construction and rehabilitation	69,043	85,836	93,393	44,607	64,048	62,266
Acquisition of major equipment:						
National defense:						
Department of Defense	174,945	178,887	173,977	171,389	170,159	162,461
Atomic energy defense activities	2,378	2,163	2,174	1,878	1,693	1,682
Subtotal, national defense	177,323	181,050	176,151	173,267	171,852	164,143
Nondefense:						
General science and basic research	576	530	551	510	503	531
Postal service	897	1,374	5,954	954	1,328	2,867
Air transportation	3,732	3,792	4,184	3,476	3,566	3,986
Water transportation (Coast Guard)	1,753	2,244	1,554	1,384	2,450	2,239
Other transportation (railroads)	2	3	261	2	3	117
Hospital and medical care for veterans	3,550	7,233	2,846	2,797	4,910	4,400
Federal law enforcement activities	2,498	2,906	1,835	2,487	2,609	1,448
Department of the Treasury (fiscal operations)	314	953	735	431	622	806
National Oceanic and Atmospheric Administration	1,339	1,356	1,969	1,554	2,184	1,649
Other	7,290	5,770	5,811	6,613	7,493	6,843
Subtotal, nondefense	21,951	26,161	25,700	20,208	25,668	24,886
Subtotal, acquisition of major equipment	199,274	207,211	201,851	193,475	197,520	189,029
Purchase or sale of land and structures:						
National defense	−29	−34	−32	−26	−25	−22
Natural resources and environment	322	424	421	253	365	408
General government	−1	....	....	−1	....	....
Other	144	157	307	15	−69	1
Subtotal, purchase or sale of land and structures	436	547	696	241	271	387
Subtotal, major public physical investment	268,753	293,594	295,940	238,323	261,839	251,682
Conduct of research and development:						
National defense:						
Defense military	60,584	63,350	62,780	57,427	62,359	63,093
Atomic energy and other	7,380	7,095	6,957	5,656	6,513	6,982
Subtotal, national defense	67,964	70,445	69,737	63,083	68,872	70,075
Nondefense:						
International affairs	226	226	226	226	226	226
General science, space, and technology:						
NASA	14,158	12,542	13,794	11,343	12,290	13,151
National Science Foundation	6,271	6,814	7,579	5,370	6,030	6,674
Department of Energy	5,424	5,335	6,027	4,810	5,542	6,202
Subtotal, general science, space, and technology	25,853	24,691	27,400	21,523	23,862	26,027
Energy	4,286	4,286	12,834	3,622	3,454	5,094
Transportation:						
Department of Transportation	896	841	1,023	932	932	1,029
NASA	595	632	723	352	576	670
Other transportation	22	40	43	26	37	41
Subtotal, transportation	1,513	1,513	1,789	1,310	1,545	1,740
Health:						
National Institutes of Health	42,664	41,726	49,373	34,830	39,582	43,246
Other health	1,246	1,447	1,488	933	996	1,051
Subtotal, health	43,910	43,173	50,861	35,763	40,578	44,297
Agriculture	1,959	2,080	2,612	1,679	1,790	2,967
Natural resources and environment	2,634	2,638	3,262	2,443	2,522	3,091
National Institute of Standards and Technology	663	833	2,058	690	743	1,970
Hospital and medical care for veterans	1,366	1,420	1,498	1,417	1,407	1,500
All other research and development	1,460	1,649	2,723	1,457	1,550	1,626
Subtotal, nondefense	83,870	82,509	105,263	70,130	77,677	88,538

Table 13–2.   FEDERAL INVESTMENT BUDGET AUTHORITY AND OUTLAYS: GRANT AND DIRECT FEDERAL PROGRAMS—Continued

(In millions of dollars)

Description	Budget Authority			Outlays		
	2020 Actual	2021 Estimate	2022 Estimate	2020 Actual	2021 Estimate	2022 Estimate
Subtotal, conduct of research and development	151,834	152,954	175,000	133,213	146,549	158,613
Conduct of education and training:						
Elementary, secondary, and vocational education	15,655	65,129	1,862	10,266	22,388	48,874
Higher education	163,220	143,467	70,698	160,280	142,654	56,040
Research and general education aids	2,596	2,684	2,687	2,312	2,627	2,651
Training and employment	2,312	2,202	8,217	2,122	2,197	3,380
Health	2,179	3,014	2,420	1,908	2,374	2,732
Veterans education, training, and rehabilitation	14,305	12,807	15,179	13,120	13,471	14,331
General science and basic research	919	1,006	1,190	777	936	1,030
International affairs	748	752	753	610	696	800
Other	1,002	1,117	2,812	900	1,024	1,447
Subtotal, conduct of education and training	202,936	232,178	105,818	192,295	188,367	131,285
Subtotal, direct Federal investment	623,523	678,726	576,758	563,831	596,755	541,580
Total, Federal investment	800,325	1,043,472	942,567	710,185	788,154	793,457

14. RESEARCH AND DEVELOPMENT

Investments in research and development (R&D) are necessary to help spur innovation across the economy and renew America's global leadership. R&D is also critical to tackling the climate crisis and driving the emerging technologies that will power future industries and create good-paying jobs across the nation. The 2022 Budget proposes $171.26 billion, a 9 percent increase, in total research and development across the Federal Government. A breakdown of the request by the major funding Department or agency is shown in the table at the end of this chapter. In addition to the 2022 Budget figures discussed in this chapter, the American Jobs Plan includes major R&D investments, including $50 billion in the National Science Foundation, $30 billion in additional funding for R&D that spurs innovation and job creation and $40 billion to upgrade research infrastructure in laboratories across the country.

FEDERAL R&D DATA

R&D is the collection of efforts directed toward gaining greater knowledge or understanding and applying knowledge toward the production of useful materials, devices, and methods. R&D investments can be characterized as basic research, applied research, experimental development, R&D equipment, or R&D facilities. The Office of Management and Budget (OMB) has used those or similar categories in its collection of R&D data since 1949. Please note that R&D crosscuts in specific topical areas as mandated by law will be reported separately in forthcoming Supplements to the President's 2022 Budget.

Background on Federal R&D Funding

More than 20 Federal agencies fund R&D in the United States. The character of the R&D that these agencies fund depends on the mission of each agency and on the role of R&D in accomplishing it. Table 14–1 shows agency-by-agency spending on basic research, applied research, experimental development, and R&D equipment and facilities.

Basic research is systematic study directed toward a fuller knowledge or understanding of the fundamental aspects of phenomena and of observable facts without specific applications toward processes or products in mind. Basic research, however, may include activities with broad applications in mind.

Applied research is systematic study to gain knowledge or understanding necessary to determine the means by which a recognized and specific need may be met.

Experimental development is creative and systematic work, drawing on knowledge gained from research and practical experience, which is directed at producing new products or processes or improving existing products or processes. Like research, experimental development will result in gaining additional knowledge.

Research and development equipment includes acquisition or design and production of movable equipment, such as spectrometers, research satellites, detectors, and other instruments. At a minimum, this category includes programs devoted to the purchase or construction of R&D equipment.

Research and development facilities include the acquisition, design, and construction of, or major repairs or alterations to, all physical facilities for use in R&D activities. Facilities include land, buildings, and fixed capital equipment, regardless of whether the facilities are to be used by the Government or by a private organization, and regardless of where title to the property may rest. This category includes such fixed facilities as reactors, wind tunnels, and particle accelerators.

Table 14–1.   FEDERAL RESEARCH AND DEVELOPMENT SPENDING
(Mandatory and discretionary budget authority [1], dollar amounts in millions)

	2020 Actual	2021 Estimate [2]	2022 Proposed [3]	Dollar Change: 2021 to 2022	Percent Change: 2021 to 2022
By Agency					
Defense [4]	62,438	63,350	62,800	−550	−1%
Health and Human Services	44,455	43,494	51,232	7,738	18%
Energy	19,476	19,312	21,452	2,140	11%
NASA	14,801	13,226	14,565	1,339	10%
National Science Foundation	6,800	7,408	8,173	765	10%
Agriculture	2,989	2,965	3,609	644	22%
Commerce	1,953	2,122	2,743	621	29%
Veterans Affairs	1,366	1,420	1,498	78	5%
Interior	1,043	1,024	1,339	315	31%
Transportation	1,094	1,033	1,221	188	18%
Homeland Security	532	590	627	37	6%
Environmental Protection Agency	516	524	585	61	12%
Education	237	445	473	28	6%
Smithsonian Institution	344	322	346	24	7%
Other	582	563	597	34	6%
TOTAL	**158,626**	**157,798**	**171,260**	**13,462**	**9%**
Basic Research					
Defense	2,546	2,651	2,362	−289	−11%
Health and Human Services	21,826	21,872	24,022	2,150	10%
Energy	5,494	5,519	5,892	373	7%
NASA	6,655	4,515	5,620	1,105	24%
National Science Foundation	5,437	5,966	6,532	566	9%
Agriculture	1,061	1,124	1,416	292	26%
Commerce	241	250	320	70	28%
Veterans Affairs	523	555	584	29	5%
Interior	82	84	171	87	104%
Transportation	16	16	16	0	0%
Homeland Security	47	53	70	17	32%
Environmental Protection Agency	....	....	....	....	....
Education	58	78	58	−20	....
Smithsonian Institution	290	288	310	22	8%
Other	14	14	14	0	0%
SUBTOTAL	**44,290**	**42,985**	**47,387**	**4,402**	**10%**
Applied Research					
Defense	6,274	6,654	5,559	−1,095	−16%
Health and Human Services	22,081	21,297	26,835	5,538	26%
Energy [5]	8,444	7,395	7,669	274	4%
NASA	2,668	2,669	2,982	313	12%
National Science Foundation	834	848	1,047	199	23%
Agriculture	1,285	1,344	1,634	290	22%
Commerce	1,074	1,150	1,353	203	18%
Veterans Affairs	813	835	882	47	6%
Interior	778	768	961	193	25%
Transportation	702	716	879	163	23%
Homeland Security	165	178	203	25	14%
Environmental Protection Agency	400	406	460	54	13%
Education	129	242	311	69	29%
Smithsonian Institution	....	....	....	....	....
Other	345	341	351	10	3%
SUBTOTAL	**45,992**	**44,843**	**51,126**	**6,283**	**14%**

Table 14–1.   FEDERAL RESEARCH AND DEVELOPMENT SPENDING—Continued

(Mandatory and discretionary budget authority [1], dollar amounts in millions)

	2020 Actual	2021 Estimate [2]	2022 Proposed [3]	Dollar Change: 2021 to 2022	Percent Change: 2021 to 2022
Experimental Development					
Defense [4]	51,764	54,045	54,859	814	2%
Health and Human Services	53	53	53	0	0%
Energy [6]	3,060	3,715	5,206	1,491	40%
NASA	5,430	5,990	5,915	−75	−1%
National Science Foundation	....	....	....	....	....
Agriculture	295	306	359	53	17%
Commerce	272	370	413	43	12%
Veterans Affairs	30	30	32	2	7%
Interior	181	170	205	35	21%
Transportation	338	269	288	19	7%
Homeland Security	320	340	345	5	1%
Environmental Protection Agency	116	118	125	7	6%
Education	50	125	104	−21	−17%
Smithsonian Institution	....	....	....	....	....
Other	215	208	232	24	12%
SUBTOTAL	**62,124**	**65,739**	**68,136**	**2,397**	**4%**
Facilities and Equipment					
Defense	1,854	0	20	20	....
Health and Human Services	495	272	322	50	18%
Energy	2,478	2,683	2,685	2	0%
NASA	48	52	48	−4	−8%
National Science Foundation	529	594	594	0	0%
Agriculture	348	191	200	9	5%
Commerce	366	352	657	305	87%
Veterans Affairs	....	....	....	....	....
Interior	2	2	2	0	0%
Transportation	38	32	38	6	19%
Homeland Security	0	19	9	−10	....
Environmental Protection Agency	....	....	....	....	....
Education	....	....	....	....	....
Smithsonian Institution	54	34	36	2	0%
Other	8	0	0	0	0%
SUBTOTAL	**6,220**	**4,231**	**4,611**	**380**	**9%**

[1] This table shows funding levels for Departments or Independent agencies with more than $200 million in R&D activities in 2022.

[2] The FY 2021 Estimate column applies the main FY 2022 President's Budget volume approach of using FY 2021 enacted appropriations.

[3] Amounts shown in FY 2022 do not include R&D funding from the American Jobs Plan.

[4] The totals for Experimental Development spending do not include the DOD Budget Activity 06 (Research, Development, Test, and Evaluation Management Support). OMB and DOD are currently evaluating whether Activity 06 may in the future be categorized as Experimental Development.

[5] Of the percent change for Energy's applied research, -5% is defense and 17% is non-defense.

[6] Of the percent change for Energy's experimental development, -3% is defense and 114% is non-defense.

15.   CREDIT AND INSURANCE

The Federal Government offers direct loans and loan guarantees to support a wide range of activities including home ownership, student loans, small business, farming, energy, infrastructure investment, and exports. In addition, Government-sponsored enterprises (GSEs) operate under Federal charters for the purpose of enhancing credit availability for targeted sectors. Through its insurance programs, the Federal Government insures deposits at depository institutions, guarantees private-sector defined-benefit pensions, and insures against some other risks such as flood and terrorism.

This chapter discusses the roles of these diverse programs. The first section discusses individual credit programs and GSEs. The second section reviews Federal deposit insurance, pension guarantees, disaster insurance, and insurance against terrorism and other security-related risks. This year's chapter includes a brief analysis of the Troubled Asset Relief Program (TARP), which was previously contained in a separate chapter.

I. CREDIT IN VARIOUS SECTORS

Housing Credit Programs

Through housing credit programs, the Federal Government promotes homeownership among various target groups, including low- and moderate-income people, veterans, and rural residents. In times of economic crisis, the Federal Government's role and target market can expand dramatically.

Coronavirus Disease 2019 (COVID-19): Impact and Federal Response

Loss of income and other hardships due to COVID-19 have left many homeowners unable to meet their financial obligations, including mortgage payments. In response, Congress and Federal agencies have provided relief in the form of foreclosure moratoriums, payment forbearance, credit reporting protections and enhanced loss mitigation. For example, the Coronavirus Aid, Relief and Economic Security (CARES) Act required a 60-day foreclosure and eviction moratorium and up to one year of payment forbearance with no additional fees for homeowners with Federally-backed mortgages. More recently, the Departments of Housing and Urban Development, Veterans Affairs and Agriculture extended the foreclosure and eviction moratorium and forbearance enrollment window through June 30, 2021, and provided up to an additional six months of forbearance for certain borrowers.

Federal Housing Administration

The Federal Housing Administration (FHA) guarantees single-family mortgages that provide access to homeownership for households who may have difficulty obtaining a conventional mortgage. In addition to traditional single-family "forward" mortgages, FHA insures "reverse" mortgages for seniors (Home Equity Conversion

Mortgages, described below) and loans for the construction, rehabilitation, and refinancing of multifamily housing, hospitals and other healthcare facilities.

FHA Single-Family Forward Mortgages

FHA has been a primary facilitator of mortgage credit for first-time and minority homebuyers, a pioneer of products such as the 30-year self-amortizing mortgage, and a vehicle to enhance credit for many low- to moderate-income households. One of the major benefits of an FHA-insured mortgage is that it provides a homeownership option for borrowers who, though they can only make a modest down-payment, can show that they are creditworthy and have sufficient income to afford the house they want to buy. In 2020, 83 percent of FHA purchase mortgages were obtained by first-time homebuyers. Of all FHA loans (purchase and refinance), 33 percent served minority borrowers and 50 percent served low- to moderate-income borrowers.

FHA Home Equity Conversion Mortgages

Home Equity Conversion Mortgages (HECMs), or "reverse" mortgages, are designed to support aging in place by enabling elderly homeowners to borrow against the equity in their homes without having to make repayments during their lifetime (unless they move, refinance or fail to meet certain requirements). A HECM is known as a "reverse" mortgage because the change in home equity over time is generally the opposite of a forward mortgage. While a traditional forward mortgage starts with a small amount of equity and builds equity with amortization of the loan, a HECM starts with a large equity cushion that declines over time as the loan accrues interest and premiums. The risk of HECMs is therefore weighted toward the end of the mortgage, while forward mortgage risk is concentrated in the first 10 years.

FHA Mutual Mortgage Insurance (MMI) Fund

FHA guarantees for forward and reverse mortgages are administered under the Mutual Mortgage Insurance (MMI) Fund. At the end of 2020, the MMI Fund had $1.295 trillion in total mortgages outstanding and a capital ratio of 6.10 percent, remaining above the 2 percent statutory minimum for the fifth straight year and increasing from the 2019 level of 4.84 percent. Although the capital ratio has improved, the serious delinquency (SDQ) rate[1], a key indicator of portfolio performance, increased from 3.9 percent to 11.6 percent as many FHA borrowers experienced financial hardship due to COVID-19. The impact of this elevated SDQ rate on the health of the MMI Fund is uncertain at this time as borrowers continue to work through available loss mitigation options. For more information on the financial status of the MMI Fund, please see the Annual Report to Congress Regarding the Financial Status of the FHA Mutual Mortgage Insurance Fund, Fiscal Year 2020.[2]

FHA's new origination volume in 2020 was $310 billion for forward mortgages and $16 billion for HECMs, and the Budget projects $247 billion and $16 billion, respectively, for 2022.

FHA Multifamily and Healthcare Guarantees

In addition to the single-family mortgage insurance provided through the MMI Fund, FHA's General Insurance and Special Risk Insurance (GISRI) loan programs continue to facilitate the construction, rehabilitation, and refinancing of multifamily housing, hospitals and other healthcare facilities. The credit enhancement provided by FHA enables borrowers to obtain long-term, fixed-rate financing, which mitigates interest rate risk and facilitates lower monthly mortgage payments. This can improve the financial sustainability of multifamily housing and healthcare facilities, and may also translate into more affordable rents and lower healthcare costs for consumers.

GISRI's new origination loan volume for all programs in 2020 was $26 billion and the Budget projects $33 billion for 2022. The total amount of guarantees outstanding on mortgages in the FHA GISRI Fund were $165 billion at the end of 2020.

VA Housing Loan Program

The Department of Veterans Affairs (VA) assists veterans, members of the Selected Reserve, and active duty personnel in purchasing homes in recognition of their service to the Nation. The VA housing loan program effectively substitutes a Federal guarantee for the borrower's down payment, meaning more favorable lending terms for veterans. Under this program, VA does not guarantee the entire mortgage loan, but typically fully guarantees the first 25 percent of losses upon default. In fiscal year 2020, VA guaranteed a total of 428,1421 new purchase home loans, providing approximately $32 billion in guarantees. Additionally, 662,065 veteran borrowers lowered interest rates on their home mortgages through streamlined refinancing. VA provided approximately $94 billion in guarantees for 1,246,816 VA loans in 2020. That followed $44 billion in guarantees for 624,546 VA loans closed in FY 2019.

VA, in cooperation with VA-guaranteed loan servicers, also assists borrowers through home retention options and alternatives to foreclosure. VA intervenes when needed to help veterans and service members avoid foreclosure through loan modifications, special forbearances, repayment plans, and acquired loans, as well as assistance to complete compromised sales or deeds-in-lieu of foreclosure. These standard efforts helped resolve over 93 percent of defaulted VA-guaranteed loans and assisted over 119,000 veterans retain homeownership or avoid foreclosure in 2020. These efforts resulted in $3.4 billion in avoided guaranteed claim payments. As noted above, VA has responded to the COVID crisis by providing special CARES Act forbearances to support otherwise-current borrowers through the pandemic. As of September 30, 2020, 200,460 VA borrowers were participating in a special CARES Act forbearance.

Rural Housing Service

The Rural Housing Service (RHS) at the U.S. Department of Agriculture (USDA) offers direct and guaranteed loans to help very-low- to moderate-income rural residents buy and maintain adequate, affordable housing. RHS housing loans and loan guarantees differ from other Federal housing loan programs in that they are means-tested, making them more accessible to low-income, rural residents. The single family housing guaranteed loan program is designed to provide home loan guarantees for moderate-income rural residents whose incomes are between 80 percent and 115 percent (maximum for the program) of area median income.

RHS has traditionally offered both direct and guaranteed homeownership loans. The direct single family housing loans have been historically funded at $1 billion a year, while the single family housing guaranteed loan program, authorized in 1990 at $100 million, has grown into a $24 billion loan program annually. USDA also offers direct and guaranteed multifamily housing loans, as well as housing repair loans.

Education Credit Programs

The Department of Education (ED) direct student loan program is one of the largest Federal credit programs, with $1.315 trillion in Direct Loan principal outstanding at the end of 2020. The Federal student loan programs provide students and their families with the funds to help meet postsecondary education costs. Because funding for the loan programs is provided through mandatory budget authority, student loans are considered separately for budget purposes from other Federal student financial assistance programs (which are largely discretionary), but

---

[1] The SDQ rate tracks the percentage of FHA-insured mortgages where the borrower is 90 or more days delinquent, including mortgages in foreclosure and bankruptcy.

[2] https://www.hud.gov/sites/dfiles/Housing/documents/2020FHAAnnualReportMMIFund.pdf

should be viewed as part of the overall Federal effort to expand access to higher education.

Loans for higher education were first authorized under the William D. Ford program, which was included in the Higher Education Act of 1965. The direct loan program was authorized by the Student Loan Reform Act of 1993 (Public Law 103–66). The enactment of the Student Aid and Fiscal Responsibility Act (SAFRA) of 2010 (Public Law 111–152) ended the guaranteed Federal Financial Education Loan (FFEL) program. On July 1, 2010, ED became the sole originator of Federal student loans through the Direct Loan program.

Under the current direct loan program, the Federal Government partners with over 6,000 institutions of higher education, which then disburse loan funds to students. Loans are available to students and parents of students regardless of income and only Parent and Graduate PLUS loans includes a minimal credit check. There are three types of Direct Loans: Federal Direct Subsidized Stafford Loans, Federal Direct Unsubsidized Stafford Loans, and Federal Direct PLUS Loans, each with different terms.

The Direct Loan program offers a variety of repayment options including income-driven repayment ones for all student borrowers. Depending on the plan, monthly payments are capped at no more than 10 or 15 percent of borrower discretionary income with any remaining balance after 20 or 25 years forgiven. In addition, borrowers working in public service professions while making 10 years of qualifying payments are eligible for Public Service Loan Forgiveness (PSLF).

Small Business and Farm Credit Programs

The Government offers direct loans and loan guarantees to small businesses and farmers, who may have difficulty obtaining credit elsewhere. It also provides guarantees of debt issued by certain investment funds that invest in small businesses. Two GSEs, the Farm Credit System and the Federal Agricultural Mortgage Corporation, increase liquidity in the agricultural lending market.

Small Business Administration

SBA ensures that small businesses across the Nation have the tools and resources needed to start, grow, and recover their business. SBA has grown significantly since the agency's creation in 1953, both in terms of the total assistance provided and the array of programs offered to small business owners. SBA's lending programs complement credit markets by offering creditworthy small businesses access to affordable credit through private lenders when they cannot otherwise obtain financing on reasonable terms or conditions.

In 2020, SBA provided $19.6 billion in loan guarantees to assist small business owners with access to affordable capital through its largest program, the 7(a) General Business Loan Guarantee program. This program provides access to financing for general business operations, such as operating and capital expenses. In addition, through the 504 Certified Development Company (CDC) and Refinance Programs, SBA supported approximately

$6.7 billion in guaranteed loans for fixed-asset financing and provided the opportunity for small businesses to refinance existing 504 CDC loans. These programs enable small businesses to secure financing for assets such as machinery and equipment, construction, and commercial real estate, and to take advantage of current low interest rates and free up resources for expansion. Furthermore, the Small Business Investment Company (SBIC) Program supports privately-owned and operated venture capital investment firms that invest in small businesses. In 2020, SBA supported $3.1 billion in SBIC venture capital investments. In addition to these guaranteed lending programs, the 7(m) Direct Microloan program supports the smallest of businesses, startups, and underserved entrepreneurs through loans of up to $50,000 made by non-profit intermediaries. In 2020, SBA recorded a record year by facilitating nearly $85 million in microlending.

SBA continues to be a valuable source for American communities who need access to low-interest loans to recover quickly in the wake of disaster, especially due to the COVID-19 pandemic. At the end of 2020, the SBA was working 275 active disaster assistance declarations and approved disaster loans totaling $195 billion in lending to businesses, homeowners, renters, and property owners. To further assist with COVID-19 relief, Congress created the Paycheck Protection Program (PPP) under the CARES Act to provide small businesses with funds to provide up to 8 weeks of payroll costs, including benefits. In 2020, the PPP provided an additional 5.2 million loans worth more than $525 billion.

Community Development Financial Institutions

Since its creation in 1994, the Department of the Treasury's Community Development Financial Institutions (CDFI) Fund has, through different grant, loan, and tax credit programs, worked to expand the availability of credit, investment capital, and financial services for underserved people and communities by supporting the growth and capacity of a national network of CDFIs, investors, and financial service providers. Today, there are over 1,000 Certified CDFIs nationwide, including a variety of loan funds, community development banks, credit unions, and venture capital funds. CDFI certification also enables some non-depository financial institutions to apply for financing programs offered by certain Federal Home Loan Banks.

Unlike other CDFI Fund programs, the CDFI Bond Guarantee Program (BGP), enacted through the Small Business Jobs Act of 2010, does not offer grants, but is instead a Federal credit program. The BGP was designed to provide CDFIs greater access to low-cost, long-term, fixed-rate capital.

Under the BGP, Treasury provides a 100-percent guarantee on long-term bonds of at least $100 million issued to qualified CDFIs, with a maximum maturity of 30 years. To date, Treasury has issued $1.7 billion in bond guarantee commitments to 25 CDFIs, $1.3 billion of which has been disbursed to help finance affordable housing, charter schools, commercial real estate, community healthcare facilities and other eligible uses in 27 States and the District of Columbia.

Farm Service Agency

Farm operating loans were first offered in 1937 by the newly created Farm Security Administration to assist family farmers who were unable to obtain credit from a commercial source to buy equipment, livestock, or seed. Farm ownership loans were authorized in 1961 to provide family farmers with financial assistance to purchase farmland. Presently, the Farm Service Agency (FSA) assists low-income family farmers in starting and maintaining viable farming operations. Emphasis is placed on aiding beginning and socially disadvantaged farmers. Legislation mandates that a portion of appropriated funds are set-aside for exclusive use by underserved groups.

FSA offers operating loans and ownership loans, both of which may be either direct or guaranteed loans. Operating loans provide credit to farmers and ranchers for annual production expenses and purchases of livestock, machinery, and equipment, while farm ownership loans assist producers in acquiring and developing their farming or ranching operations. As a condition of eligibility for direct loans, borrowers must be unable to obtain private credit at reasonable rates and terms. As FSA is the "lender of last resort," default rates on FSA direct loans are generally higher than those on private-sector loans. FSA-guaranteed farm loans are made to more creditworthy borrowers who have access to private credit markets. Because the private loan originators must retain 10 percent of the risk, they exercise care in examining the repayment ability of borrowers. The subsidy rates for the direct programs fluctuate largely because of changes in the interest component of the subsidy rate. Since the early 1990's, the majority of FSA loan assistance has been through guarantees rather than direct lending.

In 2020, FSA provided loans and loan guarantees to almost 35,000 family farmers totaling $7.5 billion. In recent years, FSA assistance has been at record levels due to various adversities in the agricultural economy. The average size of farm ownership loans remained consistent over the past few years, with new customers receiving the bulk of the direct loans. Direct and guaranteed loan programs provided assistance totaling $3.45 billion to more than 19,500 beginning farmers. The majority of assistance provided in the operating loan program during 2020 was to beginning farmers. Sixty percent of direct operating loans were made to beginning farmers. A beginning farmer is an individual or entity who: has operated a farm for not more than 10 years; substantially participates in farm operation; and, for farm ownership loans, the applicant cannot own a farm greater than 30 percent of the average size farm in the county at time of application. If the applicant is an entity, all entity members must be related by blood or marriage, and all members must be eligible beginning farmers.

Loans for socially disadvantaged farmers totaled $1.09 billion, of which $739 million was in the farm ownership program and $349 million in the farm operating program.

Lending to minority and women farmers was a significant portion of overall assistance provided, with $1.09 billion in loans and loan guarantees provided to more than 6,850 farmers. Loan assistance provided to beginning and socially disadvantaged farmers increased in 2020 compared to 2019, fulfilling an initiative of the Department to expand lending to underserved groups as a percentage of total loans made.

The FSA Microloan program increases overall direct and guaranteed lending to small niche producers and minorities. This program dramatically simplifies application procedures for small loans and implement more flexible eligibility and experience requirements. Demand for the micro-loan program continues to grow while delinquencies and defaults remain at or below those of the regular FSA operating loan program.

Energy and Infrastructure Credit Programs

The Department of Energy (DOE) administers three credit programs: Title XVII the Advanced Technology Vehicle Manufacturing (ATVM) loan program, and the Tribal Energy Loan Guarantee Program. Title XVII of the Energy Policy Act of 2005 (Public Law 109–58) authorizes DOE to issue loan guarantees for projects that employ innovative technologies to reduce air pollutants or man-made greenhouse gases. Most Title XVII loan authority requires borrowers to pay the credit subsidy cost, though Congress did appropriate $161 million for credit subsidy (net of subsequent rescissions) to support loan guarantees for renewable energy and efficient end-use technologies. The FY 2022 President's Budget requests $150 million in discretionary credit subsidy to support eligible projects. To date, DOE has issued (and amended) three loan guarantees totaling over $11 billion to support the construction of two new commercial nuclear power reactors. DOE has one active conditional commitment of $2 billion to support an innovative pet-coke to methanol facility integrated with carbon capture and storage. DOE has over $22.4 billion in available loan guarantee authority available and is actively working with applicants proceeding to conditional commitment and financial close.

The American Reinvestment and Recovery Act of 2009 (Public Law 111–5) amended the program's authorizing statute and appropriated credit subsidy to support loan guarantees on a temporary basis for commercial or advanced renewable energy systems, electric power transmission systems, and leading-edge biofuel projects. Authority for the temporary program to extend new loans expired September 30, 2011. Over $16 billion in loans and loan guarantees was disbursed under 24 of the loan guarantees issued prior to the program's expiration.

Section 136 of the Energy Independence and Security Act of 2007 (Public Law 110–140) authorizes DOE to issue loans to support the development of advanced technology vehicles and qualifying components. In 2009, the Congress appropriated $7.5 billion in credit subsidy to support a maximum of $25 billion in loans under ATVM.

From 2009 to 2011, DOE issued five loans totaling over $8 billion to support the manufacturing of advanced technology vehicles. DOE has over $2.4 billion in credit subsidy balances available to support up to $17.7 billion in loans and is actively working with applicants proceeding to conditional commitment and financial close.

Title XXVI of the Energy Policy Act of 1992, as amended (Public Law 102-486, Public Law 109-58) authorizes DOE to guarantee up to $2 billion in loans to Indian tribes for energy development. In 2017, the Congress appropriated $8.5 million in credit subsidy to support tribal energy development. DOE issued a solicitation in 2018 and is actively working with applicants proceeding to conditional commitment and financial close.

Electric and Telecommunications Loans

Rural Utilities Service (RUS) programs of the USDA provide grants and loans to support the distribution of rural electrification, telecommunications, distance learning, and broadband infrastructure systems.

In 2020, RUS delivered $6.34 billion in direct electrification loans (including $5.49 billion in FFB Electric Loans, $750 million in electric underwriting, and $104 million rural energy savings loans), $93 million in direct telecommunications loans, and $394 million in Reconnect broadband loans.

USDA Rural Infrastructure and Business Development Programs

USDA, through a variety of Rural Development (RD) programs, provides grants, direct loans, and loan guarantees to communities for constructing facilities such as healthcare clinics, police stations, and water systems, as well as to assist rural businesses and cooperatives in creating new community infrastructure (e.g., educational and healthcare networks) and to diversify the rural economy and employment opportunities. In 2020, RD provided $1.3 billion in Community Facility (CF) direct loans, which are for communities of 20,000 or less. The CF programs have the flexibility to finance more than 100 separate types of essential community infrastructure that ultimately improve access to healthcare, education, public safety and other critical facilities and services. RD also provided $1.4 billion in water and wastewater (W&W) direct loans, and guaranteed $1.7 billion in rural business loans, which will help create and save jobs in rural America. The 2018 Farm Bill gave CF and W&W loan guarantees new authorization to serve communities of 50,000 or less and allowed the programs to charge a fee to offset the loan subsidy cost. RD began executing the programs with the new authorities in 2020.

Water Infrastructure

The Environmental Protection Agency's (EPA) Water Infrastructure Finance and Innovation Act (WIFIA) program accelerates investment in the Nation's water infrastructure by providing long-term, low-cost supplemental loans for projects of regional or national significance. In 2020, EPA selected fifty-eight borrowers to apply for a WIFIA loan totaling approximately $6 billion. Those projects will leverage $7 billion in private capital, in addition to other funding sources, to help finance a total of over $15 billion in water infrastructure investments. The selected projects demonstrate the broad range of project types that the WIFIA program can finance, including wastewater, drinking water, stormwater, and water reuse projects.

Transportation Infrastructure

The Department of Transportation (DOT) administers credit programs that fund critical transportation infrastructure projects, often using innovative financing methods. The two predominant programs are the Transportation Infrastructure Finance and Innovation Act (TIFIA) and the Railroad Rehabilitation and Improvement Financing (RRIF) loan programs. DOT's Build America Bureau administers these programs, as well as Private Activity Bonds and the Nationally Significant Freight and Highway Projects (INFRA) grant program, all under one roof. The Bureau serves as the single point of contact for States, municipalities, and other project sponsors looking to utilize Federal transportation expertise, apply for Federal transportation credit and grant programs, and explore ways to access private capital in public-private partnerships. As with the 2021 Budget, the 2022 Budget will reflect the TIFIA and RRIF programs' accounts in the Office of the Secretary, where the Bureau is housed, rather than in the Federal Highway Administration and Federal Railroad Administration.

Transportation Infrastructure Finance and Innovation Act (TIFIA)

Established by the Transportation Equity Act for the 21st century (TEA–21) (Public Law 105–178) in 1998, the TIFIA program is designed to fill market gaps and leverage substantial private co-investment by providing supplemental and subordinate capital to projects of national or regional significance. Through TIFIA, DOT provides three types of Federal credit assistance to highway, transit, rail, and intermodal projects: direct loans, loan guarantees, and lines of credit.

TIFIA can help advance qualified, large-scale projects that otherwise might be delayed or deferred because of size, complexity, or uncertainty over the timing of revenues at a relatively low budgetary cost. Each dollar of subsidy provided for TIFIA can provide approximately $14 in credit assistance, and leverage additional non-Federal transportation infrastructure investment. Congress authorized $300 million for TIFIA in 2021.

Railroad Rehabilitation and Improvement Financing (RRIF)

Also established by TEA–21 in 1998, the RRIF program provides loans or loan guarantees with an interest rate equal to the Treasury rate for similar-term securities. TEA–21 also stipulates that non-Federal sources pay the subsidy cost of the loan (a "Credit Risk Premium"), thereby allowing the program to operate without Federal subsidy appropriations. The RRIF program assists projects that improve rail safety, enhance the environment, promote economic development, or enhance the capacity of the national rail network. While refinancing existing debt is an eligible use of RRIF proceeds, capital investment projects that would not occur without a RRIF loan are prioritized. Since its inception, $6.3 billion in direct loans have been made under the RRIF program.

The Fixing America's Surface Transportation (FAST) Act (Public Law 114–94) included programmatic changes to enhance the RRIF program to mirror the qualities of TIFIA, including broader eligibility, a loan term that can be as long as 35 years from project completion, and a fully subordinated loan under certain conditions. Additionally, in 2016 the Congress appropriated $1.96 million to assist Class II and Class III Railroads in preparing and applying for direct loans and loan guarantees.

In the Consolidated Appropriations Act, 2018 (Public Law 115-141), for the first time in RRIF's history, the Congress appropriated $25 million in subsidy budget authority for direct loans and loan guarantees to the RRIF program. This appropriation allows DOT to issue RRIF loans without requiring credit risk premiums from borrowers to cover the subsidy costs of the loans.

International Credit Programs

Through 2020, seven unique Federal agencies provide direct loans, loan guarantees, and insurance to a variety of private and sovereign borrowers: USDA, the Department of Defense, the Department of State, the Department of the Treasury, the Agency for International Development (USAID), the Export-Import Bank (ExIm), and the International Development Finance Corporation (DFC). These programs are intended to level the playing field for U.S. exporters, deliver robust support for U.S. goods and services, stabilize international financial markets, enhance security, and promote sustainable development.

Federal export credit programs counter official financing that foreign governments around the world, largely in Europe and Japan, but also increasingly in emerging markets such as China and Brazil, provide their exporters, usually through export credit agencies (ECAs). The U.S. Government has worked since the 1970's to constrain official credit support through a multilateral agreement in the Organization for Economic Cooperation and Development (OECD). This agreement has established standards for Government-backed financing of exports. In addition to ongoing work in keeping these OECD standards up-to-date, the U.S. Government established the International Working Group (IWG) on Export Credits to set up a new framework that will include China and other non-OECD countries, which until now have not been subject to export credit standards. The process of establishing these new standards, which is not yet complete, advances a Congressional mandate to reduce subsidized export financing programs.

Export Support Programs

When the private sector is unable or unwilling to provide financing, the Export-Import Bank, the U.S. Export Credit Agency ("ECA"), fills the gap for American businesses by equipping them with the financing support necessary to level the playing field against foreign competitors. ExIm support includes direct loans and loan guarantees for creditworthy foreign buyers to help secure export sales from U.S. exporters. It also includes working capital guarantees and export credit insurance to help U.S. exporters secure financing for overseas sales. USDA's Export Credit Guarantee Programs (also known as GSM programs) similarly help to level the playing field. Like programs of other agricultural exporting nations, GSM programs guarantee payment from countries and entities that want to import U.S. agricultural products but cannot easily obtain credit. The GSM 102 program provides guarantees for credit extended with short-term repayment terms not to exceed 18 months.

Exchange Stabilization Fund

Consistent with U.S. obligations in the International Monetary Fund regarding global financial stability, the Exchange Stabilization Fund (ESF) managed by the Department of the Treasury may provide loans or credits to a foreign entity or government of a foreign country. A loan or credit may not be made for more than six months in any 12-month period unless the President gives the Congress a written statement that unique or emergency circumstances require that the loan or credit be for more than six months. The CARES Act established within the ESF an Economic Stabilization Program with $500 billion in appropriations with temporary authority for up to $500 billion in lending and other eligible investments for: 1) airlines and certain airline industry-related businesses; 2) businesses critical to maintaining national security; and 3) programs or facilities established by the Board of Governors of the Federal Reserve System for the purpose of providing liquidity to the financial system pursuant to Section 13(3) of the Federal Reserve Act. The Consolidated Appropriations Act, 2021 (P. L. 116-260) rescinded this authority, though any loans and investments already made will remain active until obligations are fully liquidated.

Sovereign Lending and Guarantees

The U.S. Government can extend short-to-medium-term loan guarantees that cover potential losses that might be incurred by lenders if a country defaults on its borrowings; for example, the U.S. may guarantee another country's sovereign bond issuance. The purpose of this tool is to provide the Nation's sovereign international partners access to necessary, urgent, and relatively affordable financing during temporary periods of strain when they cannot access such financing in international financial markets, and to support critical reforms that will enhance long-term fiscal sustainability, often in concert with support from international financial institutions such as the International Monetary Fund. The goal of sovereign loan guarantees is to help lay the economic groundwork for the Nation's international partners to graduate to an unenhanced bond issuance in the international capital markets. For example, as part of the U.S. response to fiscal crises, the U.S. Government has extended sovereign loan guarantees to Tunisia, Jordan, Ukraine, and Iraq to enhance their access to capital markets while promoting economic policy adjustment.

Development Programs

Credit is an important tool in U.S. bilateral assistance to promote sustainable development. On January 2, 2020, the U.S. International Development Finance Corporation launched to consolidate, modernize, and reform the U.S. Government's "development finance" capabilities. The DFC provides loans, guarantees, and other investment tools such as equity and political risk insurance to facilitate and incentivize private-sector investment in emerging markets that will have positive developmental impact, and meet national security objectives. Through the DFC's equity program, the U.S. Government will partner with allies and deliver financially-sound alternatives to State-led initiatives from countries like China.

The Government-Sponsored Enterprises (GSEs)

Fannie Mae and Freddie Mac

The Federal National Mortgage Association, or Fannie Mae, created in 1938, and the Federal Home Loan Mortgage Corporation, or Freddie Mac, created in 1970, were established to support the stability and liquidity of a secondary market for residential mortgage loans. Fannie Mae's and Freddie Mac's public missions were later broadened to promote affordable housing. The Federal Home Loan Bank (FHLB) System, created in 1932, is comprised of eleven individual banks with shared liabilities. Together they lend money to financial institutions, mainly banks and thrifts, that are involved in mortgage financing to varying degrees, and they also finance some mortgages using their own funds. The mission of the FHLB System is broadly defined as promoting housing finance, and the System also has specific requirements to support affordable housing.

Together these three GSEs currently are involved, in one form or another, with approximately half of residential mortgages outstanding in the U.S. today.

History of the Conservatorship of Fannie Mae and Freddie Mac and Budgetary Effects

Growing stress and losses in the mortgage markets in 2007 and 2008 seriously eroded the capital of Fannie Mae and Freddie Mac. Legislation enacted in July 2008 strengthened regulation of the housing GSEs through the creation of the Federal Housing Finance Agency (FHFA), a new independent regulator of housing GSEs, and provided the Department of the Treasury with authorities to purchase securities from Fannie Mae and Freddie Mac.

On September 6, 2008, FHFA placed Fannie Mae and Freddie Mac under Federal conservatorship. The next day, the U.S. Treasury launched various programs to provide temporary financial support to Fannie Mae and Freddie Mac under the temporary authority to purchase securities. Treasury entered into agreements with Fannie Mae and Freddie Mac to make investments in senior preferred stock in each GSE in order to ensure that each company maintains a positive net worth. The cumulative funding commitment through these Preferred Stock Purchase Agreements (PSPAs) with Fannie Mae and Freddie Mac was set at $445.5 billion. In total, as of December 31, 2020, $191.5 billion has been invested in Fannie Mae and Freddie Mac. The remaining commitment amount is $254.1 billion.

The PSPAs also generally require that Fannie Mae and Freddie Mac pay quarterly dividends to Treasury, though the terms governing the amount of those dividends have changed several times pursuant to agreements between Treasury and Fannie Mae and Freddie Mac. The most recent changes, announced on January 14, 2021, permit the GSEs to suspend dividend payments until they achieve minimum capital levels established by FHFA through a regulatory framework published in 2020. The Budget projects those levels will not be reached during the Budget window and accordingly reflects no dividends through 2031. Through December 31, 2020, the GSEs have paid a total of $301.0 billion in dividend payments to Treasury on the senior preferred stock.

The Temporary Payroll Tax Cut Continuation Act of 2011 (Public Law 112–78) required that Fannie Mae and Freddie Mac increase their annual credit guarantee fees on single-family mortgage acquisitions between 2012 and 2021 by an average of at least 0.10 percentage point. A mortgage acquired during this time period will be subject to the fee while the loan remains outstanding. The Budget does not assume the fee will apply to loans acquired after the October 1, 2021 sunset date, but does assume the fees will apply for the life of the loans acquired prior to the sunset. The Budget estimates these fees, which are remitted directly to the Treasury and are not included in the PSPA amounts, will result in deficit reduction of $25.2 billion from 2022 through 2031.

In addition, effective January 1, 2015 FHFA directed Fannie Mae and Freddie Mac to set aside 0.042 percentage points for each dollar of the unpaid principal balance of new business purchases (including but not limited to mortgages purchased for securitization) in each year to fund several Federal affordable housing programs created by Housing and Economic Recovery act of 2008, including the Housing Trust Fund and the Capital Magnet Fund. The 2022 Budget projects these assessments will generate $4.4 billion for the affordable housing funds from 2022 through 2031. In addition, though not funded by these assessments, the Budget reflects proposals in the American Jobs Plan to provide $45 billion for the Housing Trust Fund and $12 billion for the Capital Magnet Fund over the Budget window.

Future of the Housing Finance System

Fannie Mae and Freddie Mac are in their twelfth year of conservatorship, and Congress has not yet enacted legislation to define the GSEs' long-term role in the housing finance system. The Administration is committed to housing finance policy that expands fair and equitable access to homeownership and affordable rental opportunities, protects taxpayers, and promotes financial stability. The Administration has a key role in shaping, and a key interest in the outcome of, housing finance reform, and stands ready to work with Congress in support of these goals.

The Farm Credit System (Banks and Associations)

The Farm Credit System (FCS or System) is a GSE composed of a nationwide network of borrower-owned cooperative lending institutions originally authorized by the Congress in 1916. The FCS's mission is to provide sound and dependable credit to American farmers, ranchers, producers or harvesters of aquatic products, their cooperatives, and farm-related businesses. The institutions serve rural America by providing financing for rural residential real estate; rural communication, energy, and water infrastructure; and agricultural exports. In addition, maintaining special policies and programs for the extension of credit to young, beginning, and small farmers (YBS) and ranchers is a legislative mandate for the System.

The financial condition of the System's banks and associations remains fundamentally sound. The ratio of capital to assets remained stable at 16.4 percent on December 31, 2020, compared with 16.9 percent on December 31, 2019. Capital consisted of $65.5 billion that is available to absorb losses. For the 12-month period preceding December 31, 2020, net income equaled $6.0 billion compared with $5.4 billion for the same period of the previous year.

Over the 12-month period ending December 31, 2020, System assets grew 9.7 percent, primarily due to higher cash and investment balances and increased real estate mortgage loans from continued demand by new and existing customers. During the same period, nonperforming assets as a percentage of loans and other property owned fell to 0.06 percent from 0.82 percent in 2019.

The number of FCS institutions continues to decrease due to consolidation. As of December 31, 2020, the System consisted of four banks and 67 associations, compared with seven banks and 104 associations in September 2002. Of the 71 FCS banks and associations rated under the Financial Institution Rating System (FIRS), 67 of them had one of the top two examination ratings (1 or 2 on a 1 to 5 scale) and accounted for over 98.5 percent of gross Systems assets. Four FCS institutions had a rating of 3 or lower.

The System, while continuing to record strong earnings and capital growth, remains exposed to a variety of risks associated with its portfolio concentration in agriculture and rural America. Agricultural producers in certain key crop and livestock sectors have endured several years of low prices and decreasing cash flows. The emergence of COVID-19 increased the uncertainty and risk in the general economy and the farm economy. Amid the challenging economic environment, the combination of farm commodity programs, disaster assistance, crop insurance, and the Coronavirus Food Assistance Program payments is supporting the U.S. farm sector. In fall 2020, producers started seeing improved prices for some agricultural commodities because of relatively strong demand.

FCS Performance and YBS Portfolio

Both the dollar volume of the System's total loans outstanding and the dollar volume of YBS loans outstanding increased in 2019. While young, beginning, and small farmers are not mutually exclusive groups, and thus cannot be added across categories, it is important to note the growth of activity within each group. For example, total System loan dollar volume outstanding increased by 6.3 percent in 2019, with loan dollar volume outstanding to young farmers increasing by 3.3 percent, to beginning farmers by 3.9 percent, and to small farmers by 4.6 percent.

The number of total System loans outstanding and YBS loans outstanding remained relatively flat in 2019. The number of total System loans outstanding increased by 0.5 percent. The number of loans outstanding to YBS increased by 1.0 percent, 1.8 percent, and 0.6 percent respectively.

The System's overall loan dollar volume increased by 5.4 percent, with YBS new loan dollar volume growing by 7.3 percent, 8.0 percent, and 15.9 percent, respectively. For total System loans, the number of new loans made in 2019 increased by 4.8 percent. Again, that growth is reflected across YBS loans, with the number of loans to young farmers increasing by 5.9 percent, to beginning farmers by 8.1 percent, and to small farmers by 7.8 percent.

In 2019, the System reported making a total of 269,939 new loans, totaling $90.9 billion. Out of these, loans to young farmers represented 18.2 percent of all loans made and 11.1 percent of the dollar volume of loans made. Loans made to beginning farmers represented 24.9 percent of all System loans made during the year and 15.7 percent of the dollar volume of loans made. Loans to small farmers represented 45.7 percent of all loans made during the year and 15.9 percent of the dollar volume of loans made.

Federal Agricultural Mortgage Corporation (Farmer Mac)

Farmer Mac was established in 1988 as a federally chartered instrumentality of the United States and an institution of the System to facilitate a secondary market for farm real estate and rural housing loans. Farmer Mac is not liable for any debt or obligation of the other System institutions, and no other System institutions are liable for any debt or obligation of Farmer Mac. The Farm Credit System Reform Act of 1996 expanded Farmer Mac's role from a guarantor of securities backed by loan pools to a direct purchaser of mortgages, enabling it to form pools to securitize. The Food, Conservation, and Energy Act of 2008 expanded Farmer Mac's program authorities by allowing it to purchase and guarantee securities backed by rural utility loans made by cooperatives.

Farmer Mac continues to meet core capital and regulatory risk-based capital requirements. As of September 30, 2020, Farmer Mac's total outstanding program volume (loans purchased and guaranteed, standby loan purchase commitments, and AgVantage bonds purchased and guaranteed) amounted to $22.0 billion, which represents an increase of 5.1 percent from the level a year ago. Of total program activity, $18.7 billion were on-balance sheet loans and guaranteed securities, and $3.3 billion were off-balance-sheet obligations. Total assets were $24.0 billion, with non-program investments (including cash and cash equivalents) accounting for $4.5 billion of those assets. Farmer Mac's net income attributable to common stockholders ("net income") for the first three quarters of calendar year 2020 was $59.7 million. Net income decreased compared to the same period in 2019 during which Farmer Mac reported net income of $64.6 million.

II. INSURANCE PROGRAMS

Deposit Insurance

Federal deposit insurance promotes stability in the U.S. financial system. Prior to the establishment of Federal deposit insurance, depository institution failures often caused depositors to lose confidence in the banking system and rush to withdraw deposits. Such sudden withdrawals caused serious disruption to the economy. In 1933, in the midst of the Great Depression, a system of Federal deposit insurance was established to protect depositors and to prevent bank failures from causing widespread disruption in financial markets.

Today, the Federal Deposit Insurance Corporation (FDIC) insures deposits in banks and savings associations (thrifts) using the resources available in its Deposit Insurance Fund (DIF). The National Credit Union Administration (NCUA) insures deposits (shares) in most credit unions through the National Credit Union Share Insurance Fund (SIF). (Some credit unions are privately insured.) As of September 30, 2020, the FDIC insured $8.9 trillion of deposits at 5,033 commercial banks and thrifts, and the NCUA insured nearly $1.4 trillion of shares at 5,133 credit unions.

Since its creation, the Federal deposit insurance system has undergone many reforms. As a result of the 2008 financial crisis, several reforms were enacted to protect both the immediate and longer-term integrity of the Federal deposit insurance system. The Helping Families Save Their Homes Act of 2009 (Public Law 111–22) provided NCUA with tools to protect the SIF and the financial stability of the credit union system. Notably, the Act:

- Established the Temporary Corporate Credit Union Stabilization Fund (TCCUSF), allowing NCUA to segregate the losses of corporate credit unions and providing a mechanism for assessing those losses to federally insured credit unions over an extended period of time; On September 28, 2017, the NCUA Board voted unanimously to close the TCCUSF effective October 1, 2017, ahead of its sunset date of June 30, 2021, the assets and liabilities of the TCCUSF were distributed into the SIF;

- Provided flexibility to the NCUA Board by permitting use of a restoration plan to spread insurance premium assessments over a period of up to eight years, or longer in extraordinary circumstances, if the SIF equity ratio fell below 1.2 percent; and

- Permanently increased the Share Insurance Fund's borrowing authority to $6 billion.

The Dodd-Frank Wall Street Reform and Consumer Protection (Dodd-Frank) Act of 2010 (P.L. 111–203) established new DIF reserve ratio requirements. The Act requires the FDIC to achieve a minimum DIF reserve ratio (ratio of the deposit insurance fund balance to total estimated insured deposits) of 1.35 percent by 2020, up from 1.15 percent in 2016. On September 30, 2018, the DIF reserve ratio reached 1.36 percent. In addition to raising the minimum reserve ratio, the Dodd-Frank Act also:

- Eliminated the FDIC's requirement to rebate premiums when the DIF reserve ratio is between 1.35 and 1.5 percent;

- Gave the FDIC discretion to suspend or limit rebates when the DIF reserve ratio is 1.5 percent or higher, effectively removing the 1.5 percent cap on the DIF; and

- Required the FDIC to offset the effect on small insured depository institutions (defined as banks with assets less than $10 billion) when setting assessments to raise the reserve ratio from 1.15 to 1.35 percent. In implementing the Dodd-Frank Act, the FDIC issued a final rule setting a long-term (i.e., beyond 2028) reserve ratio target of 2 percent, a goal that FDIC considers necessary to maintain a positive fund balance during economic crises while permitting steady long-term assessment rates that provide transparency and predictability to the banking sector.

The Dodd-Frank Act also permanently increased the insured deposit level to $250,000 per account at banks or credit unions insured by the FDIC or NCUA.

Recent Fund Performance

As of December 31, 2020, the FDIC DIF balance stood at $117.9 billion, a one-year increase of $7.6 billion. The growth in the DIF balance is primarily a result of assessment revenue inflows. The reserve ratio on December 31, 2020, was 1.29 percent.

As of December 31, 2020, the number of insured institutions on the FDIC's "problem list" (institutions with the highest risk ratings) totaled 56, which represented a decrease of 94 percent from December 2010, the peak year for bank failures during the financial crisis. Furthermore, the assets held by problem institutions were nearly 87 percent below the level in December 2009, the peak year for assets held by problem institutions.

The NCUA-administered SIF ended December 2020 with assets of $19.1 billion and an equity ratio of 1.26 percent. On September 28, 2017, NCUA raised the normal operating level of the SIF equity ratio to 1.39 percent and lowered it to 1.38 percent in December 2018. If the ratio exceeds the normal operating level, a distribution is normally paid to insured credit unions to reduce the equity ratio.

The health of the credit union industry has markedly improved since the financial crisis. As of December 31, 2020, NCUA reserved $177 million in the SIF to cover potential losses, an increase of 51.5 percent from the $117 million reserved as of December 31, 2019. This increase was driven by an adjustment in the application of NCUA's reserve modeling. The ratio of insured shares in problem institutions to total insured shares decreased slightly from 0.79 percent in December 2019 to 0.65 percent in December 2020. This is a significant reduction from a high of 5.7 percent in December 2009.

Restoring the Deposit Insurance Funds

As of June 30, 2020, the DIF reserve ratio fell to 1.30 percent, below the statutory minimum of 1.35 percent. The decline was a result of strong one-time growth in insured deposits. On September 15, 2020, FDIC adopted a Restoration Plan to restore the DIF reserve ratio to at least 1.35 percent within 8 years.

Budget Outlook

The Budget estimates DIF net outlays of -$62.7 billion over the current 10-year budget window (2022–2031). This $62.7 billion in net inflows to the DIF is a $9.5 billion increase of net inflows over the previous 10-year window (2021–2030) for the 2021 President's Budget. The fall in the reserve ratio and public data on the banking industry accounted for most of this change, which reflects both projections of resolution outlays, and premiums necessary to reach the historic long-run DIF target of 1.5 percent. Although the FDIC has authority to borrow up to $100 billion from Treasury to maintain sufficient DIF balances, the Budget does not anticipate FDIC utilizing its borrowing authority because the DIF is projected to maintain positive operating cash flows over the entire 10-year budget horizon.

Pension Guarantees

The Pension Benefit Guaranty Corporation (PBGC) insures the pension benefits of workers and retirees in covered defined-benefit pension plans. PBGC operates two legally and financially separated insurance programs: single-employer plans and multiemployer plans.

Single-Employer Insurance Program

Under the single-employer program, PBGC pays benefits, up to a guaranteed level, when a company's plan closes without enough assets to pay future benefits. PBGC's claims exposure is the amount by which guaranteed benefits exceed assets in insured plans. In the near term, the risk of loss stems from financially distressed firms with underfunded plans. In the longer term, loss exposure results from the possibility that well-funded plans become underfunded due to inadequate contributions, poor investment results, or increased liabilities, and that the healthy firms sponsoring those plans become distressed.

PBGC monitors companies with large underfunded plans and acts to protect the interests of the pension insurance program's stakeholders where possible. Under its Early Warning Program, PBGC works with companies to mitigate risks to pension plans posed by corporate transactions or otherwise protect the insurance program from avoidable losses. However, PBGC's authority to manage risks to the insurance program is limited. Most private insurers can diversify or reinsure their catastrophic risks as well as flexibly price these risks. Unlike private insurers, Federal law does not allow PBGC to deny insurance coverage to a defined-benefit plan or adjust premiums according to risk. Both types of PBGC premiums, the flat rate (a per person charge paid by all plans) and the variable rate (paid by underfunded plans), are set in statute.

Claims against PBGC's insurance programs are highly variable. One large pension plan termination may result in a larger claim against PBGC than the termination of many smaller plans. The future financial health of the PBGC will continue to depend largely on the termination of a limited number of very large plans and the extent to which future premiums cover future claims.

Single-employer plans generally provide benefits to the employees of one employer. When an underfunded single-employer plan terminates, usually in the bankruptcy context, PBGC becomes trustee of the plan, applies legal limits on payouts, and pays benefits over the lifetime of plan participants and beneficiaries. The amount of benefit paid is determined after taking into account (a) the benefit that a participant had accrued in the terminated plan, (b) the availability of assets from the terminated plan to cover benefits, and (c) the legal maximum benefit level set in statute. In 2021, the maximum annual payment guaranteed under the single-employer program was $72,409.08 for a retiree aged 65.

Multiemployer Insurance Program

Multiemployer plans are collectively bargained pension plans maintained by one or more labor unions and more than one unrelated employer, usually within the same or related industries. PBGC's role in the multiemployer program is more like that of a re-insurer; if a company contributing to a multiemployer plan fails, its liabilities are assumed by the other employers in the plan, not by PBGC. PBGC becomes responsible for insurance coverage when the plan runs out of money to pay benefits at the statutorily guaranteed level, which usually occurs after most or all contributing employers have withdrawn from the plan, leaving the plan without sufficient income. PBGC provides insolvent multiemployer plans with financial assistance in the form of loans sufficient to pay guaranteed benefits and administrative expenses. Since multiemployer plans do not receive PBGC assistance until their assets are fully depleted, financial assistance is almost never repaid. Guaranteed benefits under the multiemployer program are calculated based on the benefit that a participant would have received under the insolvent plan, subject to the legal multiemployer maximum set in statute. The maximum guaranteed amount depends on the participant's years of service and the rate at which benefits are accrued. For example, for a participant with 30 years of service, PBGC guarantees 100 percent of the pension benefit up to a yearly amount of $3,960. If the pension exceeds that amount, PBGC guarantees 75 percent of the rest of the pension benefit up to a total maximum guarantee of $12,870 per year for a participant with 30 years of service. This limit has been in place since 2001 and is not adjusted for inflation or cost-of-living increases.

In recent years, many multiemployer pension plans have become severely underfunded as a result of structural flaws in how these plans are funded and operated, employers withdrawing from plans, and demographic challenges. In 2001, only 15 plans covering about 80,000 participants were under 40 percent funded using estimated market rates. By 2017, this had grown to over 330 plans covering over 4 million participants. While many plans have benefited from an improving economy and will recover, about 14 million participants in the multiemployer system are in plans that, before the enactment of the American Rescue Plan Act of 2021 (ARPA) (Public Law 117–2), projected that they would become insolvent within twenty years.

As of September 30, 2020, the single-employer program reported a positive net position of $15.5 billion, while the multiemployer program reported a long-term actuarial deficit of $63.7 billion. Following enactment of ARPA on March 11, 2021, the solvency crisis in the multiemployer program is less urgent. Under ARPA, Congress established a new Special Financial Assistance program for financially troubled multiemployer plans, funded entirely by Treasury general revenues. PBGC will provide one-time payments to eligible plans to enable them to pay benefits at the plan level.

Premiums

The single-employer program's financial position is projected to continue improving over the next 10 years, in part because the Congress has raised premiums in that program several times. Before enactment of ARPA, the multiemployer program was projected to run out of funds in 2026. Particularly in the multiemployer program, premium rates remain much lower than what a private financial institution would charge for insuring the same risk.

Disaster Insurance

Flood Insurance

The Federal Government provides flood insurance through the National Flood Insurance Program (NFIP), which is administered by the Department of Homeland Security (DHS) Federal Emergency Management Agency (FEMA). Flood insurance is available to homeowners, renters, businesses, and State and local governments in communities that have adopted and enforce minimum floodplain management measures. Coverage is limited to buildings and their contents. At the end of 2020, the program had over five million policies worth $1.3 trillion in force in nearly 22,000 communities. The program is currently authorized until September 30, 2021.

The Congress established NFIP in 1968 to make flood insurance coverage widely available, to combine a program of insurance with flood mitigation measures to reduce the Nation's risk of loss from floods, and to reduce Federal disaster-assistance expenditures on flood losses. The NFIP requires participating communities to adopt certain land use ordinances consistent with FEMA's floodplain management regulations and take other mitigation efforts to reduce flood-related losses in high flood hazard areas ("Special Flood Hazard Areas") identified through partnership with FEMA, States, and local communities. These efforts have resulted in substantial reductions in the risk of flood-related losses nationwide. Since the 1970's, flood insurance rates have been based on static measurements using the Flood Insurance Rate Map. Technology has evolved, and so has FEMA's understanding of flood risk. To ensure policyholders make informed decisions on the purchase of adequate insurance and on mitigation actions to protect against flood risk, in FY 2021 FEMA introduced a new pricing methodology, Risk Rating 2.0-Equity in Action. Risk Rating 2.0-Equity in Action builds on flood hazard information and incorporates private sector data sets, catastrophe models, and evolving actuarial science. The system includes additional flood risk variables such as flood frequency, multiple flood types (riverine, storm surge, coastal, pluvial), and distance to water along with individual property characteristics. Risk Rating 2.0-Equity in Action also addresses premium inequities by taking into account the cost to rebuild as a factor in the premium, so that policyholders with low-valued home are no longer subsidizing higher-valued homes. New policies effective on or after October 1, 2021 will be subject to the new pricing methodology. and existing policyholders will be able to take advantage of immediate decreases in their premiums upon renewal. All remaining existing policyholders will be subject to the new methodology beginning April 1, 2022.

FEMA's Community Rating System offers discounts on policy premiums in communities that adopt and enforce more stringent floodplain land use ordinances than those identified in FEMA's regulations and/or engage in mitigation activities beyond those required by the NFIP. The discounts provide an incentive for communities to implement new flood protection activities that can help save lives and property when a flood occurs. Further, NFIP offers flood mitigation assistance grants for planning and carrying out activities to reduce the risk of flood damage to structures covered by NFIP, which may include demolition or relocation of a structure, elevation or flood-proofing a structure, and community-wide mitigation efforts that will reduce future flood claims for the NFIP. In particular, flood mitigation assistance grants targeted toward repetitive and severe repetitive loss properties not only help owners of high-risk property, but also reduce the disproportionate drain these properties cause on the National Flood Insurance Fund.

Due to the catastrophic nature of flooding, with hurricanes Harvey, Katrina, and Sandy as notable examples, insured flood damages can far exceed premium revenue and deplete the program's reserves. On those occasions, the NFIP exercises its borrowing authority through the Treasury to meet flood insurance claim obligations. While the program needed appropriations in the early 1980s to repay the funds borrowed during the 1970's, it was able to repay all borrowed funds with interest using only premium dollars between 1986 and 2004. In 2005, however, Hurricanes Katrina, Rita, and Wilma generated more flood insurance claims than the cumulative number of claims paid from 1968 to 2004. Hurricane Sandy in 2012 generated $8.8 billion in flood insurance claims. As a result, in 2013 the Congress increased the borrowing authority for the fund to $30.425 billion. After the estimated $2.4 billion and $670 million in flood insurance claims generated by the Louisiana flooding of August 2016 and Hurricane Matthew in October 2016, respectively, the NFIP used its borrowing authority again, bringing the total outstanding debt to Treasury to $24.6 billion.

In the fall 2017, Hurricanes Harvey and Irma struck the southern coast of the United States, resulting in catastrophic flood damage across Texas, Louisiana, and Florida. To pay claims, NFIP exhausted all borrowing authority. The Congress provided $16 billion in debt cancellation to the NFIP, bringing its debt to $20.525 billion. To pay Hurricane Harvey flood claims, NFIP also received more than $1 billion in reinsurance payments as a result of transferring risk to the private reinsurance market at the beginning of 2017. FEMA continues to mature its reinsurance program and transfer additional risk to the private market.

In July 2012, resulting largely from experiences during Hurricanes Katrina, Rita, and Wilma in 2005, the Biggert Waters Flood Insurance Reform Act of 2012 (subtitle A of title II of Public Law 112–141; BW–12) was signed into law. In addition to reauthorizing the NFIP for five years, the bill required the NFIP generally to move to full risk-based premium rates and strengthened the NFIP financially and operationally. In 2013, the NFIP began phasing in risk-based premiums for certain properties, as required by the law, and began collecting a policyholder Reserve Fund assessment that is available to meet the expected future obligations of the flood insurance program.

In March 2014, largely in reaction to premium increases initiated by BW–12, the Homeowner Flood Insurance Affordability Act of 2014 (HFIAA) (Public Law 113–89) was signed into law, further reforming the NFIP and revising many sections of BW–12. Notably, HFIAA repealed and adjusted many of the major premium increases introduced by BW–12 and required retroactive refunds of collected BW–12 premium increases, introduced a phase-in to higher full-risk premiums for structures newly mapped into the Special Flood Hazard Area until full-risk rates are achieved, and created an Office of the Flood Insurance Advocate. HFIAA also introduced a fixed annual surcharge of $25 for primary residents and $250 for all other policies to be deposited into the Reserve Fund.

The 2018-2022 FEMA Strategic Plan creates a shared vision for the NFIP and other FEMA programs to build a more prepared and resilient Nation. The Strategic Plan sets out three overarching goals: Building a culture of preparedness, Readying the Nation for catastrophic events, and reducing the complexity of FEMA. While the NFIP supports all three goals, it is central to building a culture of preparedness. To that end, FEMA is pursuing initiatives including:

1. Providing products that clearly and accurately communicate flood risk;

2. Helping individuals, businesses, and communities understand their risks and the available options like the NFIP to best manage those risks;

3. Transforming the NFIP into a simpler, customer-focused program that policyholders value and trust; and

4. Doubling the number of properties covered by flood insurance (either the NFIP or private insurance) by 2022.

Crop Insurance

Subsidized Federal crop insurance, administered by USDA's Risk Management Agency (RMA) on behalf of the Federal Crop Insurance Corporation (FCIC), assists farmers in managing yield and revenue shortfalls due to bad weather or other natural disasters. The program is a cooperative partnership between the Federal Government and the private insurance industry. Private insurance companies sell and service crop insurance policies. The Federal Government, in turn, pays private companies an administrative and operating expense subsidy to cover expenses associated with selling and servicing these policies. The Federal Government also provides reinsurance through the Standard Reinsurance Agreement (SRA) and pays companies an "underwriting gain" if they have a profitable year. For the 2022 Budget, the payments to the companies are projected to be $2.9 billion in combined subsidies. The Federal Government also subsidizes premiums for farmers as a way to encourage farmers to participate in the program.

The most basic type of crop insurance is catastrophic coverage (CAT), which compensates the farmer for losses in excess of 50 percent of the individual's average yield at

55 percent of the expected market price. The CAT premium is entirely subsidized, and farmers pay only an administrative fee. Higher levels of coverage, called "buy-up," are also available. A portion of the premium for buy-up coverage is paid by FCIC on behalf of producers and varies by coverage level – generally, the higher the coverage level, the lower the percent of premium subsidized. The remaining (unsubsidized) premium amount is owed by the producer and represents an out-of-pocket expense.

For 2020, the 5 principal crops (corn, soybeans, wheat, cotton, and sorghum) accounted for over 72 percent of total liability, and approximately 85 percent of the total U.S. planted acres of the 10 principal row crops (also including barley, peanuts, potatoes, rice, and tobacco) were covered by crop insurance. Producers can purchase both yield and revenue-based insurance products which are underwritten on the basis of a producer's actual production history (APH). Revenue insurance programs protect against loss of revenue resulting from low prices, low yields, or a combination of both. Revenue insurance has enhanced traditional yield insurance by adding price as an insurable component.

In addition to price and revenue insurance, FCIC has made available other plans of insurance to provide protection for a variety of crops grown across the United States. For example, "area plans" of insurance offer protection based on a geographic area (most commonly, a county), and do not directly insure an individual farm. Often, the loss trigger is based on an index, such as a rainfall or vegetative index, which is established by a Government entity (for example, the National Oceanic and Atmospheric Administration or United States Geological Survey). One such plan is the pilot Rainfall and Vegetation Index plan, which insures against a decline in an index value covering Pasture, Rangeland, and Forage. These pilot programs meet the needs of livestock producers who purchase insurance for protection from losses of forage produced for grazing or harvested for hay. In 2020, there were around 33 thousand Rainfall Index policies earning premiums, covering over 160 million acres of pasture, rangeland and forage. In 2020, there was about $172 million in liability for those producers who purchased livestock coverage and $13 billion in liability for those producers who purchased coverage for milk.

A crop insurance policy also contains coverage compensating farmers when they are prevented from planting their crops due to weather and other perils. When an insured farmer is unable to plant the planned crop within the planting time period because of excessive drought or moisture, the farmer may file a prevented planting claim, which pays the farmer a portion of the full coverage level. It is optional for the farmer to plant a second crop on the acreage. If the farmer does, the prevented planting claim on the first crop is reduced and the farmer's APH is recorded for that year. If the farmer does not plant a second crop, the farmer gets the full prevented planting claim, and the farmer's APH is held harmless for premium cal-culation purposes the following year. Buy-up coverage for prevented planting is limited to 5 percent.

RMA is continuously working to develop new products and to expand or improve existing products in order to cover more agricultural commodities. In 2020, RMA added new coverage for hurricanes which provided over $150 million in payments during an active hurricane season. RMA implemented a new option that allows producers to cover a portion of their policy's deductible in the event of a widespread loss. RMA also implemented new coverage for strawberries and improvements to it livestock and whole farm coverage. For more information and additional crop insurance program details, please reference RMA's website *www. rma.usda.gov*.

Farm Credit System Insurance Corporation (FCSIC)

Although not specifically disaster-related, FCSIC, an independent Government-controlled corporation, ensures the timely payment of principal and interest on FCS obligations on which the System banks are jointly and severally liable. If the Corporation does not have sufficient funds to ensure payment on insured obligations, System banks will be required to make payments under joint and several liability, as required by section 4.4(a)(2) of the Farm Credit Act (Public Law 92–181, as amended). The insurance provided by the Insurance Fund is limited to the resources in the Insurance Fund. System obligations are not guaranteed by the U.S. Government. On December 31, 2020, the assets in the Insurance Fund totaled $5.5 billion. As of December 31, 2020, the Insurance Fund as a percentage of adjusted insured debt was 1.93 percent. This was slightly below the statutory secure base amount of 2.00 percent. As of December 31, 2020, outstanding insured System obligations increased 9.9 percent compared with that of December 31, 2019, from $323 billion to $294 billion.

Insurance against Security-Related Risks

Terrorism Risk Insurance

The Terrorism Risk Insurance Program (TRIP) was authorized by the Terrorism Risk Insurance Act of 2002 to ensure the continued availability of property and casualty insurance following the terrorist attacks of September 11, 2001. TRIP's initial three-year authorization established a system of shared public and private compensation for insured property and casualty losses arising from certified acts of foreign terrorism.

TRIP was originally intended to be temporary, but has been repeatedly extended, and is currently set to expire on December 31, 2027, after it was reauthorized by the Terrorism Risk Insurance Program Reauthorization Act of 2019 (Public Law 116–94). The prior reauthorization, the Terrorism Risk Insurance Program Reauthorization Act of 2015 (Public Law 114–1), made several program changes to reduce potential Federal liability. Over the first five of those extension years, the loss threshold that triggers Federal assistance is increased by $20 million each year to $200 million in 2020, and the Government's share of losses above the deductible decreases from 85 to 80 percent over the same period. The 2015 extension also required Treasury to recoup 140 percent of all Federal payments made under the program up to a mandatory recoupment amount, which increased by $2 billion each year until 2019 when the threshold was set at $37.5 billion. Since January 1, 2020, the mandatory recoupment amount has been indexed to a running three-year average of the aggregate insurer deductible of 20 percent of direct-earned premiums.

The Budget baseline includes the estimated Federal cost of providing terrorism risk insurance, reflecting current law. Using market data synthesized through a proprietary model, the Budget projects annual outlays and recoupment for TRIP. While the Budget does not forecast any specific triggering events, the Budget includes estimates representing the weighted average of TRIP payments over a full range of possible scenarios, most of which include no notional terrorist attacks (and therefore no TRIP payments), and some of which include notional terrorist attacks of varying magnitudes. On this basis, the Budget projects net spending of $359 million over the 2022–2026 period and $518 million over the 2022–2031 period.

Aviation War Risk Insurance

In December 2014, the Congress sunset the premium aviation war risk insurance program, thereby sending U.S. air carriers back to the commercial aviation insurance market for all of their war risk insurance coverage. The non-premium program is authorized through September 30, 2023. It provides aviation insurance coverage for aircraft used in connection with certain Government contract operations by a department or agency that agrees to indemnify the Secretary of Transportation for any losses covered by the insurance.

III. BUDGETARY EFFECTS OF THE TROUBLED ASSET RELIEF PROGRAM (TARP)

This section provides analysis consistent with Sections 202 and 203 of the Emergency Economic Stabilization Act (EESA) of 2008 (P.L. 110-343), including estimates of the cost to taxpayers and the budgetary effects of TARP transactions as reflected in the Budget. This section also explains the changes in TARP costs, and includes alternative estimates as prescribed under EESA. Under EESA, Treasury has purchased different types of financial instruments with varying terms and conditions.[3] The Budget reflects the costs of these instruments using the methodology as provided by Section 123 of EESA.

The estimated costs of each transaction reflect the underlying structure of the instrument. TARP financial instruments have included direct loans, structured loans, equity, loan guarantees, and direct incentive payments. The costs of equity purchases, loans, guarantees, and loss sharing are the net present value of cash flows to and from the Government over the life of the instrument, per the Federal Credit Reform Act (FCRA) of 1990; as amended (2 U.S.C. 661 et seq.), with an EESA-required adjustment to the discount rate for market risks. Costs for the incentive payments under TARP housing programs, other than loss sharing under the FHA Refinance program, involve financial instruments without any provision for future returns and are recorded on a cash basis.[4]

Tables 15–10 through 15-16 are available online. Table 15–10 summarizes the cumulative and anticipated activity under TARP, and the estimated lifetime budgetary cost reflected in the Budget, compared to estimates from the 2021 Budget. The direct impact of TARP on the deficit is projected to be $31.6 billion, down $0.2 billion from the $31.9 billion estimate in the 2021 Budget. The total programmatic cost represents the lifetime net present value cost of TARP obligations from the date of disbursement, which is now estimated to be $50.4 billion, a figure that excludes interest on reestimates.[5]

Table 15–11 shows the current value of TARP assets through the actual balances of TARP financing accounts as of the end of each fiscal year through 2020, and projected balances for each subsequent year through 2031.[6] Based on actual net balances in financing accounts at the end of 2009, the value of TARP assets totaled $129.9 billion. As of December 31, 2020, total TARP net asset value has decreased to $17 million. The overall balance of the financing accounts is estimated to continue falling as TARP investments continue to wind down.

Table 15-12 shows the estimated impact of TARP activity on the deficit, debt held by the public and gross Federal debt following the methodology required by EESA. Direct activity under TARP is expected to increase the 2021 deficit by $0.8 billion, the major components being:

- Outlays for TARP housing programs are estimated at $0.7 billion in 2021.

- Administrative expense outlays for TARP are estimated at $43 million in 2021.

---

[3] For a more detailed analysis of the assets purchased through TARP and its budgetary effects, please see the "Budgetary Effect of the Troubled Asset Relief Program" chapter included in the *Analytical Perspectives* volume of prior budgets.

[4] Section 123 of EESA provides Treasury the authority to record TARP equity purchases pursuant to FCRA, with required adjustments to the discount rate for market risks. The Hardest Hit Fund (HHF) and Making Home Affordable (MHA) program involve the purchase of financial instruments that have no provision for repayment or other return on investment, and do not constitute direct loans or guarantees under FCRA. Therefore these purchases are recorded on a cash basis. Administrative expenses for TARP are recorded under the Office of Financial Stability and the Special Inspector General for TARP on a cash basis, consistent with other Federal administrative costs, but are recorded separately from TARP program costs.

[5] With the exception of MHA and HHF, all the other TARP investments are reflected on a present value basis pursuant to FCRA and EESA.

[6] Reestimates for TARP are calculated using actual data through September 30, 2020, and updated projections of future activity. Thus, the full impacts of TARP reestimates are reflected in the 2020 financing account balances.

- Outlays for the Special Inspector General for TARP are estimated at $19 million in 2021.

- TARP reestimates and interest on reestimates will increase the deficit by $0.8 million in 2021.

- Debt service is estimated at $759 million for 2021 and then expected to increase to $964 million by 2031, largely due to outlays for TARP housing programs. Total debt service will continue over time after TARP winds down, due to the financing of past TARP costs.

Debt net of financial assets due to TARP is estimated to be $35.6 billion as of the end of 2021. This is $2.2 billion lower than the projected debt held net of financial assets for 2021 that was reflected in the 2021 Budget.

Table 15-13 reflects the estimated effects of TARP transactions on the deficit and debt, as calculated on a cash basis. Under cash basis reporting, the 2021 deficit would be $11 million lower than the $0.8 billion estimate now reflected in the Budget. However, the impact of TARP on the Federal debt, and on debt held net of financial assets, is the same on a cash basis as under FCRA and therefore these data are not repeated in Table15-13.

Table 15-14 shows detailed information on upward and downward reestimates to program costs. The current reestimate of $0.8 million reflects an increase in estimated TARP costs from the 2021 Budget. This increase was due

in large part to interest effects and continued progress winding down TARP investments over the past year.

The 2022 Budget, as shown in table 15–15, reflects a total TARP deficit impact of $31.6 billion. This is a decrease of $0.2 billion from the 2021 Budget projection of $31.9 billion. The estimated 2021 TARP deficit impact reflected in Table 15-15 differs from the programmatic cost of $50.4 billion in the Budget because the deficit impact includes $18.8 billion in cumulative downward adjustments for interest on subsidy reestimates. See footnote 2 in Table 15-15.

Table 15-16 compares the OMB estimate for TARP's deficit impact to the deficit impact estimated by CBO in its "Report on the Troubled Asset Relief Program—March 2020."[7]

CBO estimates the total cost of TARP at $31.4 billion, based on estimated lifetime TARP disbursements of $444 billion. The Budget reflects a total deficit cost of $31.6 billion, based estimated disbursements of $449 billion. CBO and OMB cost estimates for TARP have generally converged over time as TARP equity programs have wound down.

---

[7] Available at: https://www.cbo.gov/publication/56300

Chart 15-1. Face Value of Federal Credit Outstanding

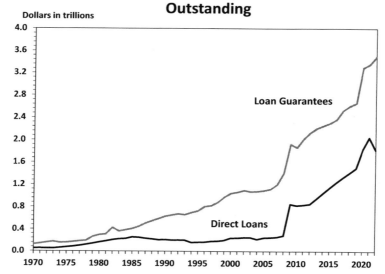

Dollars in trillions

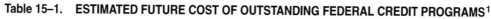

Table 15–1.   ESTIMATED FUTURE COST OF OUTSTANDING FEDERAL CREDIT PROGRAMS[1]

(In billions of dollars)

Program	Outstanding 2019	Estimated Future Costs of 2019 Outstanding[2]	Outstanding 2020	Estimated Future Costs of 2020 Outstanding[2]
Direct Loans:[2]				
Federal Student Loans	1,203	154	1,262	247
Disaster Assistance	10	2	188	6
Farm Service Agency, Rural Development, Rural Housing	60	4	63	4
Treasury Economic Stabilization Program[3]	0	0	104	0
Rural Utilities Service and Rural Telephone Bank	53	2	50	1
Education Temporary Student Loan Purchase Authority	53	7	48	11
Housing and Urban Development	38	17	43	17
Transportation Infrastructure Finance and Innovation Act Loans	20	−1	15	*
Advanced Technology Vehicle Manufacturing, Title 17 Loans	15	*	16	1
Export-Import Bank	16	2	13	2
International Assistance	9	5	9	5
Other direct loan programs[3]	22	6	20	6
Total direct loans	1,499	198	1,830	300
Guaranteed Loans:[2]				
FHA Mutual Mortgage Insurance Fund	1,288	−2	1,311	−9
Department of Veterans Affairs (VA) Mortgages	713	8	817	7
Small Business Administration (SBA) Business Loan Guarantees[4]	130	2	646	513
FHA General and Special Risk Insurance Fund	163	5	168	3
Farm Service Agency, Rural Development, Rural Housing	151	1	156	1
Federal Student Loan Guarantees	141	5	128	1
Export-Import Bank	34	*	24	1
International Assistance	25	3	30	2
Other guaranteed loan programs[3]	16	1	13	1
Total guaranteed loans[4]	2,662	22	3,294	520
Total Federal credit	**4,161**	**220**	**5,124**	**820**

* $500 million or less.

[1] Future costs represent balance sheet estimates of allowance for subsidy cost, liabilities for loan guarantees, and estimated uncollectible principal and interest.

[2] Excludes loans and guarantees by deposit insurance agencies and programs not included under credit reform, such as Tennessee Valley Authority loan guarantees. Defaulted guaranteed loans that result in loans receivable are included in direct loan amounts.

[3] As authorized by the statute, table includes TARP and SBLF equity purchases and activity with Federal Reserve 13(3) facilities authorized under the CARES Act in 2020. Future costs for TARP are calculated using the discount rate required by the Federal Credit Reform Act adjusted for market risks, as directed in legislation.

[4] To avoid double-counting, outstandings for GNMA and SBA secondary market guarantees and TARP FHA Letter of Credit program are excluded from the totals.

Table 15–2. DIRECT LOAN SUBSIDY RATES, BUDGET AUTHORITY, AND LOAN LEVELS, 2020–2022

(Dollar amounts in millions)

Agency and Program Account	2020 Actual			2021 Enacted			2022 Proposed		
	Subsidy rate [1]	Subsidy budget authority	Loan levels	Subsidy rate [1]	Subsidy budget authority	Loan levels	Subsidy rate [1]	Subsidy budget authority	Loan levels
Agriculture:									
Agricultural Credit Insurance Fund Program Account	1.39	46	3,362	–2.01	–96	4,801	–6.05	–301	4,978
Farm Storage Facility Loans Program Account	–0.23	–1	340	–1.03	–4	469	–1.84	–9	469
Rural Electrification and Telecommunications Loans Program Account ..	–3.05	–197	6,443	–3.89	–261	6,699	–3.36	–237	7,064
Distance Learning, Telemedicine, and Broadband Program	25.86	102	394	26.21	125	476	22.82	107	464
Rural Water and Waste Disposal Program Account	4.56	64	1,399	–1.53	–21	1,400	–5.16	–72	1,400
Rural Community Facilities Program Account	–4.96	–64	1,267	–6.56	–129	1,970	–5.81	–98	1,684
Multifamily Housing Revitalization Program Account	56.78	16	28	45.77	18	39	....	....	....
Rural Housing Insurance Fund Program Account	10.35	111	1,079	6.26	78	1,237	2.10	55	2,625
Rural Microenterprise Investment Program Account	14.88	1	4	3.14	1	24	–4.10	–6	150
Intermediary Relending Program Fund Account	27.63	5	19	15.56	3	19	8.07	2	19
Rural Economic Development Loans Program Account	16.78	8	48	9.55	6	59	4.68	3	64
Commerce:									
Fisheries Finance Program Account	–8.14	–8	92	–9.87	–25	249	–11.62	–24	196
Defense:									
Defense Production Act Program Account	....	....	....	[2]0.00	....	1,273	[2]4.00	28	688
Education:									
College Housing and Academic Facilities Loans Program Account	10.16	26	258	10.25	32	309	7.35	18	241
TEACH Grant Program Account	29.35	29	99	31.72	27	86	44.47	82	185
Federal Direct Student Loan Program Account	5.30	6,838	129,061	2.33	3,226	138,335	6.06	8,629	142,561
Energy:									
Title 17 Innovative Technology Loan Guarantee Program	....	....	....	....	....	....	[2]1.20	59	4,896
Advanced Technology Vehicles Manufacturing Loan Program Account	....	....	....	10.83	162	1,496	4.98	346	6,945
Homeland Security:									
Disaster Assistance Direct Loan Program Account	74.61	57	76	80.39	131	163	77.74	29	37
Housing and Urban Development:									
FHA-General and Special Risk Program Account	....	....	....	....	....	....	[2]–9.23	–61	660
Green and Resilient Retrofit Program for Multifamily Housing	....	....	....	....	....	....	[2]93.66	50	53
State:									
Repatriation Loans Program Account	48.99	2	5	55.45	1	2	46.58	1	3
Transportation:									
Railroad Rehabilitation and Improvement Program	–0.25	–2	851	0.00	....	4,196	–1.71	–10	600
TIFIA Highway Trust Fund Program Account	1.02	23	2,263	0.97	107	10,987	–1.21	–133	10,987
Maritime Guaranteed Loan (Title XI) Program Account	–0.58	–2	325	....	....	....	....	....	....
Treasury:									
Manufacturing Financing Program Account	....	....	....	....	....	....	[2]32.00	3,603	11,259
Community Development Financial Institutions Fund Program Account	–2.96	–3	103	[2]0.45	2	525	[2]0.60	3	525
Economic Stabilization Program Account	11.38	23,943	210,355	4.24	84	1,990	....	....	....
Veterans Affairs:									
Veterans Housing Benefit Program Fund	8.69	4	51	–9.24	–3	41	–9.24	–3	41
Native American Veteran Housing Loan Program Account	–4.22	–*	8	–17.16	–2	14	–17.16	–2	14
Environmental Protection Agency:									
Water Infrastructure Finance and Innovation Program Account	0.75	40	5,289	1.08	55	5,093	1.07	60	5,607
International Assistance Programs:									
Foreign Military Financing Loan Program Account	....	....	....	....	....	....	[2]0.00	....	4,000
Clean Technology Fund Program Account	....	....	....	....	....	....	39.37	270	686
Overseas Private Investment Corporation Program Account	0.50	1	110	....	....	....	....	....	....
United States International Development Finance Corporation	7.78	–276	3,607	–5.02	–225	4,483	[2]–4.34	–133	3,067
Contributions to IMF Facilities and Trust Funds	....	....	....	....	....	....	0.08	2	1,500
Small Business Administration:									
Disaster Loans Program Account	13.62	26,139	191,913	8.92	24,246	271,918	10.95	1,043	9,525
Business Loans Program Account	9.29	5	56	8.99	10	110	6.28	7	110

Table 15–2.   DIRECT LOAN SUBSIDY RATES, BUDGET AUTHORITY, AND LOAN LEVELS, 2020–2022—Continued

(Dollar amounts in millions)

Agency and Program Account	2020 Actual			2021 Enacted			2022 Proposed		
	Subsidy rate [1]	Subsidy budget authority	Loan levels	Subsidy rate [1]	Subsidy budget authority	Loan levels	Subsidy rate [1]	Subsidy budget authority	Loan levels
Export-Import Bank of the United States:									
Export-Import Bank Loans Program Account	–6.37	–1	10	....	....	....	....	....	....
Total	**N/A**	**56,906**	**558,915**	**N/A**	**27,548**	**458,463**	**N/A**	**13,306**	**223,306**

N/A = Not applicable

* $500,000 or less

[1] Additional information on credit subsidy rates is contained in the Federal Credit Supplement.

[2] Rate reflects notional estimate. Estimates will be determined at the time of execution and will reflect the terms of the contracts and other characteristics.

Table 15–3. LOAN GUARANTEE SUBSIDY RATES, BUDGET AUTHORITY, AND LOAN LEVELS, 2020–2022

(Dollar amounts in millions)

Agency and Program	2020 Actual			2021 Enacted			2022 Proposed		
	Subsidy rate [1]	Subsidy budget authority	Loan levels	Subsidy rate [1]	Subsidy budget authority	Loan levels	Subsidy rate [1]	Subsidy budget authority	Loan levels
Agriculture:									
Agricultural Credit Insurance Fund Program Account	0.10	4	4,157	0.36	21	6,172	0.12	8	6,420
Commodity Credit Corporation Export Loans Program Account	−0.21	−6	2,224	−0.40	−22	5,500	−0.45	−24	5,500
Rural Water and Waste Disposal Program Account	0.14	*	28	0.12	*	50	0.09	*	50
Rural Community Facilities Program Account	−0.51	−1	101	−0.36	−1	115	−0.29	....	111
Rural Housing Insurance Fund Program Account	−0.60	−139	23,302	−0.74	−203	27,730	−1.45	−438	30,230
Rural Business Program Account	2.06	34	1,659	1.52	28	1,869	2.01	33	1,645
Rural Energy for America Program	3.53	11	324	1.96	13	668	1	11	1,246
Biorefinery Assistance Program Account	....	....	....	16.16	51	316	....	....	....
Energy:									
Tribal Energy Loan Guarantee Program	....	....	....	....	....	....	0.56	4	735
Health and Human Services:									
Health Resources and Services	2.57	*	2	2.78	1	40	2.93	2	72
Housing and Urban Development:									
Indian Housing Loan Guarantee Fund Program Account	0.11	1	865	0.30	3	1,000	0.33	3	1,000
Native Hawaiian Housing Loan Guarantee Fund Program Account	−0.34	−*	11	−0.15	−*	21	−0.19	−*	17
Native American Housing Block Grant	6.25	1	7	6.39	1	20	5.55	1	20
Community Development Loan Guarantees Program Account	−0.01	−*	39	0.00	....	100	0.00	....	300
FHA-Mutual Mortgage Insurance Program Account	−2.16	−7,060	326,868	−3.30	−11,444	346,487	−2.66	−7,033	264,164
FHA-General and Special Risk Program Account	−3.08	−793	25,760	−2.38	−887	37,269	−2.85	−932	32,694
Interior:									
Indian Guaranteed Loan Program Account	5.56	10	183	12.33	11	83	9.84	10	103
Veterans Affairs:									
Veterans Housing Benefit Program Fund	−0.30	−1,087	362,210	−0.50	−1,969	391,280	−0.08	−241	301,013
International Assistance Programs:									
Foreign Military Financing Loan Program Account	....	....	....	....	....	....	[2]0.00	....	4,000
Loan Guarantees to Israel Program Account	....	....	....	0.00	....	500	0.00	....	500
Development Credit Authority Program Account	0.00	1	2	....	....	....	....	....	....
Overseas Private Investment Corporation Program Account	−1.13	−2	55	....	....	....	....	....	....
United State International Development Finance Corporation	−1.85	−11	585	[2]−8.24	−75	911	[2]−3.70	−34	933
Small Business Administration:									
Business Loans Program Account	96.50	532,393	551,723	78.02	290,657	372,529	0.00	....	49,000
Export-Import Bank of the United States:									
Export-Import Bank Loans Program Account	−1.15	−62	5,385	−2.07	−172	8,343	−3.68	−352	9,580
Total	**N/A**	**523,294**	**1,305,490**	**N/A**	**276,013**	**1,201,003**	**N/A**	**−8,982**	**709,333**
ADDENDUM: SECONDARY GUARANTEED LOAN COMMITMENT LIMITATIONS									
Government National Mortgage Association:									
Guarantees of Mortgage-backed Securities Loan Guarantee Program Account	−0.29	−2,171	748,518	−0.31	−2,453	791,210	−0.38	−2,340	615,663
Small Business Administration:									
Secondary Market Guarantee Program	0.00	....	6,543	0.00	....	13,000	0.00	....	13,000
Total, secondary guarantee loan commitments	**N/A**	**−2,171**	**755,061**	**N/A**	**−2,453**	**804,210**	**N/A**	**−2,340**	**628,663**

N/A = Not applicable.

* $500,000 or less

[1] Additional information on credit subsidy rates is contained in the Federal Credit Supplement.

[2] Rate reflects notional estimate. Estimates will be determined at the time of execution and will reflect the terms of the contracts and other characteristics.

Table 15–4.   SUMMARY OF FEDERAL DIRECT LOANS AND LOAN GUARANTEES[1]
(In billions of dollars)

	Actuals								Estimate	
	2013	2014	2015	2016	2017	2018	2019	2020	2021	2022
Direct Loans:										
Obligations	174.4	174.0	181.3	175.6	180.0	169.7	173.6	558.9	458.5	222.6
Disbursements	157.5	155.4	161.4	158.5	164.4	151.9	150.8	418.4	340.7	265.4
Budget authority:										
New subsidy budget authority [2,3]	−29.8	−22.4	4.9	−9.0	−1.0	−2.4	−1.2	103.4	67.7	13.3
Reestimated subsidy budget authority [2,4]	−19.7	−0.8	10.1	8.0	32.5	−10.3	29.9	67.1	21.7	....
Total subsidy budget authority	**−49.4**	**−23.2**	**15.1**	**−1.1**	**31.5**	**−12.8**	**28.7**	**170.5**	**89.4**	**13.3**
Loan guarantees:										
Commitments [5]	536.6	350.8	478.3	537.6	530.2	461.7	491.1	1,305.5	1,201.0	709.3
Lender disbursements [5]	491.3	335.6	461.6	517.6	520.6	465.1	482.7	1,287.9	1,173.5	702.0
Budget authority:										
New subsidy budget authority [2,3]	−17.9	−13.7	−11.9	−7.5	−8.8	−5.4	−9.6	531.1	281.3	−11.3
Reestimated subsidy budget authority [2,4]	20.8	1.2	−1.1	−13.6	16.8	9.4	−20.2	−15.9	−17.8	....
Total subsidy budget authority	**2.8**	**−12.5**	**−13.1**	**−21.1**	**8.0**	**4.0**	**−29.8**	**515.2**	**263.5**	**−11.3**

[1] As authorized by statute, this table includes TARP and SBLF equity purchases, International Monetary Fund (IMF) transactions resulting from the 2009 Supplemental Appropriations Act, and activity with Federal Reserve 13(3) lending facilities authorized by the CARES Act.

[2] Credit subsidy costs for TARP and IMF transactions are calculated using the discount rate required by the Federal Credit Reform Act adjusted for market risks, as directed in legislation.

[3] Includes budget authority for executing loan modifications.

[4] Includes interest on reestimate.

[5] To avoid double-counting, the face value of GNMA and SBA secondary market guarantees and TARP FHA Letter of Credit program are excluded from the totals.

16. FEDERAL DRUG CONTROL FUNDING

The 2022 Budget supports $41.0 billion for National Drug Control Program agencies to implement the Biden Administration's *Drug Policy Priorities for Year One*, including: expanding access to evidence-based treatment; advancing racial equity issues in our approach to drug policy; enhancing evidence-based harm reduction efforts; supporting evidence-based prevention efforts to reduce youth substance use; reducing the supply of illicit substances; advancing recovery-ready workplaces and expanding the addiction workforce; and expanding access to recovery support services.

The funding requested by each Department and agency in the National Drug Control Program is included in the table below.

Table 16–1. DRUG CONTROL FUNDING FY 2020—FY 2022
(Dollars in millions)

Department/Agency	FY 2020 Final[1]	FY 2021 Enacted[1]	FY 2022 President's Budget
AmeriCorps	14.550	14.550	14.550
Department of Agriculture:			
U.S. Forest Service	13.000	13.000	10.720
Office of Rural Development	21.280	11.400	11.400
Total USDA	34.280	24.400	22.120
Court Services and Offender Supervision Agency for D.C.	54.057	54.952	67.540
Department of Defense:			
Defense Security Cooperation Agency	132.264	54.897	47.515
Drug Interdiction and Counterdrug Activities[2]	4,803.802	914.429	821.908
Operations Tempo	103.727	95.880	97.798
Defense Health Program	84.575	99.023	84.763
Total DOD	5,124.368	1,164.229	1,051.984
Department of Education:			
Office of Elementary and Secondary Education	58.294	60.028	59.718
Federal Judiciary:	1,077.242	1,108.775	1,169.632
Department of Health and Human Services:			
Administration for Children and Families	30.000	20.000	27.000
Centers for Disease Control and Prevention	475.579	475.579	713.369
Centers for Medicare and Medicaid Services	8,970.000	9,790.000	10,120.000
Food and Drug Administration	64.500	64.500	100.500
Health Resources and Services Administration	653.000	650.000	705.000
Indian Health Service	132.165	135.267	142.002
National Institute on Alcohol Abuse and Alcoholism	60.591	61.499	63.193
National Institute on Drug Abuse	1,457.724	1,480.309	1,852.503
Substance Abuse and Mental Health Services Administration[3]	4,158.280	7,355.270	6,746.270
Total HHS	16,001.839	20,032.424	20,469.837
Department of Homeland Security:			
Customs and Border Protection	3,153.710	3,040.308	3,083.902
Federal Emergency Management Agency	13.500	13.500	13.500
Federal Law Enforcement Training Center	48.328	57.920	59.570
Immigration and Customs Enforcement	603.393	632.674	642.137
Science and Technology Directorate	8.500	6.000	6.300
U.S. Coast Guard	1,841.784	2,076.060	2,039.359
Total DHS	5,669.215	5,826.462	5,844.768
Department of Housing and Urban Development:	583.000	633.175	745.675

Table 16–1. DRUG CONTROL FUNDING FY 2020—FY 2022 — Continued

(Dollars in millions)

Department of the Interior:			
Bureau of Indian Affairs	14.919	14.919	14.919
Bureau of Land Management	5.100	5.100	5.100
National Park Service	3.450	3.450	3.450
Total DOI	23.469	23.469	23.469
Department of Justice:			
Assets Forfeiture Program	227.140	240.880	245.909
Bureau of Alcohol, Tobacco, Firearms, and Explosives	37.130	39.188	41.216
Bureau of Prisons	3,645.805	3,882.809	3,754.200
Criminal Division	42.573	45.081	48.042
Drug Enforcement Administration	2,717.646	2,769.132	2,920.182
Federal Bureau of Investigation	151.592	147.718	152.917
Organized Crime Drug Enforcement Task Forces	550.458	550.458	550.458
Office of Justice Programs	551.692	587.092	631.854
U.S. Attorneys	89.164	98.905	98.905
United States Marshals Service	1,042.200	1,044.414	1,082.471
Total DOJ	9,055.400	9,405.677	9,526.154
Department of Labor:			
Employment and Training Administration	26.000	26.000	26.000
Office of Inspector General	1.800	1.800	1.800
Office of Workers' Compensation Programs	7.769	7.769	7.769
Total DOL	35.569	35.569	35.569
Office of National Drug Control Policy:			
Operations	18.400	18.400	21.300
High Intensity Drug Trafficking Areas Program	285.000	290.000	293.500
Other Federal Drug Control Programs	121.715	128.182	132.617
Total ONDCP	425.115	436.582	447.417
Department of State:			
Bureau of International Narcotics and Law Enforcement Affairs [4]	425.415	425.415	406.812
United States Agency for International Development [4]	53.533	53.533	50.030
Total DOS	478.948	478.948	456.842
Department of the Transportation:			
Federal Aviation Administration	33.255	34.645	35.438
National Highway Traffic Safety Administration	14.750	12.880	11.700
Total Transportation	48.005	47.525	47.138
Department of the Treasury:			
Financial Crimes Enforcement Network	1.680	1.680	2.120
Internal Revenue Service	66.248	60.257	60.257
Office of Foreign Assets Control	0.681	0.681	0.681
Total Treasury	68.609	62.618	63.058
Department of Veterans Affairs:			
Veterans Health Administration	854.891	888.158	922.016
US Postal Inspection Service	76.434	76.434	76.434
Total Federal Drug Budget	$39,683.285	$40,373.975	$41,043.921

[1] Funding reported for FY 2020 and FY 2021 includes funding in regular and supplemental appropriations.

[2] FY 2020 includes $3.8 billion reprogrammed from other DOD programs for barrier construction along the U.S. southwest border in support of the Department of Homeland Security (DHS) under 10 U.S.C. §284(b)(7).

[3] Includes budget authority and funding through evaluation set-aside authorized by Section 241 of the Public Health Service (PHS) Act.

[4] The FY 2021 level is an estimate based on FY 2020 levels that does not reflect decisions on funding priorities. Allocations are not yet available for the enacted FY 2021 appropriation.

TECHNICAL BUDGET ANALYSES

17. CURRENT SERVICES ESTIMATES

Current services, or "baseline," estimates are designed to provide a benchmark against which Budget proposals can be measured. A baseline is not a prediction of the final outcome of the annual budget process, nor is it a proposed budget. It can be a useful tool in budgeting, however. It can be used as a benchmark against which to measure the magnitude of the policy changes in the President's Budget or other budget proposals, and it can also be used to warn of future problems if policy is not changed.

Ideally, a current services baseline would provide a projection of estimated receipts, outlays, deficits or surpluses, and budget authority reflecting this year's enacted policies and programs for each year in the future. Defining this baseline is challenging because funding for many programs in operation today expires within the 10-year budget window. Most significantly, funding for discretionary programs is provided one year at a time in annual appropriations acts. Mandatory programs are not generally subject to annual appropriations, but many operate under multiyear authorizations that expire within the budget window. The framework used to construct the baseline must address whether and how to project

forward the funding for these programs beyond their scheduled expiration dates.

Since the early 1970s, when the first requirements for the calculation of a "current services" baseline were enacted, OMB has constructed the baseline using a variety of concepts and measures. Throughout the 1990s, OMB calculated the baseline using a detailed set of rules in the Balanced Budget and Emergency Deficit Control Act of 1985 (BBEDCA), as amended by the Budget Enforcement Act of 1990 (BEA; P.L. 101-508). Although BBEDCA's baseline rules lapsed for a period when the enforcement provisions of the BEA expired in 2002, budget practitioners continued to adhere to them. The Budget Control Act of 2011 (BCA; P.L. 112-25) formally reinstated the BEA's baseline rules.

Table 17–1 shows estimates of receipts, outlays, and deficits under the Administration's baseline for 2020 through 2031.[1] The table also shows the Administration's estimates by major component of the budget. The esti-

[1] The estimates are shown on a unified budget basis; i.e., the off-budget receipts and outlays of the Social Security trust funds and the Postal Service Fund are added to the on-budget receipts and outlays to calculate the unified budget totals.

Table 17–1. CATEGORY TOTALS FOR THE BASELINE
(In billions of dollars)

	2020	2021	2022	2023	2024	2025	2026	2027	2028	2029	2030	2031
Receipts	3,421	3,580	3,988	4,304	4,451	4,640	4,991	5,272	5,506	5,724	5,958	6,205
Outlays:												
Discretionary:												
Defense	714	735	754	756	778	796	811	828	846	865	884	903
Non-defense	913	960	913	874	842	849	851	862	880	896	913	931
Subtotal, discretionary	1,627	1,696	1,667	1,630	1,621	1,645	1,661	1,689	1,726	1,760	1,797	1,834
Mandatory:												
Social Security	1,090	1,135	1,196	1,261	1,333	1,410	1,493	1,580	1,673	1,769	1,868	1,969
Medicare	769	709	767	842	842	948	1,016	1,087	1,229	1,181	1,328	1,415
Medicaid and CHIP	475	538	535	547	582	612	642	676	717	757	798	843
Other mandatory	2,244	2,868	1,238	852	776	764	785	791	859	831	885	923
Subtotal, mandatory	4,578	5,251	3,735	3,503	3,533	3,735	3,935	4,135	4,478	4,537	4,879	5,149
Net interest	345	303	305	319	365	436	509	581	649	717	798	883
Total, outlays	6,550	7,249	5,707	5,453	5,519	5,816	6,106	6,405	6,854	7,015	7,475	7,866
Unified deficit(+)/surplus(−)	3,129	3,670	1,719	1,148	1,068	1,176	1,115	1,134	1,348	1,291	1,517	1,660
On-budget	(3,142)	(3,597)	(1,670)	(1,074)	(969)	(1,041)	(955)	(938)	(1,122)	(1,021)	(1,205)	(1,307)
Off-budget	(−13)	(73)	(48)	(74)	(99)	(135)	(160)	(195)	(226)	(270)	(312)	(354)
Memorandum:												
Baseline deficit	3,129	3,670	1,719	1,148	1,068	1,176	1,115	1,134	1,348	1,291	1,517	1,660
Extension of certain emergency funding [1]	....	....	58	112	176	190	196	201	205	210	214	218
Related debt service	....	....	*	*	2	5	9	14	19	24	32	41
Baseline deficit including extension of all emergency funding	3,129	3,670	1,777	1,261	1,246	1,371	1,321	1,349	1,572	1,525	1,763	1,919

*Less than $500 million.

[1] Extends and inflates funding that was provided and designated as emergency funding for 2021 in Division M of Public Law 116-260 to address the public health and economic effects of the COVID-19 public health emergency.

mates are based on the economic assumptions underlying the Budget, which, as discussed later in this chapter, were developed on the assumption that the Administration's budget proposals will be enacted. Additionally, as discussed below, the baseline removes the extension of certain emergency spending provided to address the public health and economic effects of the COVID-19 public health emergency. The memorandum bank on Table 17-1 provides additional detail about the effects of removing the extension of this funding.

Conceptual Basis for Estimates

Receipts and outlays are divided into two categories that are important for calculating the baseline: those controlled by authorizing legislation (receipts and direct or mandatory spending) and those controlled through the annual appropriations process (discretionary spending). Different estimating rules apply to each category.

Direct spending and receipts.—Direct spending includes the major entitlement programs, such as Social Security, Medicare, Medicaid, Federal employee retirement, unemployment compensation, and the Supplemental Nutrition Assistance Program (SNAP). It also includes such programs as deposit insurance and farm price and income supports, where the Government is legally obligated to make payments under certain conditions. Taxes and other receipts are like direct spending in that they involve ongoing activities that generally operate under permanent or long-standing authority, and the underlying statutes generally specify the tax rates or benefit levels that must be collected or paid, and who must pay or who is eligible to receive benefits.

The baseline generally—but not always—assumes that receipts and direct spending programs continue in the future as specified by current law. The budgetary effects of anticipated regulatory and administrative actions that are permissible under current law are also reflected in the estimates. BBEDCA requires several exemptions to this general rule. Exceptions in BBEDCA are described below:

- Expiring excise taxes dedicated to a trust fund are assumed to be extended at the rates in effect at the time of expiration. During the projection period of 2021 through 2031, the taxes affected by this exception are:

  — taxes deposited in the Airport and Airway Trust Fund, which expire on September 30, 2023;

  — taxes deposited in the Oil Spill Liability Trust Fund, which expire on December 31, 2025;

  — taxes deposited in the Patient-Centered Outcomes Research Trust Fund, which expire on September 30, 2029;

  — taxes deposited in the Sport Fish Restoration and Boating Resources Trust Fund, which expire on September 30, 2022; and

  — taxes deposited in the Highway Trust Fund and the Leaking Underground Storage Tank Trust Fund, which expire on September 30, 2022.

- Expiring authorizations for direct spending programs that were enacted on or before the date of enactment of the Balanced Budget Act of 1997 are assumed to be extended if their current year outlays exceed $50 million. For example, even though the Environmental Quality Incentives Program, which was authorized prior to the Balanced Budget Act of 1997, continues only through 2023 under current law, the baseline estimates assume continuation of this program through the projection period, because the program's current year outlays exceed the $50 million threshold.[2]

Discretionary spending.—Discretionary programs differ in one important aspect from direct spending programs: the Congress provides spending authority for almost all discretionary programs one year at a time. The spending authority is normally provided in the form of annual appropriations. Absent appropriations of additional funds in the future, discretionary programs would cease to operate after existing balances were spent. If the baseline were intended strictly to reflect current law, then a baseline would reflect only the expenditure of remaining balances from appropriations laws already enacted. Instead, the BBEDCA baseline provides a mechanical definition to reflect the continuing costs of discretionary programs. Under BBEDCA, the baseline estimates for discretionary programs in the current year are based on that year's enacted appropriations, or on the annualized levels provided by a continuing resolution if final full-year appropriations have not been enacted. For the budget year and beyond, the spending authority in the current year is adjusted for inflation, using specified inflation rates.[3] The definition attempts to keep discretionary spending for each program roughly level in real terms.

As noted above, the baseline does not include the extension and inflation of all emergency spending. Specifically, funding that was provided and designated as emergency funding for 2021 in Division M of Public Law 116-260 to address the public health and economic effects of the COVID-19 public health emergency has been removed from the baseline beginning in 2022. Removing the extension and inflation of this funding allows the baseline to provide a more meaningful benchmark for discretionary spending than a baseline strictly following the BBEDCA rules.

Joint Committee Enforcement / BBEDCA § 251A sequestration.—The Joint Select Committee process under the

---

[2] If enacted after the Balanced Budget Act of 1997 (P.L. 105-33), programs that are expressly temporary in nature expire in the baseline as provided by current law, even if their current year outlays exceed the $50 million threshold.

[3] The Administration's baseline uses the inflation rates for discretionary spending required by BBEDCA. This requirement results in an overcompensation in the calculation for Federal pay as a result of the calendar-year timing of Federal pay adjustments. Updating the calculation to address this annual timing discrepancy would have only a small effect on the discretionary baseline.

BCA stipulated that, absent intervening legislation, enforcement procedures would be invoked annually through 2021 to reduce the levels of discretionary and mandatory spending to accomplish certain deficit reduction. The reductions to mandatory spending were subsequently extended through 2030.[4] The BBEDCA baseline includes the effects of the across-the-board reductions ("sequestration") already invoked by Joint Committee sequestration orders for 2013 through 2021, the BBEDCA § 251A sequestration order for mandatory spending for 2022 issued with the transmittal of the 2022 Budget, and the extension of sequestration of mandatory spending through 2030.[5] For discretionary programs, the enforcement procedures ended in 2021 along with the discretionary caps.

Economic Assumptions

As discussed above, an important purpose of the baseline is to serve as a benchmark against which policy proposals are measured. By convention, the President's Budget constructs baseline and policy estimates under the same set of economic and technical assumptions.

---

[4] Since enactment of the BCA, the Congress has extended sequestration of mandatory spending through a series of amendments to section 251A of BBEDCA (2 U.S.C. 901a). Most recently, the CARES Act (P.L. 116-136) extended it through 2030. Subsequently, P.L. 117-7 adjusted the sequestration percentages for Medicare spending in 2030.

[5] The effects of the sequestration reductions are reflected in the detailed schedules for the affected budget accounts for all years. See Chapter 6, "Budget Concepts," of this volume for a more thorough discussion of sequestration procedures.

These assumptions are developed on the basis that the President's Budget proposals will be enacted.

Of course, the economy and the budget interact. Government tax and spending policies can influence prices, economic growth, consumption, savings, and investment. In turn, changes in economic conditions due to the enactment of proposals affect tax receipts and spending, including for unemployment benefits, entitlement payments that receive automatic cost-of-living adjustments (COLAs), income support programs for low-income individuals, and interest on the Federal debt.

Because of these interactions, it would be reasonable, from an economic perspective, to assume different economic paths for the baseline projection and the President's Budget. However, this would greatly complicate the process of producing the Budget, which normally includes a large number of proposals that could have potential economic feedback effects. Agencies would have to produce two sets of estimates for programs sensitive to economic assumptions even if those programs were not directly affected by any proposal in the Budget. Using different economic assumptions for baseline and policy estimates would also diminish the value of the baseline estimates as a benchmark for measuring proposed policy changes, because it would be difficult to separate the effects of proposed policy changes from the effects of different economic assumptions. Using the same economic assumptions for the baseline and the President's Budget eliminates this potential source of confusion.

The economic assumptions underlying the Budget and the Administration's baseline are summarized in Table 17–2. The economic outlook underlying these assump-

Table 17–2. SUMMARY OF ECONOMIC ASSUMPTIONS

(Fiscal years; in billions of dollars)

	2020	2021	2022	2023	2024	2025	2026	2027	2028	2029	2030	2031
Gross Domestic Product (GDP):												
Levels, in billions of dollars:												
Current dollars	21,000	22,030	23,500	24,563	25,537	26,516	27,533	28,590	29,697	30,867	32,094	33,391
Real, chained (2012) dollars	18,541	19,131	20,040	20,550	20,945	21,322	21,706	22,097	22,503	22,931	23,375	23,843
Percent change, year over year:												
Current dollars	−1.1	4.9	6.7	4.5	4.0	3.8	3.8	3.8	3.9	3.9	4.0	4.0
Real, chained (2012) dollars	−2.3	3.2	4.8	2.5	1.9	1.8	1.8	1.8	1.8	1.9	1.9	2.0
Inflation measures (percent change, year over year):												
GDP chained price index	1.3	1.7	1.8	1.9	2.0	2.0	2.0	2.0	2.0	2.0	2.0	2.0
Consumer price index (all urban)	1.5	1.9	2.0	2.1	2.2	2.3	2.3	2.3	2.3	2.3	2.3	2.3
Unemployment rate, civilian (percent)	7.3	6.0	4.3	3.9	3.8	3.8	3.8	3.8	3.8	3.8	3.8	3.8
Interest rates (percent):												
91-day Treasury bills	0.7	0.1	0.2	0.3	0.6	1.1	1.4	1.6	1.6	1.8	2.0	2.2
10-year Treasury notes	1.1	1.1	1.3	1.6	2.0	2.3	2.6	2.7	2.7	2.8	2.8	2.8
MEMORANDUM:												
Related program assumptions:												
Automatic benefit increases (percent):												
Social security and veterans pensions	1.6	1.3	2.3	2.1	2.2	2.2	2.3	2.3	2.3	2.3	2.3	2.3
Federal employee retirement	1.6	1.3	2.3	2.1	2.2	2.2	2.3	2.3	2.3	2.3	2.3	2.3
Supplemental Nutrition Assistance Program	....	....	....	1.7	2.2	2.2	2.3	2.3	2.3	2.3	2.3	2.3
Insured unemployment rate	6.1	2.7	1.4	1.2	1.2	1.2	1.2	1.2	1.2	1.2	1.2	1.2

Table 17–3.   BASELINE BENEFICIARY PROJECTIONS FOR MAJOR BENEFIT PROGRAMS

(Annual average, in thousands)

	Actual 2020	Estimate										
		2021	2022	2023	2024	2025	2026	2027	2028	2029	2030	2031
Farmers receiving Federal payments	1,439	1,434	1,429	1,424	1,419	1,414	1,409	1,404	1,399	1,394	1,389	1,384
Federal direct student loans	7,207	7,358	7,381	7,380	7,417	7,423	7,435	7,466	7,467	7,490	7,508	7,510
Federal Pell Grants	6,303	6,456	6,857	7,169	7,741	7,634	7,809	7,991	8,175	8,354	8,538	8,730
Medicaid/Children's Health Insurance Program [1]	81,700	82,623	82,935	83,215	83,922	84,522	85,322	86,022	86,525	86,813	87,626	88,337
Medicare-eligible military retiree health benefits	2,456	2,479	2,503	2,524	2,545	2,571	2,596	2,618	2,637	2,650	2,654	2,653
Medicare [2]:												
Hospital insurance	62,008	63,170	64,621	66,256	67,863	69,458	71,094	72,648	74,127	75,531	76,791	77,853
Supplementary medical insurance:												
Part B	56,981	58,185	59,532	61,056	62,570	64,077	65,614	67,096	68,506	69,854	71,074	72,140
Part D	48,303	49,605	50,991	52,490	53,946	55,365	56,773	58,072	59,301	60,470	61,527	62,429
Prescription Drug Plans and Medicare:												
Advantage Prescription Drug Plans	47,063	48,623	50,166	51,752	53,268	54,721	56,124	57,408	58,623	59,779	60,824	61,715
Retiree Drug Subsidy	1,240	981	825	738	678	644	649	664	678	691	703	713
Managed Care Enrollment [3]	24,530	26,825	28,823	30,149	31,303	32,472	33,650	34,796	35,897	36,953	37,939	38,832
Railroad retirement	499	493	486	479	471	464	457	449	442	435	428	421
Federal civil service retirement	2,747	2,775	2,803	2,829	2,851	2,873	2,897	2,919	2,941	2,963	2,982	3,000
Military retirement	2,325	2,335	2,342	2,349	2,354	2,356	2,357	2,355	2,352	2,347	2,342	2,335
Unemployment insurance	29,799	8,598	5,745	5,318	5,267	5,300	5,334	5,365	5,397	5,420	5,461	5,499
Unemployment insurance—RUIA	41	44	25	24	22	21	20	20	20	20	19	19
Supplemental Nutrition Assistance Program	39,885	43,932	45,367	44,514	43,059	41,209	39,209	38,709	39,009	39,309	39,609	39,709
Child nutrition	29,766	30,027	36,953	37,231	37,438	37,648	37,860	38,075	38,293	38,513	38,737	38,963
Foster care, Adoption Assistance and Guardianship Assistance	675	807	910	1,005	1,045	1,087	1,132	1,180	1,230	1,290	1,345	1,405
Supplemental security income (SSI):												
Aged	1,109	1,084	1,100	1,107	1,113	1,122	1,133	1,144	1,158	1,173	1,188	1,205
Blind/disabled	6,802	6,704	6,791	6,811	6,819	6,836	6,847	6,855	6,867	6,884	6,908	6,939
Total, SSI	7,911	7,789	7,891	7,918	7,932	7,958	7,980	7,999	8,025	8,057	8,096	8,143
Child care and development fund [4]	2,275	2,225	2,359	2,689	2,614	2,554	2,522	2,488	2,455	2,424	2,392	2,360
Social security (OASDI):												
Old age and survivors insurance	54,463	55,467	56,560	57,808	59,182	60,575	61,974	63,360	64,851	66,261	67,583	68,806
Disability insurance	9,882	9,657	9,685	9,724	9,756	9,815	9,875	9,945	9,941	9,942	9,954	9,969
Total, OASDI	64,345	65,124	66,245	67,532	68,938	70,390	71,849	73,305	74,792	76,203	77,537	78,775
Veterans compensation:												
Veterans	5,034	5,246	5,504	5,724	5,932	6,125	6,305	6,478	6,645	6,807	6,963	7,114
Survivors (non-veterans)	440	455	475	493	512	533	556	580	605	631	657	685
Total, Veterans compensation	5,474	5,701	5,979	6,217	6,444	6,659	6,861	7,058	7,250	7,438	7,620	7,798
Veterans pensions:												
Veterans	230	215	209	205	203	201	201	200	200	199	199	199
Survivors (non-veterans)	164	155	147	143	140	138	136	135	133	132	131	129
Total, Veterans pensions	393	370	357	348	342	339	337	335	333	331	330	328

[1] Medicaid enrollment excludes territories.

[2] Medicare figures (Hospital Insurance, Part B, and Part D) do not sum to total Medicare enrollment due to enrollment in multiple programs.

[3] Enrollment figures include only beneficiaries who receive both Part A and Part B services through managed care.

[4] These levels include children served through CCDF (including TANF transfers) and through funds spent directly on child care in the Social Services Block Grant and TANF programs.

Table 17–5. RECEIPTS BY SOURCE IN THE PROJECTION OF BASELINE

(In billions of dollars)

	2020 Actual	Estimate										
		2021	2022	2023	2024	2025	2026	2027	2028	2029	2030	2031
Individual income taxes	1,608.7	1,703.7	2,005.3	2,173.9	2,209.9	2,346.8	2,645.8	2,851.5	2,986.4	3,127.5	3,274.7	3,431.4
Corporation income taxes	211.8	268.5	265.9	367.2	412.0	432.3	424.6	423.7	432.9	431.6	433.3	438.5
Social insurance and retirement receipts	1,310.0	1,296.2	1,416.7	1,467.1	1,526.4	1,577.1	1,639.1	1,699.5	1,778.6	1,845.4	1,921.8	1,996.3
(On-budget)	(344.5)	(352.0)	(385.1)	(399.5)	(413.2)	(423.7)	(437.2)	(452.6)	(473.7)	(490.5)	(511.7)	(528.9)
(Off-budget)	(965.4)	(944.1)	(1,031.6)	(1,067.6)	(1,113.2)	(1,153.4)	(1,201.8)	(1,246.9)	(1,304.9)	(1,354.9)	(1,410.1)	(1,467.4)
Excise taxes	86.8	74.1	81.9	85.5	90.1	90.2	91.1	92.0	91.8	93.9	96.6	97.3
Estate and gift taxes	17.6	17.6	20.8	22.3	23.6	24.6	25.1	37.8	39.0	40.7	43.2	45.9
Customs duties	68.6	84.8	57.4	45.2	45.5	46.5	47.8	49.2	50.8	52.6	54.6	56.8
Miscellaneous receipts	117.7	134.7	140.2	143.1	143.1	122.9	117.3	117.8	126.3	132.0	133.6	139.1
Total, receipts	**3,421.2**	**3,579.5**	**3,988.2**	**4,304.2**	**4,450.6**	**4,640.3**	**4,990.8**	**5,271.5**	**5,505.7**	**5,723.7**	**5,957.8**	**6,205.3**
(On-budget)	(2,455.7)	(2,635.4)	(2,956.6)	(3,236.6)	(3,337.4)	(3,486.9)	(3,789.0)	(4,024.7)	(4,200.8)	(4,368.8)	(4,547.8)	(4,737.9)
(Off-budget)	(965.4)	(944.1)	(1,031.6)	(1,067.6)	(1,113.2)	(1,153.4)	(1,201.8)	(1,246.9)	(1,304.9)	(1,354.9)	(1,410.1)	(1,467.4)

tions is discussed in greater detail in Chapter 2 of this volume.

Major Programmatic Assumptions

A number of programmatic assumptions must be made to calculate the baseline estimates. These include assumptions about annual cost-of-living adjustments in the indexed programs and the number of beneficiaries who will receive payments from the major benefit programs. Assumptions about various automatic cost-of-living-adjustments are shown in Table 17–2, and assumptions about baseline caseload projections for the major benefit programs are shown in Table 17–3. These assumptions affect baseline estimates of direct spending for each of these programs, and they also affect estimates of the discretionary baseline for a limited number of programs. For the administrative expenses for Medicare, Railroad Retirement, and unemployment insurance, the discretionary baseline is increased (or decreased) for changes in the number of beneficiaries in addition to the adjustments for inflation described earlier. It is also necessary to make assumptions about the continuation of expiring programs and provisions. As explained above, in the baseline estimates provided here, expiring excise taxes dedicated to a trust fund are extended at current rates. In general, mandatory programs with spending of at least $50 million in the current year are also assumed to continue, unless the programs are explicitly temporary in nature. Table 17–4, available at *https://www.whitehouse.gov/omb/analytical-perspectives/*, provides a listing of mandatory programs and taxes assumed to continue in the baseline after their expiration.[6] Many other important assumptions must be made in order to calculate the baseline estimates. These include the timing and content of

regulations that will be issued over the projection period, the use of administrative discretion under current law, and other assumptions about the way programs operate. Table 17–4 lists many of these assumptions and their effects on the baseline estimates. The list is not intended to be exhaustive; the variety and complexity of Government programs are too great to provide a complete list. Instead, the table shows some of the more important assumptions.

Current Services Receipts, Outlays, and Budget Authority

Receipts.—Table 17–5 shows the Administration's baseline receipts by major source. Table 17–6 shows the scheduled increases in the Social Security taxable earnings base, which affect both payroll tax receipts for the program and the initial benefit levels for certain retirees.

Outlays.—Table 17–7 shows the growth from 2021 to 2022 and average annual growth over the five-year and ten-year periods for certain discretionary and major mandatory programs. Tables 17–8 and 17–9 show the Administration's baseline outlays by function and by agency, respectively. A more detailed presentation of these outlays (by function, category, subfunction, and program) is available on the internet as part of Table 17–12 at *https://www.whitehouse.gov/omb/analytical-perspectives/*.

Budget authority.—Tables 17–10 and 17–11 show estimates of budget authority in the Administration's baseline by function and by agency, respectively. A more detailed presentation of this budget authority with program-level estimates is also available on the internet as part of Table 17–12 at *https://www.whitehouse.gov/omb/analytical-perspectives/*.

---

[6] All discretionary programs with enacted non-emergency appropriations in the current year, as well as emergency appropriations other than those enacted in in Division M of Public Law 116-260, are assumed to continue, and are therefore not presented in Table 17-4.

Table 17–6. EFFECT ON RECEIPTS OF CHANGES IN THE SOCIAL SECURITY TAXABLE EARNINGS BASE

(In billions of dollars)

	2022	2023	2024	2025	2026	2027	2028	2029	2030	2031
Social security (OASDI) taxable earnings base increases:										
$142,800 to $145,500 on Jan. 1, 2022	1.5	3.8	4.1	4.4	4.7	5.1	5.6	6.0	6.5	7.0
$145,500 to $153,000 on Jan. 1, 2023	....	4.3	10.6	11.4	12.3	13.2	14.3	15.5	16.8	18.2
$153,000 to $159,000 on Jan. 1, 2024	....	....	3.4	8.3	8.9	9.7	10.5	11.3	12.3	13.3
$159,000 to $164,700 on Jan. 1, 2025	....	....	....	3.2	7.9	8.5	9.2	10.0	10.8	11.7
$164,700 to $171,300 on Jan. 1, 2026	....	....	....	....	3.7	9.1	9.9	10.7	11.6	12.6
$171,300 to $176,400 on Jan. 1, 2027	....	....	....	....	....	2.9	7.1	7.7	8.3	9.0
$176,400 to $182,400 on Jan. 1, 2028	....	....	....	....	....	....	3.4	8.5	9.2	10.0
$182,400 to $189,000 on Jan. 1, 2029	....	....	....	....	....	....	....	3.8	9.4	10.2
$189,000 to $195,600 on Jan. 1, 2030	....	....	....	....	....	....	....	....	3.9	9.5
$195,600 to $203,100 on Jan. 1, 2031	....	....	....	....	....	....	....	....	....	4.4

Table 17–7. CHANGE IN OUTLAY ESTIMATES BY CATEGORY IN THE BASELINE

(In billions of dollars)

	2021	2022	2023	2024	2025	2026	2027	2028	2029	2030	2031	Change 2021 to 2022		Change 2021 to 2026		Change 2021 to 2031	
												Amount	Percent	Amount	Average annual rate	Amount	Average annual rate
Outlays:																	
Discretionary:																	
Defense	735	754	756	778	796	811	828	846	865	884	903	18	2.5%	75	2.0%	167	2.1%
Non-defense	960	913	874	842	849	851	862	880	896	913	931	–47	–4.9%	–110	–2.4%	–29	–0.3%
Subtotal, discretionary	1,696	1,667	1,630	1,621	1,645	1,661	1,689	1,726	1,760	1,797	1,834	–29	–1.7%	–34	–0.4%	139	0.8%
Mandatory:																	
Farm programs	52	20	21	21	21	18	18	18	18	18	17	–31	–60.6%	–34	–19.4%	–34	–10.3%
GSE support	–5	–4	–4	–3	–3	–2	–2	–2	–2	–2	–1	–*	–6.9%	2	–12.6%	3	–11.5%
Medicaid	521	518	529	563	592	621	654	698	741	783	828	–3	–0.7%	100	3.6%	307	4.7%
Other health care	168	161	124	116	112	115	119	122	125	127	129	–7	–4.1%	–53	–7.3%	–39	–2.6%
Medicare	709	767	842	842	948	1,016	1,087	1,229	1,181	1,328	1,415	58	8.1%	307	7.5%	706	7.2%
Federal employee retirement and disability	158	167	167	167	178	183	188	199	193	205	212	10	6.1%	25	3.0%	54	3.0%
Unemployment compensation	539	50	22	23	27	32	35	42	44	45	47	–489	–90.8%	–507	–43.1%	–492	–21.6%
Food and nutrition assistance	196	157	110	108	107	106	108	111	114	118	121	–39	–19.9%	–89	–11.4%	–75	–4.7%
Other income security programs	942	421	228	205	201	206	189	197	190	198	202	–521	–55.3%	–736	–26.2%	–740	–14.3%
Social Security	1,135	1,196	1,261	1,333	1,410	1,493	1,580	1,673	1,769	1,868	1,969	61	5.3%	358	5.6%	834	5.7%
Veterans programs	133	177	161	158	182	194	206	236	216	245	260	43	32.4%	60	7.7%	126	6.9%
Other mandatory programs	906	250	162	123	86	85	87	91	91	90	99	–656	–72.4%	–822	–37.8%	–807	–19.8%
Undistributed offsetting receipts	–204	–144	–121	–124	–127	–131	–134	–138	–141	–144	–148	60	–29.4%	73	–8.5%	55	–3.1%
Subtotal, mandatory	5,251	3,735	3,503	3,533	3,735	3,935	4,135	4,478	4,537	4,879	5,149	–1,516	–28.9%	–1,315	–5.6%	–102	–0.2%
Net interest	303	305	319	365	436	509	581	649	717	798	883	2	0.6%	206	10.9%	580	11.3%
Total, outlays	7,249	5,707	5,453	5,519	5,816	6,106	6,405	6,854	7,015	7,475	7,866	–1,543	–21.3%	–1,144	–3.4%	616	0.8%

*Less than $500 million.

Table 17–8. OUTLAYS BY FUNCTION IN THE BASELINE

(In billions of dollars)

Function	2020 Actual	Estimate										
		2021	2022	2023	2024	2025	2026	2027	2028	2029	2030	2031
National Defense:												
Department of Defense—Military	690.4	712.4	727.5	730.6	751.7	769.4	783.1	799.0	816.9	834.6	853.2	872.2
Other	34.2	36.0	40.8	41.2	41.1	41.9	42.8	43.8	44.7	45.7	46.7	47.6
Total, National Defense	724.6	748.4	768.3	771.9	792.8	811.3	825.8	842.8	861.6	880.4	899.9	919.8
International Affairs	67.7	51.7	59.3	62.0	63.0	62.5	64.7	66.4	67.9	69.4	70.7	71.5
General Science, Space, and Technology	34.0	38.2	39.5	39.6	40.7	41.9	41.9	42.6	43.3	44.2	45.1	46.1
Energy	7.1	6.1	7.6	5.5	4.6	4.9	5.2	4.1	7.5	8.0	8.7	8.7
Natural Resources and Environment	42.5	47.1	49.6	54.5	56.8	55.4	55.3	54.8	55.1	55.6	56.7	57.0
Agriculture	47.3	65.6	32.6	33.9	31.1	30.5	27.5	27.5	27.9	28.1	28.5	28.3
Commerce and Housing Credit	568.9	384.7	20.1	12.4	11.5	13.4	14.3	16.9	16.9	15.5	15.5	17.6
On-Budget	(574.5)	(380.2)	(12.7)	(9.9)	(11.2)	(13.2)	(14.0)	(16.6)	(16.6)	(15.2)	(15.2)	(17.3)
Off-Budget	(−5.6)	(4.4)	(7.4)	(2.6)	(0.3)	(0.3)	(0.3)	(0.3)	(0.3)	(0.3)	(0.3)	(0.3)
Transportation	145.6	178.1	138.4	125.6	121.3	117.7	117.2	119.1	123.4	126.2	127.6	131.2
Community and Regional Development	81.9	92.9	58.1	45.8	44.3	44.7	41.2	40.7	40.9	38.2	37.1	37.3
Education, Training, Employment, and Social Services	237.8	271.1	235.7	217.2	173.6	144.0	148.5	152.5	155.6	159.1	161.4	164.3
Health	747.6	836.2	803.7	770.4	781.6	801.6	824.6	858.9	908.3	955.7	1,001.4	1,049.9
Medicare	776.2	716.9	774.9	849.6	849.6	956.7	1,024.4	1,096.2	1,238.4	1,190.0	1,337.2	1,424.4
Income Security	1,263.6	1,926.5	884.3	617.6	590.7	602.3	617.6	611.0	642.2	634.3	662.5	679.8
Social Security	1,095.8	1,141.2	1,203.3	1,267.4	1,339.5	1,416.7	1,499.6	1,587.2	1,680.3	1,776.3	1,875.0	1,976.1
On-Budget	(39.9)	(34.9)	(44.3)	(47.4)	(51.2)	(55.5)	(67.1)	(75.2)	(81.2)	(87.6)	(94.3)	(101.5)
Off-Budget	(1,055.9)	(1,106.3)	(1,159.0)	(1,220.0)	(1,288.4)	(1,361.2)	(1,432.5)	(1,512.0)	(1,599.0)	(1,688.7)	(1,780.7)	(1,874.6)
Veterans Benefits and Services	218.7	236.3	287.9	276.5	274.0	298.9	313.1	328.5	361.0	343.7	376.6	394.1
Administration of Justice	72.0	83.4	73.9	73.3	72.8	74.2	75.6	77.5	79.2	80.9	82.7	90.6
General Government	180.1	325.6	108.0	31.4	30.2	30.5	30.9	31.4	32.5	32.9	33.8	34.6
Net Interest	345.5	303.0	304.9	319.4	365.2	436.4	509.0	581.1	649.3	717.2	798.3	882.5
On-Budget	(424.3)	(376.3)	(370.6)	(378.7)	(419.6)	(487.2)	(556.8)	(626.9)	(692.3)	(755.5)	(831.3)	(909.1)
Off-Budget	(−78.8)	(−73.3)	(−65.7)	(−59.3)	(−54.5)	(−50.8)	(−47.8)	(−45.8)	(−43.0)	(−38.3)	(−32.9)	(−26.6)
Allowances	....	....	0.3	....	....	....	....	....	....	....	....	....
Undistributed Offsetting Receipts:												
Employer share, employee retirement (on-budget)	−80.9	−89.8	−96.9	−95.1	−97.2	−99.5	−101.9	−104.3	−106.7	−109.3	−111.8	−114.7
Employer share, employee retirement (off-budget)	−19.1	−19.9	−20.9	−21.4	−22.0	−22.8	−23.5	−24.2	−25.0	−25.4	−26.4	−27.1
Rents and royalties on the Outer Continental Shelf	−3.6	−3.8	−5.0	−4.6	−5.2	−5.2	−5.4	−5.6	−5.8	−5.9	−6.1	−6.3
Sale of major assets	....	....	....	....	....	....	....	....	....	....	....	....
Other undistributed offsetting receipts	−2.7	−90.1	−21.0	−0.1	−0.1	−*	−*	−*	−*	−*	−*	−*
Total, Undistributed Offsetting Receipts	−106.4	−203.6	−143.8	−121.2	−124.4	−127.5	−130.7	−134.0	−137.5	−140.7	−144.2	−148.1
On-Budget	(−87.2)	(−183.7)	(−122.9)	(−99.8)	(−102.4)	(−104.7)	(−107.3)	(−109.9)	(−112.5)	(−115.2)	(−117.9)	(−121.0)
Off-Budget	(−19.1)	(−19.9)	(−20.9)	(−21.4)	(−22.0)	(−22.8)	(−23.5)	(−24.2)	(−25.0)	(−25.4)	(−26.4)	(−27.1)
Total	**6,550.4**	**7,249.5**	**5,706.7**	**5,452.6**	**5,518.9**	**5,816.1**	**6,105.8**	**6,405.2**	**6,853.9**	**7,015.0**	**7,474.6**	**7,865.8**
On-Budget	(5,598.0)	(6,231.9)	(4,626.9)	(4,310.6)	(4,306.7)	(4,528.2)	(4,744.2)	(4,962.9)	(5,322.6)	(5,389.8)	(5,752.9)	(6,044.6)
Off-Budget	(952.4)	(1,017.5)	(1,079.8)	(1,141.9)	(1,212.2)	(1,287.9)	(1,361.5)	(1,442.3)	(1,531.3)	(1,625.2)	(1,721.7)	(1,821.2)

*Less than $500 million.

Table 17–9. OUTLAYS BY AGENCY IN THE BASELINE
(In billions of dollars)

Agency	2020 Actual	Estimate										
		2021	2022	2023	2024	2025	2026	2027	2028	2029	2030	2031
Legislative Branch	5.4	6.4	5.8	5.9	6.0	6.1	6.2	6.4	6.5	6.7	6.8	7.0
Judicial Branch	8.3	8.7	9.1	9.3	9.6	9.7	10.0	10.3	10.4	10.7	10.9	11.2
Agriculture	184.2	288.7	218.3	174.4	169.2	168.3	164.6	166.5	170.6	173.9	178.8	182.4
Commerce	15.9	16.1	14.1	11.8	11.4	11.2	10.6	10.8	11.0	11.2	11.5	11.8
Defense—Military Programs	690.4	712.4	727.5	730.6	751.7	769.4	783.1	799.0	816.9	834.6	853.2	872.2
Education	204.4	232.0	195.0	178.7	135.0	105.1	109.4	112.9	115.4	118.2	119.8	121.8
Energy	32.0	35.0	41.5	40.4	39.4	40.2	40.7	40.3	43.6	44.8	45.8	46.6
Health and Human Services	1,504.0	1,547.4	1,590.9	1,630.5	1,628.5	1,752.7	1,840.2	1,944.5	2,131.8	2,127.4	2,320.0	2,456.3
Homeland Security	92.0	122.7	79.0	74.8	75.3	77.5	76.8	78.6	82.1	84.2	85.5	93.3
Housing and Urban Development	33.2	55.8	59.7	59.6	60.6	61.4	60.3	59.4	59.7	56.8	55.7	56.5
Interior	16.4	17.7	18.3	19.3	19.7	19.6	19.7	19.3	19.1	19.2	19.6	20.2
Justice	39.6	45.3	39.8	39.1	38.2	39.0	39.6	40.6	41.4	42.4	43.3	44.4
Labor	477.5	552.6	107.8	63.0	50.9	45.2	55.0	47.9	55.3	57.1	59.1	61.6
State	32.9	35.8	35.0	35.1	36.3	37.6	38.3	39.0	39.9	40.7	41.6	42.5
Transportation	100.3	125.7	119.9	106.9	102.0	99.4	97.8	98.4	100.2	102.0	103.7	105.7
Treasury	1,151.7	1,681.8	846.4	602.1	646.3	714.5	778.9	854.9	927.6	991.0	1,072.2	1,156.1
Veterans Affairs	218.4	235.9	287.6	276.1	273.6	298.4	312.7	328.1	360.5	343.3	376.1	393.6
Corps of Engineers—Civil Works	7.6	7.1	7.7	10.4	11.4	9.6	9.3	9.1	8.9	8.8	8.9	7.9
Other Defense Civil Programs	65.2	68.3	72.0	68.8	65.4	73.2	78.2	78.3	86.2	77.6	86.9	89.8
Environmental Protection Agency	8.7	7.5	8.5	8.9	9.4	9.8	10.1	10.3	10.5	10.8	11.0	11.3
Executive Office of the President	0.4	0.5	0.5	0.5	0.5	0.5	0.5	0.5	0.5	0.5	0.5	0.5
General Services Administration	−0.3	2.1	1.7	−0.1	0.1	−0.1	0.0	0.1	0.1	0.1	0.1	0.1
International Assistance Programs	21.7	25.6	23.1	25.5	25.1	23.3	24.8	25.8	26.6	27.2	27.7	27.7
National Aeronautics and Space Administration	21.5	23.6	23.9	23.9	24.5	25.0	25.5	26.1	26.6	27.2	27.8	28.4
National Science Foundation	7.3	8.3	8.9	9.1	9.5	9.7	9.6	9.7	9.6	9.8	10.0	10.2
Office of Personnel Management	105.6	107.9	111.8	116.6	121.3	125.6	130.4	135.0	140.2	145.1	147.8	149.5
Small Business Administration	577.4	372.3	11.5	3.0	3.1	3.2	3.2	3.3	3.3	3.4	3.5	3.5
Social Security Administration	1,153.9	1,199.2	1,267.9	1,330.8	1,400.6	1,484.3	1,569.3	1,658.8	1,759.1	1,846.8	1,953.0	2,056.4
On-Budget	(98.0)	(93.0)	(108.9)	(110.7)	(112.2)	(123.1)	(136.8)	(146.8)	(160.1)	(158.1)	(172.3)	(181.8)
Off-Budget	(1,055.9)	(1,106.3)	(1,159.0)	(1,220.0)	(1,288.4)	(1,361.2)	(1,432.5)	(1,512.0)	(1,599.0)	(1,688.7)	(1,780.7)	(1,874.6)
Other Independent Agencies	16.2	35.0	42.0	38.5	37.4	39.7	40.1	43.3	44.4	43.8	44.7	46.6
On-Budget	(21.8)	(30.6)	(34.6)	(35.9)	(37.1)	(39.4)	(39.8)	(43.0)	(44.1)	(43.5)	(44.4)	(46.3)
Off-Budget	(−5.6)	(4.4)	(7.4)	(2.6)	(0.3)	(0.3)	(0.3)	(0.3)	(0.3)	(0.3)	(0.3)	(0.3)
Allowances	....	....	0.3	....	....	....	....	....	....	....	....	....
Undistributed Offsetting Receipts	−241.6	−327.8	−268.4	−241.0	−242.9	−242.8	−238.9	−251.6	−254.3	−249.9	−251.0	−249.3
On-Budget	(−143.6)	(−234.6)	(−181.8)	(−160.4)	(−166.5)	(−169.2)	(−167.7)	(−181.7)	(−186.3)	(−186.1)	(−191.7)	(−195.6)
Off-Budget	(−97.9)	(−93.2)	(−86.6)	(−80.7)	(−76.5)	(−73.5)	(−71.3)	(−70.0)	(−68.0)	(−63.8)	(−59.3)	(−53.7)
Total	**6,550.4**	**7,249.5**	**5,706.7**	**5,452.6**	**5,518.9**	**5,816.1**	**6,105.8**	**6,405.2**	**6,853.9**	**7,015.0**	**7,474.6**	**7,865.8**
On-Budget	(5,598.0)	(6,231.9)	(4,626.9)	(4,310.6)	(4,306.7)	(4,528.2)	(4,744.2)	(4,962.9)	(5,322.6)	(5,389.8)	(5,752.9)	(6,044.6)
Off-Budget	(952.4)	(1,017.5)	(1,079.8)	(1,141.9)	(1,212.2)	(1,287.9)	(1,361.5)	(1,442.3)	(1,531.3)	(1,625.2)	(1,721.7)	(1,821.2)

Table 17–10. BUDGET AUTHORITY BY FUNCTION IN THE BASELINE

(In billions of dollars)

Function	2020 Actual	Estimate 2021	2022	2023	2024	2025	2026	2027	2028	2029	2030	2031
National Defense:												
Department of Defense—Military	738.8	713.8	732.7	749.1	765.3	782.4	799.7	817.2	835.2	853.9	873.0	893.1
Other	35.7	40.2	40.4	41.2	42.0	42.9	43.8	44.6	45.5	46.4	47.3	48.3
Total, National Defense	774.5	754.0	773.0	790.3	807.3	825.3	843.5	861.8	880.8	900.4	920.4	941.4
International Affairs	73.2	84.5	78.9	81.9	84.7	87.1	94.0	99.3	101.4	103.5	105.7	107.2
General Science, Space, and Technology	37.5	38.6	38.9	39.7	40.5	41.4	42.3	43.1	44.1	45.0	45.9	46.9
Energy	6.6	5.3	8.0	5.4	5.7	5.0	5.2	4.6	7.9	8.6	9.1	9.3
Natural Resources and Environment	54.2	49.5	51.0	52.7	53.8	54.5	53.6	54.6	55.8	57.1	58.0	59.8
Agriculture	70.6	46.2	25.4	25.9	26.4	26.5	26.6	26.7	27.0	27.3	27.6	27.0
Commerce and Housing Credit	1,247.4	−211.1	19.4	21.9	26.1	29.6	33.2	35.2	36.3	37.4	38.6	41.1
On-Budget	(1,247.1)	(−221.4)	(19.2)	(21.6)	(25.8)	(29.3)	(32.9)	(34.9)	(36.1)	(37.1)	(38.3)	(40.8)
Off-Budget	(0.3)	(10.3)	(0.3)	(0.3)	(0.3)	(0.3)	(0.3)	(0.3)	(0.3)	(0.3)	(0.3)	(0.3)
Transportation	171.9	209.1	106.8	107.8	108.8	108.5	110.3	112.3	115.4	117.1	117.5	119.8
Community and Regional Development	134.4	80.8	32.1	32.7	33.4	34.1	35.8	36.5	37.0	37.6	38.3	38.9
Education, Training, Employment, and Social Services	268.6	477.8	129.1	134.4	140.7	145.7	151.0	155.1	158.2	161.8	164.1	167.2
Health	923.7	903.7	740.3	728.3	758.1	793.4	829.2	868.9	918.6	965.7	1,010.8	1,060.8
Medicare	819.8	703.4	839.1	830.5	850.9	957.9	1,025.6	1,097.4	1,239.6	1,191.2	1,338.4	1,425.8
Income Security	1,329.1	1,974.5	827.0	607.3	602.8	616.3	622.8	622.2	647.5	652.6	674.5	692.5
Social Security	1,099.2	1,145.0	1,207.3	1,273.3	1,345.8	1,423.4	1,506.8	1,594.8	1,688.2	1,784.4	1,883.4	1,984.7
On-Budget	(39.9)	(34.9)	(44.3)	(47.4)	(51.2)	(55.5)	(67.1)	(75.2)	(81.2)	(87.6)	(94.3)	(101.5)
Off-Budget	(1,059.3)	(1,110.1)	(1,163.0)	(1,225.9)	(1,294.6)	(1,367.9)	(1,439.6)	(1,519.6)	(1,606.9)	(1,696.9)	(1,789.0)	(1,883.2)
Veterans Benefits and Services	233.6	256.0	263.4	269.9	288.8	303.0	317.4	332.9	348.9	365.0	381.4	399.2
Administration of Justice	70.3	72.6	75.7	74.5	75.0	77.0	78.8	80.6	82.4	84.2	86.0	93.8
General Government	182.1	400.8	29.6	29.9	30.5	31.1	31.8	32.4	33.1	33.7	34.4	35.4
Net Interest	344.8	303.0	304.9	319.4	365.1	436.4	509.0	581.1	649.3	717.2	798.3	882.5
On-Budget	(423.6)	(376.3)	(370.5)	(378.7)	(419.6)	(487.2)	(556.8)	(626.9)	(692.3)	(755.5)	(831.3)	(909.1)
Off-Budget	(−78.8)	(−73.3)	(−65.7)	(−59.3)	(−54.5)	(−50.8)	(−47.8)	(−45.8)	(−43.0)	(−38.3)	(−32.9)	(−26.6)
Allowances	....	....	0.3	....	....	....	....	....	....	....	....	....
Undistributed Offsetting Receipts:												
Employer share, employee retirement (on-budget)	−80.9	−89.8	−96.9	−95.1	−97.2	−99.5	−101.9	−104.3	−106.7	−109.3	−111.8	−114.7
Employer share, employee retirement (off-budget)	−19.1	−19.9	−20.9	−21.4	−22.0	−22.8	−23.5	−24.2	−25.0	−25.4	−26.4	−27.1
Rents and royalties on the Outer Continental Shelf	−3.6	−3.8	−5.0	−4.6	−5.2	−5.2	−5.4	−5.6	−5.8	−5.9	−6.1	−6.3
Sale of major assets	....	....	....	....	....	....	....	....	....	....	....	....
Other undistributed offsetting receipts	−2.7	−90.1	−21.0	−0.1	−0.1	−*	−*	−*	−*	−*	−*	−*
Total, Undistributed Offsetting Receipts	−106.4	−203.6	−143.8	−121.2	−124.4	−127.5	−130.7	−134.0	−137.5	−140.7	−144.2	−148.1
On-Budget	(−87.2)	(−183.7)	(−122.9)	(−99.8)	(−102.4)	(−104.7)	(−107.3)	(−109.9)	(−112.5)	(−115.2)	(−117.9)	(−121.0)
Off-Budget	(−19.1)	(−19.9)	(−20.9)	(−21.4)	(−22.0)	(−22.8)	(−23.5)	(−24.2)	(−25.0)	(−25.4)	(−26.4)	(−27.1)
Total	**7,735.3**	**7,090.1**	**5,406.5**	**5,304.6**	**5,520.1**	**5,868.8**	**6,186.1**	**6,505.4**	**6,933.9**	**7,149.1**	**7,588.4**	**7,985.4**
On-Budget	(6,773.7)	(6,062.8)	(4,329.8)	(4,159.1)	(4,301.6)	(4,574.1)	(4,817.4)	(5,055.5)	(5,394.7)	(5,515.7)	(5,858.3)	(6,155.6)
Off-Budget	(961.6)	(1,027.2)	(1,076.7)	(1,145.5)	(1,218.5)	(1,294.7)	(1,368.7)	(1,449.9)	(1,539.2)	(1,633.4)	(1,730.0)	(1,829.8)
MEMORANDUM												
Discretionary Budget Authority:												
National Defense	756.6	740.8	758.9	775.7	792.9	810.5	828.5	846.8	865.6	884.9	904.6	924.7
International Affairs	59.2	62.6	63.8	65.1	66.4	67.8	69.2	70.7	72.1	73.6	75.1	76.7
Domestic	1,082.5	812.8	655.6	669.3	684.0	699.2	714.8	730.7	746.8	763.4	780.2	797.5
Total, Discretionary	1,898.3	1,616.2	1,478.3	1,510.1	1,543.3	1,577.5	1,612.5	1,648.2	1,684.6	1,721.9	1,759.9	1,798.9

*Less than $500 million.

Table 17–11. BUDGET AUTHORITY BY AGENCY IN THE BASELINE

(In billions of dollars)

Agency	2020 Actual	Estimate										
		2021	2022	2023	2024	2025	2026	2027	2028	2029	2030	2031
Legislative Branch	5.4	5.6	5.7	5.9	6.0	6.1	6.3	6.4	6.6	6.8	6.9	7.1
Judicial Branch	8.4	8.6	9.0	9.2	9.4	9.7	9.9	10.1	10.3	10.5	10.8	11.0
Agriculture	235.2	261.1	204.7	164.7	166.1	166.3	166.0	168.6	173.0	177.4	181.2	184.8
Commerce	17.4	14.3	9.7	10.0	10.2	10.4	10.7	10.9	11.1	11.4	11.6	11.9
Defense—Military Programs	738.8	713.8	732.7	749.1	765.3	782.4	799.7	817.2	835.2	853.9	873.0	893.1
Education	230.8	434.2	92.1	96.7	102.5	106.9	111.6	115.0	117.5	120.4	122.0	124.2
Energy	35.9	36.9	40.6	39.1	40.3	39.9	41.2	41.4	44.6	45.9	46.8	47.8
Health and Human Services	1,721.4	1,639.3	1,564.9	1,552.6	1,602.8	1,743.1	1,844.9	1,954.2	2,142.0	2,136.6	2,329.7	2,467.6
Homeland Security	114.2	124.3	71.2	72.2	73.9	75.6	78.3	80.0	83.4	85.4	87.2	94.7
Housing and Urban Development	73.8	69.2	60.4	61.4	62.4	63.4	64.6	65.7	66.8	67.9	69.0	70.1
Interior	19.3	21.0	18.8	18.9	19.2	19.4	18.2	18.5	18.9	19.3	19.5	20.2
Justice	37.3	38.7	42.0	40.7	40.5	41.6	42.6	43.6	44.6	45.6	46.6	47.8
Labor	506.6	549.8	99.6	68.2	56.6	56.8	55.0	53.5	60.6	62.5	64.6	67.1
State	31.8	35.4	36.0	36.8	37.5	38.3	39.1	40.0	40.8	41.7	42.5	43.4
Transportation	122.0	157.7	88.2	88.8	89.4	90.0	90.7	91.3	92.0	92.7	93.4	94.2
Treasury	1,635.4	1,309.1	752.0	599.0	646.4	714.8	779.6	855.8	928.1	991.8	1,072.8	1,157.1
Veterans Affairs	233.3	255.6	262.9	269.5	288.4	302.5	317.0	332.5	348.4	364.6	380.9	398.6
Corps of Engineers—Civil Works	7.6	7.8	7.9	8.1	8.3	8.5	8.7	8.9	9.1	9.3	9.5	9.7
Other Defense Civil Programs	65.4	68.4	67.1	69.0	70.8	73.5	78.5	78.6	80.5	83.9	87.2	90.2
Environmental Protection Agency	9.4	9.4	9.5	9.7	9.9	10.2	10.4	10.6	10.9	11.1	11.3	11.6
Executive Office of the President	0.5	0.6	0.4	0.5	0.5	0.5	0.5	0.5	0.5	0.5	0.6	0.6
General Services Administration	−0.8	0.1	0.6	0.3	0.3	0.3	0.3	0.3	0.3	0.4	0.4	0.4
International Assistance Programs	39.9	46.1	41.5	43.6	45.6	47.2	53.3	57.7	58.9	60.1	61.4	61.9
National Aeronautics and Space Administration	22.6	23.3	23.8	24.3	24.8	25.3	25.8	26.4	26.9	27.5	28.1	28.7
National Science Foundation	8.5	9.2	8.8	9.0	9.2	9.3	9.5	9.7	9.9	10.1	10.3	10.5
Office of Personnel Management	107.4	110.8	114.5	119.0	123.7	128.3	133.2	138.2	143.3	148.6	151.5	153.6
Small Business Administration	759.6	208.8	3.0	3.0	3.1	3.1	3.2	3.3	3.3	3.4	3.5	3.5
Social Security Administration	1,157.9	1,202.3	1,269.8	1,336.7	1,406.8	1,491.0	1,576.5	1,666.5	1,767.1	1,855.0	1,961.3	2,065.0
On-Budget	(98.7)	(92.1)	(106.9)	(110.8)	(112.2)	(123.1)	(136.8)	(146.8)	(160.1)	(158.1)	(172.3)	(181.8)
Off-Budget	(1,059.3)	(1,110.1)	(1,163.0)	(1,225.9)	(1,294.6)	(1,367.9)	(1,439.6)	(1,519.6)	(1,606.9)	(1,696.9)	(1,789.0)	(1,883.2)
Other Independent Agencies	32.0	56.4	37.3	39.7	43.2	46.9	49.8	51.7	53.5	54.8	55.6	58.0
On-Budget	(31.7)	(46.2)	(37.0)	(39.4)	(42.9)	(46.6)	(49.6)	(51.4)	(53.2)	(54.5)	(55.3)	(57.8)
Off-Budget	(0.3)	(10.3)	(0.3)	(0.3)	(0.3)	(0.3)	(0.3)	(0.3)	(0.3)	(0.3)	(0.3)	(0.3)
Allowances	....	....	0.3	....	....	....	....	....	....	....	....	....
Undistributed Offsetting Receipts	−241.6	−327.8	−268.4	−241.0	−242.9	−242.8	−238.9	−251.6	−254.3	−249.9	−251.0	−249.3
On-Budget	(−143.6)	(−234.6)	(−181.8)	(−160.4)	(−166.5)	(−169.2)	(−167.7)	(−181.7)	(−186.3)	(−186.1)	(−191.7)	(−195.6)
Off-Budget	(−97.9)	(−93.2)	(−86.6)	(−80.7)	(−76.5)	(−73.5)	(−71.3)	(−70.0)	(−68.0)	(−63.8)	(−59.3)	(−53.7)
Total	**7,735.3**	**7,090.1**	**5,406.5**	**5,304.6**	**5,520.1**	**5,868.8**	**6,186.1**	**6,505.4**	**6,933.9**	**7,149.1**	**7,588.4**	**7,985.4**
On-Budget	(6,773.7)	(6,062.8)	(4,329.8)	(4,159.1)	(4,301.6)	(4,574.1)	(4,817.4)	(5,055.5)	(5,394.7)	(5,515.7)	(5,858.3)	(6,155.6)
Off-Budget	(961.6)	(1,027.2)	(1,076.7)	(1,145.5)	(1,218.5)	(1,294.7)	(1,368.7)	(1,449.9)	(1,539.2)	(1,633.4)	(1,730.0)	(1,829.8)

18. TRUST FUNDS AND FEDERAL FUNDS

As is common for State and local government budgets, the budget for the Federal Government contains information about collections and expenditures for different types of funds. This chapter presents summary information about the transactions of the two major fund groups used by the Federal Government, trust funds and Federal funds. It also presents information about the income and outgo of the major trust funds and certain Federal funds that are financed by dedicated collections in a manner similar to trust funds.

The Federal Funds Group

The Federal funds group includes all financial transactions of the Government that are not required by law to be recorded in trust funds. It accounts for a larger share of the budget than the trust funds group.

The Federal funds group includes the "general fund," which is used for the general purposes of Government rather than being restricted by law to a specific program. The general fund is the largest fund in the Government and it receives all collections not dedicated for some other fund, including virtually all income taxes and many excise taxes. The general fund is used for all programs that are not supported by trust, special, or revolving funds.

The Federal funds group also includes special funds and revolving funds, both of which receive collections that are dedicated by law for specific purposes. Where the law requires that Federal fund collections be dedicated to a particular program, the collections and associated disbursements are recorded in special fund receipt and expenditure accounts.[1] An example is the portion of the Outer Continental Shelf mineral leasing receipts deposited into the Land and Water Conservation Fund. Money in special fund receipt accounts must be appropriated before it can be obligated and spent. The majority of special fund collections are derived from the Government's power to impose taxes or fines, or otherwise compel payment, as in the case of the Crime Victims Fund. In addition, a significant amount of collections credited to special funds is derived from certain types of business-like activity, such as the sale of Government land or other assets or the use of Government property. These collections include receipts from timber sales and royalties from oil and gas extraction.

Revolving funds are used to conduct continuing cycles of business-like activity. Revolving funds receive proceeds from the sale of products or services, and these proceeds finance ongoing activities that continue to provide products or services. Instead of being deposited in receipt accounts, the proceeds are recorded in revolving fund expenditure accounts. The proceeds are generally available for obligation and expenditure without further legislative action. Outlays for programs with revolving funds are reported both gross and net of these proceeds; gross outlays include the expenditures from the proceeds and net program outlays are derived by subtracting the proceeds from gross outlays. Because the proceeds of these sales are recorded as offsets to outlays within expenditure accounts rather than receipt accounts, the proceeds are known as "offsetting collections."[2] There are two classes of revolving funds in the Federal funds group. Public enterprise funds, such as the Postal Service Fund, conduct business-like operations mainly with the public. Intragovernmental funds, such as the Federal Buildings Fund, conduct business-like operations mainly within and between Government agencies.

The Trust Funds Group

The trust funds group consists of funds that are designated by law as trust funds. Like special funds and revolving funds, trust funds receive collections that are dedicated by law for specific purposes. Some of the larger trust funds are used to budget for social insurance programs, such as Social Security, Medicare, and unemployment compensation. Other large trust funds are used to budget for military and Federal civilian employees' retirement benefits, highway and transit construction and maintenance, and airport and airway development and maintenance. There are a few trust revolving funds that are credited with collections earmarked by law to carry out a cycle of business-type operations. There are also a few small trust funds that have been established to carry out the terms of a conditional gift or bequest.

There is no substantive difference between special funds in the Federal funds group and trust funds, or between revolving funds in the Federal funds group and trust revolving funds. Whether a particular fund is designated in law as a trust fund is, in many cases, arbitrary. For example, the National Service Life Insurance Fund is a trust fund, but the Servicemen's Group Life Insurance Fund is a Federal fund, even though both receive dedicated collections from veterans and both provide life insurance payments to veterans' beneficiaries.

The Federal Government uses the term "trust fund" differently than the way in which it is commonly used. In common usage, the term is used to refer to a private fund that has a beneficiary who owns the trust's income and may also own the trust's assets. A custodian or trustee manages

---

[1] There are two types of budget accounts: expenditure (or appropriation) accounts and receipt accounts. Expenditure accounts are used to record outlays and receipt accounts are used to record governmental receipts and offsetting receipts. For further detail on expenditure and receipt accounts, see Chapter 6, "Budget Concepts," in this volume.

[2] See Chapter 9 in this volume for more information on offsetting collections and offsetting receipts.

the assets on behalf of the beneficiary according to the terms of the trust agreement, as established by a trustor. Neither the trustee nor the beneficiary can change the terms of the trust agreement; only the trustor can change the terms of the agreement. In contrast, the Federal Government owns and manages the assets and the earnings of most Federal trust funds, and can unilaterally change the law to raise or lower future trust fund collections and payments or change the purpose for which the collections are used. Only a few small Federal trust funds are managed pursuant to a trust agreement whereby the Government acts as the trustee; even then, the Government generally owns the funds and has some ability to alter the amount deposited into or paid out of the funds.

Deposit funds, which are funds held by the Government as a custodian on behalf of individuals or a non-Federal entity, are similar to private-sector trust funds. The Government makes no decisions about the amount of money placed in deposit funds or about how the proceeds are spent. For this reason, these funds are not classified as Federal trust funds, but are instead considered to be non-budgetary and excluded from the Federal budget.[3]

The income of a Federal Government trust fund must be used for the purposes specified in law. The income of some trust funds, such as the Federal Employees Health Benefits fund, is spent almost as quickly as it is collected. In other cases, such as the military and Federal civilian employees' retirement trust funds, the trust fund income is not spent as quickly as it is collected. Currently, these funds do not use all of their annual income (which includes intragovernmental interest income). This surplus of income over outgo adds to the trust fund's balance, which is available for future expenditures. Trust fund balances are generally required by law to be invested in Federal securities issued by the Department of the Treasury.[4] The National Railroad Retirement Investment Trust is a rare example of a Government trust fund authorized to invest balances in equity markets.

A trust fund normally consists of one or more receipt accounts (to record income) and an expenditure account (to record outgo). However, a few trust funds, such as the Veterans Special Life Insurance fund, are established by law as trust revolving funds. Such a fund is similar to a revolving fund in the Federal funds group in that it may consist of a single account to record both income and outgo. Trust revolving funds are used to conduct cycle of business-type operations; offsetting collections are credited to the funds (which are also expenditure accounts) and the funds' outlays are displayed net of the offsetting collections.

Income and Outgo by Fund Group

Table 18–1 shows income, outgo, and the surplus or deficit by fund group and in the aggregate (netted to avoid double-counting) from which the total unified budget re-

ceipts, outlays, and surplus or deficit are derived. Income consists mostly of governmental receipts (derived from governmental activity, primarily income, payroll, and excise taxes). Income also includes offsetting receipts, which include proprietary receipts (derived from business-like transactions with the public), interfund collections (derived from payments from a fund in one fund group to a fund in the other fund group), and gifts. Outgo consists of payments made to the public or to a fund in the other fund group.

Two types of transactions are treated specially in the table. First, income and outgo for each fund group exclude all transactions that occur between funds within the same fund group.[5] These intrafund transactions constitute outgo and income for the individual funds that make and collect the payments, but they are offsetting within the fund group as a whole. The totals for each fund group measure only the group's transactions with the public and the other fund group. Second, outgo is calculated net of the collections from Federal sources that are credited to expenditure accounts (which, as noted above, are referred to as offsetting collections); the spending that is financed by those collections is included in outgo and the collections from Federal sources are subsequently subtracted from outgo.[6] Although it would be conceptually correct to add interfund offsetting collections from Federal sources to income for a particular fund, this cannot be done at the present time because the budget data do not provide this type of detail. As a result, both interfund and intrafund offsetting collections from Federal sources are offset against outgo in Table 18–1 and are not shown separately.

The vast majority of the interfund transactions in the table are payments by the Federal funds to the trust funds. These payments include interest payments from the general fund to the trust funds for interest earned on trust fund balances invested in interest-bearing Treasury securities. The payments also include payments by Federal agencies to Federal employee benefits trust funds and Social Security trust funds on behalf of current employees and general fund transfers to employee retirement trust funds to amortize the unfunded liabilities of these funds. In addition, the payments include general fund transfers to the Supplementary Medical Insurance trust fund for the cost of Medicare Parts B (outpatient and physician benefits) and D (prescription drug benefits) that is not covered by premiums or other income from the public.

In addition to investing their balances with the Treasury, some funds in the Federal funds group and

[3] Deposit funds are also discussed in Chapter 7 of this volume, "Coverage of the Budget."

[4] Securities held by trust funds (and by other Government accounts), debt held by the public, and gross Federal debt are discussed in Chapter 4 of this volume, "Federal Borrowing and Debt."

[5] For example, the railroad retirement trust funds pay the equivalent of Social Security benefits to railroad retirees in addition to the regular railroad pension. These benefits are financed by a payment from the Federal Old-Age and Survivors Insurance trust fund to the railroad retirement trust funds. The payment and collection are not included in Table 18–1 so that the total trust fund income and outgo shown in the table reflect transactions with the public and with Federal funds.

[6] Collections from non-Federal sources are shown as income and spending that is financed by those collections is shown as outgo. For example, postage stamp fees are deposited as offsetting collections in the Postal Service Fund. As a result, the Fund's income reported in Table 18–1 includes postage stamp fees and the Fund's outgo is gross disbursements, including disbursements financed by those fees.

Table 18–1.   RECEIPTS, OUTLAYS AND SURPLUS OR DEFICIT BY FUND GROUP

(In billions of dollars)

	2020 Actual	Estimate					
		2021	2022	2023	2024	2025	2026
Receipts:							
Federal funds cash income:							
From the public	2,428.0	2,698.5	2,989.8	3,395.5	3,524.2	3,692.7	3,915.1
From trust funds	1.2	2.0	1.9	1.7	1.6	1.6	1.5
Total, Federal funds cash income	2,429.1	2,700.5	2,991.7	3,397.3	3,525.9	3,694.3	3,916.6
Trust funds cash income:							
From the public	1,618.5	1,591.8	1,774.5	1,857.7	1,940.5	2,012.4	2,091.0
From Federal funds:							
Interest	135.2	124.2	124.6	119.8	118.6	115.3	108.3
Other	758.7	1,022.4	774.7	817.0	864.2	915.3	980.3
Total, Trust funds cash income	2,512.4	2,738.4	2,673.7	2,794.6	2,923.3	3,043.0	3,179.6
Offsetting collections from the public and offsetting receipts:							
Federal funds	−378.4	−473.7	−347.0	−353.1	−361.7	−376.2	−370.3
Trust funds	−1,142.0	−1,384.4	−1,144.2	−1,197.7	−1,259.7	−1,323.2	−1,393.8
Total, offsetting collections from the public and offsetting receipts	−1,520.4	−1,858.1	−1,491.3	−1,550.8	−1,621.4	−1,699.4	−1,764.1
Unified budget receipts:							
Federal funds	2,050.7	2,226.8	2,644.7	3,044.1	3,164.2	3,318.0	3,546.3
Trust funds	1,370.4	1,354.0	1,529.5	1,596.9	1,663.6	1,719.9	1,785.8
Total, unified budget receipts	3,421.2	3,580.8	4,174.2	4,641.0	4,827.8	5,037.9	5,332.1
Outlays:							
Federal funds cash outgo	5,505.5	6,483.8	4,975.0	4,901.5	5,053.7	5,235.7	5,362.4
Trust funds cash outgo	2,565.3	2,623.8	2,527.4	2,662.3	2,754.5	2,971.5	3,147.9
Offsetting collections from the public and offsetting receipts:							
Federal funds	−378.4	−473.7	−347.0	−353.1	−361.7	−376.2	−370.3
Trust funds	−1,142.0	−1,384.4	−1,144.2	−1,197.7	−1,259.7	−1,323.2	−1,393.8
Total, offsetting collections from the public and offsetting receipts	−1,520.4	−1,858.1	−1,491.3	−1,550.8	−1,621.4	−1,699.4	−1,764.1
Unified budget outlays:							
Federal funds	5,127.1	6,010.1	4,627.9	4,548.4	4,692.0	4,859.4	4,992.2
Trust funds	1,423.3	1,239.3	1,383.2	1,464.6	1,494.8	1,648.3	1,754.1
Total, unified budget outlays	6,550.4	7,249.5	6,011.1	6,013.0	6,186.8	6,507.7	6,746.3
Surplus or deficit(−):							
Federal funds	−3,076.4	−3,783.4	−1,983.2	−1,504.2	−1,527.9	−1,541.4	−1,445.8
Trust funds	−52.8	114.7	146.3	132.3	168.9	71.6	31.7
Total, unified surplus/deficit(−)	−3,129.2	−3,668.7	−1,837.0	−1,371.9	−1,359.0	−1,469.8	−1,414.2

Note: Receipts include governmental, interfund, and proprietary, and exclude intrafund receipts (which are offset against intrafund payments so that cash income and cash outgo are not overstated).

most trust funds are authorized to borrow from the general fund of the Treasury.[7] Similar to the treatment of funds invested with the Treasury, borrowed funds are not recorded as receipts of the fund or included in the income of the fund. Rather, the borrowed funds finance outlays by the fund in excess of available receipts. Subsequently, any excess fund receipts are transferred from the fund to the general fund in repayment of the borrowing. The repayment is not recorded as an outlay of the fund or included in fund outgo. This treatment is consistent with the broad principle that borrowing and debt redemption are not budgetary transactions but rather a means of financing deficits or disposing of surpluses.[8]

Some income in both Federal funds and trust funds consists of offsetting receipts.[9] Offsetting receipts are not considered governmental receipts (such as taxes), but they are instead recorded on the outlay side of the budget.[10] Expenditures resulting from offsetting receipts are recorded as gross outlays and the collections of offsetting receipts are then subtracted from gross outlays to derive

---

[7] For example, the Unemployment Trust Fund is authorized to borrow from the general fund for unemployment benefits; the Bonneville Power Administration Fund, a revolving fund in the Department of Energy, is authorized to borrow from the general fund; and the Black Lung Disability Trust Fund, a trust fund in the Department of Labor, is authorized to receive appropriations of repayable advances from the general fund, which constitute a form of borrowing.

[8] Borrowing and debt repayment are discussed in Chapter 4 of this volume, "Federal Borrowing and Debt," and Chapter 6 of this volume, "Budget Concepts."

[9] Interest on borrowed funds is an example of an intragovernmental offsetting receipt and Medicare Part B's premiums are an example of offsetting receipts from the public.

[10] For further discussion of offsetting receipts, see Chapter 9 of this volume, "Offsetting Collections and Offsetting Receipts."

Table 18–2. COMPARISON OF TOTAL FEDERAL FUND AND TRUST FUND RECEIPTS TO UNIFIED BUDGET RECEIPTS, FISCAL YEAR 2020

(In billions of dollars)

Gross Federal fund and Trust fund cash income:	
Federal funds	2,787.1
Trust funds	2,573.5
Total, gross Federal fund and Trust fund cash income	5,360.6
Deduct: intrabudgetary offsetting collections (from funds within same fund group):	
Federal funds	−327.8
Trust funds	−53.8
Subtotal, intrabudgetary offsetting collections	−381.6
Deduct: intrafund receipts (from funds within same fund group):	
Federal funds	−30.2
Trust funds	−7.3
Subtotal, intrafund receipts	−37.5
Federal fund and Trust fund cash income net of intrabudgetary offsetting collections and intrafund receipts:	
Federal funds	2,429.1
Trust funds	2,512.4
Total, Federal fund and Trust fund cash income net of intrafund receipts	4,941.6
Deduct: offsetting collections from the public:	
Federal funds	−246.2
Trust funds	−61.4
Subtotal, offsetting collections from the public	−307.5
Deduct other offsetting receipts:	
Federal fund receipts from Trust funds	−1.2
Trust fund receipts from Federal funds:	
Interest in receipt accounts	−135.2
General fund payments to Medicare Parts B and D	−359.5
Employing agencies' payments for pensions, Social Security, and Medicare	−91.9
General fund payments for unfunded liabilities of Federal employees' retirement funds	−138.7
Transfer of taxation of Social Security and RRB benefits to OASDI, HI, and RRB	−67.2
Other receipts from Federal funds	−101.4
Subtotal, Trust fund receipts from Federal funds	−893.9
Proprietary receipts:	
Federal funds	−116.6
Trust funds	−186.7
Subtotal, proprietary receipts	−303.4
Offsetting governmental receipts:	
Federal funds	−14.4
Trust funds	−*
Subtotal, offsetting governmental receipts	−14.5
Subtotal, other offsetting receipts	−1,212.9
Unified budget receipts:	
Federal funds	2,050.7
Trust funds	1,370.4
Total, unified budget receipts	3,421.2
Memoradum:	
Gross receipts:[1]	
Federal funds	2,213.2
Trust funds	2,458.4
Total, gross receipts	4,671.5

* $50 million or less.

[1] Gross income excluding offsetting collections.

net outlays. Net outlays reflect the Government's net transactions with the public.

As shown in Table 18–1, 40 percent of all governmental receipts were deposited in trust funds in 2020 and the remaining 60 percent of governmental receipts were deposited in Federal funds, which, as noted above, include the general fund. As noted above, most outlays between the trust fund and Federal fund groups (interfund outlays) flow from Federal funds to trust funds, rather than from trust funds to Federal funds. As a result, while trust funds accounted for 22 percent of total 2020 outlays, they accounted for 25 percent of 2020 outlays net of interfund transactions.

Because the income for Federal funds and trust funds recorded in Table 18–1 includes offsetting receipts and offsetting collections from the public, offsetting receipts and offsetting collections from the public must be deducted from the two fund groups' combined gross income in order to reconcile to total governmental receipts in the unified budget. Similarly, because the outgo for Federal funds and trust funds in Table 18–1 consists of outlays gross of offsetting receipts and offsetting collections from the public, the amount of the offsetting receipts and offsetting collections from the public must be deducted from the sum of the Federal funds' and the trust funds' gross outgo in order to reconcile to total (net) unified budget outlays. Table 18–2 reconciles, for fiscal year 2020, the gross total of all trust fund and Federal fund receipts with the receipt total of the unified budget.

Income, Outgo, and Balances of Trust Funds

Table 18–3 shows, for the trust funds group as a whole, the funds' balance at the start of each year, income and outgo during the year, and the end-of-year balance. Income and outgo are divided between transactions with the public and transactions with Federal funds. Receipts from Federal funds are divided between interest and other interfund receipts.

The definitions of income and outgo in this table differ from those in Table 18–1 in one important way. Trust fund collections that are offset against outgo (offsetting collections from Federal sources) within expenditure accounts instead of being deposited in separate receipt accounts are classified as income in this table, but not in Table 18–1. This classification is consistent with the definitions of income and outgo for trust funds used elsewhere in the budget. It has the effect of increasing both income and outgo by the amount of the offsetting collections from Federal sources. The difference was approximately $54 billion in 2020. Table 18–3, therefore, provides a more complete summary of trust fund income and outgo.

In 2020, the trust funds group ran a deficit of $53 billion. This was the first time in several decades that the trust fund group ran a deficit rather than a surplus. The net deficit was largely the result of the impacts of the Coronavirus pandemic and the Government's response to the pandemic on the Unemployment Insurance and Medicare trust funds. The trust fund group is expected to run a $115 billion surplus in 2021 and to continue to run surpluses over the next several years. The resulting

Table 18–3. INCOME, OUTGO, AND BALANCES OF TRUST FUNDS GROUP

(In billions of dollars)

	2020 Actual	Estimate					
		2021	2022	2023	2024	2025	2026
Balance, start of year	5,300.1	5,247.4	5,362.3	5,508.9	5,641.2	5,810.1	5,881.7
Adjustments to balances	*	....	....	....	....	....	....
Total balance, start of year	5,300.1	5,247.4	5,362.3	5,508.9	5,641.2	5,810.1	5,881.7
Income:							
Governmental receipts	1,370.4	1,354.0	1,529.5	1,596.9	1,663.6	1,719.9	1,785.8
Offsetting governmental	0.1	4.5	*	*	*	*	*
Proprietary	246.6	230.1	244.0	260.0	276.1	291.8	304.5
From Federal funds:							
Interest	137.6	128.6	126.4	121.6	120.2	117.0	110.1
Other	811.5	1,081.1	832.5	877.4	927.3	981.0	1,048.9
Total income during the year	2,566.3	2,798.4	2,732.5	2,855.8	2,987.2	3,109.6	3,249.3
Outgo (–)	–2,619.1	–2,683.7	–2,586.2	–2,723.5	–2,818.4	–3,038.0	–3,217.7
Change in fund balance:							
Surplus or deficit(–):							
Excluding interest	–190.5	–14.0	19.9	10.7	48.7	–45.4	–78.5
Interest	137.6	128.6	126.4	121.6	120.2	117.0	110.1
Subtotal, surplus or deficit (–)	–52.8	114.7	146.3	132.3	168.9	71.6	31.7
Borrowing, transfers, lapses, & other adjustments	0.1	0.2	0.3	....	....	....	....
Total change in fund balance	–52.7	114.9	146.6	132.3	168.9	71.6	31.7
Balance, end of year	5,247.4	5,362.3	5,508.9	5,641.2	5,810.1	5,881.7	5,913.3

* $50 million or less.

Note: In contrast to Table 18–1, income also includes income that is offset within expenditure accounts as offsetting collections from Federal sources, instead of being deposited in receipt accounts.

projected growth in trust fund balances in 2021 through 2026 continues a trend that has persisted over the past several decades.

The size of the trust fund balances is largely the consequence of the way some trust funds are financed. Some of the larger trust funds (primarily Social Security and the Federal retirement funds) are fully or partially advance funded, with collections on behalf of individual participants received by the funds years earlier than when the associated benefits are paid. For example, under the Federal military and civilian retirement programs, Federal agencies and employees together are required to pay the retirement trust funds an amount equal to accruing retirement benefits. Since many years pass between the time when benefits are accrued and when they are paid, the trust funds accumulate substantial balances over time. [11]

Due to advance funding and economic growth (both real and nominal), trust fund balances increased from $205 billion in 1982 to $5.2 trillion in 2020. Based on the estimates in the 2022 Budget, which include the ef-

fect of the Budget's proposals, the balances are estimated to increase by approximately 13 percent by the year 2026, rising to $5.9 trillion. Almost all of these balances are invested in Treasury securities and earn interest.

From the perspective of the trust fund, these balances are assets that represent the value, in today's dollars, of past taxes, fees, and other income from the public and from other Government accounts that the trust fund has received in excess of past spending. Trust fund assets held in Treasury securities are legal claims on the Treasury, similar to Treasury securities issued to the public. Like all other fund assets, these are available to the fund for future benefit payments and other expenditures. From the perspective of the Government as a whole, however, the trust fund balances do not represent net additions to the Government's balance sheet. The trust fund balances are assets of the agencies responsible for administering the trust fund programs and liabilities of the Department of the Treasury. These assets and liabilities cancel each other out in the Government-wide balance sheet. The effects of Treasury debt held by trust funds and other Government accounts are discussed further in Chapter 4 of this volume, "Federal Borrowing and Debt."

Table 18–4 shows estimates of income, outgo, surplus or deficit, and balances for 2020 through 2026 for the major trust funds. With the exception of transactions between trust funds, the data for the individual trust funds are conceptually the same as the data in Table 18–3 for the trust funds group. As explained previously, transactions between trust funds are shown as outgo of the fund

---

[11] Until the 1980s, most trust funds operated on a pay-as-you-go basis as distinct from a pre-funded basis. Taxes and fees were set at levels sufficient to finance current program expenditures and administrative expenses, and to maintain balances generally equal to one year's worth of expenditures (to provide for unexpected events). As a result, trust fund balances tended to grow at about the same rate as the funds' annual expenditures. In the 1980s, pay-as-you-go financing was replaced by full or partial advance funding for some of the larger trust funds. The Social Security Amendments of 1983 (P.L. 98-21) raised payroll taxes above the levels necessary to finance then-current expenditures. Legislation enacted in the mid-1980s established the requirement for full accrual basis funding of Federal military and civilian retirement benefits.

that makes the payment and as income of the fund that collects it in the data for an individual trust fund, but the collections are offset against outgo in the data for the trust fund group as a whole.

As noted above, trust funds are funded by a combination of payments from the public and payments from Federal funds, including payments directly from the general fund and payments from agency appropriations. Similarly, the fund outgo amounts in Table 18–4 represent both outflows to the public—such as for the provision of benefit payments or the purchase of goods or services— and outflows to other Government accounts—such as for reimbursement for services provided by other agencies or payment of interest on borrowing from Treasury.

Because trust funds and Federal special and revolving funds conduct transactions both with the public and with other Government accounts, the surplus or deficit of an individual fund may differ from the fund's impact on the surplus or deficit of the Federal Government. Transactions with the public affect both the surplus or deficit of an individual fund and the Federal Government surplus or deficit. Transactions with other Government accounts affect the surplus or deficit of the particular fund. However, because that same transaction is offset in another Government account, there is no net impact on the total Federal Government surplus or deficit.

A brief description of the major trust funds is given below; additional information for these and other trust funds can be found in the Status of Funds tables in the Budget *Appendix*.

- Social Security Trust Funds: The Social Security trust funds consist of the Old Age and Survivors Insurance (OASI) trust fund and the Disability Insurance (DI) trust fund. The trust funds are funded by payroll taxes from employers and employees, interest earnings on trust fund balances, Federal agency payments as employers, and a portion of the income taxes paid on Social Security benefits.

- Medicare Trust Funds: Like the Social Security trust funds, the Medicare Hospital Insurance (HI) trust fund is funded by payroll taxes from employers and employees, Federal agency payments as employers, and a portion of the income taxes paid on Social Security benefits. The HI trust fund also receives transfers from the general fund of the Treasury for certain HI benefits and premiums from certain voluntary participants. The other Medicare trust fund, Supplementary Medical Insurance (SMI), finances Part B (outpatient and physician benefits) and Part

D (prescription drug benefits). SMI receives premium payments from covered individuals, transfers from States toward Part D benefits, excise taxes on manufacturers and importers of brand-name prescription drugs, and transfers from the general fund of the Treasury for the portion of Part B and Part D costs not covered by premiums or transfers from States. In addition, like other trust funds, these two trust funds receive interest earnings on their trust fund balances.

- Highway Trust Fund: The fund finances Federal highway and transit infrastructure projects, as well as highway and vehicle safety activities. The Highway Trust Fund is financed by Federal motor fuel taxes and associated fees, and, in recent years, by general fund transfers, as those taxes and fees have been inadequate to support current levels of spending.

- Unemployment Trust Fund: The Unemployment Trust Fund is funded by Federal and State taxes on employers, payments from Federal agencies, taxes on certain employees, and interest earnings on trust fund balances. Unemployment insurance is administered largely by the States, following Federal guidelines. The Unemployment Trust Fund is composed of individual accounts for each State and several Federal accounts, including accounts related to the separate unemployment insurance program for railroad employees.

- Civilian and military retirement trust funds: The Civil Service Retirement and Disability Fund is funded by employee and agency payments, general fund transfers for the unfunded portion of retirement costs, and interest earnings on trust fund balances. The Military Retirement Fund likewise is funded by payments from the Department of Defense, general fund transfers for unfunded retirement costs, and interest earnings on trust fund balances.

Table 18–5 shows income, outgo, and balances of two Federal funds that are designated as special funds. These funds are similar to trust funds in that they are financed by dedicated receipts, the excess of income over outgo is invested in Treasury securities, the interest earnings add to fund balances, and the balances remain available to cover future expenditures. The table is illustrative of the Federal funds group, which includes many revolving funds and special funds.

Table 18–4. INCOME, OUTGO, AND BALANCES OF MAJOR TRUST FUNDS

(In billions of dollars)

	2020 Actual	Estimate					
		2021	2022	2023	2024	2025	2026
Airport and Airway Trust Fund							
Balance, start of year	17.9	9.0	15.3	14.5	14.8	16.1	18.3
Adjustments to balances	−1.4	....	....	....	....	....	....
Total balance, start of year	16.5	9.0	15.3	14.5	14.8	16.1	18.3
Income:							
Governmental receipts	9.0	9.3	15.3	17.8	18.7	19.6	20.3
Offsetting governmental	....	....	....	....	....	....	....
Proprietary	0.1	0.1	0.1	0.1	0.1	0.1	0.1
Intrabudgetary:							
Intrafund	....	....	....	....	....	....	....
Interest	0.4	0.2	0.2	0.2	0.2	0.3	0.3
Other intrabudgetary	0.1	14.0	*	*	*	0.1	0.1
Total income during the year	9.5	23.7	15.6	18.1	19.0	20.0	20.8
Outgo (−)	−17.1	−17.3	−16.5	−17.8	−17.7	−17.8	−17.0
Change in fund balance:							
Surplus or deficit(−):							
Excluding interest	−7.9	6.1	−1.1	0.2	1.1	1.9	3.4
Interest	0.4	0.2	0.2	0.2	0.2	0.3	0.3
Subtotal, surplus or deficit (−)	−7.5	6.3	−0.9	0.3	1.3	2.2	3.7
Borrowing, transfers, lapses, & other adjustments	*	....	....	....	....	....	....
Total change in fund balance	−7.5	6.3	−0.9	0.3	1.3	2.2	3.7
Balance, end of year	9.0	15.3	14.5	14.8	16.1	18.3	22.1
Civil Service Retirement and Disability Fund							
Balance, start of year	939.7	962.1	982.7	1,002.1	1,014.6	1,025.0	1,033.5
Adjustments to balances	....	....	....	....	....	....	....
Total balance, start of year	939.7	962.1	982.7	1,002.1	1,014.6	1,025.0	1,033.5
Income:							
Governmental receipts	5.1	5.7	6.1	6.5	6.9	7.4	7.8
Offsetting governmental	....	....	....	....	....	....	....
Proprietary	....	....	....	....	....	....	....
Intrabudgetary:							
Intrafund	....	....	....	....	....	....	....
Interest	25.1	21.8	19.7	18.7	18.2	18.1	18.2
Other intrabudgetary	83.3	86.6	90.4	87.4	88.7	90.0	91.5
Total income during the year	113.5	114.1	116.2	112.6	113.8	115.4	117.6
Outgo (−)	−91.2	−93.5	−96.8	−100.1	−103.5	−106.9	−110.4
Change in fund balance:							
Surplus or deficit(−):							
Excluding interest	−2.7	−1.3	−0.3	−6.2	−7.8	−9.5	−11.0
Interest	25.1	21.8	19.7	18.7	18.2	18.1	18.2
Subtotal, surplus or deficit (−)	22.4	20.6	19.5	12.5	10.4	8.6	7.2
Borrowing, transfers, lapses, & other adjustments	....	....	....	....	....	....	....
Total change in fund balance	22.4	20.6	19.5	12.5	10.4	8.6	7.2
Balance, end of year	962.1	982.7	1,002.1	1,014.6	1,025.0	1,033.5	1,040.7
Employees and Retired Employees Health Benefits Funds							
Balance, start of year	27.5	28.1	29.6	30.9	32.1	33.0	34.3
Adjustments to balances	....	....	....	....	....	....	....
Total balance, start of year	27.5	28.1	29.6	30.9	32.1	33.0	34.3
Income:							
Governmental receipts	....	....	....	....	....	....	....

Table 18–4.   INCOME, OUTGO, AND BALANCES OF MAJOR TRUST FUNDS—Continued
(In billions of dollars)

	2020 Actual	Estimate					
		2021	2022	2023	2024	2025	2026
Offsetting governmental	....	....	....	....	....	....	....
Proprietary	17.1	17.8	18.6	19.4	20.5	21.5	22.6
Intrabudgetary:							
Intrafund	....	....	....	....	....	....	....
Interest	0.4	0.4	0.3	0.3	0.3	0.3	0.4
Other intrabudgetary	39.2	39.8	41.6	43.7	46.0	48.5	51.0
Total income during the year	56.7	58.1	60.4	63.5	66.8	70.4	74.1
Outgo (–)	–56.1	–56.6	–59.1	–62.3	–65.8	–69.1	–72.9
Change in fund balance:							
Surplus or deficit(–):							
Excluding interest	0.2	1.1	1.0	0.9	0.7	0.9	0.7
Interest	0.4	0.4	0.3	0.3	0.3	0.3	0.4
Subtotal, surplus or deficit (–)	0.6	1.5	1.3	1.2	1.0	1.3	1.2
Borrowing, transfers, lapses, & other adjustments	....	....	....	....	....	....	....
Total change in fund balance	0.6	1.5	1.3	1.2	1.0	1.3	1.2
Balance, end of year	28.1	29.6	30.9	32.1	33.0	34.3	35.5
Employees Life Insurance Fund							
Balance, start of year	47.7	48.7	50.0	51.1	52.2	53.3	54.4
Adjustments to balances	....	....	....	....	....	....	....
Total balance, start of year	47.7	48.7	50.0	51.1	52.2	53.3	54.4
Income:							
Governmental receipts	....	....	....	....	....	....	....
Offsetting governmental	....	....	....	....	....	....	....
Proprietary	3.1	3.3	3.4	3.5	3.6	3.7	3.8
Intrabudgetary:							
Intrafund	....	....	....	....	....	....	....
Interest	0.6	0.7	0.6	0.5	0.4	0.5	0.6
Other intrabudgetary	0.6	0.6	0.6	0.6	0.7	0.7	0.7
Total income during the year	4.3	4.6	4.6	4.6	4.7	4.8	5.1
Outgo (–)	–3.3	–3.4	–3.5	–3.5	–3.6	–3.7	–3.8
Change in fund balance:							
Surplus or deficit(–):							
Excluding interest	0.4	0.6	0.5	0.6	0.6	0.7	0.7
Interest	0.6	0.7	0.6	0.5	0.4	0.5	0.6
Subtotal, surplus or deficit (–)	1.0	1.3	1.1	1.1	1.1	1.1	1.3
Borrowing, transfers, lapses, & other adjustments	*	....	....	....	....	....	....
Total change in fund balance	1.0	1.3	1.1	1.1	1.1	1.1	1.3
Balance, end of year	48.7	50.0	51.1	52.2	53.3	54.4	55.7
Foreign Military Sales Trust Fund							
Balance, start of year	32.5	34.9	34.8	39.4	42.2	44.3	47.0
Adjustments to balances	....	....	....	....	....	....	....
Total balance, start of year	32.5	34.9	34.8	39.4	42.2	44.3	47.0
Income:							
Governmental receipts	....	....	....	....	....	....	....
Offsetting governmental	....	....	....	....	....	....	....
Proprietary	78.5	54.1	51.5	49.9	49.2	48.9	44.1
Intrabudgetary:							
Intrafund	....	....	....	....	....	....	....
Interest	....	....	....	....	....	....	....
Other intrabudgetary	....	....	....	....	....	....	....
Total income during the year	78.5	54.1	51.5	49.9	49.2	48.9	44.1

Table 18–4.   INCOME, OUTGO, AND BALANCES OF MAJOR TRUST FUNDS—Continued

(In billions of dollars)

	2020 Actual	Estimate					
		2021	2022	2023	2024	2025	2026
Outgo (–)	–76.2	–54.2	–46.8	–47.1	–47.0	–46.2	–42.4
Change in fund balance:							
Surplus or deficit(–):							
Excluding interest	2.3	–0.1	4.6	2.8	2.1	2.7	1.7
Interest	....	....	....	....	....	....	....
Subtotal, surplus or deficit (–)	2.3	–0.1	4.6	2.8	2.1	2.7	1.7
Borrowing, transfers, lapses, & other adjustments	*	....	....	....	....	....	....
Total change in fund balance	2.3	–0.1	4.6	2.8	2.1	2.7	1.7
Balance, end of year	34.9	34.8	39.4	42.2	44.3	47.0	48.8
Foreign Service Retirement and Disability Fund							
Balance, start of year	19.3	20.0	20.4	20.7	21.1	21.5	21.8
Adjustments to balances	....	....	....	....	....	....	....
Total balance, start of year	19.3	20.0	20.4	20.7	21.1	21.5	21.8
Income:							
Governmental receipts	*	*	*	*	*	*	*
Offsetting governmental	....	....	....	....	....	....	....
Proprietary	....	....	....	....	....	....	....
Intrabudgetary:							
Intrafund	*	*	*	*	*	*	*
Interest	0.5	0.5	0.6	0.6	0.6	0.6	0.6
Other intrabudgetary	1.1	0.8	0.8	0.9	0.9	0.9	0.9
Total income during the year	1.7	1.4	1.4	1.5	1.5	1.5	1.5
Outgo (–)	–1.0	–1.0	–1.1	–1.1	–1.1	–1.1	–1.2
Change in fund balance:							
Surplus or deficit(–):							
Excluding interest	0.1	–0.2	–0.2	–0.2	–0.2	–0.2	–0.3
Interest	0.5	0.5	0.6	0.6	0.6	0.6	0.6
Subtotal, surplus or deficit (–)	0.7	0.4	0.4	0.4	0.4	0.4	0.4
Borrowing, transfers, lapses, & other adjustments	*	....	....	....	....	....	....
Total change in fund balance	0.7	0.4	0.4	0.4	0.4	0.4	0.4
Balance, end of year	20.0	20.4	20.7	21.1	21.5	21.8	22.2
Highway Trust Fund							
Balance, start of year	32.9	17.8	12.7	–4.9	–23.8	–43.2	–62.7
Adjustments to balances	–*	....	....	....	....	....	....
Total balance, start of year	32.9	17.8	12.7	–4.9	–23.8	–43.2	–62.7
Income:							
Governmental receipts	42.8	39.8	40.9	41.3	41.4	41.7	41.7
Offsetting governmental	....	....	....	....	....	....	....
Proprietary	0.1	....	....	....	....	....	....
Intrabudgetary:							
Intrafund	....	....	....	....	....	....	....
Interest	0.2	*	*	*	*	*	*
Other intrabudgetary	0.1	14.6	1.0	1.0	1.0	1.0	1.0
Total income during the year	43.2	54.4	41.9	42.2	42.4	42.7	42.8
Outgo (–)	–58.5	–59.5	–59.5	–61.2	–61.8	–62.2	–62.6
Change in fund balance:							
Surplus or deficit(–):							
Excluding interest	–15.5	–5.1	–17.7	–18.9	–19.4	–19.5	–19.8
Interest	0.2	*	*	*	*	*	*
Subtotal, surplus or deficit (–)	–15.3	–5.1	–17.6	–18.9	–19.4	–19.5	–19.8
Borrowing, transfers, lapses, & other adjustments	0.2	....	–*	....	....	....	....

Table 18–4.   INCOME, OUTGO, AND BALANCES OF MAJOR TRUST FUNDS—Continued

(In billions of dollars)

	2020 Actual	Estimate					
		2021	2022	2023	2024	2025	2026
Total change in fund balance	−15.1	−5.1	−17.6	−18.9	−19.4	−19.5	−19.8
Balance, end of year	17.8	12.7	−4.9	−23.8	−43.2	−62.7	−82.5
Medicare: Hospital Insurance (HI) Trust Fund							
Balance, start of year	198.9	134.4	113.5	160.7	183.3	221.2	240.1
Adjustments to balances	....	....	....	....	....	....	....
Total balance, start of year	198.9	134.4	113.5	160.7	183.3	221.2	240.1
Income:							
Governmental receipts	292.6	287.8	359.3	383.2	400.6	418.8	436.5
Offsetting governmental	....	....	....	....	....	....	....
Proprietary	13.5	12.2	12.6	12.9	13.2	13.6	14.0
Intrabudgetary:							
Intrafund	....	....	....	....	....	....	....
Interest	5.3	2.4	2.4	2.4	1.9	1.1	0.1
Other intrabudgetary	33.8	33.5	36.7	39.3	42.2	45.5	52.6
Total income during the year	345.3	335.9	411.0	437.8	458.0	479.1	503.3
Outgo (−)	−409.8	−356.8	−363.8	−415.2	−420.1	−460.2	−487.8
Change in fund balance:							
Surplus or deficit(−):							
Excluding interest	−69.9	−23.2	44.8	20.2	36.0	17.7	15.3
Interest	5.3	2.4	2.4	2.4	1.9	1.1	0.1
Subtotal, surplus or deficit (−)	−64.5	−20.9	47.2	22.6	37.9	18.8	15.5
Borrowing, transfers, lapses, & other adjustments	....	....	....	....	....	....	....
Total change in fund balance	−64.5	−20.9	47.2	22.6	37.9	18.8	15.5
Balance, end of year	134.4	113.5	160.7	183.3	221.2	240.1	255.5
Medicare: Supplementary Insurance (SMI) Trust Fund							
Balance, start of year	104.1	88.9	179.3	187.3	207.9	271.7	303.4
Adjustments to balances	....	....	....	....	....	....	....
Total balance, start of year	104.1	88.9	179.3	187.3	207.9	271.7	303.4
Income:							
Governmental receipts	3.2	2.7	2.8	1.6	4.0	2.8	2.8
Offsetting governmental	....	....	....	....	....	....	....
Proprietary	129.7	137.3	153.2	169.3	184.8	199.3	215.1
Intrabudgetary:							
Intrafund	....	....	....	....	....	....	....
Interest	2.2	2.4	5.0	5.4	6.0	5.2	5.3
Other intrabudgetary	359.5	461.1	423.2	459.8	495.5	532.6	572.2
Total income during the year	494.5	603.5	584.1	636.1	690.4	739.8	795.4
Outgo (−)	−509.7	−513.1	−576.1	−615.6	−626.5	−708.1	−764.3
Change in fund balance:							
Surplus or deficit(−):							
Excluding interest	−17.4	88.0	3.0	15.1	57.8	26.6	25.9
Interest	2.2	2.4	5.0	5.4	6.0	5.2	5.3
Subtotal, surplus or deficit (−)	−15.1	90.4	8.0	20.6	63.8	31.7	31.1
Borrowing, transfers, lapses, & other adjustments	*	....	....	....	....	....	....
Total change in fund balance	−15.1	90.4	8.0	20.6	63.8	31.7	31.1
Balance, end of year	88.9	179.3	187.3	207.9	271.7	303.4	334.5
Military Retirement Fund							
Balance, start of year	818.5	898.1	989.6	1,091.1	1,200.8	1,320.5	1,439.3
Adjustments to balances	....	....	....	....	....	....	....
Total balance, start of year	818.5	898.1	989.6	1,091.1	1,200.8	1,320.5	1,439.3

Table 18–4. INCOME, OUTGO, AND BALANCES OF MAJOR TRUST FUNDS—Continued

(In billions of dollars)

	2020 Actual	Estimate					
		2021	2022	2023	2024	2025	2026
Income:							
Governmental receipts	....	....	....	....	....	....	....
Offsetting governmental	....	....	....	....	....	....	....
Proprietary	....	....	....	....	....	....	....
Intrabudgetary:							
Intrafund	....	....	....	....	....	....	....
Interest	19.7	21.8	29.4	31.6	35.3	37.3	33.6
Other intrabudgetary	122.2	133.3	142.5	145.1	147.9	152.0	156.3
Total income during the year	141.9	155.1	171.9	176.7	183.1	189.3	189.8
Outgo (–)	–62.3	–63.6	–70.4	–66.9	–63.5	–70.4	–72.2
Change in fund balance:							
Surplus or deficit(–):							
Excluding interest	59.9	69.7	72.1	78.1	84.4	81.6	84.0
Interest	19.7	21.8	29.4	31.6	35.3	37.3	33.6
Subtotal, surplus or deficit (–)	79.6	91.5	101.5	109.8	119.6	118.9	117.6
Borrowing, transfers, lapses, & other adjustments	....	....	....	....	....	....	....
Total change in fund balance	79.6	91.5	101.5	109.8	119.6	118.9	117.6
Balance, end of year	898.1	989.6	1,091.1	1,200.8	1,320.5	1,439.3	1,557.0
Railroad Retirement Trust Funds							
Balance, start of year	23.3	21.3	20.7	19.1	17.1	15.1	13.1
Adjustments to balances	–0.1	....	....	....	....	....	....
Total balance, start of year	23.2	21.3	20.7	19.1	17.1	15.1	13.1
Income:							
Governmental receipts	4.4	4.6	5.2	5.3	5.4	5.5	5.5
Offsetting governmental	....	....	....	....	....	....	....
Proprietary	*	....	....	....	....	....	....
Intrabudgetary:							
Intrafund	5.0	5.2	5.7	5.5	5.6	5.6	5.7
Interest	1.5	3.2	0.3	0.4	0.4	0.4	0.4
Other intrabudgetary	0.7	0.8	0.8	0.8	0.8	0.8	1.0
Total income during the year	11.6	13.8	11.9	12.0	12.2	12.4	12.7
Outgo (–)	–13.5	–14.4	–13.7	–14.0	–14.2	–14.3	–14.5
Change in fund balance:							
Surplus or deficit(–):							
Excluding interest	–3.3	–3.8	–2.1	–2.4	–2.4	–2.4	–2.3
Interest	1.5	3.2	0.3	0.4	0.4	0.4	0.4
Subtotal, surplus or deficit (–)	–1.8	–0.6	–1.7	–2.0	–1.9	–2.0	–1.8
Borrowing, transfers, lapses, & other adjustments	–*	–0.1	0.1	....	....	....	....
Total change in fund balance	–1.9	–0.7	–1.6	–2.0	–1.9	–2.0	–1.8
Balance, end of year	21.3	20.7	19.1	17.1	15.1	13.1	11.3
Social Security: Disability Insurance (DI) Trust Fund							
Balance, start of year	96.4	97.1	92.9	96.4	101.0	107.8	114.6
Adjustments to balances	....	....	....	....	....	....	....
Total balance, start of year	96.4	97.1	92.9	96.4	101.0	107.8	114.6
Income:							
Governmental receipts	140.1	137.1	149.9	155.6	162.2	168.2	175.2
Offsetting governmental	....	....	....	....	....	....	....
Proprietary	0.1	0.1	0.1	0.1	0.1	0.1	0.1
Intrabudgetary:							
Intrafund	....	....	....	....	....	....	....
Interest	2.8	2.7	2.4	2.1	2.0	2.1	2.2

Table 18–4. INCOME, OUTGO, AND BALANCES OF MAJOR TRUST FUNDS—Continued
(In billions of dollars)

	2020 Actual	Estimate					
		2021	2022	2023	2024	2025	2026
Other intrabudgetary	4.5	3.4	4.6	4.7	4.9	5.2	5.6
Total income during the year	147.5	143.3	156.9	162.5	169.2	175.5	183.1
Outgo (–)	−146.8	−147.5	−153.6	−157.8	−162.4	−168.7	−175.5
Change in fund balance:							
Surplus or deficit(–):							
Excluding interest	−2.2	−6.9	1.0	2.6	4.8	4.7	5.4
Interest	2.8	2.7	2.4	2.1	2.0	2.1	2.2
Subtotal, surplus or deficit (–)	0.7	−4.2	3.4	4.7	6.8	6.8	7.6
Borrowing, transfers, lapses, & other adjustments	....	*	0.1	....	....	....	....
Total change in fund balance	0.7	−4.1	3.4	4.7	6.8	6.8	7.6
Balance, end of year	97.1	92.9	96.4	101.0	107.8	114.6	122.3
Social Security: Old Age and Survivors Insurance (OASI) Trust Fund							
Balance, start of year	2,804.3	2,811.1	2,746.3	2,704.6	2,632.2	2,531.5	2,396.2
Adjustments to balances	....	....	....	....	....	....	....
Total balance, start of year	2,804.3	2,811.1	2,746.3	2,704.6	2,632.2	2,531.5	2,396.2
Income:							
Governmental receipts	825.3	807.0	882.7	916.0	955.4	990.4	1,031.6
Offsetting governmental	....	....	....	....	....	....	....
Proprietary	*	*	*	*	*	*	*
Intrabudgetary:							
Intrafund	....	....	....	....	....	....	....
Interest	76.0	70.6	63.3	57.2	52.5	48.7	45.6
Other intrabudgetary	54.3	51.3	60.6	64.0	68.2	73.1	84.9
Total income during the year	955.6	929.0	1,006.6	1,037.3	1,076.1	1,112.2	1,162.2
Outgo (–)	−948.7	−993.8	−1,048.4	−1,109.7	−1,176.8	−1,247.5	−1,323.3
Change in fund balance:							
Surplus or deficit(–):							
Excluding interest	−69.1	−135.4	−105.1	−129.6	−153.2	−184.0	−206.7
Interest	76.0	70.6	63.3	57.2	52.5	48.7	45.6
Subtotal, surplus or deficit (–)	6.9	−64.8	−41.8	−72.4	−100.6	−135.3	−161.2
Borrowing, transfers, lapses, & other adjustments	−0.1	0.1	*	....	....	....	....
Total change in fund balance	6.8	−64.8	−41.8	−72.4	−100.6	−135.3	−161.2
Balance, end of year	2,811.1	2,746.3	2,704.6	2,632.2	2,531.5	2,396.2	2,235.0
Unemployment Trust Fund							
Balance, start of year	84.8	14.2	9.5	23.6	61.0	96.1	123.5
Adjustments to balances	....	....	....	....	....	....	....
Total balance, start of year	84.8	14.2	9.5	23.6	61.0	96.1	123.5
Income:							
Governmental receipts	43.1	54.6	59.5	61.1	60.2	56.9	55.3
Offsetting governmental	....	....	....	....	....	....	....
Proprietary	*	*	*	*	*	*	*
Intrabudgetary:							
Intrafund	....	....	....	....	....	....	....
Interest	2.1	1.0	1.5	1.4	1.5	1.7	1.8
Other intrabudgetary	84.8	221.7	0.7	0.5	0.5	0.5	0.6
Total income during the year	130.0	277.2	61.6	63.1	62.3	59.1	57.7
Outgo (–)	−200.6	−282.0	−47.3	−25.7	−27.2	−31.7	−37.0
Change in fund balance:							
Surplus or deficit(–):							
Excluding interest	−72.7	−5.8	12.8	36.0	33.5	25.8	18.9
Interest	2.1	1.0	1.5	1.4	1.5	1.7	1.8

Table 18–4. INCOME, OUTGO, AND BALANCES OF MAJOR TRUST FUNDS—Continued

(In billions of dollars)

	2020 Actual	Estimate					
		2021	2022	2023	2024	2025	2026
Subtotal, surplus or deficit (–)	−70.6	−4.8	14.2	37.4	35.1	27.4	20.7
Borrowing, transfers, lapses, & other adjustments	*	0.1	−0.1	....	....	....	....
Total change in fund balance	−70.6	−4.7	14.1	37.4	35.1	27.4	20.7
Balance, end of year	14.2	9.5	23.6	61.0	96.1	123.5	144.2
All Other Trust Funds							
Balance, start of year	52.2	61.8	65.1	72.4	84.8	96.1	104.6
Adjustments to balances	1.5	....	....	....	....	....	....
Total balance, start of year	53.7	61.8	65.1	72.4	84.8	96.1	104.6
Income:							
Governmental receipts	4.7	5.3	7.8	8.4	8.7	8.7	8.9
Offsetting governmental	0.1	4.5	*	*	*	*	*
Proprietary	4.3	5.2	4.6	4.7	4.6	4.6	4.6
Intrabudgetary:							
Intrafund	....	....	....	....	....	....	....
Interest	0.8	0.8	0.8	0.8	0.8	0.8	0.8
Other intrabudgetary	27.5	19.5	29.1	29.6	29.9	30.1	30.5
Total income during the year	37.4	35.4	42.5	43.5	44.1	44.3	44.9
Outgo (–)	−29.3	−32.2	−35.3	−31.1	−32.7	−35.9	−38.5
Change in fund balance:							
Surplus or deficit(–):							
Excluding interest	7.3	2.3	6.3	11.5	10.5	7.6	5.6
Interest	0.8	0.8	0.8	0.8	0.8	0.8	0.8
Subtotal, surplus or deficit (–)	8.1	3.2	7.2	12.3	11.4	8.4	6.4
Borrowing, transfers, lapses, & other adjustments	*	0.1	0.2	....	....	....	....
Total change in fund balance	8.1	3.3	7.3	12.3	11.4	8.4	6.4
Balance, end of year	61.8	65.1	72.4	84.8	96.1	104.6	111.0

* $50 million or less.

Table 18–5. INCOME, OUTGO, AND BALANCES OF SELECTED SPECIAL FUNDS

(In billions of dollars)

	2020 Actual	Estimate					
		2021	2022	2023	2024	2025	2026
Abandoned Mine Reclamation Fund							
Balance, start of year	2.7	2.6	2.4	2.2	1.9	1.6	1.4
Adjustments to balances	....	....	....	....	....	....	....
Total balance, start of year	2.7	2.6	2.4	2.2	1.9	1.6	1.4
Income:							
Governmental receipts	0.1	0.1	....	....	....	....	....
Offsetting governmental	....	....	....	....	....	....	....
Proprietary	....	....	....	....	....	....	....
Intrabudgetary:							
Intrafund	....	....	....	....	....	....	....
Interest	0.1	*	*	*	*	*	*
Other intrabudgetary	....	....	....	....	....	....	....
Total income during the year	0.2	0.1	*	*	*	*	*
Outgo (–)	–0.3	–0.3	–0.3	–0.3	–0.3	–0.3	–0.3
Change in fund balance:							
Surplus or deficit(–):							
Excluding interest	–0.1	–0.2	–0.3	–0.3	–0.3	–0.3	–0.3
Interest	0.1	*	*	*	*	*	*
Subtotal, surplus or deficit (–)	–0.1	–0.1	–0.3	–0.3	–0.3	–0.3	–0.3
Borrowing, transfers, lapses, & other adjustments	....	–*	....	....	....	....	....
Total change in fund balance	–0.1	–0.2	–0.3	–0.3	–0.3	–0.3	–0.3
Balance, end of year	2.6	2.4	2.2	1.9	1.6	1.4	1.1
Department of Defense Medicare-Eligible Retiree Health Care Fund							
Balance, start of year	252.2	264.2	275.5	291.1	307.0	323.6	340.1
Adjustments to balances	....	....	....	....	....	....	....
Total balance, start of year	252.2	264.2	275.5	291.1	307.0	323.6	340.1
Income:							
Governmental receipts	....	....	....	....	....	....	....
Offsetting governmental	....	....	....	....	....	....	....
Proprietary	....	....	....	....	....	....	....
Intrabudgetary:							
Intrafund	14.7	15.6	16.8	17.5	18.2	19.0	19.8
Interest	7.8	7.1	10.7	11.0	11.6	11.4	8.9
Other intrabudgetary	....	....	....	....	....	....	....
Total income during the year	22.5	22.7	27.5	28.5	29.8	30.4	28.7
Outgo (–)	–10.6	–11.4	–11.9	–12.6	–13.2	–13.9	–14.6
Change in fund balance:							
Surplus or deficit(–):							
Excluding interest	4.1	4.2	4.9	4.9	5.0	5.1	5.2
Interest	7.8	7.1	10.7	11.0	11.6	11.4	8.9
Subtotal, surplus or deficit (–)	12.0	11.3	15.5	16.0	16.6	16.5	14.1
Borrowing, transfers, lapses, & other adjustments	....	....	....	....	....	....	....
Total change in fund balance	12.0	11.3	15.5	16.0	16.6	16.5	14.1
Balance, end of year	264.2	275.5	291.1	307.0	323.6	340.1	354.2

* $50 million or less.

19. COMPARISON OF ACTUAL TO ESTIMATED TOTALS

The Budget is required by statute to compare budget year estimates of receipts and outlays with the subsequent actual receipts and outlays for that year. This chapter meets that requirement by comparing the actual receipts, outlays, and deficit for 2020 with the current services estimates shown in the 2020 Budget, published in March 2019.[1] It also presents a more detailed comparison for mandatory and related programs, and reconciles the actual receipts, outlays, and deficit totals shown here with the figures for 2020 previously published by the Department of the Treasury.

Receipts

Actual receipts for 2020 were $3,421 billion, $221 billion less than the $3,643 billion current services estimate in the 2020 Budget, which was published in March 2019. As shown in Table 19-1, this decrease was the net effect of legislative changes, economic conditions that differed from what had been expected, and technical factors that resulted in different tax liabilities and collection patterns than had been assumed.

Policy differences. Legislated tax changes enacted after March 2019 reduced 2020 receipts by a net $173 billion relative to the 2020 Budget current services estimate. The Taxpayer First Act (P.L. 116-25) changed management and oversight of the Internal Revenue Service to improve customer service, expanded the use of electronic information systems in part by relaxing restrictions to mandate electronic filing based on the number of returns to be filed by a taxpayer, and increased the penalty for late returns, among other provisions; it was signed into law on July 1, 2019, and increased 2020 receipts by an estimated $5 million. The Further Consolidated Appropriations Act, 2020 (P.L. 116-94), repealed the medical device excise tax, the annual fee on health insurance providers, and the excise tax on high cost employer-sponsored health coverage; modified required distribution rules for designated beneficiaries of defined contribution retirement plans; reduced the medical expense deduction floor from 10 percent to 7.5 percent of a taxpayer's adjusted gross income; and included tax incentives for economic growth and community development, energy production and efficiency, and green economy jobs. It also extended a number of provisions set to expire at the end of 2019, including the New Markets Tax Credit; Work Opportunity Credit; and excise tax rates on beer, wine, and distilled spirits; among others. Finally, it provided tax relief for taxpayers affected by federally-declared disasters that occurred in 2018 or 2019. This Act was signed into law on December 20, 2019, and reduced 2020 receipts by an estimated $26 billion. The United States-Mexico-Canada Agreement Implementation Act (P.L. 116-113) revised certain tariffs and addressed trade barriers; it was signed into law on January 29, 2020, and increased 2020 receipts by an estimate $1 million. The Families First Coronavirus Response Act (P.L. 116-127) provided fully refundable credits against payroll taxes to compensate employers (including self-employed individuals) for paid sick leave and family and medical leave mandated in the Act; it was signed into law on March 18, 2020, and decreased 2020 receipts by an estimated $1 billion. The Coronavirus Aid, Relief, and Economic Security (CARES) Act (P.L. 116-136), allowed employers and self-employed individuals to defer payment of the employer's share of Social Security taxes incurred from March 27 through December 31, 2020; provided a refundable

---

[1] The current services concept is discussed in Chapter 17, "Current Services Estimates." For mandatory programs and receipts, the March 2019 current services estimate was based on laws then in place, adjusted for certain expiring provisions. For discretionary programs, the current services estimate was based on the discretionary spending limits enacted in the Budget Control Act of 2011 (BCA). Spending for Overseas Contingency Operations, was estimated based on annualizing the amounts provided in the 2019 appropriations and increasing for inflation. The current services estimates also reflected the effects of discretionary and mandatory sequestration as required by the BCA following failure of the Joint Select Committee on Deficit Reduction to meet its deficit reduction target. For a detailed explanation of the 2019 estimate, see "Current Services Estimates," Chapter 26 in Analytical Perspectives, Budget of the United States Government, Fiscal Year 2020.

Table 19–1. COMPARISON OF ACTUAL 2020 RECEIPTS WITH THE INITIAL CURRENT SERVICES ESTIMATES
(In billions of dollars)

	Estimate (March 2019)	Changes			Total Changes	Actual
		Policy	Economic	Technical		
Individual income taxes	1,822	−139	−102	28	−213	1,609
Corporation income taxes	256	−19	−24	−1	−44	212
Social insurance and retirement receipts	1,296	....	−38	53	14	1,310
Excise taxes	108	−15	−1	−5	−22	87
Estate and gift taxes	19	....	−0	−1	−2	18
Customs duties	48	0	−4	24	20	69
Miscellaneous receipts	94	0	37	−12	24	118
Total receipts	3,643	−173	−133	84	−221	3,421

* $500 million or less

Employee Retention Credit against payroll taxes for employers who kept employees on payroll during mandated shut-downs; permitted business to offset 100 percent of taxable income for net operating losses incurred over the three-year period from 2018 to 2020, and allowed corporations to carry back recently incurred losses for refunds of tax liabilities for the prior five years; allowed taxpayers to use their business losses to offset non-business income for tax years 2018 through 2020, or for farm losses for tax years 2018 through 2025; waived penalties for certain early withdrawals from retirement accounts in 2020; created a partial above-the-line deduction for taxpayers who do not itemize deductions in 2020 but make charitable contributions of up to $300 in cash; and excluded from taxation certain employer payments for employees' student loans; among other provisions. This Act was signed into law on March 27, 2020, and reduced 2020 receipts by an estimated $147 billion.

Economic differences. Differences between the economic assumptions upon which the current services estimates were based and actual economic performance decreased 2020 receipts by a net $133 billion below the March 2019 current services estimate. Wage and salary income was lower in 2020 than initially projected, which decreased individual income tax and social insurance receipts by $102 billion and $24 billion below the March 2019 estimate, respectively, and accounted for most of the net decrease in receipts attributable to economic differences. Different economic factors than those assumed in March 2019 had a smaller effect on other sources of receipts, increasing collections by a net $8 billion.

Technical factors. Technical factors increased receipts by a net $84 billion relative to the March 2019 current services estimate. These factors had the greatest effect on social insurance and retirement receipts, increasing collections by $53 billion. Increases in individual income taxes and customs duties of $28 billion and $24 billion, respectively, accounted for most of the remaining changes in 2020 receipts attributable to technical factors, partially offset by a decrease in miscellaneous receipts of $12 billion. The models used to prepare the March 2019 estimates of individual income taxes were based on historical economic data and then-current tax and collections data that were all subsequently revised and account for the net

increase in this source of receipts attributable to technical factors. New tariffs imposed on imports accounted for the increase in customs duties.

Outlays

Outlays for 2020 were $6,550 billion, $1,839 billion more than the $4,711 billion current services estimate in the 2020 Budget. Table 19–2 distributes the $1,839 billion net increase in outlays among discretionary and mandatory programs and net interest.[2] The table also shows rough estimates according to three reasons for the changes: policy; economic conditions; and technical estimating differences, a residual.

Policy differences. Policy changes are the result of legislative actions that change spending levels, primarily through higher or lower appropriations or changes in authorizing legislation, which may themselves be in response to changed economic conditions. For 2020, policy changes increased outlays by $1,814 billion relative to the initial current services estimates, which included increased spending to counter the impacts of the COVID-19 pandemic through the Families First Coronavirus Response Act (Public Law 116-127), Coronavirus Aid, Relief and Economic Security Act (Public Law 116-136) and the Paycheck Protection Program and Health Care Enhancement Act (Public Law 116-139). The combined policy changes from final 2019 and 2020 appropriations increased discretionary outlays by $310 billion. Policy changes increased mandatory outlays by a net $1,490 billion above current law, largely due to legislation mentioned above which funded a broad set of programs aimed at combating the COVID-19 pandemic. Debt service costs associated with all policy changes increased outlays by than $14 billion.

Economic and technical factors. Economic and technical estimating factors resulted in a net increase in outlays of $25 billion. Technical changes result from changes in such factors as the number of beneficiaries for entitlement

---

[2] Discretionary programs are controlled by annual appropriations, while mandatory programs are generally controlled by authorizing legislation. Mandatory programs are primarily formula benefit or entitlement programs with permanent spending authority that depends on eligibility criteria, benefit levels, and other factors.

Table 19–2. COMPARISON OF ACTUAL 2020 OUTLAYS WITH THE INITIAL CURRENT SERVICES ESTIMATES

(In billions of dollars)

	Estimate (March 2019)	Changes			Total Changes	Actual
		Policy	Economic	Technical		
Discretionary:						
Defense	671	62	....	–19	43	714
Nondefense	671	248	....	–6	242	913
Subtotal, discretionary	1,342	310	....	–25	285	1,627
Mandatory:						
Social Security	1,102	....	–3	–9	–12	1,090
Other programs	1,785	1,490	143	70	1,703	3,488
Subtotal, mandatory	2,887	1,490	140	61	1,691	4,578
Net interest	482	14	–98	–52	–137	345
Total outlays	4,711	1,814	42	–16	1,839	6,550

* $500 million or less

Table 19–3. COMPARISON OF THE ACTUAL 2020 DEFICIT WITH THE INITIAL CURRENT SERVICES ESTIMATE

(In billions of dollars)

	Estimate (March 2019)	Changes			Total Changes	Actual
		Policy	Economic	Technical		
Receipts	3,643	−173	−133	84	−221	3,421
Outlays	4,711	1,814	42	−16	1,839	6,550
Deficit	1,068	1,987	175	−101	2,061	3,129

* $500 million or less

Note: Deficit changes are outlays minus receipts. For these changes, a positive number indicates an increase in the deficit.

programs, crop conditions, or other factors not associated with policy changes or economic conditions. Defense discretionary spending decreased relative to the current services estimate largely due to slower-than-estimated spending of both new and prior-year authority, while overall non-defense spending decreased slightly, likely attributable to several factors, including overstated outlay assumptions in the 2020 budget, a 35-day lapse in appropriations and disruption due to the COVID-19 pandemic. Increases in discretionary outlays due to legislation, as discussed above, were offset by a $25 billion decrease in net outlays resulting from these technical changes. Outlays for mandatory programs increased $201 billion due to economic and technical factors. There was a net increase in outlays of $140 billion as a result of differences between actual economic conditions versus those forecast in March 2019.

Outlays for Social Security were $12 billion lower than anticipated in the 2020 Budget largely due to lower-than-estimated number of beneficiaries and cost-of-living adjustments. Income security programs and higher education programs were a combined $221 billion higher than anticipated; the remaining changes were spread throughout government programs and lowered outlays by $20 billion. Outlays for net interest were approximately $137 billion lower due to economic and technical factors, primarily due to lower interest rates than originally assumed.

Deficit

The preceding two sections discussed the differences between the initial current services estimates and the actual Federal Government receipts and outlays for 2020. This section combines these effects to show the net deficit impact of these differences.

As shown in Table 19–3, the 2020 current services deficit was initially estimated to be $1,068 billion. The actual deficit was $3,129 billion, which was a $2,061 billion increase from the initial estimate. Receipts were $221 billion lower and outlays were $1,839 billion higher than the initial estimate. The table shows the distribution of the changes according to the categories in the preceding two sections. The net effect of policy changes for receipts and outlays increased the deficit by $1,987 billion. Economic conditions that differed from the initial assumptions in March 2019 increased the deficit by $175 billion. Technical factors decreased the deficit by an estimated $101 billion.

Comparison of the Actual and Estimated Outlays for Mandatory and Related Programs for 2019

This section compares the original 2020 outlay estimates for mandatory and related programs in the current services estimates of the 2020 Budget with the actual outlays. Major examples of these programs include Social Security and Medicare benefits, Medicaid and unemployment compensation payments, and deposit insurance for banks and thrift institutions. This category also includes net interest outlays and undistributed offsetting receipts.

A number of factors may cause differences between the amounts estimated in the Budget and the actual mandatory outlays. For example, legislation may change benefit rates or coverage, the actual number of beneficiaries may differ from the number estimated, or economic conditions (such as inflation or interest rates) may differ from what was assumed in making the original estimates.

Table 19–4 shows the differences between the actual outlays for these programs in 2020 and the current services estimates included in the 2020 Budget. Actual outlays for mandatory spending and net interest in 2020 were $4,923 billion, which was $1,554 billion more than the current services estimate of $3,369 billion in March 2019.

As Table 19–4 shows, actual outlays for mandatory human resources programs were $3,865 billion, $911 billion higher than originally estimated. This increase was the net effect of legislative action, differences between actual and assumed economic conditions, differences between the anticipated and actual number of beneficiaries, and other technical differences.

The overall increase in outlays for these programs was mainly driven by the legislative response to the COVID-19 pandemic. Income security, other advancement of commerce programs, and other functions accounted for an increase of outlays of $1,499 billion. In addition, outlays in higher education programs were $108 billion higher than estimate primarily due to loan modification costs largely related to emergency COVID-19 relief and net upward reestimates due largely to reductions in forecasted income of borrowers in income-driven repayment. Outlays for net interest were $345 billion, or $137 billion lower than the original estimate. As shown on Table 19–4, interest payments on Treasury debt securities decreased by $160 billion. Interest earnings of trust funds decreased by $12 billion, increasing net outlays, while net outlays for other interest further increased net outlays by $11 billion.

Table 19–4. COMPARISON OF ACTUAL AND ESTIMATED OUTLAYS FOR MANDATORY AND RELATED PROGRAMS UNDER CURRENT LAW

(In billions of dollars)

	2020		
	Estimate	Actual	Change
Mandatory outlays:			
Human resources programs:			
Education, training, employment, and social services:			
Higher Education	18	125	108
Other	7	6	−1
Total, education, training, employment, and social services	25	131	107
Health:			
Medicaid	426	458	32
Other	108	110	2
Total, health	534	569	35
Medicare	702	769	67
Income security:			
Retirement and disability	160	156	−4
Unemployment compensation	27	472	444
Food and nutrition assistance	91	109	18
Other	187	448	261
Total, income security	465	1184	719
Social security	1102	1090	−12
Veterans benefits and services:			
Income security for veterans	110	110	−0
Other	16	11	−5
Total, veterans benefits and services	126	121	−5
Total, mandatory human resources programs	2,954	3,865	911
Other functions:			
Agriculture	14	31	17
International	−1	8	9
Mortgage credit	−24	−17	7
Deposit insurance	−4	−7	−3
Other advancement of commerce	21	600	579
Other functions	35	205	171
Total, other functions	39	819	780
Undistributed offsetting receipts:			
Employer share, employee retirement	−102	−100	2
Rents and royalties on the outer continental shelf	−5	−4	2
Other undistributed offsetting receipts	1	−3	−4
Total, undistributed offsetting receipts	−106	−106	−0
Total, mandatory	2,887	4,578	1691
Net interest:			
Interest on Treasury debt securities (gross)	683	523	−160
Interest received by trust funds	−147	−135	12
Other interest	−53	−42	11
Total, net interest	482	345	−137
Total, outlays for mandatory and net interest	3,369	4,923	1554

* $500 million or less

Reconciliation of Differences with Amounts Published by the Treasury for 2020

Table 19-5 provides a reconciliation of the receipts, outlays, and deficit totals for 2019 published by the Department of the Treasury in the September 2020 Monthly Treasury Statement (MTS) and those published in this Budget. The Department of the Treasury made no adjustments to the estimates for the Combined Statement of Receipts, Outlays, and Balances. Additional adjustments for the 2022 Budget increased receipts by $1,207 million and decreased outlays by $1,476 million. Some of these adjustments were for financial transactions that are not reported to the Department of the Treasury but are included in the Budget, including those for the Affordable Housing Program, the Electric Reliability Organization, the Federal Financial Institutions Examination Council Appraisal Subcommittee, Federal Retirement Thrift Investment Board Program Expenses, the National Oilheat Research Alliance, the Public Company Accounting Oversight Board, the Puerto Rico Oversight Board, the Securities Investor Protection Corporation, fees and payments related to the Standard Setting Body, and the United Mine Workers of America benefit funds. There was also an adjustment for the National Railroad Retirement Investment Trust (NRRIT), which relates to a conceptual difference in reporting. NRRIT reports to the Department of the Treasury with a one-month lag so that the fiscal year total provided in the Treasury Combined Statement covers September 2019 through August 2020. The Budget has been adjusted to reflect NRRIT transactions that occurred during the actual fiscal year, which begins October 1. In addition, the Budget also reflects agency adjustments to 2020 outlays reported to Treasury after preparation of the Treasury Combined Statement.

Table 19–5. RECONCILIATION OF FINAL AMOUNTS FOR 2020
(In millions of dollars)

	Receipts	Outlays	Deficit
Totals published by Treasury (September MTS)	3,419,955	6,551,872	3,131,917
Miscellaneous Treasury adjustments	....	....	....
Totals published by Treasury in Combined Statement	3,419,955	6,551,872	3,131,917
Affordable Housing Program	343	343	....
Electric Reliability Organization	100	100	....
Federal Financial Institutions Examination Council Appraisal Subcommittee	14	14	....
Federal Retirement Thrift Investment Board Program Expenses	....	–21	–21
National Oilheat Research Alliance	7	7	....
National Railroad Retirement Investment Trust	....	822	822
Postal Service	....	–3,205	–3,205
Public Company Accounting Oversight Board	270	266	–4
Puerto Rico Oversight Board	58	58	....
Securities Investor Protection Corporation	373	82	–291
Standard Setting Body	31	31	....
United Mine Workers of America benefit funds	14	13	–1
Other	–3	14	17
Total adjustments, net	1,207	–1,476	–2,683
Totals in the Budget	3,421,162	6,550,396	3,129,234
MEMORANDUM:			
Total change since year-end statement	1,207	–1,476	–2,683